Public Speaking

for College & Career

The McGraw·Hill Companies

Connect
Learn
Succeed™

PUBLIC SPEAKING FOR COLLEGE & CAREER, TENTH EDITION

Published by McGraw-Hill, a business unit of The McGraw-Hill Companies, Inc., 1221 Avenue of the Americas, New York, NY 10020. Copyright © 2013 by Hamilton Gregory. All rights reserved. Printed in the United States of America. Previous editions © 2010, 2008, and 2005. No part of this publication may be reproduced or distributed in any form or by any means, or stored in a database or retrieval system, without the prior written consent of The McGraw-Hill Companies, Inc., including, but not limited to, in any network or other electronic storage or transmission, or broadcast for distance learning.

Some ancillaries, including electronic and print components, may not be available to customers outside the United States.

This book is printed on acid-free paper.

2 3 4 5 6 7 8 9 0 DOW/DOW 1 0 9 8 7 6 5 4 3

ISBN 978-0-07-803682-8
MHID 0-07-803682-8

Senior Vice President, Products & Markets: *Kurt L. Strand*
Vice President, General Manager, Products & Markets: *Michael Ryan*
Vice President, Content Production & Technology Services: *Kimberly Meriwether David*
Managing Director: *David Patterson*
Brand Manager: *Susan Gouijnstook*
Director of Development: *Rhona Robbin*
Development Editor: *Sarah Remington*
Digital Product Analyst: *Janet Smith*
Marketing Manager: *Clare Cashen*
Content Project Manager: *Jennifer Gehl*
Senior Buyer: *Sandy Ludovissy*
Senior Designer: *David W. Hash*
Cover/Interior Designer: *Greg Nettles/SquareCrow Creative*
Cover Image: *young man © Ocean/Corbis, young woman © Hill Street Studios/Blend Images/Corbis, crowd scene © Bob Daemmrich/Alamy*
Content Licensing Specialist: *Ann Marie Jannette*
Photo Research: *Jennifer Blankenship*
Compositor: *Laserwords Private Limited*
Typeface: *10/12 Minion Pro*
Printer: *R. R. Donnelley*

All credits appearing on page or at the end of the book are considered to be an extension of the copyright page.

Library of Congress Cataloging-in-Publication Data

Gregory, Hamilton.
    Public speaking for college & career/Hamilton Gregory.—10th ed.
        p. cm.
    Includes index.
    ISBN 978-0-07-803682-8—ISBN 0-07-803682-8 (acid-free paper) 1. Public speaking. I. Title.
    II. Title: Public speaking for college and career.
    PN4121.G716 2013
    808.5'1–dc23
                                                                                    2012020023

www.mhhe.com

Dedicated to the memory of
Merrell,
my beloved wife and best friend,
who left this world much too soon

Brief Contents

Contents

Part 4
Organizing the Speech

Part 5
Presenting the Speech

Part 6
Types of Public Speaking

Preface

What if you had a tool that gave you and your students more time for practice in the classroom? What if you could significantly increase student retention and success? What if your students had access to a suite of videos that illustrate public speaking techniques in action? *Public Speaking for College and Career* is an integrated program that helps students connect to practice, build confidence and achieve success in public speaking.

Practice for College

Public Speaking for College and Career speaks to busy students. It gives them the tools they need to be successful in the classroom and exercise their skills as often as possible.

The Gregory text has a reputation for being highly accessible to students. In fact, in an article in the journal *Communication Teacher*, this book was rated #1 in readability in an analysis of 22 leading college textbooks on public speaking.[1]

Connect Public Speaking is a highly interactive learning environment designed to help students connect to the speech preparation tools and resources they will need to achieve success. Through engaging media and study resources, students improve their performance on exams and speech assignments. *Connect Public Speaking* makes managing and completing assignments easier.

Connect Public Speaking Plus offers all of this with the addition of an integrated, interactive e-book. The e-book optimized for the Web immerses students in a flexible, interactive environment. Assign e-book exercises to ensure your students are reading, or direct them to the embedded activities and multimedia for a more memorable and engaging homework assignment.

Build Confidence as a Speaker

Because most students who take a public speaking course need guidance on how to build confidence and conquer their fears, this book offers a great deal of reassurance and practical tips.

- **Managing nervousness** is the focus of Chapter 2. Mastering its contents will be a great confidence builder for students. The chapter explores why so many people are afraid of public speaking, how to manage anxiety, and how to turn nervousness into an energizer, not a spoiler.

- **Speech Capture** is a new, cutting-edge tool that lets students upload their own videos for self-review and/or peer review. Instructors are able to evaluate speeches live, using a fully customizable rubric. Instructors can also upload speech videos on behalf of students, as well as create and manage peer review assignments.

- *LearnSmart,* McGraw-Hill's adaptive learning system, helps assess student knowledge of course content and maps out a personalized study plan for success. Accessible within Connect Public Speaking, *LearnSmart* uses a series of adaptive questions to pinpoint the concepts students understand—and those they don't. The result is an online tool that helps students learn faster and study more efficiently and that enables instructors to customize classroom lectures and activities to meet their students' needs.

Prepare Effective Speeches

Careful preparation is a key ingredient in planning, organizing, and delivering effective speeches. Features in the book and in Connect Public Speaking help students develop plans and organize their thoughts so that their speeches are as successful as they can be.

- **The Connect Outline Tool, with an enhanced user interface** guides students systematically through the process of organizing and outlining their speeches. Instructors can customize parts of the outliner, and also turn it off if they don't want their students to use it.

Prepare for a Career

Public Speaking for College and Career has students' aspirations in mind, with technology tools and features that will serve students wherever their future careers take them.

Anticipate Real-World Situations

A variety of features give students skills and techniques for communicating in the real world.

- **The Speech Prep App** is a mobile tool designed to help users build confidence in their public speaking skills through practice. Users can view sample speech clips; create and organize note cards; and time, record, and review their own speeches. Students can continue to use the app after they complete their public speaking course—it will come in handy for any speech they have to give in their personal and professional lives. Go to www.mhhe.com/speechprep to purchase the App for Apple or Android devices.

- **New speech videos and clips** give students tangible examples to learn from, including one new example of a speech that needs improvement. The new video topics are instructive in a variety of areas, including speaking with notes; using words effectively; conversational style; and employing examples, testimony, visual aids. There are six new full-length speeches and thirteen new speeches. When viewed in Connect, instructors can opt to assign multiple-choice assessment questions to ensure student engagement.

- **"Tips for Your Career"** in every chapter give students a heads-up about the types of things they will need to think about as presenters in their professional lives.

- **How to create effective PowerPoint slides,** in Chapter 9, helps students master this tricky but critical skill. At the end of the chapter, an appendix, "How to Avoid 'Death by PowerPoint,'" vividly illustrates the six most common Power-Point blunders and how to avoid them.

- **Special sections on leading and participating in business meetings** are included in Chapter 19 ("Speaking in Groups").

Skill-Building Features

Critical-thinking skills are vital in the classroom, on the job, and in the community. Students who build these skills will be better speakers, listeners, and citizens as they strive to understand and evaluate what they see, hear, and read.

- **Ethical Issue Quizzes** are new to this edition. These provide real-world scenarios that pose ethical dilemmas, and ask students to make a choice. Students can check their answers at the end of the chapter.

- **"Your Thoughts?" questions** appear several times in each chapter, and will provoke both thought and discussion.

- **"Building Critical-Thinking Skills" exercises** at the end of each chapter give students practice in this valuable skill.

Chapter-by-Chapter Changes

Chapter 1: Introduction to Public Speaking

- Revised "Tips for Your Career" about the five biggest mistakes made by speakers, revealing that PowerPoint blunders rank #2 in a new survey of 370 business and professional leaders
- New "Ethical Issues Quiz" on distorting information
- Revised sections on interference, situation, and stereotyping and scapegoating
- New speech example in "Quick Guide to Public Speaking"
- Revised critical-thinking resources, including one new "Building Critical-Thinking Skills" question

Chapter 2: Managing Nervousness

- Renaming of the chapter to emphasize *managing* nervousness instead of controlling it
- Revised sections on reasons for nervousness and adrenaline, and numerous updated tips and tricks for harnessing nervousness
- New "Ethical Issues Quiz" about creating your own speech

Chapter 3: Listening

- New "Introduction to Listening" section
- Expanded coverage of listening analytically, taking notes, and resisting distractions
- New section on "Multitasking can hurt you professionally"
- Expanded instruction on how to handle intrusion of electronic devices
- Revised section on evaluating others' speeches
- New "Ethical Issues Quiz" about handling inattentive listeners
- Revised critical-thinking resources, including one new "Building Critical-Thinking Skills" question and two new "Your Thoughts?" questions

Chapter 4: Reaching the Audience

- New graphic showing a sample survey
- Revised and updated sections about conducting research, being sensitive to listeners with disabilities, and accommodating audiences' differing levels of knowledge and interest
- New section about audience expectations
- A new "Tips for Your Career" about being sensitive to audience discomfort
- New "Ethical Issues Quiz" about presenting to an audience that might not be receptive to your message

Chapter 5: Selecting Topic, Purpose, and Central Idea

- Revised sections on choosing topics that interest the audience
- Expanded coverage of technology and how it factors into the topic-selection and topic-narrowing processes; includes new coverage of specific social media and websites, using smartphones and other devices
- New graphics for Personal Inventory and Brainstorming Guide
- New "Ethical Issues Quiz" about recycling one's own material for a speech
- Revised critical-thinking activities, including three new "Your Thoughts?" questions

Chapter 6: Finding Information

- Revised section on misconceptions about research
- Throughout the chapter, research tips now include more information about electronic resources and technology, including e-books
- New information about field research, including investigations and using Facebook for research
- Tips on using smartphones and camcorders to record interviews
- Refreshed technology references and suggested websites in the chapter appendix ("Tips for Finding Materials")
- Revised "Tips for Your Career" about keeping track of good ideas
- New "Ethical Issues Quiz" about disclosing research findings

Chapter 7: Evaluating Information and Avoiding Plagiarism

- New section about being an honest investigator
- Fifteen new examples and stories to illustrate points throughout the chapter
- Revised section about judging anecdotal evidence, including the claim that domestic violence increases on Super Bowl Sunday
- Revised "Tips for Your Career" about questioning facts reported by media outlets
- Two new "Ethical Issues Quiz" boxes, one on plagiarism and the other on giving credit to others for their ideas
- Updated coverage about research technology, including an updated list of websites that are reliable for fact-checking and a revised section on "cutting and pasting"
- Shortened and updated section on copyright infringement

Chapter 8: Supporting Your Ideas

- Expanded section on supporting a speech with the use of a narrative
- Eight new examples and stories to illustrate points in the chapter

- New "Tips for Your Career" about providing supporting materials for the audience
- New "Ethical Issues Quiz" about using statistics
- Revised critical-thinking activities, including one new "Building Critical-Thinking Skills" question and two new "Your Thoughts?" questions

Chapter 9: Presentation Aids

- Updated coverage of new technology for presentation aids
- New extended example in the step-by-step method for creating PowerPoint slides
- New section "Using Color Carefully," including how to meet the needs of color-blind listeners and the best color combinations for all audiences
- New sample slides in the chapter appendix (How to Avoid "Death by Power-Point"), comparing good and bad graphics
- New sample speech available online ("Failed to Get the Job?" which shows the wrong way to use PowerPoint, followed by an improved version that shows the correct way)
- Revised critical-thinking activities, including one new "Your Thoughts?" question

Chapter 15: Speaking to Inform

- New example illustrating how to use the familiar to explain the unfamiliar
- New sample speech, with outline, commentary, and transcript ("Gold Fever")
- New "Ethical Issues Quiz" about selecting an informative speech topic
- Revised critical-thinking activities, including one new "Building Critical-Thinking Skills" question and one new "Your Thoughts?" question

Chapter 16: Speaking to Persuade

- New sections on using smartphones, social media, and online petitions at the end of a presentation
- New sample persuasive speech, with outline, commentary, and transcript ("House Arrest")
- New "Ethical Issues Quiz" about full disclosure
- Revised "Tips for Your Career" about persuasion as a long-term process
- New examples of the Statement-of-Reasons pattern and the Comparative Advantages pattern
- Revised critical-thinking activities, including one new "Your Thoughts?" question

Chapter 17: Persuasive Strategies

- New type of logical fallacy – slippery slope
- New example of the "straw man" fallacy

- New sample persuasive speech, with outline, commentary, and transcript ("Sleep Deficiency")
- New "Ethical Issues Quiz" about using fear as a motivator
- Revised critical-thinking activities, including one new "Building Teamwork Skills" question and two new "Your Thoughts?" questions

Chapter 18: Special Types of Speeches

- New "Ethical Issues Quiz" about making appropriate remarks during a wedding speech
- Four new images

Chapter 19: Speaking in Groups

- New "Ethical Issues Quiz" about respectfully disagreeing with group members
- Revised sample agenda
- Streamlined section on the Reflective-Thinking Method outlining the method in seven specific steps
- Revised critical-thinking activities, including one new "Your Thoughts?" question

Appendix

- New sample informative speech ("One Slip—and You're Dead")

Course Solutions

Speeches for Analysis DVD: Videos for *Public Speaking for College and Career*

High resolution versions of all of the videos that accompany this book—full-length speeches and speech excerpts—have been placed on a DVD as an option for instructors. Because they are high resolution, the videos are ideal for viewing on a large screen in a classroom or auditorium. The DVD includes 22 videos and 33 speech excerpts, 19 of which are new to this edition.

Design your ideal course materials with McGraw-Hill's Create—www.mcgrawhillcreate.com! Rearrange or omit chapters, combine material from other sources, and/or upload your syllabus or any other content you have written to make the perfect resources for your students. Search thousands of leading McGraw-Hill textbooks to find the best content for your students, then arrange it to fit your teaching style. You can even personalize your book's appearance by selecting the cover and adding your name, school, and course information. When you order a Create book, you receive a complimentary review copy. Get a printed copy in 3 to 5 business days or an electronic copy (eComp) via e-mail in about an hour.

Register today at www.mcgrawhillcreate.com, and craft your course resources to match the way you teach.

 CourseSmart offers thousands of the most commonly adopted textbooks across hundreds of courses from a wide variety of higher education publishers. It is the only place for faculty to review and compare the full text of a textbook online, providing immediate access without the environmental impact of requesting a printed exam copy. At CourseSmart, students can save up to 50% off the cost of a printed book, reduce their impact on the environment, and gain access to powerful Web tools for learning, including full text search, notes and highlighting, and e-mail tools for sharing notes among classmates. Learn more at www.coursesmart.com.

 McGraw-Hill Campus is the first of its kind institutional service providing faculty with true single sign-on access to all of McGraw-Hill's course content, digital tools, and other high-quality learning resources from any learning management system (LMS). This innovative offering allows for secure and deep integration and seamless access to any of our course solutions such as McGraw-Hill Connect®, McGraw-Hill Create™, McGraw-Hill LearnSmart™, or Tegrity®. McGraw-Hill Campus includes access to our entire content library, including e-books, assessment tools, presentation slides, and multimedia content, among other resources, providing faculty open and unlimited access to prepare for class, create tests/quizzes, develop lecture material, integrate interactive content, and much more.

Instructor Resources

The **Instructor's Manual and Resource Integrator** is a suite of resources for both novice and experienced instructors and includes dozens of ready-to-reproduce worksheets and forms for classroom use, tips for videotaping classroom speeches, sample course outlines, speech evaluation forms, chapter resources, and test items. A special feature in the manual is a Resource Integrator that describes textbook features, activities, and multimedia materials that are relevant to each chapter.

Chapter Highlights on PowerPoint slides highlight key points in each chapter in the book. Instructors can choose a version that has no videos or a version that includes video clips (speech excerpts). The program is designed to reflect best practices in using slides effectively in presentations. As a result, many of the slides have graphics but no words; instructors can use or adapt the accompanying scripts to provide narration.

A **Test Bank** offers multiple-choice, true or false, and essay questions for each chapter. McGraw-Hill's computerized EZ Test allows the instructor to create customized exams using the publisher's supplied test items or the instructor's own questions. A version of the test bank is also provided in Microsoft Word files for instructors who prefer that format.

Instructor resources are available online at http://www.mhhe.com/gregory10e.

Acknowledgments

Over 200 instructors have reviewed this book in its successive editions. Their advice has not only shown me how to improve the book but also helped me improve my own classroom teaching. I am grateful to the reviewers for their insights, encouragement, and willingness to help a colleague.

For this edition, reviewers include Pamela Baldwin, Community College of Beaver County; Carole Bennett, Oakland Community College; Cynthia Brown El, Macomb Community College; Kenneth R. Chase, Wheaton College; Nickolas Dixon, Southeastern University; Joan Geller, Johnson & Wales University; Mayra Holzer, Valencia College; Joshua Misner, North Idaho College; Teresa Moore, Brevard Community College; Marjorie Keeshan Nadler, Miami University of Ohio; Debbie Nicolai, Lindenwood University; Kekeli Nuviadenu, Bethune-Cookman University; Karen O'Donnell, Finger Lakes Community College; Maria Parnell, Brevard Community College; Terri Piazza, Allen County Community College; Cynthia Stout, Midlands Technical College; Charlene Widener, Hutchinson Community College, and Elvinet Wilson, Indiana University East.

From the earliest days of this book, Betty Dvorson, an inspiring and popular instructor at City College of San Francisco, has given me lots of valuable advice and enthusiastic support. For their creative ideas, special thanks to Michael N. Anhar of California State University, Sacramento; Barbara Guess, Forsyth Technical Community College; Ruth Bennett, Betty Farmer, and Jim Manning, all of Western Carolina University; Tom W. Gregory, Trinity College in Washington, DC; Jim McDiarmid, speech instructor on U.S. Navy ships under PACE (Program of Afloat College Education); members of the Speech Communication faculty at Mesa Community College (Jim Mancuso, Christine Beckman, Loretta Kissell, Linda Larson, Stacey Nordhues, Tracey Powers, Erin Rawson, and Gary Stephens); and instructors at Butler Community College, especially Pat Lowrance and Alexis Hopkins.

For this edition, I had the pleasure of working with Sarah Remington, a savvy, supportive editor who brought her good judgment and keen intelligence to my book, and rescued me from more than one blunder. My book also profited from the support and vision of Executive Editor Susan Gouijnstook, Director of Development Rhona Robbin, and Marketing Manager Clare Cashen. I also appreciate the wholehearted backing I have received from David Patterson, managing director for products & markets, and Michael Ryan, vice president and general manager of McGraw-Hill Higher Education.

Content Product Manager Jennifer Gehl displayed admirable skill and care (and patience with me!) in guiding the book through the production stages, aided by Kathryn DiBernardo, copyeditor; Lauren Timmer, first proofreader, and Kay Brimeyer, second proofreader. Others who provided valuable assistance included Jennifer Blankenship, photo researcher; Sarah Hill, media project manager; Janet Byrne Smith, digital product analyst; Jamie Daron, editorial coordinator, and Elizabeth Murphy, freelance developer. The physical beauty of this book is due to the creative efforts of David W. Hash, senior designer, and Greg Nettles of SquareCrowCreative.

Speech Capture and Speech Tools are a reality today thanks to the following people, who designed and built the new tools: Vicki Splaine, Debabrata Acharya, Pravarna Besa, Manish Gupta, Irina Reznik, Sanjay Shinde, Sujoy Banerjee, John Brady, Priscila Encarnacion, Nidhi Kumari, and Suzy Cho. And, since Speech Capture is a living tool, special thanks go out to the following people who work daily to support and enhance it: Jeremy Partacz, Daniel Hazelett, Ralph Mitek, Vijay Kapu, Erica Eatmon, Stephanie Hom, Jatin Kalra, Sri Kiran Poolla, and Srini Mogalipuvvu.

I wish to thank the following colleagues for ideas, inspiration, and support: Kenet Adamson, Kara Allen, Jennifer Browning, Jan Caldwell, Angela Calhoun, Loretta Carlton, Jim Cavener, Patricia Cutspec, Rebecca Davis, Michael Flynn, Lynne Gabai, Deborah L. Harmon, Cris Harshman, Melody Hays, David Holcombe, Rusty Holmes, Lisa Johnson, Erika Lytle, Deb Maddox, Mary McClurkin, Stephanie O'Brien, Jim Olsen, Rolfe Olsen, Susan Paterson, Ellen Perry, Beth Stewart, Mary Sugeir, Heather Vaughn, and Lloyd Weinberg.

I am indebted to the hundreds of students in my public speaking classes over the years who have made teaching this course a pleasant and rewarding task. From them I have drawn most of the examples of classroom speeches.

And for their support and patience, special thanks to my late wife Merrell and to our children, Jess, Jim, and June.

—Hamilton Gregory

Public Speaking

for College & Career

Introduction to Public Speaking

OUTLINE

Benefits of a Public Speaking Course

The Speech Communication Process

The Speaker's Responsibilities

Speech Introducing Yourself or a Classmate

Quick Guide to Public Speaking

OBJECTIVES

After studying this chapter, you should be able to:

1. Explain at least three benefits of a public speaking course.
2. Identify and explain the seven elements of the speech communication process.
3. Describe the main responsibilities that speakers have toward their listeners.
4. Prepare a speech introducing yourself or a classmate.

BORN WITH A LARGE PURPLE BIRTHMARK on her face, Abigail Hardin cannot remember a time when people didn't "stare, point, whisper, or ask me if I had been hit in the face." Throughout her childhood in Clinton, Mississippi, she hated the notoriety of being "the girl with the birthmark," and she remembers "many nights of crying and begging for answers as to why I had this defect on my face."[1]

Hardin is now a student at the University of Alabama, and her facial appearance has changed, thanks to eight laser surgeries and skilled use of makeup. But she has not forgotten the hurt and insecurities of her childhood. She gives talks to schoolchildren to encourage them "to look past the differences we all have and accept each other for who we are." She also wants to instill a sense of self-worth in those kids "who feel like they don't fit in." During her talks, she reads from a book she has written, *Look at Me; I Am Just Like You,* about a hippo named Lucie who has a birthmark.[2]

University of Alabama student Abigail Hardin shares the story of Lucie, a hippo with a birthmark.

Her presentations—given to more than 3,000 children in schools in Mississippi and Alabama—have drawn praise from many educators. "She became an inspiration and heroine to our whole school," says Judith Sharpe, a school principal in Ridgeland, Mississippi.[3]

Abigail Hardin is a powerful demonstration that public speaking can touch lives and make a contribution to society.

3

Benefits of a Public Speaking Course

Many college graduates say that of all the courses they took, public speaking proved to be one of the most valuable.[4] Here are some of the reasons:

1. **You learn how to speak to an audience.** Being able to stand up and give a talk to a group of people is a rewarding skill you can use throughout your life. Imagine yourself in these public speaking scenarios:

   - In one of your college classes, you must give a 30-minute presentation on a research project.
   - To 50 colleagues at work, you give a brief speech appealing for contributions to the United Way charity drive.
   - In court you explain to a jury why a traffic accident was not your fault.

2. **You learn skills that apply to one-on-one communication.** Although the emphasis of this course is on speaking to groups, the principles that you learn also apply to communication with individuals.[5] Throughout your lifetime you will be obliged to talk in situations such as these:

   - In a job interview, a human resources manager says, "We've got 50 well-qualified applicants for this job. Why should we hire you?" If you know how to give a reply that is brief, interesting, and convincing, you obviously improve your chances of getting the job. In a public speaking course, you learn how to organize and present persuasive messages.
   - You sit down with a bank executive to ask for a loan so that you can buy a new car. The skills of nonverbal communication (such as eye contact and facial expression) that you learn in a public speaking course should help you convey to the banker that you are a trustworthy and reliable person who will repay the loan.

   After taking a public speaking course, many students report that their new skills help them as much in talking to one person as in addressing a large audience.

3. **You develop the oral communication skills that are prized in the job market.** When you go to a job interview, which of the following is most likely to influence the employer when he or she decides whether to hire you?

   - The reputation of your school
   - Your grade-point average
   - Letters of reference
   - Technical knowledge in your field
   - Oral communication skills—speaking and listening
   - Written communication skills—reading and writing

   Research shows that "oral communication skills" is the correct answer—a finding that surprises many students.[6] Surely "technical knowledge in your field" is the most important factor for jobs in science and technology, isn't it? Not according to employers. You can be brilliant in your field, says one executive, but if you can't communicate successfully with co-workers and the public, your brilliance is of little value.[7]

   Once you have a job, being a good communicator can help you win advancement. "If a dozen equally skilled technicians are competing for the job of manager, the winner is most likely to be the one with the best communication skills," says Cristina Silva, human resources manager of a plant in Los Angeles.[8]

You never know when you may be asked to give a speech. Because he was the youngest motorcycle racer to enter the Dakar off-road endurance race in 2010, Rodrigo Caballero, 19, an engineering student at a university in Chile, was asked to speak to over 1,000 contestants at the start of the grueling 4,500-mile race in South America. Thanks to a public speaking course he had taken, he was able to organize and deliver his remarks effectively.

4. **You learn in an ideal environment for gaining experience and building confidence.** The classroom is a perfect place to practice and develop your skills. No one will deny you a job or a loan on the basis of your classroom speeches. Your audience is friendly and sympathetic—all your classmates are going through the same experience.

   The critiques given by your instructor and by fellow students are valuable parts of the course. If, for example, you say "um" or "uh" so often that it distracts your listeners, you are probably unaware of this unconscious habit. Being told of the problem is the first step toward correcting it.

   If you are like most students, your public speaking class will help you gain self-confidence. You will enjoy the pride that comes from meeting a challenge and handling it successfully.

5. **You can make a contribution to the lives of other people.** While attending a funeral service for a beloved aunt, Karen Walker heard the minister give a brief eulogy and then say, "Would anyone like to say a few words at our 'open mic'?"

Your Thoughts

Who is the most engaging public communicator (politician, teacher, minister, etc.) you have ever encountered? What are the reasons for his or her success?

A few people went to the microphone and shared some memories, but most audience members were silent. "I wanted to pay tribute to my aunt, but I was too scared," said Walker. "I felt really bad because there were a lot of important things about my aunt and her life that were never said." A few years later, Walker took a public speaking class, and a year or so afterward, she attended another funeral—for her grandfather. "This time I vowed that I would not pass up the opportunity to honor a wonderful person. I asked to be part of the service, and I spoke about my childhood memories of my grandfather."

The eulogy, said Walker, was appreciated by her family members, who told her that she had expressed beautifully what they would have said if they had possessed the courage and the skills to stand up and speak. "It gave me a good feeling to know that I could represent the family in this way," she said.

Being able to speak in public—offering a toast, sharing information, providing encouragement, attempting persuasion—can bring pleasure and joy to yourself and to others. Walker said that her success was possible because of what she had learned in her public speaking class.[9]

The Speech Communication Process

When a speaker gives a speech, does communication take place?

Sometimes yes, sometimes no—because *speaking and communicating are not the same thing.* You can speak to a listener, but if the listener does not understand your message in the way you meant it to be understood, you have failed to communicate it.[10] Here's an example given by Michael O'Malley in his book *Creating Commitment: How to Attract and Retain Talented Employees:*

> A job recruiter coached one young woman on how to present herself at a job interview. She was told to "dress your best." On the day of the interview, she showed up wearing a prom dress.
> The recruiter had meant "wear your best business attire," but the young woman had interpreted the advice as "wear the fanciest clothes you own."[11]

This incident illustrates that speaking and communicating are not synonymous. As a slogan of the Hitachi Corporation puts it: "Communication is not simply sending a message. It is creating true understanding—swiftly, clearly, and precisely."[12]

To help you send messages that truly communicate, it is helpful to understand the process of speech communication. As we discuss the process, use Figure 1.1 as a visual reference.

Elements of the Process

The speech communication process has seven distinct components.

Speaker

speaker
the originator of a message sent to a listener

When you are a **speaker,** you are the source of a message that is transmitted to a listener. Whether you are speaking to a dozen people or 500, you bear a great responsibility for the success of the communication. The key question that you must constantly ask yourself is not "Am I giving out good information?" or "Am I performing well?" but, rather, "Am I getting through to my listeners?"

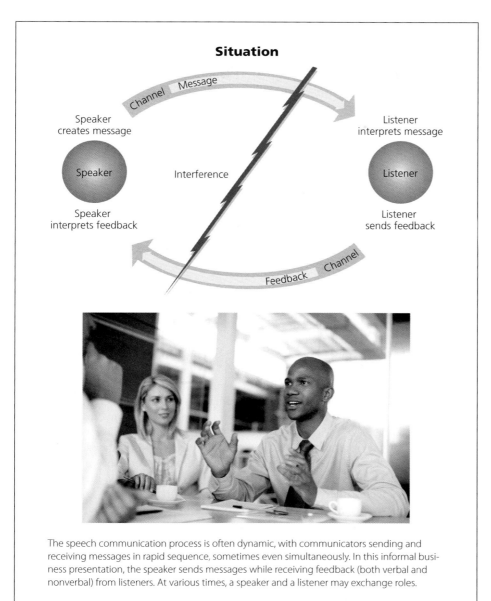

Figure 1.1
The Speech Communication Process
In this model of the speech communication process, a **speaker** creates a **message** and sends it via a **channel** to the **listener,** who interprets it and sends **feedback** via a channel to the speaker. **Interference** is whatever impedes accurate communication. The **situation** refers to the time and place in which communication takes place.

The speech communication process is often dynamic, with communicators sending and receiving messages in rapid sequence, sometimes even simultaneously. In this informal business presentation, the speaker sends messages while receiving feedback (both verbal and nonverbal) from listeners. At various times, a speaker and a listener may exchange roles.

Listener

The **listener** is the recipient of the message sent by the speaker. The true test of communication is not whether a message is delivered by the speaker but whether it is accurately received by the listener. "A speech," says management consultant David W. Richardson of Westport, Connecticut, "takes place in the minds of the audience."[13]

If communication fails, who is to blame—the speaker or the listener? It could be either, or both. Although speakers share part of the responsibility for communication, listeners also must bear some of the burden. They must focus on the speaker, not daydream or text a friend. They must listen with an open mind, avoiding the tendency to prejudge the speaker or discount a speaker's views without a fair hearing.

listener
the receiver of the speaker's message

Message

message
whatever is communicated verbally and nonverbally to the listener

The **message** is whatever the speaker communicates to the listeners. The message is sent in the form of *symbols*—either *verbal* or *nonverbal.*

Verbal symbols are words. It's important for you to recognize that words are not things; they are *symbols* of things. If you give me an apple, you transfer a solid object from your hand to mine. But if you're making a speech and you mention the word "apple," you are not transferring a concrete thing. You are transferring a verbal symbol.

Nonverbal symbols are what you convey with your tone of voice, eyes, facial expression, gestures, posture, and appearance.

Your Thoughts

When nonverbal and verbal messages are contradictory, why do you think listeners tend to accept the nonverbal as the true message?

So far, the process sounds simple, but now we enter a danger zone. As a speaker transmits verbal and nonverbal symbols, the listeners must receive and interpret them. Unfortunately, listeners may end up with a variety of interpretations, some of them quite different from what the speaker intended. Consider our simple word *apple.* One listener may think of a small green fruit, while another conjures an image of a big red fruit. One listener may think of crisp tartness, while another thinks of juicy sweetness.

If such a simple word can evoke a variety of mental pictures, imagine the confusion and misunderstanding that can arise when abstract words such as *imperialism, patriotism,* and *censorship* are used. The term *censorship* may mean "stamping out filth" to some listeners, but it may mean "total government control of the news media" to others.

As a speaker, use symbols that are clear and specific. Don't say, "Smoking may cause you a lot of trouble." The phrase "a lot of trouble" is vague, and might be interpreted by some listeners to mean "coughing," by others to mean "stained teeth," or by still others to mean "cancer." Be specific: "Smoking is the leading cause of lung cancer."

Sometimes a speaker's verbal symbols contradict his or her nonverbal symbols. If you say to an audience at the end of a speech, "Now I would like to hear your views on this subject," but your expression is tense and your voice sounds irritated, the listeners are getting a mixed message. Which will they believe, your words or your nonverbal behavior? Listeners usually accept the nonverbal behavior as the true message. In this case, they will conclude that you do *not* welcome comments.

Make sure the nonverbal part of your message reinforces, rather than contradicts, the verbal part. In other words, smile and use a friendly tone of voice when you ask for audience participation.

Channel

channel
the pathway used to transmit a message

The **channel** is the medium used to communicate the message. In everyday life, you receive messages via television, phones, internet, and direct voice communication. For public speaking, your main channels are auditory (your voice) and visual (gestures, facial expressions, visual aids). You can also use other channels—taste, smell, touch, and physical activity—which will be discussed in Chapter 9.

Feedback

feedback
verbal and nonverbal responses made by a listener to a speaker

Feedback is the response that the listeners give the speaker. Sometimes it is *verbal,* as when a listener asks questions or makes comments. In most public speeches and certainly in the ones you will give in the classroom, listeners wait to give verbal feedback until the question-and-answer period.

Listeners also give *nonverbal* feedback. If they are smiling and nodding their heads, they are obviously in agreement with your remarks. If they are frowning and sitting with their arms folded, they more than likely disagree with what you are saying.

Tips for Your Career

Seek Feedback*

Some speakers develop unconscious habits when they speak, such as smoothing their hair or straightening their clothes. The best way to discover and discard these quirks is to get feedback from your listeners in the form of an evaluation. Although feedback is valuable for pinpointing delivery problems, it is even more important as a way to assess the *content* of your speech: Are your remarks enlightening or confusing to the listeners?

You don't need an evaluation of every speech in your career, but you should seek feedback occasionally. Strive to get both positive input and constructive suggestions, so that you can keep the good and eliminate the bad. Here are four good methods:

1. **Ask several friends or colleagues to critique your speech.** Don't make an imprecise request like "Tell me how I do on this" because your evaluators will probably say at the end of your speech, "You did fine—good speech," regardless of what they thought of it, to avoid hurting your feelings. Instead give them a specific assignment: "Please make a note of at least three things that you like about the speech and my delivery, and at least three things that you feel need

improvement." Now your listeners know exactly what you need. As a result, you are likely to get helpful feedback.

2. **Use an evaluation form.** Distribute sheets to all listeners, asking for responses to a series of questions about your delivery and the content of your speech. To protect anonymity, you can have someone collect the forms.

3. **Ask a small group of listeners to sit down with you after a meeting to share their reactions.** This is especially useful in finding out whether the listeners understood and accepted your message. Try to listen and learn without becoming argumentative or defensive.

4. **Record your presentation on video.** Invite colleagues to watch the video with you and help you evaluate it. Because many people are *never* pleased with either themselves or their speeches on video, colleagues often can provide objectivity. For example, an introduction that now seems dull to you might strike your colleagues as interesting and captivating.

*The sources for Tips are cited in the Notes section at the end of the book.

If they are yawning, they are probably bored or weary. ("A yawn," wrote English author G. K. Chesterton, "is a silent shout.")

If you receive negative feedback, try to help your listeners. If, for example, you are explaining a concept, but some of your listeners are shaking their heads and giving you looks that seem to say, "I don't understand," try again, using different words, to make your ideas clear.

interference
anything that obstructs accurate communication of a message

Interference

Interference is anything that blocks or hinders the accurate communication of a message. There are three types:

- *External* interference comes from outside the listener: someone coughing, people talking loudly in the hall, or broken air-conditioning that leaves the listeners hot and sticky.

- *Internal* interference comes from within the listener. Some listeners might be hungry or tired or sick, or they might be daydreaming or worrying about a personal problem. As a speaker, you can help such listeners by making your speech so engaging that the audience wants to listen to you.

- *Speaker-generated* interference can occur if you distract your listeners with unfamiliar words, confusing concepts, or bizarre clothing.

Interference can be caused by a daydreaming listener.

Sometimes listeners will try to overcome interference—for example, straining to hear the speaker's words over the noise of a truck outside. But too often, listeners will fail to make the extra effort.

When you are a speaker, stay alert for signs of interference and respond immediately. For example, if a plane roars overhead, you can either speak louder or pause while it passes.

Situation

situation

the setting in which communication takes place

The **situation** is the context—the time, place, and circumstances—in which communication occurs. Different situations call for different behaviors. In some settings, speakers can crack jokes and audiences can laugh, while in others, speakers must be serious and listeners should remain silent.

Time of day determines how receptive an audience is. Many listeners, for example, become sluggish and sleepy about an hour after a big meal. If you give a presentation during that period, you can enliven it by using colorful visual aids and hands-on activities.

When you prepare a speech, find out as much as possible about the situation: What is the nature of the occasion? How many people are likely to be present? Will the speech be given indoors or outdoors? Once you assess these variables, you can adapt your speech to make it effective for the situation.

The Process in Everyday Life

So far, our discussion might suggest that speech communication is a simple process: a speaker sends a message, a listener provides feedback—back and forth, like a tennis match. But in everyday life, the process is usually complex and dynamic. Instead of speaker and listener taking turns, communicators often send and receive messages at the same time.

For example, you go into your boss's office to ask for a raise. As you start your (verbal) message, she is giving you a friendly, accepting smile, a (nonverbal) message that seems to say that she is glad to see you. But as your message is spelled out, her smile fades and is replaced by a grim expression of regret—negative feedback. "I wish I could give you a big raise," she says, "but I can't even give you a little one." As she is saying these last words, she interprets your facial expression as displaying disbelief, so she hastily adds, "Our departmental budget just won't permit it. My hands are tied." And so on . . . a lively give-and-take of verbal and nonverbal communication.

The Speaker's Responsibilities

When you give a speech, you should accept certain responsibilities.

Maintain High Ethical Standards

The standards of conduct and moral judgment that are generally accepted in a society are called *ethics*. In public speaking, the focus on ethics is on how speakers handle their material and how they treat their listeners.[14] Speakers should be honest and straightforward with listeners, avoiding all methods and goals that are deceitful, unscrupulous, or unfair. "Ethical Issue Quiz" boxes throughout the book will help you exercise your skills at points where ethical issues are discussed.

Let's examine three important ethical responsibilities of the speaker.

Never Distort Information

As an ethical speaker, you should always be honest about facts and figures. Distorting information is not only dishonest—it's foolish. Let's say that in your career, you persuade some colleagues to take a certain course of action but it is later discovered that you got your way by distorting facts and statistics. In the future, your colleagues will distrust everything you propose—even if you have sound logic and impeccable evidence on your side. "A liar will not be believed," said the ancient Greek writer Aesop, "even when he [or she] speaks the truth."[15]

Ethical Issue Quiz

Suppose you are speaking in support of a good cause, but the statistics you want to use in your speech are complicated and hard to explain. You could convince your audience more easily if you made up some simplified statistics. Is it okay to fabricate a small amount of data so that it is easier for your audience to understand?

A. Yes, if the data is close to being accurate.
B. No, it is not okay.
C. Sometimes yes, sometimes no—it depends on the context.

For the answer, see the last page of this chapter.

Respect Your Audience

Some speakers talk down to their listeners. Speaking in a scolding, condescending tone, one speaker told an audience of young job-seekers, "I know you people don't believe me, but you're wasting your time and money if you pay a consultant to critique your résumé."

Humorist Will Rogers said it well: "Everybody is ignorant, only on different subjects" and "There is nothing as stupid as an educated man if you get him off the thing he was educated in."[16] When you are the expert on a subject, remember that your "ignorant" listeners are experts on topics within their own realm of knowledge and experience.

Reject Stereotyping and Scapegoating

A **stereotype** is a simplistic or exaggerated image that humans carry in their minds about groups of people. If you were asked to give a speech to raise funds for a shelter for homeless people, you might have difficulty in generating sympathy because many people have a negative stereotype of the homeless, referring to them as "bums" and assuming them to be addicted to alcohol or drugs.

stereotype
an oversimplified or exaggerated image

Like all stereotypes, this one is unfair, as illustrated by the story of Dave Talley, a homeless man in Tempe, Arizona, who found a backpack containing a laptop computer and $3,300 in cash. He turned in the backpack, which had been lost by Bryan Belanger, a student at Arizona State University. Belanger said he had withdrawn the money from his bank account to buy a new car after his old one had been wrecked. As for Dave Talley, he said he had no hesitation about turning in the lost items. "Not everybody on the streets is a criminal," he said. "Most of us have honor and integrity."[17]

You should reject stereotypes because they force all people in a group into the same simple pattern. They fail to account for individual differences and the wide range of characteristics among members of any group. For example, a popular stereotype depicts lawyers as dishonest. Some lawyers are dishonest, yes, but many are sincere advocates who make positive contributions to society.

While avoiding stereotyping, you also should reject its close cousin, scapegoating. A **scapegoat** is a person or a group unfairly blamed for some real or imagined wrong. In recent years, the alleged decline in the quality of education in the United States has been blamed on public school teachers, who have been vilified as incompetent and uncaring. While there may be some teachers who deserve such labels, most are dedicated professionals who care deeply about their students.

scapegoat
an individual or a group that innocently bears the blame of others

Enrich Listeners' Lives

Before a speech, some speakers make remarks such as these to their friends:

- "I hope not many people show up."
- "When I ask for questions, I hope nobody has any."
- "I want to get this over with."

Often a speaker makes these comments out of nervousness. As you will see in Chapter 2, speech anxiety is a normal occurrence that can be motivated by a variety of understandable reasons. However, such remarks show that the speaker is focused on his or her own emotions rather than on the audience.

Instead of viewing a speech as an ordeal, consider it an opportunity to enrich the lives of your listeners. One of my students, Mary Crosby, gave a classroom speech on poisonous spiders—what they look like, how to avoid them, and what to do if bitten. She had spent 6 hours researching the topic. If the 17 of us in the audience had duplicated her research, spending 6 hours apiece, we would have labored for 102 hours. Thus, Crosby saved us a great deal of time and effort and, more importantly, gave us important information. (Most of us, of course, probably never would have taken the time to do this research, so her speech was all the more valuable.)

Take Every Speech Seriously

Consider two situations that some speakers erroneously assume are not worth taking seriously: classroom speeches and small audiences.

Classroom speeches.   Contrary to what some students think, your classroom speeches are as important as any speeches that you may give in your career or community, and they deserve to be taken seriously. They deal with real human issues and they are given by real human beings. As a teacher, I look forward to classroom speeches because I learn a lot from them. I have learned how to save the life of a person choking on food, how to garden without using pesticides, how to set up a tax-free savings account for my children, and so much more.

Small audiences.   Some speakers mistakenly think that if an audience is small, they need not put forth their best effort. Wrong. You should try as hard to communicate with an audience of 5 as you would with an audience of 500. James "Doc" Blakely of Wharton, Texas, tells of a colleague who traveled to a small town in the Canadian province of Saskatchewan to give a speech and found that only one person had shown up to hear him. He gave the lone listener his best efforts, and later that listener started a national movement based on the speaker's ideas.[18]

Speech Introducing Yourself or a Classmate

A speech introducing yourself or a classmate to the audience is often assigned early in a public speaking class. The speech gives you an opportunity to use an easy topic to gain experience. It also gives you and other members of the class a chance to learn key information about one another—so that future classroom speeches can be tailored to the needs and interests of the audience.

Strive to show your audience what makes you or your classmate interesting and unique. Unless your instructor advises otherwise, you may include the following items.

Background Information
- Name
- Hometown
- Family information
- Work experience
- Academic plans
- Post-graduation goals

Unique Features
- Special interests (hobbies, sports, clubs, etc.)
- One interesting or unusual thing about you or your classmate
- One interesting or unusual experience

The last three items are especially important because they give the audience a glimpse into the qualities, interests, and experiences that make you or your classmate unique.

Sample Self-Introduction Speech

Robert Schnitzhofer introduces himself to a public speaking class.

With a Name Like This . . .

INTRODUCTION

I'm Robert Schnitzhofer, and yes, I know, Schnitzhofer is a strange name. When I was a kid, I wished I had a name like Brad Pitt—short and tough-sounding. But now I see my name as an advantage, which I will explain in a few minutes.

BODY

I am enrolled in the culinary program, and after I graduate, I hope to open a bakery that specializes in wedding and birthday cakes. Not ordinary cakes—I want to offer sophisticated and elegant desserts.

I like a lot of different types of music. Some of my favorites are Gnarls Barkley, the White Stripes, Erykah Badu, and Drive-By Truckers. My favorite website is YouTube.com. My favorite movie of all time is *Jerry Maguire*.

Going back to my name: I was teased as a child, but now I enjoy having an odd name that people have never heard before. It's a good conversation starter. I tell people about my great-great grandfather Albert Schnitzhofer, who emigrated from Switzerland. I found out that he owned a bakery in Zurich. It's kind of intriguing to think that my interest in baking might be genetic. From a business point of view, I think having an unusual name will be an advantage. It will catch people's attention—stand out in the crowd.

CONCLUSION

Smucker's is a company that makes jams and jellies, and they have a slogan that you have probably heard on TV: "With a name like Smucker's, it has to be good." Someday when I open my business, I will call it Schnitzhofer Bakery, and I already have a slogan: "With a name like Schnitzhofer, we have to be good."

Sample Speech Introducing a Classmate

In this speech, Sara Newton introduces classmate Elizabeth Hernandez.

A Life-Changing Gift

INTRODUCTION

When Elizabeth Hernandez graduated from high school, she received a present that changed her life. It was a digital camera system, with several different lenses—including a zoom telephoto lens.

BODY

Elizabeth began going to soccer games, tennis matches, and other sports events, taking pictures with the telephoto lens. Some of her pictures were so good, she submitted them to the local newspaper. To her surprise, the paper printed all of them. The photo editor at the paper told Elizabeth that she ought to consider a career in photojournalism.

That's exactly what Elizabeth has decided to do. She is a photojournalism major, and she makes money on the side with freelance photography. Last summer she landed an assignment taking publicity pictures for a basketball camp.

Elizabeth loves to hike in wilderness areas, and of course she always takes her camera with her. Her other special interests are chatting with friends on Facebook and searching the Internet for—you guessed it—interesting photos.

CONCLUSION

Thanks to a wonderful high school graduation gift, Elizabeth Hernandez has found her passion and her career.

Quick Guide to Public Speaking

If you love the sport of snowshoe boulder jumping, it would make a good topic.

To help you with any major speeches that you must give before you have had time to study this entire book, we will take a look at the key principles of preparation and delivery.

The guide below assumes that you will use the most popular method of speaking—extemporaneous—which means that you carefully prepare your speech but you don't read or memorize a script. Instead you look directly at your listeners and talk in a natural, conversational way, occasionally glancing at notes to stay on track.

The extemporaneous style and three other methods of speaking—manuscript (reading a document), memorization (speaking from memory), and impromptu (speaking with little or no time to prepare)—will be fully discussed in Chapter 14.

Preparation

Audience.   The goal of public speaking is to gain a response from your listeners—to get them to think, feel, or act in a certain way. To reach the listeners, find out as much as you can about them. What are their ages, genders, racial and ethnic backgrounds, and educational levels? What are their attitudes toward you and the subject? How much do they already know about the subject? When you have completed a thorough analysis of your listeners, adapt your speech to meet their needs and interests.

Topic.   Choose a topic that is interesting to you and about which you know a lot (either now or after doing research). Your topic also should be interesting to the listeners—one they

Tips for Your Career

Avoid the Five Biggest Mistakes Made by Speakers

In a survey by the author, 370 business and professional leaders were asked to name the most common mistakes made by public speakers in the United States today. Here are the most common ones:

1. **Failing to tailor one's speech to the needs and interests of the audience.** A *poor* speaker bores listeners with information that is stale or useless. A *good* speaker sizes up the listeners in advance and gives them material that is interesting and useful.

2. **Using PowerPoint ineffectively.** If used wisely, PowerPoint slides can be wonderful, but if used poorly, they can irritate an audience. "How to Avoid Death by PowerPoint," an appendix at the end of Chapter 9, contrasts bad slides with good ones.

3. **Speaking too long.** If you want to avoid alienating an audience, stay within your time limit. Time yourself when you practice, and when you give your speech, refrain from ad-libbing and going off on tangents.

4. **Being poorly prepared.** A good speech does not just happen. The speaker must spend hours researching the topic, organizing material, and rehearsing the speech before he or she rises to speak. Therese Myers, head of Quarterdeck Office Systems, says, "I've learned that slapping together a presentation during an hour on the plane the day before doesn't cut it. Now I take at least two weeks to prepare a talk."

5. **Being dull.** A speech can be made boring by poor content or by poor delivery. To avoid being dull, you should (a) choose a subject about which you are enthusiastic, (b) prepare interesting material, (c) have a strong desire to communicate your message to the audience, and (d) let your enthusiasm shine during your delivery of the speech.

Listeners get bored if a speech is uninteresting or too long.

will consider timely and worthwhile. Narrow the topic so that you can comfortably and adequately cover it within the time allotted.

Purposes and central idea.   Select a general purpose (to inform, to persuade, etc.), a specific purpose (a statement of exactly what you want to achieve with your audience), and a central idea (the message of your speech boiled down to one sentence). For example, suppose you want to persuade your listeners to safeguard their dental health. You could create objectives such as these:

General Purpose: To persuade

Specific Purpose: To persuade my listeners to take good care of their teeth and gums

Next, ask yourself, "What is my essential message? What big idea do I want to leave in the minds of my listeners?" Your answer is your central idea. Here is one possibility:

Central Idea: Keeping your mouth healthy can contribute to your overall health.

This central idea is what you want your listeners to remember if they forget everything else.

Finding materials.   Gather information by reading books and periodicals (such as magazines and journals), searching for information on the Internet, interviewing knowledgeable people, or drawing from your own personal experiences. Look for interesting items such as examples, statistics, stories, and quotations. Consider using visual aids to help the audience understand and remember key points.

Organization.   Organize the body of your speech by devising two or three main points that explain or prove the central idea. To continue the example from above, ask yourself this question: "How can I get my audience to understand and accept my central idea?" Here are two main points that could be made:

I. Medical researchers say that poor oral health can lead to diabetes, heart disease, pneumonia, and some types of cancer.
II. Know how to protect your teeth and gums.

The next step is to develop each main point with support material such as examples, statistics, and quotations from experts. Underneath the first main point, these two items could be used to illustrate the health risks of poor oral health:

- Researchers at Columbia University's School of Public Health tracked 9,296 men and women for 20 years and found that those participants who developed gum disease had a much greater risk of becoming diabetic than participants without gum disease.
- A recent study published in the *New England Journal of Medicine* established that having gum disease significantly increases the chances of developing heart disease.

Under the second main point, discuss the need to brush and floss daily, use antibacterial mouthwash, and get a professional cleaning from a dental hygienist twice a year.

Transitions.   To carry your listeners smoothly from one part of the speech to another, use transitional words or phrases, such as "Let's begin by looking at the problem," "Now for my second reason," and "Let me summarize what we've covered."

Introduction.   In the first part of your introduction, grab the attention of the listeners and make them want to listen to the rest of the speech. Attention-getters include fascinating stories, intriguing questions, and interesting facts or statistics. Next, prepare listeners for the body of the speech (by stating the central idea and/or by previewing the main points). Give any background information or definitions that the audience would need in order to understand the speech. Establish credibility by stating your own expertise or by citing reliable sources.

Conclusion.   Summarize your key points, and then close with a clincher (such as a quotation or a story) to drive home the central idea of the speech.

Outline.   Put together all parts of the speech (introduction, body, conclusion, and transitions) in an outline. Make sure that everything in the outline serves to explain, illustrate, or prove the central idea.

Speaking notes.   Prepare brief speaking notes based on your outline. These notes should be the only cues you take with you to the lectern.

Practice.   Rehearse your speech several times. Don't memorize the speech, but strive to rehearse ideas (as cued by your brief speaking notes). Trim the speech if you are in danger of exceeding the time limit.

Delivery

McGraw-Hill **Speech Prep**
http://www.mhhe.com/ speechprep/

Self-confidence.   Develop a positive attitude about yourself, your speech, and your audience. Don't let fear cripple you: nervousness is normal for most speakers. Rather than trying to banish your jitters, use nervousness as a source of energy—it actually can help you to come across as a vital, enthusiastic speaker.

Approach and beginning.   When you are called to speak, leave your seat without sighing or mumbling, walk confidently to the front of the room, spend a few moments standing in silence (this is a good time to arrange your notes and get your first sentences firmly in mind), and then look directly at the audience as you begin your speech.

Eye contact.   Look at all parts of the audience throughout the speech, glancing down at your notes only occasionally. Avoid staring at a wall or the floor; avoid looking out a window.

Speaking rate.   Speak at a rate that makes it easy for the audience to absorb your ideas—neither too slow nor too fast.

Expressiveness.   Your voice should sound as animated as it does when you carry on a conversation with a friend.

Clarity and volume.   Pronounce your words distinctly and speak loud enough so that all listeners can clearly hear you. Avoid verbal fillers such as *uh, ah, um, er, okay, ya know.*

Gestures and movement.   If it is appropriate and feels natural, use gestures to accompany your words. They should add to, rather than distract from, your message. You may move about during your speech, as long as your movements are purposeful and confident—not random and nervous. Don't do anything that distracts the audience, such as jingling keys or riffling note cards.

Posture and poise.   Stand up straight. Try to be comfortable, yet poised and alert. Avoid leaning on the lectern or slouching on a desk.

Use of notes.   Glance at your notes occasionally to pick up the next point. Don't read them or absentmindedly stare at them.

Stand up straight, look at your listeners, and use gestures.

Enthusiasm.   Don't simply go through the motions of "giving a speech." Your whole manner—eyes, facial expression, posture, voice—should show enthusiasm for your subject, and you should seem genuinely interested in communicating your ideas.

Ending and departure.   Say your conclusion, pause a few moments, and then ask—in a tone that shows that you sincerely mean it—"Are there any questions?" Don't give the appearance of being anxious to get back to your seat (by pocketing your notes or by taking a step toward your seat).

Resources for Review and Skill Building

Summary

A public speaking course helps you develop the key oral communication skills (speaking well and listening intelligently) that are highly prized in business, technical, and professional careers. You gain both confidence and experience as you practice those skills in an ideal environment—the classroom—where your audience is friendly and supportive.

The speech communication process consists of seven elements: speaker, listener, message, channel, feedback, interference, and situation. Communication does not necessarily take place just because a speaker transmits a message; the message must be accurately received by the listener. When the speaker sends a message, he or she must make sure that the two components of a message—verbal and nonverbal—don't contradict each other.

Communicators often send and receive messages at the same time, creating a lively give-and-take of verbal and nonverbal communication.

Speakers should maintain high ethical standards, never distorting information, even for a good cause. They should respect their audiences and avoid a condescending attitude. They reject stereotyping and scapegoating.

Good communicators don't view a speech as an ordeal to be endured, but as an opportunity to enrich the lives of their listeners. For this reason, they take every speech seriously, even if the audience is small.

Key Terms

channel, *8*

feedback, *8*

interference, *9*

listener, *7*

message, *8*

scapegoat, *11*

situation, *10*

speaker, *6*

stereotype, *11*

Review Questions

1. Why are communication skills important to your career?

2. Name five personal benefits of a public speaking course.

3. What are the seven elements of the speech communication process?

4. Why is speaking not necessarily the same thing as communicating?

5. If there is a contradiction between the verbal and non-verbal components of a speaker's message, which component is a listener likely to accept as the true message?

6. If communication fails, who is to blame—the speaker or the listener?

7. What two channels are most frequently used for classroom speeches?

8. What are the three types of interference?

9. What are stereotypes? Give some examples.

10. According to a survey, what is the number one mistake made by public speakers?

Building Critical-Thinking Skills

1. Describe an instance of miscommunication between you and another person (friend, relative, salesperson, etc.). Discuss what caused the problem, and how the interchange could have been handled better.

2. Interference can block effective communication. Imagine you are a supervisor and you are giving important instructions at a staff meeting. You notice that a few employees are not receiving your message because they are carrying on a whispered conversation. What would you do? Justify your approach.

Building Teamwork Skills

1. Working in a group, analyze a particular room (your classroom or some other site that everyone is familiar with) as a setting for speeches (consider size of the room, seating, equipment, and potential distractions). Prepare a list of tips that speakers can follow to minimize interference and maximize communication.

2. Taking turns, each member of a group states his or her chosen (or probable) career, and then group members work together to imagine scenarios (in that career) in which oral communication skills play an important part.

Ethical Issues

Answer for p. 11: B. Making up data is never acceptable or ethical. It is okay to summarize complicated data for your audience, but be sure to tell them that you did so, and never alter data to suit your agenda.

Managing Nervousness

OUTLINE

Reasons for Nervousness

The Value of Fear

Guidelines for Managing Nervousness

OBJECTIVES

After studying this chapter, you should be able to:

1. Identify and describe the five fears that can cause nervousness.
2. Explain why nervousness can actually help a public speaker.
3. Apply techniques that can be used before and during a speech to manage nervousness.

RACING HIS CAR as fast as 137 miles per hour, Carl Edwards has won over 20 NASCAR races in the past decade. Because he seems fearless in a dangerous sport, you might assume that he has always been fearless in other areas of his life. Not so.

Before he entered NASCAR competition, he worked eight months as a teacher at a middle school in Columbia, Missouri. His first day in the classroom, he says, "I was petrified." He feared making a fool of himself, and he was scared he wouldn't know the material well enough to answer students' questions.[1]

He soon found a way to calm himself down and become a confident teacher. His solution? Spend a lot of time preparing for each class. "I learned that being totally prepared is the best way to handle your nerves in all areas of life, whether it's public speaking or NASCAR racing."[2]

Carl Edwards speaks at a NASCAR event.

If you experience nervousness as a public speaker, you are not alone. Most people—even public figures like Edwards—suffer from stage fright when called upon to speak in public.[3] In fact, when researchers ask Americans to name their greatest fears, the fear of speaking to a group of strangers is listed more often than fear of snakes, insects, lightning, deep water, heights, or flying in airplanes.[4]

With the tips offered in this chapter, you should be able to manage your nervousness and become a confident speaker.

Reasons for Nervousness

Is it ridiculous to be afraid to give a speech? I used to think so, back when I first began public speaking. I was a nervous wreck, and I would often chide myself by saying, "Come on, there's no good reason to be scared." But I was wrong. There *is* good reason to be scared; in fact, there are many good reasons, including the five below.

1. **Fear of being stared at.** If you haven't had experience in being the center of attention, it can be unnerving to have all eyes in a room focused on you.

2. **Fear of failure or rejection.** If you are like most people, you are afraid of looking stupid. You ask yourself, "What if I make a fool of myself?" or "What if I say something really dumb?"

3. **Fear of the unknown.** New events, such as your first job interview, can be scary because you cannot anticipate the outcome. Fortunately, this fear usually eases in public speaking as you gain experience. You develop enough confidence to know that nothing terrible will happen.

4. **A traumatic experience in the past.** You may have painful memories of a humiliating event in a classroom, or a presentation that flopped.

5. **Social anxiety.** Because of your genetic makeup or temperament, you may be awkward, uneasy, or apprehensive in public. You may feel defensive around other people, and fearful of being evaluated and judged.

All of these reasons are understandable, and you need not feel ashamed if any of them apply to you. Recognizing them is an important step in learning how to manage your nervousness.

The Value of Fear

In the first hour of my public speaking class, many students tell me that one of their goals is to eliminate all traces of nervousness. My response may surprise you as much as it surprises them: *You should not try to banish all your fear and nervousness. You need a certain amount of fear to give a good speech.*

You *need* fear? Yes. When accepted and managed, fear energizes you; it makes you think fast. It gives you vitality and enthusiasm. Here is why: When you stand up to give a speech and fear hits you, your body's biological survival mechanisms kick in. You experience the same feeling of high alert that saved our cave-dwelling ancestors when they faced hungry wolves and either had to fight or flee to survive. Though these mechanisms are not as crucial in our day-to-day lives as they were to our ancestors, this system is still nice to have for emergencies: if you were walking down a deserted street one night and someone threatened you, your body would release a burst of **adrenaline** into your bloodstream, causing freshly oxygenated blood to rush to your muscles, and you would be able to fight ferociously or retreat quickly. The benefit of adrenaline can be seen in competitive sports: athletes *must* get their adrenaline flowing before a game begins. The great home-run slugger Reggie Jackson said during his heyday, "I have butterflies in my stomach almost every time I step up to the plate. When I don't have them, I get worried because it means I won't hit the ball very well."[5]

Many musicians, actors, and public speakers have the same attitude. Singer Garth Brooks says, "If I ever stop getting nervous before a performance, it's time for me to quit."[6] In public speaking, adrenaline infuses you with energy. It enables you to think with greater clarity and quickness. It makes you come across to your audience as someone who is alive and vibrant. Elayne Snyder, a speech teacher, uses the term

adrenaline

a hormone, triggered by stress, that stimulates heart, lungs, and muscles and prepares the body for "fright, flight, or fight"

positive nervousness, which she describes in this way: "It's a zesty, enthusiastic, lively feeling with a slight edge to it. Positive nervousness is the state you'll achieve by converting your anxiety into constructive energy. . . . It's still nervousness, but you're no longer victimized by it; instead you're vitalized by it."[7]

positive nervousness
useful energy

If you want proof that nervousness is beneficial, observe speakers who have absolutely no butterflies at all. Because they are 100 percent relaxed, they usually give speeches that are dull and flat, with no energy, no zest. There is an old saying: "Speakers who say they are as cool as a cucumber usually give speeches about as interesting as a cucumber." One speaker, the novelist I. A. R. Wylie, said, "I rarely rise to my feet without a throat constricted with terror and a furiously thumping heart. When, for some reason, I *am* cool and self-assured, the speech is always a failure. I need fear to spur me on."[8]

Another danger of being too relaxed: you might get hit with a sudden bolt of panic. A hospital official told me that she gave an orientation speech to new employees every week for several years. "It became so routine that I lost all of my stage fright," she said. Then one day, while in the middle of her talk, she was suddenly and inexplicably struck with paralyzing fear. "I got all choked up and had to take a break to pull myself together."

I have had a similar experience, and so have many other speakers. We get too relaxed, and then we get blindsided by sudden panic. For this reason, if I find myself overly calm before a speech, I tell myself to be alert for danger. I try to encourage "positive nervousness," and this helps me to avoid being caught off-guard.

Your Thoughts ?

Many musicians make a distinction between "good nervousness" and "bad nervousness." What does this distinction mean? How does it apply to public speakers?

Guidelines for Managing Nervousness

A complete lack of fear is undesirable, but what about the other extreme? Is *too much* nervousness bad for you? Of course it is, especially if you are so incapacitated that you forget what you were planning to say, or if your breathing is so labored that you cannot get your words out. Your goal is to keep your nervousness under control so that you have just the right amount—enough to energize you, but not enough to cripple you. You can achieve a good balance by following the tips below.

In the Planning Stage

By giving time and energy to planning your speech, you can bypass many anxieties.

Choose a Topic You Know Well

Nothing will unsettle you more than speaking on a subject that is unfamiliar to you. If you are asked to do so, I suggest you decline the invitation (unless, of course, it is an assignment from an instructor or a boss who gives you no choice). Choose a topic you are interested in and know a lot about–or want to learn more about. This will give you enormous self-confidence; if something terrible happens, like losing your notes, you can improvise because you know your subject. Also, familiarity with the topic will allow you to handle yourself well in the question-and-answer period after the speech.

Prepare Yourself Thoroughly

Here is a piece of advice given by many experienced speakers: *The very best precaution against excessive stage fright is thorough, careful preparation.* You may have heard the expression "I came unglued." In public speaking, solid preparation is the "glue" that will hold you together.[9] Joel Weldon of Scottsdale, Arizona (who quips that he used to be so frightened of audiences that he was "unable to lead a church group in silent prayer"), gives his personal formula for managing fear: "I prepare and then prepare, and then when I think I'm ready, I prepare some more."[10] Weldon recommends five to eight hours of preparation for each hour in front of an audience.[11]

Start your preparation far in advance of the speech date so that you have plenty of time to gather ideas, create an outline, and prepare speaking notes. Then practice, practice, practice. Don't just look over your notes—actually stand up and rehearse your talk in whatever way suits you: in front of a mirror, a camcorder, or a live audience of family or friends. Don't rehearse just once—run through your entire speech at least four times. If you "give" your speech four times at home, you will find that your fifth delivery—before a live audience—will be smoother and more self-assured than if you had not practiced at all.

Never Memorize a Speech

Giving a speech from memory courts disaster. Winston Churchill, the British prime minister during World War II who is considered one of the greatest orators of the twentieth century, learned this lesson as a young man. In the beginning of his career, he would write out and memorize his speeches. One day, while giving a memorized talk to Parliament, he suddenly stopped. His mind went blank. He began his last sentence all over. Again his mind went blank. He sat down in embarrassment and shame. Never again did Churchill try to memorize a speech. This same thing has happened to many others who have tried to commit a speech to memory. Everything goes smoothly until they get derailed, and then they are hopelessly off the track.

Even if you avoid derailment, there is another reason for not memorizing: you will probably sound mechanical. Your audience will sense that you are speaking from your memory and not from your heart, and this will undermine your impact.

Visualize Yourself Giving an Effective Speech

Let yourself daydream a bit: picture yourself going up to the lectern, a bit nervous but in control of yourself, then giving a forceful talk to an appreciative audience. This visualization technique may sound silly, but it has worked for many speakers and it may work for you. Notice that the daydream includes nervousness. You need to have a realistic image in your mind: nervous, but nevertheless in command of the situation and capable of delivering a strong, effective speech.

This technique, often called **positive imagery,** has been used by athletes for years. Have you ever watched professional golf on TV? Before each stroke, golfers carefully study the distance from the ball to the hole, the rise and fall of the terrain, and so on. Many of them report that just before swinging, they imagine themselves hitting the ball with the right amount of force and watching it go straight into the cup. Then they try to execute the play just as they imagined it. The imagery, many pros say, improves their game.

positive imagery
visualization of successful actions

Positive imagery works best when you can couple it with *believing* that you will give a successful speech. Is it absurd to hold such a belief? If you fail to prepare, yes, it is absurd. But if you spend time in solid preparation and rehearsal, you are justified in believing in success.

Whatever you do, don't let yourself imagine the opposite—a bad speech or poor delivery. Negative thinking will add unnecessary fear to your life in the days before your speech, and rob you of creative energy—energy that you need for preparing and practicing.[12]

Know That Shyness Is No Barrier

Some shy people think that their temperament blocks them from becoming good speakers, but this is erroneous. Many shy introverts have succeeded in show business: Brad Pitt, Gwyneth Paltrow, Nicole Kidman, Jim Carrey, Blake Lively, Robert Pattinson, Johnny Depp, and Keira Knightley, to name just a few.[13] Many less-famous people also have succeeded. "I used to stammer," says Joe W. Boyd of Bellingham, Washington, "and I used to be petrified at the thought of speaking before a group of any size." Despite his shyness, Boyd joined a Toastmasters club to develop his speaking skills. Two years later, he won the Toastmasters International Public Speaking Contest by giving a superb speech to an audience of more than 2,000 listeners.[14]

Brad Pitt is a shy introvert.

Shift Focus from Self to Audience

Before a speech, some speakers worry about whether listeners will like them. This is a big mistake, says Johnny Lee, a specialist in preventing workplace violence, who manages his nervousness by focusing on his audience rather than on himself. To worry about yourself and your image, he says, "is a kind of vanity—you are putting yourself above your audience and your message."[15]

Carlos Jimenez, a member of a Toastmasters club in Northern California, says that focusing on himself is an act of inexcusable selfishness. "Who am I to worry about whether I will be perceived as a brilliant, eloquent expert. Who am I to think that the way I look and talk is more important than the people who are sitting in the audience? I look at public speaking as a way to help people, and I can't really help people if my mind is filled with 'me, me, me' instead of 'you, you, you.'"[16]

One good way to shift the focus from self to audience is to change your "self-talk." Whenever you have a self-centered thought such as, "I will make a total idiot out of myself," substitute an audience-centered thought such as, "I will give my listeners information that will be useful in their lives." This approach eases your anxiety and also empowers you to connect with your audience.

Plan Visual Aids

In addition to adding spice and interest to a speech, visual aids reduce anxiety because you can shift the audience's stares from you to your illustrations.[17] Also, moving about as you display your aids siphons off some of your excess nervous energy. Your aids don't have to be elaborate, and you don't need many—sometimes one or two will suffice.

Make Arrangements

At least several days before you give your speech, inspect the location and anticipate any problems: Is there an extension cord for the multimedia projector? Do the windows have curtains or blinds so that the room can be darkened? Is there a whiteboard and a marker? Some talks have been ruined and some speakers turned into nervous wrecks because, at the last moment, they discover that there isn't an extension cord in the entire building.

Devote Extra Practice to the Introduction

Because you will probably have the most anxiety at the beginning of your speech, you should spend a lot of time practicing your introduction.

Most speakers, actors, and musicians report that after the first minute or two, their nervousness eases and the rest of the event is relatively easy. Ernestine Schumann-Heink, the German opera singer, said, "I grow so nervous before a performance, I become sick. I want to go home. But after I have been on the stage for a few minutes, I am so happy that nobody can drag me off." Perhaps happiness is too strong a word for what you will feel, but if you are a typical speaker, the rest of your speech will be smooth sailing once you have weathered the turbulent waters of the first few minutes.

Immediately before the Speech

Here are a few tips for the hours preceding your speech:

Verify Equipment and Materials

On the day of your speech, arrive early and inspect every detail of the arrangements you have made. Is the equipment you need in place and in good working order? If there is a public-address system, test your voice on it before the audience arrives so that you can feel at ease with it. Learn how to adjust the microphone.

Get Acclimated to Audience and Setting

It can be frightening to arrive at the meeting place at the last moment and confront a sea of strange faces waiting to hear you talk. If you arrive at least one hour early, you can get acclimated to the setting and chat with people as they come into

Greet listeners as they arrive.

the room. In this way, you will see them not as a hostile pack of strangers but as ordinary people who wish you well.

Henry Heimlich is the creator of the famed Heimlich Maneuver for rescuing people who are choking. Even though he frequently gives lectures throughout the world, Dr. Heimlich says, "I am always a little nervous wondering how a particular audience will accept me and my thoughts. It is good to meet some of the audience socially before lecturing to them, in order to relate to their cultural and intellectual backgrounds. You are then their 'friend.'"[18]

Danielle Kennedy of Sun Valley, Idaho, says that when she began her speaking career, she was so nervous she would hide out in a bathroom until it was time for her to speak. Now, she says, she mingles with the listeners as they arrive and engages them in conversation. "This reminds me that they are just nice people who want to be informed. I also give myself pleasant thoughts. Things like: 'Can you imagine, these people drove 100 miles just to hear me. I am so lucky. These people are wonderful.' I get real warm thoughts going by the time I get up there."[19]

Use Physical Actions to Release Tension

Adrenaline can be beneficial, providing athletes and public speakers with helpful energy, but it also has a downside. When your body goes on high alert, you get pumped up and ready for action, but you also get a racing heart, trembling hands, and jittery knees. If you are an athlete, this is no problem because you will soon be engaged in vigorous play that will drain off excess nervous energy. As a public speaker, you don't have that outlet. Nevertheless, there are several tension releasers you can use:

- Take three slow, deep breaths and hold them. To prevent hyperventilating, be sure to inhale slowly and exhale slowly.
- Do exercises that can be performed without calling attention to yourself. Here are some examples: (1) Tighten and then relax your leg muscles. (2) Push your arm or hand muscles against a hard object (such as a desktop or a chair) for a few moments, then release the pressure. (3) Press the palms of your hands against each other in the same way: tension, release . . . tension, release . . .

During the Speech

Here are proven pointers to keep in mind as you deliver a speech.

Pause before You Start

All good speakers pause a few seconds before they begin their talk. This silence is effective because (1) it is dramatic, building up the audience's interest and curiosity; (2) it makes you look poised and in control; (3) it calms you; and (4) it gives you a chance to look at your notes and get your first two or three sentences firmly in mind.

Many tense, inexperienced speakers rush up to the lectern and begin their speech at once, thus getting off to a frenzied, flustered start. They think that silence is an undesirable void that must be filled up immediately. To the contrary, silence is a good breathing space between what went before and what comes next. It helps the audience to focus.

Deal Rationally with Your Body's Turmoil

If you are a typical beginning speaker, you will suffer from some or all of the following symptoms as you begin your talk:

- Pounding heart
- Trembling hands
- Shaky knees

Figure 2.1
The alternative paths that a speaker feeling stressed might take.

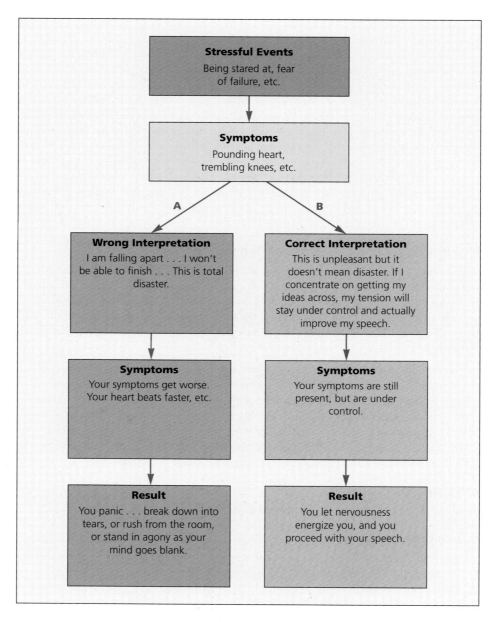

- Dry, constricted throat
- Difficulty in breathing
- Quivering voice
- Flushed face

You are likely to suffer the most during the first few minutes of a speech, and then things get better. However, if your symptoms get worse as you proceed, it might be because your mind has taken a wrong path. Examine the two paths diagrammed in Figure 2.1. If you take Route A, you are trapped in a vicious circle. Your mind tells your body that disaster is upon you, and your body responds by feeling worse. This, in turn, increases your brain's perception of disaster.

You can avoid this rocky road by choosing Route B, in which your mind helps your body stay in control. The mental trick is to remind yourself that nervousness is an ally that can help energize you. Tell yourself that your symptoms, rather than being a prelude to disaster, are evidence that you are keyed up enough to give a good speech.

Think of Communication, Not Performance

Regard your challenge as *communication* rather than *performance*. Dr. Michael T. Motley of the University of California, Davis, says that speakers who suffer from excessive anxiety make the mistake of thinking of themselves as *performing* for listeners, whom they see as hostile evaluators. Such people say, "The audience will ridicule me if I make a mistake. I'll be embarrassed to death." But in fact, says Dr. Motley, audiences are more interested in hearing what you have to say "than in analyzing or criticizing how [you] say it." Audiences "usually ignore errors and awkwardness as long as they get something out of a speech."[20]

Your Thoughts

"It is folly for a speaker to focus on his or her personal appearance." Do you agree? Defend your answer.

When you stop worrying about "How well am I performing?" and start thinking about "How can I share my ideas with these people?" two things usually happen: (1) your anxiety comes down to a manageable level and (2) your delivery improves dramatically. If you treat speechmaking as a dialogue with your listeners rather than as a performance, you will tend to talk *with* them, instead of *to* them; you will tend to speak conversationally rather than in a stiff, unnatural way.

When one of my students, Maxine Jones, began her first classroom speech, her voice sounded artificial and cold; but after a few moments, she sounded animated and warm, as if she were carrying on a lively conversation. This caused her to become more interesting and easier to follow. Later she explained her transformation: "At first I was scared to death, but then I noticed that everyone in the room was looking at me with curiosity in their eyes, and I could tell that they really wanted to hear what I was saying. I told myself, 'They really *care* about this information—I can't let them down.' So I settled down and talked to them as if they were my friends. I got so involved with explaining things to them that I didn't worry too much about being scared."

What Jones discovered is confirmed by athletes. Most tennis players, for example, are gripped by nervous tension before a match, but if they concentrate on hitting the ball, their tension recedes into the background. Likewise, public speakers may be filled with anxiety before a speech, but if they concentrate on communicating with the audience, their anxiety moves to a back burner, where it provides energy for the task.

Know That Most Symptoms Are Not Seen

Some speakers get rattled because they think the audience is keenly aware of their thumping heart and quaking hands. You, of course, are painfully aware of those symptoms, but—believe it or not—your audience is usually oblivious to your body's distress. Remember that people are sitting out there wanting to hear your ideas. They are not saying to themselves, "Let's see, what signs of nervousness is this person displaying?"

I have had students tell me after a speech that they were embarrassed about their jittery performance, yet I and the other listeners in the class saw no signs of nervousness. We were listening to the ideas and failed to notice the speaker's discomfort. Various studies have found the same thing to be true: audiences are unaware of the symptoms that the speakers think are embarrassingly obvious.[21] In other words, you are probably the only one who knows that your knees are shaking and your heart is pounding.

TV talk show host Dick Cavett notes that a TV performer's level of stage fright "varies from night to night. The best thing to do is tell yourself it doesn't show one-eighth

Tips for Your Career

Prepare for Memory Lapses

A psychologist tells of the time when he was speaking at a convention as the presiding officer. At one point, he wanted to praise an associate, who was sitting next to him at the head table, for her hard work in planning the convention. "As I began my words of tribute," he said, "my mind suddenly went blank, and I couldn't remember her name! It was awful. This was a woman I had worked with for years. She was like a sister."

Fortunately, he said, everyone was wearing name tags, so he leaned over, saw her name, and used it in his remarks—without the audience suspecting his memory lapse.

Such lapses are common, but don't be alarmed. There is a simple solution: Prepare a card with all basic information—names, dates, phone numbers—and keep the card with your other notes for easy access.

This "card trick" is used by many ministers, politicians, and other public speakers. "When I perform weddings, even if I'm an old friend of the couple," says one minister, "I have their names printed in big letters on a card that I keep in front of me."

Use a card for any familiar passages, such as the Lord's Prayer or the Pledge of Allegiance, that you are supposed to recite or to lead the audience in reciting. You may never need to read the card, but it's nice to have a backup in case of emergency.

Please don't misinterpret this tip to mean that you should write out an entire speech. Brief notes—a few words or phrases—are still recommended. Use the "card trick" only for names, numbers, and wordings that must be recalled with complete accuracy.

At public ceremonies like this wedding in Chicago, many ministers avoid embarrassment by having key information (such as the names of bride and groom) on a card in front of them.

as much as you feel. If you're a little nervous, you don't look nervous at all. If you're very nervous, you look slightly nervous. And if you're totally out of control, you look troubled. It scales down on the screen." People who appear on a talk show, says Cavett, should always remind themselves that everything they are doing *looks* better than it *feels*. "Your nervous system may be giving you a thousand shocks, but the viewer can only see a few of them."[22] The same thing holds true for a speech: you look better than you feel.

Never Mention Nervousness or Apologize

Despite what I've just said, there may be times when an audience does notice your nervousness—when, for example, your breathing is audibly labored. In such a case, resist the temptation to comment or apologize. Everyone knows that most people get nervous when they talk in public, so why call attention to it or apologize for it?

Commenting about nervousness can create two big dangers. First of all, you might get yourself more rattled than you were to begin with. I remember listening to a teacher who was giving a talk to a PTA meeting one night. In the middle of her remarks, she suddenly blurted out, "Oh my god, I knew I would fall apart." Up to that time, I had not been aware of any discomfort or nervousness. She tried to continue her talk, but she was too flustered. She gave up the effort and sat down with a red face. I don't know what kind of internal distress she was suffering, of course, but I am certain that if she had said nothing about her nervousness, she could have dragged herself through the speech. When she sat down, I felt irritated and disappointed because I had been keenly interested in her remarks. How selfish of her, I thought, to deprive me of the second half of her speech simply because she was nervous. I know that my reaction sounds insensitive, but it underscores an important point: your listeners don't care about your emotional distress; they only want to hear your ideas.

The second risk in mentioning symptoms is that your audience might have been unaware of your nervousness before you brought it up, but now you have distracted them from your speech and they are watching the very thing you don't want them to scrutinize: your body's behavior. If you say, "I'm sorry that my hands are shaking," what do you think the audience will pay close attention to, at least for the next few minutes? Your hands, of course, instead of your speech. Keep your audience's attention focused on your ideas, and they will pay little or no attention to your emotional and physical distress.

Don't Let Your Audience Upset You

If you are like some speakers, you get rattled when you look out at the audience and observe that most listeners are poker-faced and unsmiling. Does this mean they are displeased with your speech? No. Their solemn faces have nothing to do with you and your speech. This is just one of those peculiarities of human nature: in a conversation, people will smile and nod and encourage you, but when listening to a speech in an audience, most of them wear a blank mask. The way to deal with those stony faces is to remind yourself that your listeners want you to succeed; they hope that you will give them a worthwhile message. If you are lucky, you will notice two or three listeners who obviously appreciate your speech—they nod in agreement or give you looks of approval. Let your eyes go to them frequently. They will give you courage and confidence.

Actress Moran Rosenblatt listens to a speaker at a film festival in Berlin. Is she displeased with the speaker's remarks? Is she bored? Don't jump to conclusions. Perhaps this is just her habitual expression when she's absorbed in listening to an interesting topic. Speakers should not let such expressions upset them. Some listeners who look displeased are actually quite pleased.

If you are an inexperienced speaker, you may get upset if you see members of an audience whispering to one another. You may wonder, "Are these people making negative comments about me?" If the listeners are smiling, it's even worse: You ask yourself, "Did I say something dumb? Is there something wrong with my clothes?" If this happens to you, keep in mind that your rude listeners are probably just sharing some personal gossip. If they *are* whispering about something you've said, it's not necessarily negative. They may be whispering that they agree with you 100 percent.

What if you see faces that look angry or displeased? Don't assume the worst. Some people get a troubled look on their face whenever they concentrate on a speaker's message. Michelle Roberts, a defense attorney in Washington, DC, studies the facial expressions of every juror when she addresses the jury during a trial, but she has learned that frowning faces do not necessarily signify disapproval. "Sometimes jurors seem like they're scowling and actually they're with you."[23]

What if a listener stands up and walks out of the room? For some inexperienced speakers, this feels like a stunning personal defeat. Before you jump to conclusions, bear in mind that the listener's behavior is probably not a response to your speech: he or she may have another meeting to attend or may need to use the rest room or may have become ill suddenly. But what if the listener is indeed storming out of the room in a huff, obviously rejecting your speech? In such a case, advises veteran speaker Earl Nightingale, "don't worry about it. On controversial subjects, you're bound to have listeners who are not in agreement with you—unless you're giving them pure, unadulterated pap. Trying to win over every member of the audience is an impossible and thankless task. Remember, there were those who disagreed with wise, kind Socrates."[24]

Act Poised

To develop confidence when you face an audience, act as if you already are confident. Why? Because playing the role of the self-assured speaker can often transform you into a speaker who is genuinely confident and poised. In various wars, soldiers have reported that they were terrified before going into combat, but nevertheless they acted brave in front of their buddies. During the battle, to their surprise, what started off as a pretense became a reality. Instead of pretending to be courageous, they actually became so. The same thing often happens to public speakers.

Look Directly at the Audience

If you are frightened of your audience, it is tempting to stare at your notes or the back wall or the window, but these evasions will only add to your nervousness, not reduce it.

Force yourself to establish eye contact, especially at the beginning of your speech. Good eye contact means more than just a quick, furtive glance at various faces in front of you; it means "locking" your eyes with a listener's for a couple of seconds. Locking eyes may sound frightening, but it actually helps to calm you. In an article about a public speaking course that she took, writer Maggie Paley said, "When you make contact with one other set of eyes, it's a connection; you can relax and concentrate. The first time I did it, I calmed down 90 percent, and spoke . . . fluently."[25]

Don't Speak Too Fast

Because of nervous tension and a desire to "get it over with," many speakers race through their speeches. "Take it slow and easy," advises Dr. Michael T. Motley of the University of California, Davis. "People in an audience have a tremendous job of information-processing to do. They need your help. Slow down, pause, and guide the audience through your talk by delineating major and minor points carefully. Remember that your objective is to help the audience understand what you are saying, not to present your information in record time."[26]

To help yourself slow down, rehearse your speech in front of friends or relatives and ask them to raise their hands whenever you talk too rapidly. For the actual delivery of the speech, write yourself reminders in large letters on your notes (such as "SLOW DOWN"). While you are speaking, look at your listeners and talk directly to them in the same calm, patient, deliberate manner you would use if you were explaining an idea to a friend.

Get Audience Action Early in the Speech

I said earlier that it's a bit unnerving to see your listeners' expressionless faces. In some speeches, you can change those faces from blank to animated by asking a question. (Tips on how to ask questions will be discussed in Chapter 11.) When the listeners respond with answers or a show of hands, they show themselves to be friendly and cooperative, and this reduces your apprehension. When they loosen up, you loosen up.

Eliminate Excess Energy

For siphoning off excess energy during the speech, you can use visual aids (as mentioned earlier) and these two tension releasers:

- Let your hands make gestures. You will not have any trouble making gestures if you simply allow your hands to be free. Don't clutch note cards or thrust your hands into your pockets or grip the lectern. If you let your hands hang by your side or rest on the lectern, you will find that they will make gestures naturally. You will not have to think about it.
- Walk about. Though you obviously should not pace back and forth like a caged animal, you can walk a few steps at a time. For example, you can walk a few steps to the left of the lectern to make a point, move back to the lectern to look at your notes for your next point, and then walk to the right of the lectern as you speak.

In addition to reducing tension, gestures and movement make you a more exciting and interesting speaker than someone who stands frozen in one spot.

Accept Imperfection

If you think that you must give a perfect, polished speech, you put enormous—and unnecessary—pressure on yourself. Your listeners don't care whether your delivery is perfect; they simply hope that your words will enlighten or entertain them. Think of yourself as a package deliverer; the audience is more interested in the package than in how skillfully you hand it over.

Making a mistake is not the end of the world. Even experienced speakers commit a fair number of blunders and bloopers. If you completely flub a sentence or mangle an idea, you might say something like, "No, wait. That's not the way I wanted to explain this. Let me try again." If you momentarily forget what you were planning to say, don't despair. Pause a few moments to regain your composure and find your place in your notes. If you can't find your place, ask the audience for help: "I've lost my train of thought—where was I?" There is no need to apologize. In conversation, you pause and correct yourself all the time; to do so in a speech makes you sound spontaneous and natural.

If you make a mistake that causes your audience to snicker or laugh, try to join in. If you can laugh at yourself, your audience will love you—they will see that you are no "stuffed shirt." Some comedians deliberately plan "mistakes" as a technique for gaining rapport with their audiences.

Welcome Experience

If you are an inexperienced speaker, please know that you will learn to manage your nervousness as you get more and more practice in public speaking, both in your speech class and in your career. You should welcome this experience as a way to further your personal and professional growth.

One of my students told me at the beginning of the course that she just *knew* she would drop out of the class right before her first speech. She stayed, though, and developed into a fine speaker. She later got a promotion in her company partly because of her speaking ability. "I never thought I'd say this," she admitted, "but the experience of giving speeches—plus learning how to handle nervousness—helped me enormously. Before I took the course, I used to panic whenever I started off a talk. I had this enormous lump in my throat, and I thought I was doing terrible. I would hurry through my talk just to get it over with." But as a result of the course, she said, "I learned to control my nervousness and use it to my advantage. Now I'm as nervous as ever when I give a speech, but I make the nervousness work *for* me instead of *against* me."

In your career, rather than shying away from speaking opportunities, seek them out. An old saying is true: experience is the best teacher.

Resources for Review and Skill Building

Summary

Nervousness is a normal, understandable emotion experienced by most public speakers. There are many reasons for jitters, but five of the most common are fear of being stared at, fear of failure or rejection, fear of the unknown, a traumatic experience in the past, and social anxiety. There is no reason to be ashamed if any of them apply to you.

Instead of trying to eliminate nervousness, welcome it as a source of energy. Properly channeled, it can help you give a better speech than you would deliver if you were completely relaxed.

The best way to avoid excessive, crippling nervousness is to pour time and energy into preparing and practicing your speech. Then, when you stand up to speak, deal rationally with your nervous symptoms (such as trembling knees and dry throat); remind yourself that the symptoms are not a prelude to disaster but instead are evidence that you are keyed up enough to give a good speech. Never call attention to your nervousness and never apologize for it; the listeners don't care about your emotional state—they just want to hear your message. Concentrate on getting your ideas across to the audience; this will get your mind where it belongs—on your listeners and not on yourself—and it will help you move your nervousness to a back burner, where it can still simmer and energize you without hindering your effectiveness.

Key Terms

adrenaline, *22*

positive imagery, *25*

positive nervousness, *23*

Review Questions

1. What are the five common reasons for speakers' nervousness?

2. Why are fear and nervousness beneficial to the public speaker?

3. Why is delivering a speech from memory a bad method?

4. Is shyness a liability for a speaker? Explain your answer.

5. How can a speaker reduce excessive tension before a speech?

6. Does an audience detect most of a speaker's nervous symptoms? Explain your answer.

7. Why should you never call attention to your nervousness?

8. Explain the idea "Think of communication, not performance."

9. Why should speakers not be upset when they see the unsmiling faces of their listeners?

10. Why should a speaker act as if he or she is confident?

Building Critical-Thinking Skills

1. In an experiment, psychologist Rowland Miller asked college students to do something embarrassing, such as singing "The Star-Spangled Banner," while classmates watched. Those students who reported a great degree of embarrassment thought that their classmates would consider them fools and like them less, but Miller found just the opposite: The classmates expressed greater regard for the easily embarrassed students after the performance than before. What lessons can a public speaker draw from this research?

2. Imagine that while you are speaking to an audience, you notice that (a) everyone is very quiet, (b) a man in the front is rubbing his neck, and (c) a woman is looking in her purse. Using two columns on a piece of paper, give a negative interpretation of these events in the first column, and then give a positive interpretation in the adjacent column.

Building Teamwork Skills

1. In a group, make a list of the nervous symptoms that group members have experienced before and during oral communication in public. (This may include being asked for comments during a class discussion.) Then discuss ways to control nervousness.

2. Worrying about future events, say mental-health therapists, can be helpful at certain times and harmful at other times. In a group, discuss the pros and cons of worrying, giving examples from everyday life. Then decide which aspects of speech preparation and delivery deserve to be worried about and which do not.

Ethical Issues

Answer for p. 24: A, B, and C. Not knowing much about the topic can worsen speech anxiety and can cause embarrassment in the question-and-answer period. Plagiarism is a form of theft and is always unethical.

Listening

OBJECTIVES

After studying this chapter, you should be able to:

1. Explain the difference between hearing and listening.
2. Describe eight keys to effective listening.
3. Define three major responsibilities that listeners have toward speakers.
4. Know how to give and receive evaluations of speeches.

AIR FORCE TECHNICAL SERGEANT Marquis Mullins and his daughter Anya (on the opposite page) are giving their full attention to a speaker at an Independence Day celebration in Washington, DC. They are displaying the attributes of ideal listeners—eyes focused on speaker, mind engaged with what the speaker is saying.

They also illustrate one of the key points of this chapter: When listeners are absorbed and attentive, they not only learn a lot—they also help to energize and encourage the speaker.

When listeners are fully engaged,
they help to energize the speaker.

Figure 3.1
Samantha Rudolph tries to recruit college students to work for ESPN, but a listening error by some students blocks effective communication.

Introduction to Listening

Can you remember key ideas from a speaker's presentation 24 hours after you listen to it? Before you answer, consider this:

Samantha Rudolph gives presentations on college campuses throughout the United States to try to recruit students to work at ESPN, the popular sports network (Figure 3.1). During a presentation at one college, she spent most of her time talking about the many ESPN jobs that are available at headquarters in Connecticut, but at one point, she mentioned that there are also a number of positions available in other states.[1]

The next day a professor, who had sent her Mass Communication class to listen to the presentation, discussed ESPN opportunities with her students, and she was surprised to learn that at least half the class believed that Rudolph had given the following message (as expressed by one student): "If you can't live in Connecticut, you can forget about working for ESPN."[2]

The students who failed to listen carefully were not stupid, and we should not feel superior to them. All of us face a challenge when we listen to a presentation. We don't have printed words to linger over and re-read if necessary. All we have is oral communication, which is written on the wind—fast-moving and impermanent.

Although listening effectively is a challenging task, you can become a better listener by employing the techniques discussed in this chapter. These techniques should also help you become a better speaker. As you gain more awareness of the difficulties of the listening process, you will be able to plan your presentations to ensure that you give listeners messages that are clear and memorable.

The Problem of Poor Listening Skills

A parent says to a child, "Are you listening to me?"

The child replies, "I hear you. I hear you."

Although in conversation we sometimes use the words "hear" and "listen" interchangeably, we should not treat them as synonyms. **Hearing** occurs when your ears pick up sound waves being transmitted by a speaker. **Listening** involves making sense out of what is being transmitted. In the words of Keith Davis, a business professor at Arizona State University, "Hearing is with the ears, listening is with the mind."[3]

Listening is a major part of daily life. We spend an estimated 50 to 70 percent of our communication time listening, but research shows that most of us are not very effective as listeners. According to tests by Dr. Lyman K. Steil of the University of Minnesota in St. Paul, here is what happens after the average person listens to a 10-minute oral presentation:

- Ten minutes later: The listener has heard, understood, properly evaluated, and retained only about 50 percent of what was said.

- Two days later: The listener's comprehension and retention have dropped to only 25 percent of what was said.[4]

You might think that our chief problem is failing to retain information, but actually our biggest error is miscomprehending and distorting what we hear. The results can be disastrous. Throughout the world, instructions are misunderstood, equipment breaks down from improper use, productivity declines, profits sag, sales are lost, relationships are damaged, morale is lowered, rumors get started, and health is harmed.[5]

How to Listen Effectively

Many businesses have discovered that they can boost productivity and sales by teaching their employees to listen more effectively. Here are some key techniques:

Prepare Yourself

Listening to difficult material is hard work, so prepare yourself as thoroughly as a runner prepares for a race.

Prepare yourself *physically.* Get enough sleep the night before. Consider exercising right before the speech or lecture. For example, if you suspect you will become drowsy in a warm classroom mid-afternoon, take a brisk walk beforehand to make yourself alert.

Prepare yourself *intellectually.* If the subject matter of the speech is new or complex, conduct research or do background reading beforehand. In this way, the speech will be much easier to understand. The American philosopher Henry David Thoreau once said, "We hear and apprehend only what we already half know."

Be Willing to Expend Energy

When you watch a comedian on TV, do you have to work hard to pay attention? Of course not. You simply sit back and enjoy the humor. It is easy, effortless, and fun. If you are like many listeners, you assume that when you go to a presentation on a difficult subject, you should be able to sit back and absorb the content just as easily as you grasp a comedian's jokes. But this is a major misconception. Listening effectively to difficult material requires work. You must be alert and energetic, giving total concentration with your eyes, ears, and mind.

hearing
the process by which sound waves are received by the ear

listening
the act of interpreting and evaluating what is being said

Listening often requires intense concentration.

According to Dr. Ralph G. Nichols, who did pioneering work on listening skills at the University of Minnesota, listening "is characterized by faster heart action, quicker circulation of the blood, and a small rise in body temperature."[6]

If you tend to drift away mentally whenever a speaker begins to talk about unfamiliar or difficult material, try to break yourself of the habit. Vow to put as much energy as necessary into paying attention.

Listen Analytically

You should analyze a speech, not to nitpick or poke holes in it, but to help you understand and remember the speaker's message. Here are two elements to analyze:

Focus on main ideas.   After a speech, some listeners remember the interesting stories and fascinating visuals, but they can't tell you the points that the speaker was trying to make. Look for the key ideas of the speech.

Evaluate supports.   Effective speakers use stories, statistics, and quotations to explain, illustrate, or prove their main points. As a listener, you should evaluate those supports, asking yourself these questions:

- Do the supports seem to be accurate and up-to-date?
- Are they derived from reliable sources or are they merely hearsay?
- Do they truly explain or prove a point?

Listening analytically helps you become a better listener, and it also helps you improve the quality of your own speeches because you can avoid the mistakes you see in the speeches of others. For an example of how to analyze, see Figure 3.2, which involves note-taking, our next subject.

Take Notes

Note taking facilitates effective listening in two key ways:

1. *Note taking helps you remember.* Studies show that people who take notes in meetings and lectures retain far more information than people who don't take notes.[7]

2. *Note taking helps you stay focused on the speaker.* Because it prevents your mind from wandering, it is a good idea to take notes on *all* speeches, even if you eventually throw the notes away. One of the author's colleagues explains:

   I take notes at any talk I go to. I review the notes right after the meeting to solidify the key points in my mind. Afterwards, I may save the notes for my files or for some sort of follow-up, but I usually throw them away. This doesn't mean that I had wasted my time by taking notes. The act of writing them helped me to listen analytically. It also—I must confess—kept me from daydreaming.

Note taking is effective only if you take notes systematically. Follow these strategies:

Don't try to write down everything.   Jot down just the key information. If you try to record one sentence after another, you will wear your hand out, or worse, you might fall into the habit of transcribing without evaluating.

Figure 3.2

Two methods of note taking are shown as Option A and Option B.

Speaker's Words

"Hackers are able to get into e-mail, Facebook, and bank accounts because most people use easy-to-guess passwords, according to the *New York Times*. Amichai Shulman is the chief technology officer at Imperva, a company that makes software to block hackers. He says that the most popular passwords are 123456, iloveyou, password, abc123, and america. The solution is to use a long password that mixes letters and numbers. But be careful. The password should be complex—for example, tp38jqx72wkw—instead of something simple, such as ilovemycat6789."

Option A
The speaker's message is analyzed and sorted. (See text for details.)

Main ideas	Support	Follow-up
Hackers can access accounts	email, Facebook, bank	
Passwords too simple	123456, iloveyou, america	Are people just lazy?
Solution – long, with letters & numbers	tp38jqx72wkw	Too hard to memorize?

Option B
Because it is sometimes hard to distinguish between main ideas and subpoints while a speaker is talking, some listeners jot down one item per line.

Hackers can access accounts
email, Facebook, bank
Passwords too simple
123456, iloveyou, america – Are people just lazy?
Solution – long, with letters & numbers
tp38jqx72wkw – Too hard to memorize?

Later, the listener can analyze the notes, using a highlighter to focus on key ideas and a red pen for follow-up items.

Hackers can access accounts
email, Facebook, bank
Passwords too simple
123456, iloveyou, america – (Are people just lazy?)
Solution – long, with letters & numbers
tp38jqx72wkw – (Too hard to memorize?)

Tips for Your Career

TIP 3.1

Take Notes in Important Conversations and Small-Group Meetings

Whenever your supervisors and colleagues talk to you (either one-on-one or in a group meeting) about work-related matters, take notes. Not only does this give you a written record of important discussions, but it also is a compliment, a nonverbal way of saying, "Your ideas are important to me—so important that I want to make sure I get them down correctly." Contrary to what some may think, taking notes does *not* signify to others that you have a poor memory.

One of the most common complaints of employees is that "the boss never listens to what we say." So, if you are ever in a supervisory position, take notes when an employee comes to you with a suggestion. Doing so demonstrates that you value the employee's comments and are prepared to take action if necessary. Even if you can't take action, you have shown that you truly listen and value input.

Summarize.　Put the speaker's ideas into your own words. This will help to ensure that you understand the speaker's message.

Use a note taking method.　If you have not already developed a method that works well for you, consider using one of the two methods in Figure 3.2. In Option A, the first column is labeled "Main Ideas," and the second column "Supports." The third column is entitled "Follow-up," which you can use to ask questions during the question-and-answer period, or use to conduct research later (for example, you might remind yourself: "Get more info on this"). Obviously you should use the Follow-up column only as needed.

Option B is a good choice when a speaker talks fast or does not clearly distinguish between main points and supports. Write one note per line. Later use a highlighter to mark the key ideas. In pen, circle any items that you need to follow up on.

Soon after a presentation, review your notes.　If necessary, clarify them while the speaker's words are still fresh in your mind. If any parts of your notes are vague or confusing, seek help from another listener or, if available, the speaker—he or she will be flattered.

Resist Distractions

Four common types of distractions make concentrating on a speech difficult:

- **Auditory** – people coughing or whispering, a cell phone ringing, loud noises in the hallway
- **Visual** – an interesting poster left over from a previous meeting, an intriguing listener seated nearby, people walking into or out of the room
- **Physical** – hunger, a headache or stuffy nose, a seat that is uncomfortable, a room that is too hot or too cold
- **Mental** – daydreams, worries, and preoccupations

Mental distractions are often caused by the fact that your mind runs faster than a speaker's words. As a listener, you can process speech at about 500 words per minute, while most speakers talk at 125 to 150 words a minute. This gap creates a lot of mental spare time, and we can easily start daydreaming or thinking of unrelated matters.

How can you resist distractions? By using rigorous self-discipline. Prepare yourself for active listening by arriving in the room a few minutes early and getting yourself situated. Find a seat that is free from such distractions as blinding sunlight or friends who

Tips for Your Career

Learn How Listeners Show Respect in Different Cultures

While Gail Opp-Kemp, an American artist, was giving a speech on the art of Japanese brush painting to an audience that included visitors from Japan, she was disconcerted to see that many of her Japanese listeners had their eyes closed. Were they turned off because an American had the audacity to instruct Japanese in their own art form? Were they deliberately trying to signal their rejection of her?

Opp-Kemp later found out that her listeners were not being disrespectful. Japanese listeners sometimes close their eyes to enhance concentration. Her listeners were paying tribute to her by meditating upon her words.

Someday you may be either a speaker or a listener in a situation involving people from other countries or backgrounds. Learning how different cultures signal respect can help you avoid misunderstandings. Here are some examples:

- In the deaf culture of North America, many listeners signify applause not by clapping their hands but by waving them in the air.
- In some cultures (both overseas and in some groups in North America), listeners are considered disrespectful if they look directly at the speaker. Respect is shown by looking in the general direction but avoiding direct eye contact.
- In some countries, whistling by listeners is a sign of approval, while in other countries, it is a form of jeering.

For detailed information about different cultures, simply type the name of the nation or group into Google or another browser of your choice. Add the search terms "culture" and "customs." For example, for India, your search terms would be "India culture customs."

---

might want to whisper to you. Make yourself comfortable, lay out paper and pen for taking notes, and clear your mind of personal matters. When the speech begins, concentrate all your mental energies on the speaker's message.

Avoid Fake Listening

Many members of an audience look directly at a speaker and seem to be listening, but in reality they are just pretending. Their minds are far away.

If you engage in fake listening, you might miss a lot of important information, but even worse, you risk embarrassment and ridicule. Imagine that you are engaged in fake listening during a meeting and your boss suddenly asks you to comment on a statement that has just been made. You don't have a clue. You've been caught.

If you have the habit of tuning speakers out while pretending to listen, one of the best ways to force yourself to pay attention is to take notes, as discussed earlier.

Give Every Speaker a Fair Chance

Don't reject speakers because you dislike their looks or their clothes or the organization they represent. Instead, focus on their message, which might be interesting and worthwhile.

If speakers have ragged delivery, or they seem shaky and lacking in confidence, don't be too quick to discount the content of their speech.

Your Thoughts

The Chinese character for "the act of listening" includes (1) ear, (2) self, (3) eyes, (4) undivided attention, and (5) heart. Why do you think these components are included?

Wyatt Rangel, a stockbroker, relates an incident:

> At a dinner meeting of my investment club, one of the speakers was a woman from Thailand who had lived in the U.S. only a year or so, and she spoke English with a heavy accent. It took a lot of concentration to understand what she was saying, and frankly I didn't think a recent immigrant could give me any worthwhile information. I was tempted to tune her out, but I made the effort, and I'm glad I did. She had some good insights into Asian corporations, and I was able to parlay her tips into financial gain a few months later.

Give every speaker a fair chance. You may be pleasantly surprised by what you learn.

Control Emotions

Some listeners don't listen well because they have a powerful emotional reaction to a topic or to some comment the speaker makes. Their strong emotions cut off intelligent listening for the rest of the speech. Instead of paying attention to the speaker's words, they "argue" with the speaker inside their heads or think of ways to retaliate in the question-and-answer period. They often jump to conclusions, convincing themselves that the speaker is saying something that he or she really is not.

During many question-and-answer periods, I have seen listeners verbally attack a speaker for espousing a position that any careful listener would know was not the speaker's true position.

When you are listening to speakers who seem to be arguing against some of your ideas or beliefs, make sure you understand exactly what they are saying. Hear them out, and *then* prepare your counterarguments.

The Listener's Responsibilities

As we discussed in Chapter 1, the speaker who is honest and fair has ethical and moral obligations to his or her listeners. The converse is also true: the honest and fair listener has ethical and moral obligations to the speaker. Let's examine three of the listener's primary responsibilities.

Show Courtesy and Respect

Are you a polite listener? To make sure that you are not committing acts of rudeness, keep the following points in mind:

Your Thoughts

Is this woman justified in being upset because her date is talking to a friend during lunch? What should she say to him?

Follow the Golden Rule of Listening

If you were engaged in conversation with a friend, how would you feel if your friend yawned and fell asleep? Or started reading a book? Or talked on a cell phone? You would be upset by your friend's rudeness, wouldn't you?

Many people would never dream of being so rude to a friend in conversation, yet when they sit in an audience, they are terribly rude to the speaker. They fall asleep, study for a test, check their e-mail or text messages, or carry on a whispered conversation with their friends.

Fortunately, a public speaking class cures some people of their rudeness. As one student put it:

> I had been sitting in classrooms for 12 years and until now, I never realized how much a speaker sees. I always thought a listener is hidden and anonymous out there in a sea of faces. Now that I've been a speaker, I realize that when

you look out at an audience, you are well aware of the least little thing somebody does. I am ashamed now at how I used to carry on conversations in the back of class. I was very rude, and I didn't even know it.

Follow the Golden Rule of Listening: "Listen unto others as you would have others listen unto you." When you are a speaker, you want an audience that listens attentively and courteously. So when you are a listener, you should provide the same response.

Reject Electronic Intrusion

During a meeting or presentation, if you read and send text messages, play games on your phone, or browse the Internet on your laptop, you are sending a strong, clear message to the speaker: "You are not important to me, and your comments don't merit my respect and my attention."

To be courteous, keep your eyes and attention on the speaker. Follow these rules:

- Before a meeting begins, turn off any electronics that might beep or chirp. Remove headphones or earbuds, even if they are not connected to devices.
- Never talk on a cellphone or headset. Even whispers are distracting.
- Don't send or read text messages. "People mistakenly think that tapping is not as distracting as talking," says Nancy Flynn, executive director of the ePolicy Institute. "In fact, it can be more distracting. And it's pretty insulting to the speaker."[8]
- Unless you have an emergency situation (see the next section), turn off vibrate mode on your phone. A vibrating phone can still be noisy and distracting. Also, if you get up and leave the room to respond to a friend's routine call, you are creating an unnecessary disruption.

Sometimes the rules above can be broken, such as in cases like these:

- If you ask a speaker for permission beforehand, you may take notes on a tablet, laptop computer, or smartphone. Show the speaker that you are paying attention by looking at him or her frequently (rather than keeping your eyes focused nonstop on your computer). If you play games, text, or browse, the speaker will sense what you are doing and think that you are being disrespectful.
- In some classes or training sessions, you will be encouraged or even required to use an electronic device as part of the learning process. As suggested above, look at the speaker frequently to convey that you are connected to him or her.
- If you are on call (for example, if you are a firefighter or a paramedic), or if you are awaiting news related to an ongoing emergency, go to the speaker in advance and explain the situation. Set your phone to vibrate and sit near the door if you can. If you get a call, leave the room quietly and answer it well away from the door.

Beware the Pitfalls of Multitasking

We all multitask every day, combining such simple acts as driving a car and listening to music. When the tasks are easy and routine, there is no problem, but multitasking

---

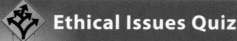

Ethical Issues Quiz

Suppose that a classmate is rude and inattentive when you are giving a speech. When he gives his speech, which of the following is the best approach for listening to him?

A. As he speaks, show him how awful distractions are for a speaker by staring him down with a disapproving facial expression.
B. Ask him unfriendly and difficult questions during the question-and-answer period.
C. Listen to his speech attentively and politely.

For the answer, see the last page of this chapter.

Tips for Your Career

Confront Electronic Rudeness

If you are like most speakers, you will be irritated or even unnerved if you see listeners who are immersed in their private world of electronic devices. It is hard to communicate effectively with people who are tuning you out.

What can you do to capture their full attention?

If possible, forbid the use of electronic devices. Many speakers—including corporate executives and military officers—ban the use of smartphones and tablets during meetings and presentations. Some companies require employees to put their electronic devices on a table as they enter a conference room.

What if you lack the power to order a ban? If possible, ask the person in charge of a group to request—before you rise to speak—that all equipment be turned off. But what if those strategies aren't possible, and you see that some of your listeners are using electronic equipment? Try saying something like this: "I hate to inconvenience anyone, but I have a problem. I have trouble concentrating on what I want to say when I look out and see people working on their computers or talking on their cell phones. I would appreciate it if you would help me out and turn off your equipment while I'm speaking." By emphasizing *your* difficulties rather than attacking *their* rudeness, you enhance your chances of gaining compliance.

One final strategy that has been used successfully by some speakers: In the introduction of your speech, use an attention getter that is so compelling that listeners become totally absorbed in listening to you. (Samples of attention getters are presented in Chapter 11.)

If you were this speaker, how would you handle the rude listeners?

is a bad strategy in two situations: (1) when the tasks are complex, and (2) when you may insult or alienate other people. Here is some important information that you need to know:

Multitasking can mar your performance.   Although multitaskers think they are performing all activities effectively, studies show that their comprehension suffers. For example, researchers at Cornell University arranged for two groups of students to listen to the same lecture and then take a test immediately afterward. One group was allowed to use their laptops to browse the Internet during the lecture, while the other group was asked to keep their laptops closed. When tested, the students with open laptops remembered significantly less information from the lecture than did the students with closed laptops.[9]

Many other research studies show that in complex tasks, multitaskers of all ages are more likely to misunderstand information and make mistakes.[10] René Marois, a psychology researcher at Vanderbilt University, says, "Our research offers neurological evidence that the brain cannot effectively do two things at once."[11] Note the key word: *effectively.*

Multitasking can hurt you professionally.   Because they are considered discourteous or inattentive, multitaskers may be given extra work or unpleasant assignments, passed over for promotion, or even fired.[12] Here are some recent incidents:

- An executive at a top hospital lost her job because she "disrespected" the board of directors by "working on her laptop during presentations, firing off e-mails, and focusing on her own projects instead of participating or listening to the chair and other speakers," according to *The Cost of Bad Behavior,* a book by professors Christine Pearson of the Thunderbird School of Global Management and Christine Porath of the University of Southern California.[13]

- Tom Golisano, a billionaire and power broker in New York State politics, pushed to remove Malcolm A. Smith as the State Senate majority leader after a budget meeting in which the senator spent the time reading e-mail on his smartphone instead of listening respectfully to Golisano, according to the *New York Times.*[14]

- Danielle Gregory, a judge in Marion County (Indiana) Juvenile Court, lost her job because while she was "on the bench conducting court sessions," she sent "multiple text messages" to friends instead of giving her full attention to the discourse in the courtroom, reports WTHR-TV Eyewitness News in Indianapolis.[15]

Rude employees are sometimes given extra work.

What if nobody complains to you about texting? Is it okay? Hank London of Pacifica, California, who leads workshops on career development, says, "Just because coworkers, supervisors or clients don't say anything about your texting while in meetings, this doesn't mean they haven't taken notice." Your rudeness, he warns, can come back to haunt you.[16] In some cases, people may develop a dislike for you without being aware of the subconscious reason for their antagonism.

Provide Encouragement

Encourage the speaker as much as possible—by giving your full attention, taking notes, leaning slightly forward instead of slouching back in your seat, looking directly at the speaker instead of at the floor, and letting your face show interest and animation. If the speaker says something you particularly like, nod in agreement or smile approvingly. (If the speaker says something that offends you or puzzles you, obviously you should not give positive feedback; I am not recommending hypocrisy.)

The more encouragement a speaker receives, the better his or her delivery is likely to be. Most entertainers and professional speakers say that if an audience is lively and enthusiastic, they do a much better job than if the audience is sullen or apathetic. From my own experience, I feel that I always do better in giving a speech if I get encouragement. Maybe just a few people are displaying lively interest, but their nods and smiles and eager eyes inspire me and energize me.

When we help a speaker to give a good speech, we are doing more than an act of kindness; we are creating a payoff for ourselves: the better the speaker, the easier it is to listen. And the easier it is to listen, the better we will understand, remember, and gain knowledge.

Find Value in Every Speech

Sometimes you will be obliged to hear a speech that you feel is boring and worthless. Instead of tuning the speaker out, try to exploit the speech for something worthwhile. Make a game of it: see how many diamonds you can pluck from the mud. Is there any new information that might be useful to you in the future? Is the speaker using techniques of delivery that are worth noting and emulating?

If a speech is so bad that you honestly cannot find anything worthwhile in it, use it as a how-not-to-do-it lesson. Ask yourself, "What can I learn from this speaker's mistakes?" Here is an example of how one business executive profited from a poor speech:

> At a convention recently I found myself in an extremely boring seminar (on listening, ironically enough). After spending the first half-hour wishing I had never signed up, I decided to take advantage of the situation. I turned my thought, "This guy isn't teaching me how to run a seminar on listening," into a question: "What is he teaching me about how *not* to run a seminar?" While providing a negative example was not the presenter's goal, I got a useful lesson.[17]

"When life hands you a lemon, make lemonade," some wise person once advised. If you look for value or a how-*not*-to-do-it lesson in every poor speech, you will find that the sourest oratorical lemon can be turned into lemonade. "Know how to listen," the Greek writer Plutarch said 20 centuries ago, "and you will profit even from those who talk badly."

Speech Evaluations

Both evaluators and speakers profit from a speech evaluation. Evaluators gain insights into what works and what doesn't work in speechmaking. Speakers can use suggestions to improve their speaking skills.

When Evaluating

Evaluating speeches should not be limited to a public speaking class. You also can apply these techniques to speeches that you hear in your career.

Establish criteria.   Before you listen to a speech, decide upon the criteria for judging it. This will keep you from omitting important elements. For classroom speeches, your instructor may give you a checklist or tell you to analyze certain features of a speech. Otherwise, you can use the "Quick Guide to Public Speaking" in Chapter 1 for your criteria.

Listen objectively.   Keep an open mind. Don't let yourself be swayed emotionally by the speaker's delivery or appearance. If, for example, a speaker sounds ill at ease and uncertain, this doesn't necessarily mean that her arguments are inferior. Don't let your own biases influence your criticism; for example, if you are strongly against gun control, but the speaker argues in favor of it, be careful to criticize the speaker's ideas fairly and objectively.

Tips for Your Career

Express Appreciation to a Speaker

Whenever you find a speech enjoyable or profitable, let the speaker know. No matter how busy or important he or she is, genuine feedback will be greatly appreciated.

After giving a speech, some speakers are physically and emotionally exhausted, and they sit down with a nagging doubt: Did it go okay? A word of thanks or a compliment from a listener is refreshing and gratifying. (If you can't express your appreciation in person right after the speech, write the speaker a brief note or e-mail.)

Be sure to say something positive and specific about the *content* of the speech. A corporation president told me of a commencement address he had delivered to a college several years before. "I sweated blood for a whole month putting that speech together and then rehearsing it dozens of times—it was my first commencement speech," he said. "When I delivered the speech, I tried to speak straight from my heart. I thought I did a good job, and I thought my speech had some real nuggets of wisdom. But afterwards, only two people came by to thank me. And you know what? They both paid me the same compliment: they said they were grateful that I had kept the speech short! They said not one word about the ideas in my speech. Not one word about whether they enjoyed the speech itself. It's depressing to think that the only thing noteworthy about my speech was its brevity."

Sad to say, there were probably dozens of people in the audience whose hearts and minds were touched by the eloquent wisdom of the speaker—but they never told him.

Take notes.   Jot down your observations throughout the speech so that you capture key elements.

Look for both positive and negative aspects.   Emphasize the positive (so that the speaker will continue doing what works well) as well as pointing out opportunities for improvement.

Give positive comments first.   When it comes to public speaking, most people have easily bruised egos. If you start out a critique with negative remarks, you can damage the speaker's confidence and self-esteem. Always begin by discussing his or her strengths. Point out positive attributes that might seem obvious to you but may not be obvious to the speaker. For example, "You looked poised and confident."

Couple negative comments with positive alternatives.   When you point out a flaw, immediately give a constructive alternative. For example, you can inform a speaker that she seems to be reading long sentences from a script, and then you can suggest an alternative: "Use note cards with just a few words on each card so that you can look at the audience most of the time and sound conversational."

In most cases, ignore nervousness.   Because most people cannot help being jittery, don't criticize nervousness—unless you can give a useful tip. For example, it is unhelpful to say, "You looked tense and scared," but it is helpful to say, "Your hands trembled when you held your piece of paper (notes), and this was distracting, so next time, put your notes on the lectern."

Be specific   Instead of saying, "You need to improve your eye contact," say, "You looked too much at the floor." Instead of "You did great," say, "Your introduction captivated me and your stories were extremely interesting."

When Receiving Evaluations

To get maximum benefit from evaluations, follow these guidelines:

Don't be defensive.   Try to understand criticism and consider its merits. Don't argue or counterattack.

Seek clarification.   If an evaluator makes a comment that you don't understand, ask for an explanation.

Strive for improvement.   In your next speech, try to correct problem areas. But don't feel that you must eliminate all errors or bad habits at once.

Resources for Review and Skill Building

Summary

Listening effectively is often a difficult task, but it can be rewarding if you are willing to make the effort. Guidelines for effective listening include:

1. Prepare yourself intellectually and physically. Do background research to maximize your understanding of the new material in the speech. Get some exercise before the speech if necessary.

2. Listen analytically. Focus on main ideas and evaluate supports.

3. Take notes, not only to record key points, but also to keep your mind from wandering.

4. Resist distractions, both external and internal. Use rigorous self-discipline to focus on the speaker's remarks.

5. Avoid fakery. Don't pretend to be listening when in fact your mind is wandering. This kind of behavior can settle into a hard-to-break habit.

6. Give every speaker a fair chance. Don't discount a speaker because of personal appearance or the organization he or she represents.

7. Control your emotions. Don't mentally argue with a speaker because you might misunderstand what he or she is really saying.

As a listener you have three important obligations to a speaker: show courtesy and respect, provide encouragement, and find value in every speech. The more support you give a speaker, the better the speech will be, and the more you will profit from it.

Evaluating speeches can help you improve your own speechmaking skills. Look for both positive and negative aspects of a speech, and give specific, constructive suggestions. When you are on the receiving end of evaluations, don't be defensive. Try to understand the criticism and then make improvements.

Key Terms

hearing, *39*

listening, *39*

Review Questions

1. What is the difference between *hearing* and *listening?*

2. Name at least four problems caused by ineffective listening in business.

3. What is the difference between listening to easy material and listening to complex material?

4. List at least two ways in which you can prepare yourself physically and intellectually to listen to a speech.

5. The text lists four types of distractions: auditory, visual, physical, and mental. Give two examples of each type.

6. What two speech elements should a listener examine analytically?

7. List two advantages of taking notes during a speech.

8. How can texting during a meeting hurt you in your career?

9. When you are a listener, how can you encourage a speaker?

10. When you evaluate a speech, how should you handle both the positive and the negative aspects that you observe?

Building Critical-Thinking Skills

1. When a person is truly and deeply listening to you, what behaviors do you detect in his or her tone of voice, facial expression, eyes, and overall body language?

2. Science writer Judith Stone wrote, "There are two ways to approach a subject that frightens you and makes you feel stupid: you can embrace it with humility and an open mind, or you can ridicule it mercilessly." Translate this idea into advice for listeners of speeches.

Building Teamwork Skills

1. In a group, conduct this role play: One student gives an impromptu speech describing his or her classes this term, while all the other group members exhibit rude behaviors (such as texting, chatting, reading a magazine). Then the speaker discusses how he or she felt about the rudeness. (If time permits, let other group members play the speaker's role.)

2. Working in a group, compile a list of the attributes that would describe "the ideal listener" for a speech. Then do likewise for a conversation. In what ways are the lists similar and different?

Ethical Issues

Answer for p. 45: C. Nothing can be gained by engaging in retaliation. You can hope that your responsive behavior will be a good model for others.

Reaching the Audience

OUTLINE

OBJECTIVES

After studying this chapter, you should be able to:

1. Describe the difference between a speaker who is audience-centered and one who is not.
2. Define audience analysis and audience adaptation and state why they are important.
3. Use interviews and surveys to gain information about an audience in advance.
4. Explain how speakers can be responsive to diverse audiences.
5. Describe how speakers can adapt to varying levels of audience knowledge, attitudes, interest, and needs and desires.
6. Explain how speakers should adapt to the occasion (time limit, purpose, and size of audience).
7. Describe how a speaker can adapt to the audience during a speech.

WHAT IS THE MOST IMPORTANT RULE for public speaking? Many veteran speakers would say that it is to care deeply about your audience.

One speaker who has a reputation for caring deeply about his audiences is Apolo Ohno, an Olympic Gold Medalist speed skater, who speaks to audiences throughout the United States on such topics as childhood obesity and the dangers of underage drinking. Ohno prepares for a presentation by asking the organizers a bit about themselves and the audience. For any speaker, it is helpful to ask about basic information ahead of time, such as how old the listeners will be, what they all have in common, and why they are motivated to attend the presentation. Once Ohno knows more about the concerns and interests of his audience, he can tailor his speaking style to accommodate them. A friendly, energetic

Apolo Ohno leans forward as a student asks a question at a school in Chicago.

speaker, he begins at a lectern but soon walks into the midst of his listeners to get close to them, and he frequently asks for comments and questions. Often he stays behind long after an event is over—to keep talking to audience members.[1]

Ohno gets favorable reviews from students and other observers. A newspaper reporter in Seattle said "he seemed to speak from the heart, and appeared to be genuinely interested in making a connection with students."[2]

The Audience-Centered Speaker

Some speeches are ineffective because the speaker is self-centered, focusing on "How do I look?" and "Am I doing a good job?" and "Does everyone like me?" The self-centered speaker fails to focus on the audience and their needs.

audience-centered speaker
one who tries to establish a meaningful connection with listeners

A better approach is taken by the **audience-centered speaker**—one who tries to connect with listeners and offer them a meaningful experience. If you are an audience-centered speaker, you learn everything you can about your listeners in advance, and then you tailor your speech to their needs and interests. You look directly at the audience, speak with enthusiasm, and try to reach every listener.

Consider the experience of Jill Sieburg, a health educator who gives presentations aimed at persuading people to become organ donors. Before every talk, she sends an e-mail to people who will be in the audience to find out their views. Are some of them, for example, opposed to organ donation because they fear their bodies will be disfigured? If yes, she will spend time in her talk explaining how organ donation is like any other kind of surgery—"Your body is sewed up afterwards and you are not disfigured."

audience analysis
collecting information about audience characteristics

adaptation
adjusting one's material and delivery to meet listeners' needs

Sieburg demonstrates two important tasks that all audience-centered speakers should perform: (1) **analyze** the listeners to find out exactly who they are and where they stand on the issues to be discussed, and (2) **adapt** the speech to the listeners' knowledge level and viewpoints.

customize
to make or alter to a customer's specifications

This process of analysis and adaptation is sometimes called **customizing,** a crucial strategy in the business world. If you sell customized vans, you find out what features each customer needs and then outfit the van accordingly. For a person with paralyzed legs, you provide brake controls that are operated by hand; for a carpenter, you furnish special compartments for lumber and tools; and for a rock band, you provide storage space for drums and guitars. Customizing in public speaking means tailoring a speech to fit a particular audience.

Here are some guidelines for customizing speeches.

Prepare a separate analysis of each audience. Don't assume that if a speech works well with one group, it will surely succeed with another. Sometimes it will, but sometimes it won't.

I once delivered a speech that was received with much laughter and applause. So sweet was the success that I delivered the same speech a month later to another group. It was a dud. If I had not been so giddy with success, I would have seen that the second audience had a different educational background and a different set of attitudes. They needed a different speech.

Customize for different segments of the same audience. Many audiences contain subgroups, with the people in each subgroup sharing the same needs and level of understanding. Try to reach all the subgroups.

Ethical Issues Quiz

A registered nurse is scheduled to give a presentation to a group of college freshmen about maintaining healthy lifestyles while in school. She plans to inform them that tanning beds can cause premature skin aging as well as increase the risk of skin cancer. As she gathers information about her audience in advance, she discovers that several of her future listeners visit tanning salons regularly. What should she do?

A. Drop the information about tanning beds to avoid offending some listeners.

B. Mention the issue but downplay it and recommend that listeners do research and decide for themselves.

C. Keep the information and emphasize medical studies about the harm caused by tanning beds.

For the answer, see the last page of this chapter.

Tips for Your Career

Be Sensitive to Audience Discomfort

New York Governor Andrew Cuomo gave a lengthy State of the State address in a convention center that was so cold, listeners had to wear their winter hats and coats, and at least one ski parka was spotted. "My feet were like two blocks of ice," State Senator Diane Savino told the *New York Times*. "I actually think he would've gotten more applause, but people were sitting on their hands to keep them warm."

The governor "prefers a chilly environment for big speeches" according to a *Times* reporter, who speculated that he "wanted to make sure his audience stayed alert." Alertness is a good goal, of course, but audiences can't be alert to a speaker's message if they are miserable.

Don't let audience discomfort undermine the effectiveness of your speech. Keep the room temperature from being too hot or too cold. Make sure the microphone amplification is neither too loud nor too soft (you can ask listeners for feedback). If a meeting lasts a long time, give periodic breaks. If your presentation is right before a scheduled meal, be sure to end on time (even if it means shortening your remarks)—hungry listeners quickly become irritated with a speaker who keeps them from a meal.

For example, in a speech on traveling abroad, one subgroup—young parents—may want information on recreation options for children, while another subgroup—older travelers—may want information on discounts for seniors.

Never sacrifice ethical principles.   Customizing does not mean telling listeners whatever would make them happy—regardless of truth. An ethical speaker never lies or distorts information.

Getting Information about the Audience

A speaker's worst nightmare is being laughed at by listeners. This came true for Lawrence B. Gibbs. When he was Internal Revenue Commissioner, he spoke to an audience of 1,000 tax preparers at a convention in Las Vegas, and he tried to brag about how smoothly the latest tax preparation season had been. Some people, he said, had made "gloomy predictions that this tax-filing season would drive taxpayers crazy, confuse them unmercifully, or break them financially." [*Dramatic pause*] "It just hasn't happened, folks!"[3]

The convention hall exploded with laughter. The tax preparers had just finished a tax season in which the scenario that Gibbs dismissed as nonexistent had (from their perspective) actually occurred. Regardless of whose viewpoint was accurate, Gibbs had revealed that he knew nothing about his listeners' feelings and experience. If he had spoken with just a few of the members of the audience beforehand, he could have escaped public ridicule.[4]

You can avoid this kind of blunder by finding out as much as possible about your listeners—their backgrounds and what they know and don't know. Two good ways to collect information about them are interviews and surveys.

Interviews

Start with the person who invited you to speak. Find out all that you can about listeners' knowledge level, attitudes, needs, interests, and backgrounds. Get details about the occasion, such as the purpose of the event, other speakers on the program, size of audience, and most importantly, your time limit. Next, ask for the names and contact information of a few prospective listeners and interview them to find out what they already know about your subject, what ideas and information they are hoping to receive from your speech, and whether any particular approach (such as visual aids) works well with this group. When you start your speech, you can thank the people you interviewed by name. Doing so will add to your credibility because it shows your desire to meet the needs and interests of your listeners.

Surveys

Another good way to get information about your audience is to conduct a survey in advance of your speech, using a questionnaire to poll listeners' knowledge, interests, and attitudes. For a classroom speech, work with your instructor to decide how and when to distribute the questionnaire. For a career or community speech, try to get permission to contact your future listeners through an electronic channel that is common among them, such as an e-mail distribution list, Twitter handle, or Facebook or LinkedIn group.

open-ended question
a question that permits a broad range of responses

closed question
a question requiring only a short, specific response

A questionnaire can have two kinds of questions: **open-ended questions,** which encourage respondents to elaborate on their views, and **closed questions,** which give respondents pre-selected options, such as yes/no, true/false, and multiple choice. In Figure 4.1, the first question is open-ended, while all the rest are closed.

Let's suppose you are planning a speech on why most people need to add more vegetables to their daily diet, and you want to find out what your listeners know about vegetables and what their attitudes are. The questionnaire in Figure 4.1 shows some sample questions.

The first question is open-ended so that you can get a picture of how your future listeners view vegetables. Do they dislike them? It is helpful to know the listeners' attitudes. The rest of the questions are designed to help you decide what to include in your speech. For example, the second question probes whether the listeners know that a multivitamin pill does not substitute for vegetables. If all respondents indicate that they already know this, you can omit it from your speech. The fourth question investigates whether your listeners understand what vegetables can and cannot do. In this case, vegetables do *not* cause higher intelligence or improved vision.

Here are some guidelines for surveys:

- Keep it short. One page is ideal. Most people will not fill out a long document.
- Phrase questions in a way that doesn't suggest the answer you want or anticipate. Instead of "Do you resist eating vegetables because your parents tried to force them on you?" ask, "If you don't like to eat vegetables, can you explain why?"
- Pre-test your questionnaire with a few friends or colleagues, who can point out any confusing questions.

Sometimes the results of a survey can be included in a speech as a point of interest.

Open-ended	1.	What is your emotional reaction when you hear the word vegetables? (Jot down a few words or sentences.)
Simple options	2.	Do vitamin supplements provide all of the necessary nutrients that are contained in vegetables? Yes ☐ No ☐ Not sure ☐
Multiple choice	3.	Which one of the following statements is correct? ☐ Iceberg lettuce contains no nutrients. ☐ Fresh foods are always healthier than frozen foods. ☐ Cooked carrots are healthier than raw carrots. ☐ Colorless foods like white cabbage have low nutritional value.
Checklist	4.	What are the health benefits of a diet rich in vegetables? (Check all that are true.) ☐ Lower blood pressure ☐ Reduced risk of some cancers ☐ Improved vision ☐ Higher intelligence ☐ Improved digestion
Scale	5.	"The average person does not eat as many vegetables as he or she should." Strongly Agree Agree Not sure Disagree Strongly Disagree ○ ○ ○ ○ ○
Ranking	6.	Which of these vegetables do you eat most often? Rank them in order, from 1 (most often) to 5 (least often). _____ Corn _____ Carrots _____ Onions _____ Tomatoes _____ Potatoes

Figure 4.1
Types of Survey Questions

In your speech on vegetables, for example, you can say, "According to my survey, half of you think that fresh foods are always healthier than frozen foods. But nutrition researchers have found that frozen vegetables are often healthier than fresh produce sold in supermarkets. Why? Because vegetables chosen for freezing tend to be processed at their peak ripeness. That's the time when they are loaded with maximum nutrients."

Audience Diversity

In most presentations, you are likely to see a wide diversity of listeners: men and women of different ages, races, nationalities, ethnic groups, religions, economic levels, educational backgrounds, and physical abilities. To be a successful communicator, you should welcome the opportunity to meet the needs of *all* listeners, not just those who are like you.

Gender

The gender of your listeners may give you some clues about their social and economic situation. For example, despite the advances made by women in the workplace in recent decades, many females still receive a lower wage than male co-workers who perform the same job. A speaker trying to persuade workers to join a labor union could stress such inequities if some of the listeners are women.

Although gender can sometimes give clues, you should avoid making assumptions based on gender stereotypes. Men may become irritated by a speaker who assumes that only females are interested in issues concerning the health of babies. And women would be annoyed by a speaker who suggests that only men are interested in new mechanical technologies for jet engines. Listeners can lose respect for a speaker who uses **sexist language**—that is, words that convey stereotypes about men or women. Instead of saying "the girl at the front desk," say "Ms. Martinez" or "Maria Martinez." Instead of "the best man for the job," say "the best person for the job." (Sexist language will be discussed further in Chapter 13.)

Don't make assumptions about marriage and sexual orientation. For example, Kitty O. Locker, who teaches business communication at Ohio State University, advises speakers to "avoid terms that assume that everyone is married or is heterosexual." Instead of announcing to employees, "You and your husband or wife are cordially invited to the company picnic," say, "You and your guest are cordially invited to the company picnic."[5]

sexist language
words based on gender stereotypes

Age

If you have a variety of ages represented in your audience, be sensitive to the interests, attitudes, and knowledge of all your listeners, giving explanations or background whenever necessary. If, for example, you talk about a new trend in music that is popular with young people, give a brief explanation for the benefit of older members of the audience.

Be careful about making generalizations concerning any age group. For an audience of older people, for example, you are wise to consider the fact that many people suffer hearing loss as they age, but you shouldn't jump to the conclusion that you must shout during your speech. Not all older people are hard of hearing, and those who are might be wearing hearing aids.

Educational Background

Find out the educational level of your listeners. Avoid talking over their heads, using concepts that they may not understand. Also avoid the other extreme: talking down to your listeners and treating them as if they are ignorant.

Define terms whenever necessary. Fred Ebel, past president of a Toastmasters club in Orlando, Florida, talks about his experience with one audience: "I told a joke which referred to an insect called a praying mantis. I thought everyone knew what a praying mantis was. But I was greeted by silence that would have made the dropping of a pin sound like a thunderclap. Several listeners came up to me and asked, 'What is a praying mantis?'"[6]

Occupation

Knowing your listeners' occupational background can help you shape your remarks. Let's say you give speeches on résumé padding. To a group of students, you might want to point out how one's career can be ruined if an employee is found to have lied on a résumé. To a group of human resources managers, you can give tips on how to detect false information. To a group of lawyers, you can discuss legal action that can be taken against someone who has lied on a résumé.

Religious Affiliation

Knowing the religious affiliations of your audience will give you good clues about their beliefs and attitudes. Most Seventh-Day Adventists, for example, are very knowledgeable about nutrition because of the strong emphasis the denomination places on health and diet. If you are asked to speak to an Adventist group on a health-related issue, you can assume that the audience has a higher level of background knowledge on the subject than the average audience. You can therefore avoid going over basic information they already know.

Although religious background can give you clues about your audience, be cautious. You cannot assume that all members of a religious group subscribe to official doctrines and pronouncements. A denomination's hierarchy, for example, may call for a stop to the production of nuclear weapons, but the majority of the members of that denomination may not agree with their leaders' views.

Economic and Social Status

Be sensitive to the economic and social status of your listeners so that you can adapt your speech accordingly. Suppose you are going to speak in favor of an economic stimulus package intended to create new manufacturing jobs. If your listeners are blue-collar workers or unemployed, they will probably be favorably disposed to your ideas before you even begin. You therefore might want to aim your speech at encouraging them to support political candidates who endorse the stimulus program. However, if your listeners are wealthy members of the business community, many of them may be opposed to your ideas because they fear higher taxes, or they cannot easily relate to the people whom the stimulus would most benefit. Therefore, you could aim your speech at showing how new manufacturing jobs can contribute to the overall prosperity of the community, and you could spend time discussing the facts that concern the audience members most, such as taxes, labor union involvement, or political implications.

taboo
an act, word, or object that is forbidden on grounds of morality or taste

International Listeners

The world today is a "global village," with interlocking interests and economies, and you must know how to interact with customers and associates from many different countries. Whether you are speaking on campus, in the community, or in your career, any audience you face is likely to include people for whom English is a second language.

To reach international listeners, consider the following:

Respect taboos.   Every culture has its own set of **taboos,** and violating them can undermine a speaker's credibility. Stacie Krajchir of Venice Beach, California, who works around the world as a television producer, says, "I have a habit of putting my hands on my hips when I talk." In Indonesia, she was told that "when you stand that way, it's seen as a sign of rudeness or defiance."[7]

You can avoid taboos by educating yourself about a culture—a task that will be discussed below.

In American culture, this posture is fine, but in some cultures, putting hands on hips signals disrespect.

Learn nonverbal signals.   Body language cues such as eye contact vary from country to country. American business executives assume a person who won't look them in the eye is evasive and dishonest, but in many parts of Latin America, Asia, and Africa, keeping your eyes lowered is a sign of respect.[8] A few years ago, some Americans who were trying to negotiate a contract with Japanese executives were happy to see nods of assent

At a victory celebration after being elected Thailand's first female prime minister, Yingluck Shinawatra gives a traditional Thai gesture to convey respect for her audience. Often Thais use the gesture as a form of greeting, instead of the Western practice of shaking hands.

throughout the meeting but were later stunned when the Japanese rejected their proposal. The Americans were unaware that in Japan a nod of assent doesn't mean agreement; it signifies only that the listener understands what is being said.[9]

Although nonverbal cues vary from culture to culture, there are some cues that are recognizable everywhere. First and foremost is the smile, which Roger Axtell, an international behavior expert, calls the most understood and most useful form of communication in the world.[10] As a Mexican-American proverb puts it: *Todos en el mundo sonreimos en la misma lengua*—"Everyone in the world smiles in the same language." (The smile discussed here is the natural involuntary expression that all people make when they are happy—not variations such as the embarrassed smile of someone caught in a shameful act.)

Conduct research.   If you are like most people, you don't have time to become well-versed in all the cultures in the world, but you can focus on cultures that are likely to be represented in an upcoming presentation. Here's how:

1. Get insights by conducting Internet searches and by browsing websites specializing in international cultures. Books and articles also can be good sources, but make sure they are recent, because cultural information can become outdated.

2. Contact knowledgeable people. You can use social media and online discussion groups to consult people who live in or visit the country you have questions about. Or, you can find an expert on your campus or in your community whom you can interview face-to-face.

Tips for Your Career

Work Closely with Interpreters

Use interpreters if there is a chance that some listeners will not hear or understand your message. For example, you might use a sign-language interpreter for deaf listeners and a foreign-language interpreter for non-English-speaking listeners. Here are some tips on using interpreters effectively:

- Because interpreters say that they stumble less and make fewer misinterpretations when they know the speaker's message in advance, provide a copy of your outline to the interpreter well before the event.
- If possible, ask him or her to rehearse with you several times, and to alert you if any elements in your speech are likely to be misunderstood.
- In your opening remarks, introduce the interpreter to the audience and express your appreciation for his or her assistance.
- When using a foreign-language interpreter, you will probably employ the popular *consecutive interpretation* method, in which you and the interpreter take turns. Say only a few sentences at a time, so that neither language group gets weary of waiting its turn. A less-frequent method is *simultaneous interpretation,* in which your words are rendered into a separate microphone a few seconds later for listeners wearing headphones. At large international meetings, a speech may be rendered into many languages simultaneously.
- To demonstrate your desire to connect with all listeners, learn a few words and phrases from sign language and/or a foreign language to sprinkle into your presentation. Practice with a fluent user to make sure you are giving an accurate rendition.
- Even if all listeners are using the services of a sign-language interpreter, you should still talk directly to the listeners, not to the interpreter.

Gayle Robertson is a sign-language interpreter in Salem, Oregon. Before a speech, she appreciates receiving a copy of the speaker's outline.

Be careful with jargon and slang.   Avoid using idiomatic expressions such as "cramming for an exam," "bite the bullet," and "the ball is in your court." If you must use jargon, such as "interface" or "virtual reality," explain or illustrate each term.

Maintain a serious, formal tone.   Americans are accustomed to speakers using a humorous and informal approach to public speaking, but American presenters who adopt this tone with international audiences are often viewed as frivolous and disrespectful. "Most foreign audiences," says Richard Crum, senior editor for Berlitz Translation Services in Woodland Hills, California, "expect seriousness. An important presentation can be undermined by a presenter who is joking or boastful."[11]

If possible, provide handouts covering some of your main points a day or two before a presentation. (But don't give out lengthy material immediately before or during a meeting—for reasons to be discussed in Chapter 9.) Most nonnative speakers of English have greater comprehension when reading than when listening.[12] If they read the material beforehand, they can find out the meaning of any terms they don't understand, and when they come to the actual presentation, they will have a knowledge base that will maximize their understanding of your remarks.

Provide visual and tactile learning. Can you use visual aids or demonstrations to illuminate your ideas? Can you provide any hands-on experiences?

America's Diverse Cultures

The same sensitivity you show toward international listeners should be extended to ethnic, racial, religious, and other groups in the United States.

Here are some suggestions.

ethnocentrism

judging other cultures as inferior to one's own culture

Avoid ethnocentrism. The belief that one's own cultural group is superior to other groups is known as **ethnocentrism.** People who are ethnocentric view the customs and standards of other groups as inferior or wrong.

In most cases, different customs are not a matter of right and wrong but of choice and tradition. In some African-American churches, listeners shout affirmative responses during a sermon, while in some other churches, listeners remain silent. One custom is not superior to the other; they are simply different.

Learn the expectations and viewpoints of different cultures and groups. Let's say you are a manager giving an informal training talk to a group of employees and you try to encourage them to ask questions as you go along. Some of the Asian-American employees, however, never ask questions. Before you conclude that these employees are uninvolved and uninterested, keep in mind that for some Asian Americans, asking questions is considered a disrespectful challenge to the speaker's authority.

If you don't know much about the attitudes and viewpoints of an American ethnic group, interview a few representative audience members beforehand to learn about their backgrounds and needs. Also, ask for advice from associates who have had experience communicating with the kinds of listeners to whom you will be speaking.

Focus on individuality. Although becoming informed about group differences is important, treat your knowledge as possible clues, not as absolute certainties. In the example above, notice that I spoke of *some* Asian Americans—not all. If you have Asian Americans in your audience, be sensitive to possible cultural differences, but you should treat these listeners primarily as individuals who may have characteristics that do not coincide with those of other Asian Americans. In dealing with diverse groups, be sensitive to possible differences and special needs, but as much as possible, focus on the individuality of each listener.

Never ridicule any group. Some people think that if no members of a particular group (such as women, gays and lesbians, or minorities) are present, it is okay to make insulting jokes. It is *never* okay. Such slurs are offensive and unfunny to many men and women who don't belong to the group being ridiculed, and they will automatically lose respect for a speaker who uses them.

Listeners with Disabilities

People with disabilities are active in the workplace and in their communities. How can speakers know what accommodations to make? Scott H. Lewis, who describes himself as "a blind Toastmaster" (he's a member of a Toastmasters club in Port Angeles, Washington), has a simple answer: "Ask." Fearful of making a social blunder, some speakers shy away from the best source of information. Lewis says, "Persons of disability know what they need . . . and are the best and most qualified resources to consult when making reasonable accommodations."[13]

Here are some general tips for being sensitive to listeners with disabilities:

- Before you ask your audience to gather around you for a demonstration, or involve them in an activity, be sure to determine if listeners with disabilities can participate. Encourage them to do so.

- Many people, without realizing it, treat adults with disabilities as if they were children. Don't use first names unless you are using first names with all others present. Don't speak in an exaggerated, condescending manner. Don't talk down to them.

- Don't equate physical limitations with mental limitations. The fact that a listener is in a wheelchair has nothing to do with his or her mental abilities.

- The Easter Seals campaign gives this advice: "It's okay to offer help to a person with a disability if it seems needed, but don't overdo it or insist on helping. Always ask first."[14]

- Never take the arm of a person with a mobility or visual impairment. Instead, offer your arm.

Now let's look at tips for specific types of disabilities.

Listeners with Mobility Impairments

- Try to remove barriers that would limit wheelchair access. Whenever there is a choice, ask the listener where he or she would like to sit—don't assume that he or she would prefer to be in the back or the front of the room.

- Never patronize people in wheelchairs by patting them on the head or shoulder.

- Shake hands with people in wheelchairs like you would with anyone else.

- Don't lean against or hang on someone's wheelchair. It is viewed by the person as part of his or her personal space.[15]

Listeners Who Are Deaf or Hearing-Impaired

- If hearing-impaired listeners must see your mouth to understand your words, try to avoid turning away. At the same time, don't put them in a spotlight by standing directly in front of them and looking at only them.

- "It is not necessary to exaggerate your words," says Deborah L. Harmon, a college counselor for students with disabilities, "although it may be appropriate to slow your rate of speech slightly when talking with people who are hearing-impaired."[16]

Your Thoughts

Why is it insulting to assume that all persons in a wheelchair want to sit in the back of a room?

- Whenever possible, speakers should augment their remarks with visual aids, says Harmon. "Write technical terms on a board when first introduced" so that deaf audience members can see how the terms are spelled and thus can figure out their pronunciation.[17]
- Be aware that "people in the deaf community and culture," writes social worker Helen Sloss Luey, "tend to perceive deafness not as a disability, but as an alternate lifestyle and culture."[18]

Listeners Who Are Blind or Visually Impaired

- Talk in a normal voice. Just because a person has limited vision, don't assume that he or she has a hearing impairment, too.
- Don't touch or call a guide dog, says Harmon. Trying to play with it interferes with the performance of its duties. These animals are highly trained work dogs that will not disrupt a speech. They don't need to be soothed or distracted by you.[19]
- Don't assume that listeners who are blind or visually impaired will not want copies of your handouts. "Even if they can't read them at the meeting," says Sharon Lynn Campbell of St. Louis, Missouri, "they may want to have them read aloud later."[20]
- If you say to a listener who is blind, "Do you see what I mean?" or a similar phrase, there is no need to become flustered or apologetic. The listener realizes that you are using a common phrase out of habit and that you intend no insult. She probably uses it herself.

Audience Knowledge

Thomas Leech, a business consultant in San Diego, California, tells of a manager at an electronics firm who was asked to explain a new electronics program to a group of visiting Explorer Scouts. "He pulled two dozen visuals used for working meetings, went into great detail about technical aspects, and spoke of FLMs and MOKFLTPAC," says Leech. "He was enthusiastic, knowledgeable, and totally ineffective, since his audience was lost for about 44 of his 45 minutes."[21]

For a speech on gambling, don't assume that all your listeners know what blackjack is. Find out in advance.

This man made a common mistake: failing to speak at the knowledge level of his listeners. To avoid this mistake, find out what your listeners know and don't know about your subject, and then adapt your remarks to their level.

If your pre-speech analysis shows that your listeners know a lot about your topic, you can skip an explanation of basic concepts and go straight into advanced material. On the other hand, if your analysis shows that listeners know little or nothing about your topic, you will need to start at a basic level and add advanced material as you go along. Avoid overwhelming them with more information than they can comfortably absorb.

So far, so good, but now comes the tricky part. What should you do if some of your listeners know a lot about your subject and others know nothing? Whenever possible, the solution is to start off at a simple level and add complexity as you go along (and tell your audience that this is what you will do). For example, if you are speaking on identity theft to a mixed audience, you can hold the attention of everyone by saying something like this: "I realize that some of you know little about identity theft, while some of you have already been victims. So, to bring everyone up to speed, I want to begin by defining what identity theft is, and then

I'll get into the nitty-gritty of how you can prevent the crime." Regardless of their level of knowledge, listeners usually appreciate this kind of sensitivity.

Audience Psychology

Your listeners do not see the world the same way you do, because they have lived a different life, with different experiences, different mistakes, and different successes. To further your understanding of your listeners, assess their level of interest and their attitudes.

Interest Level

Through interviews or surveys, ask your listeners whether they are interested in your topic. If they seem indifferent or bored, your challenge is to generate interest during the speech. One student prepared a speech on handwriting analysis, a topic that she knew well; however, in her prespeech interviews she discovered that her classmates considered the topic boring. So she began her speech by saying, "Did you know that when you fill out papers for a job interview, some employers send the papers to handwriting experts who claim that they can determine whether you are honest and reliable?" Now the audience found the topic interesting because it obviously had a potential impact on their lives.

To keep an audience interested throughout the entire speech, avoid getting bogged down in tedious, technical material. Use interesting examples, lively stories, and captivating visuals. All of these techniques will be discussed in more detail in later chapters.

Attitudes

Attitudes are the emotional inclinations—the favorable or unfavorable predispositions— that listeners bring to a speech. Each listener's attitudes are derived from a complex inner web of values, beliefs, experiences, and biases.

Before your speech, try to determine your listeners' attitudes—negative, neutral, or positive—toward your goal, yourself as speaker, and the occasion.

attitude
a predisposition to respond favorably or unfavorably toward a person or an idea

Attitudes toward the Goal

Unfavorable.   If listeners are negative toward your goal or objective, you should design your speech either to win them over to your views or—if that is unrealistic—to move them closer to your position.

When Najuana Dorsey, a student at Georgia Southern University, planned a speech on the desirability of insects as a source of protein for low-income people in impoverished countries, she knew (from a questionnaire) that her classmates were repulsed by the idea of anyone eating insects. So she devised a plan to change their attitude. In the early part of her speech, she gave solid scientific data about the nutritional value of insects. Near the end, she pulled out a cricket cake and said, "The crickets are roasted, and they taste like pecans. Why don't you try just one bite?" Despite initial squeamishness, all but one of her classmates ended up eating an entire piece, finding the cake to be surprisingly delicious. On after-speech evaluation sheets, students indicated that they now agreed with Dorsey's contention that insects could help alleviate hunger in the world.[22] (See Figure 4.2.)

Neutral.   If your listeners are apathetic or neutral, try to involve them in the issue, and then win them over to your side. For example, if an audience seems unconcerned about the extinction of hundreds of species of plants every year, you can tell them of the many

Figure 4.2
When student speaker Najuana Dorsey invited her classmates at Georgia Southern University to try some cricket cake, how did they respond? See text on the previous page for the answer.

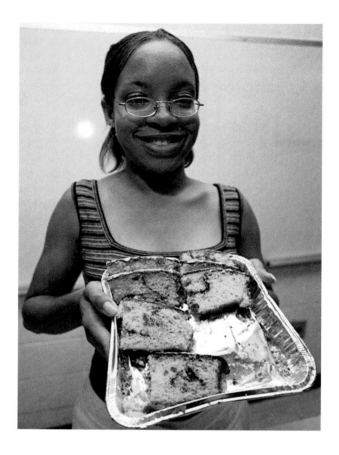

medicines that are derived from plants. Digitalis, which is derived from the leaves of the foxglove plant, is used to treat heart disease. "Who knows," you can say, "if one of the many plants that will disappear from earth this year contains an ingredient that could have saved your life someday?" What you are trying to do, of course, is show that the issue is not a faraway abstraction but a real concern that could affect listeners' own lives.

Favorable.   If your audience is favorably disposed toward your ideas, your task is to reinforce their positive views and even motivate them to take action. For example, you might give a pep talk to members of a political party in your community, urging them to campaign on behalf of the party's candidate in an upcoming election.

Attitudes toward the Speaker

Listeners will have a negative attitude toward a speaker if they suspect that he or she is unqualified to speak on a particular subject. This skepticism can be overcome if the person introducing you states your credentials and expertise. Otherwise, you can establish your credibility yourself at the beginning of your speech. Angie Chen, a student speaker, gave a classroom speech on acupuncture. During her introduction, she revealed that she had grown up in China and had undergone acupuncture treatment herself and had watched it performed on friends and relatives. Though Chen did not claim to be a medical expert, her summary of her experiences showed that she knew a great deal about the subject.

You also can enhance your credibility by explaining how you got your information. Let's say you give a report on recovery programs for drug addicts in your community. In your introduction, it is appropriate to mention that you have read two books on the subject and interviewed a local expert on chemical dependency. This is not bragging; it is simply a way to let the audience know that your information is based on solid research.

Attitudes toward the Occasion

Sometimes listeners are irritated because they have been ordered to attend—they are a "captive audience"—and because they think the meeting is unnecessary. With such audiences, give a lively presentation geared to their precise needs. If possible, show an awareness of their situation and your desire to help.

One speaker had to address a group of disgruntled employees who were required to attend a 4 P.M. meeting to listen to her suggestions about filling out employee self-evaluation—a topic they felt was a waste of time. At the beginning she said, "I know you'd rather be somewhere else right now, and I know you think this meeting is pointless, but let's make the best use of our time that we can. I have talked to several of you about your concerns, and I'd like to zero in on them and see if we can improve the situation. And I promise to be finished by 5, so we can all go home." Her comments, she said, caused the listeners to lean forward and listen attentively to her presentation.

The Occasion

Find out as much as you can about the occasion and the setting of your speech, especially when you are giving a speech in your community or at a career-related meeting. Here are some issues to ask about; pay special attention to the first one.

Time Limit

Many public occasions are marred by long-winded speakers who drone on and on, oblivious to the lateness of the hour and the restlessness of the audience. Always find out how much time has been allotted for your speech, and *never* exceed the limit. This rule applies when you are the sole speaker and especially when you are one of several speakers. If four speakers on a program are supposed to speak for only 10 minutes apiece, imagine what happens when each speaks for 30 minutes. The audience becomes fatigued and inattentive.

Some speakers have absolutely no concept of time. For a 5-minute speech, some of my students talk for 20 minutes and then swear later that they could not have talked for more than 5—something must have been wrong with my stopwatch. As we will see later, practicing your speech at home and clocking yourself will help you keep within time limits. If you tend to be a talkative speaker, follow the wise speechmaking formula of President Franklin D. Roosevelt:

- Be sincere.
- Be brief.
- Be seated.

Expectations

Actor Steve Martin upset a lot of listeners one evening when he appeared at the 92nd Street Y in New York City and talked about art history. The audience of 900, who had paid $50 each to hear him, had assumed he would talk about his film and television

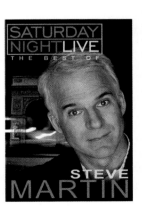

Tips for Your Career

Be Prepared to Trim Your Remarks

One of the most exasperating situations you can face is this: Because of circumstances beyond your control, your speech comes at the end of a long, tedious meeting when listeners are weary and ready to leave. Often the best response is to trim your speech. As the following incident shows, the audience will be grateful:

> An all-day professional conference was supposed to end at 3:30 P.M. so that participants would have plenty of daylight for driving back to their hometowns. Unfortunately, most of the speakers on the program exceeded their time limit, and the final speaker found himself starting at 3:18. Without commenting on the insensitivity of the other speakers, he started out by

saying, "How many of you would like to leave at 3:30?" Every hand went up. "I will end at 3:30," he promised. Though it meant omitting most of his prepared remarks, the speaker kept his promise. One of the participants said later: "We appreciated his sensitivity to us and his awareness of the time. And he showed class in not lambasting the earlier speakers who stole most of his time. He showed no anger or resentment."

Here's a technique to consider: When I am invited to speak at meetings where there are several speakers, I prepare two versions of my speech—a full-length one to use if the other speakers respect their time limits and a shorter version if events dictate that I trim my remarks.

career as a comedian. Many of the listeners complained by phone and e-mail the next day, and the Y issued an apology and promised to send a $50 gift certificate to any unhappy listener.[23]

If listeners expect one thing, and you present another, they may be disappointed, even angry. Find out in advance the purpose of a meeting or presentation, and then make sure you give listeners the kind of material they are expecting.

Other Events on the Program

Find out all that you can about other events on a program. Are there other speakers on the agenda? If so, on what topic will they speak? It would be disconcerting to prepare a speech on the life of Martin Luther King and then discover during the ceremony that the speaker ahead of you is talking on the same subject.

Even more alarming is to come to a meeting and find out that you are not just giving a speech but also debating someone on your topic. Obviously you need to know such information in advance so that you can anticipate the other speaker's argument and prepare your rebuttal.

Your Thoughts

While you are waiting to give a speech, you discover that the person speaking just before you is covering the same topic. When you stand up, what will you do and say?

Audience Size

It can be unsettling to walk into a room expecting an audience of 20 but instead finding 200. Knowing the size of your audience ahead of time will help you not only to prepare yourself psychologically but also to plan your presentation. Will you need extra-large visual aids? Will you need a microphone?

It's easier to connect with your listeners if they are close to you physically. If you have relatively few listeners, and they are scattered throughout a big room or they are all clumped together in the back rows, ask them to move to the front and center. Because some listeners dislike having to move, you may have to appeal for their cooperation by saying something like, "I hate to bother you, but it will save my throat if I don't have to shout."

Adapting during the Speech

Adapting your speech to your audience, so important during the preparation stages, also must take place during the actual delivery of the speech. Be sensitive to your listeners' moods and reactions, and then make any appropriate adjustments that you can. Here is an example.

> Using a portable chef's stove, Lester Petchenik, a student speaker, was demonstrating how to cook green beans *amandine*. At one point he sprinkled a large amount of salt into his pan—an action that caused several members of the audience to exchange glances of surprise. Noticing this reaction, Petchenik ad-libbed, "I know it looks like I put too much salt in, but remember that I've got three pounds of green beans in this pan. In just a moment, when you taste this, you'll see that it's not too salty." (He was right.)

Try to overcome any barriers to communication.   John Naber of Pasadena, California, an Olympic gold medalist in swimming, says that he once gave a speech in a room with poor acoustics. Realizing the audience would have trouble understanding him if he stayed at the lectern, he said, "I moved into the middle of the group and walked among them as I spoke."[24]

Be sensitive to the mood of the audience.   You can tell if listeners are bored, drowsy, or restless by observing their body language. Are they yawning, letting their head droop down, averting their eyes from the speaker, or fidgeting in their seats? Sometimes they are listless not because your speech is boring but because of circumstances beyond your control. It is eight o'clock in the morning, for example, and you have to explain a technical process to a group of conventioneers who have stayed up partying half the night.

Many effective speakers encourage a lively interaction with their listeners, listening to them as much as speaking. One such speaker is Nick Clegg, deputy prime minister of the United Kingdom, who is shown here interacting with students at Oxford Brookes University in England.

Try to "wake up" a listless audience.   For droopy listeners, here are some techniques you can use: (1) Invite audience participation (by asking for examples of what you are talking about or by asking for a show of hands of those who agree with you). (2) Rev up your delivery (by moving about, by speaking slightly louder at certain points, or by speaking occasionally in a more dramatic tone).

Resources for Review and Skill Building

Summary

To be an effective speaker, concentrate your attention and energies on your audience, and have a strong desire to communicate your message to them. Analyze the listeners beforehand and adapt your materials and presentation to their needs and interests.

To get information about an audience, you can interview the program director, you can interview a few future listeners, or you can conduct a survey of your listeners.

A wide diversity of listeners—men and women of different ages, races, nationalities, ethnic groups, religions, economic levels, and physical abilities—are likely to be in your audiences.

When speaking to international audiences, learn as much as you can about the culture of the listeners. Learn nonverbal signals, be careful with jargon and slang, and maintain a serious, formal tone. If possible, provide handouts covering some of your main points a day or two before a presentation.

Extend the same sensitivity to America's diverse cultures. Avoid ethnocentrism, the belief that one's own cultural group is superior to other groups. Learn the expectations and viewpoints of different cultures, but treat your knowledge as possible clues, not absolute certainties. As much as possible, treat listeners primarily as individuals who may have characteristics that do not coincide with those of others in their cultural group.

Try to accommodate the needs of listeners with disabilities. If you are in doubt about what they need, simply ask them. Never treat adults with disabilities as if they were children, and don't equate physical limitations with mental limitations.

Analyze and adapt your presentations to such factors as age, gender, educational levels, occupations, religious affiliations, and economic and social status.

Consider your listeners' level of knowledge about your material, their level of interest in your subject matter, and their attitudes toward the goal, the speaker, and the occasion.

Analyze the occasion to gather details about the time limit, audience expectations, other events on the program, and the number of people who will attend.

Be prepared to adapt to the needs of the listeners during the speech itself. Be sensitive to the cues that indicate boredom, restlessness, or lack of understanding.

Key Terms

adaptation, *54*

attitude, *65*

audience analysis, *54*

audience-centered speaker, *54*

closed question, *56*

customize, *54*

ethnocentrism, *62*

open-ended question, *56*

sexist language, *58*

taboo, *59*

Review Questions

1. What is an *audience-centered* speaker?

2. What is meant by audience analysis and adaptation?

3. How can a speaker get advance information about an audience?

4. What are taboos, and why are they an important concern for a speaker?

5. Do international audiences usually prefer a presentation that is humorous and informal or one that is serious and formal? Explain your answer.

6. What is ethnocentrism?

7. Who is the best source of information about the needs of listeners with disabilities, and why?

8. What approach should you take if listeners have an unfavorable attitude toward your speech goal?

9. What guidelines should be followed for a speech to an audience that knows little or nothing about your topic?

10. What might happen if you give a speech that is different from the one the audience was expecting?

Building Critical-Thinking Skills

1. Several websites provide ready-made speeches that public speakers are welcome to use as their own. Aside from the dishonesty involved, why would using such speeches be a mistake?

2. At what time of day are you normally least alert? What conditions in a room (such as temperature and noise) cause you to be inattentive? Now imagine that you are a listener in these circumstances. What would a speaker need to do to keep you awake and engaged?

Building Teamwork Skills

1. Work with a group to create a questionnaire aimed at finding out where an audience stands concerning one of these issues: (a) Should "vicious" breeds of dogs such as pit bulls be outlawed? (b) Should the legal drinking age be changed? (c) Should pain sufferers be given medical marijuana? Use all the types of questions shown in Figure 4.1.

2. In a group, create a list of 10 examples of American slang or jargon that might be misunderstood by visiting physicians from Hong Kong who speak British English.

Ethical Issues

Answer for p. 54: C. The speaker should neither omit nor water down her information, especially since she believes it can prevent long-term harm.

Selecting Topic, Purpose, and Central Idea

OUTLINE

OBJECTIVES

After studying this chapter, you should be able to:

1. Select appropriate and interesting speech topics.
2. Specify the general purpose of a speech.
3. Develop a clear, concise specific purpose statement for every speech you prepare.
4. Develop a clear, coherent central idea for every speech you prepare.
5. Understand how the specific purpose and the central idea fit into the overall design of a speech.

CHRISTO COETZER, a student at the University of Pretoria in South Africa, has unicycled hundreds of miles across several countries, and he loves to give presentations on his passion for unicycles.[1]

For Coetzer, choosing a topic for a speech is easy, but some speakers—on campus and beyond—speak on topics they are not passionate about, and they end up boring the audience. Other speakers are enthusiastic about their topics, but they fail to have clear objectives. They meander and roam, causing listeners to become irritated and confused.

To help you avoid these mistakes, the first half of this chapter shows how to choose a good topic, and the second half explains how to develop clear objectives, using three valuable tools—general purpose, specific purpose, and central idea.

Coetzer hopes that by sharing his enthusiasm, he can entice student listeners into trying his sport.

Selecting a Topic

For some speeches that you will give as part of a job, your topic will be chosen by someone else. Your boss, for example, tells you to present a new policy to your fellow employees.

In most public speaking classes, students are permitted to choose their own topics—a freedom that causes some students a great deal of agony, as they moan to friends, "I have to give a speech next week and I can't think of a thing to speak on." Don't let yourself get stuck at this stage. Choose your topic far in advance, because you will need to spend your time and energy on researching, outlining, and practicing. If you are indecisive and delay, you may find yourself without enough time to prepare the speech adequately.

While you are taking this course, keep a notepad or smartphone handy and record ideas for topics as they come to you so that you will have a stockpile from which to draw. In the weeks ahead, you can add to your list as you come up with more ideas.

Here are some important points to bear in mind as you look for a topic.

Select a Topic You Care About

Has anything ever happened to you that was so exciting or interesting or infuriating you could hardly wait to tell your friends about it? That's the way you should feel about your speech topic. It should be something you care about, something you are eager to communicate to others. Are you exhilarated by the sport of kayaking? Speak on how to get started in kayaking. Are you angry over the rising number of car thefts in your community? Speak on how to foil car thieves.

Enthusiasm is contagious. If you are excited, your excitement will spread to your listeners. If you are not excited about your topic, you are likely to do a lackluster job of preparing the speech, and when you deliver it, you will probably come across as dull and unconvincing.

Select a Topic You Can Master

A nightmare scenario: You give a speech on a subject about which you know very little. In the question-and-answer period, some listeners (who know the subject well) point out your omissions and errors.

This nightmare happened to me once in college, and it has happened to other speakers, but it need not happen to you. Make things easy for yourself. Speak on a subject with which you are already thoroughly familiar—or about which you can learn through research.

Here are several ways to probe for topics about which you know a lot (or can learn).

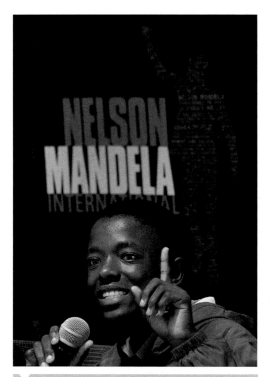

Thando Sithebe, a student in Johannesburg, South Africa, had always wanted to know more about Nelson Mandela, the man who was imprisoned for 27 years before becoming South Africa's first black president, so he researched and delivered a classroom speech about Mandela's life and influence. Impressed by the speech, his instructor arranged for Sithebe to give it at a "Nelson Mandela International Day" event.

Personal Experiences

If you are permitted to choose your own topic, start your search with the subject on which you are the world's foremost expert—your own life.

"But my life isn't very interesting or exciting," you might say. Not so. Maybe you are not an international celebrity, but there are dozens of aspects of your life that could make interesting speeches. Here are some examples, all involving students:

- After a friend was defrauded by a student-loan scam, Christina Morales researched the crime and told classmates how to find honest, reliable lenders for student loans.
- Michael Kaplan demonstrated how to make a thin crepe (pancake) filled with spinach, cheese, and tomato.
- Rachel Keller gave a classroom speech on the joys of rising into the sky in a hot-air balloon.

These students were *ordinary* people who chose to speak on *ordinary* aspects of their lives, but their speeches turned out the way all good speeches should turn out—interesting. When you are searching for a topic, start by looking for interesting experiences in your own life.

To help you assess your interests, you can create a personal inventory, using the categories shown in Figure 5.1 (which is an example of how one student, Lisa Lorenzo, used the technique). After you have filled in the inventory, go back and analyze the list for possible speech topics. You may want to ask a friend or an instructor to help you.

All the items in Lorenzo's inventory are potentially good speech topics. The best one would be whichever she is most eager to share with the audience.

Exploring Interests

Can you identify a topic that intrigues you—a topic that you have always wanted to know more about? If you choose such a topic, you not only get a subject that is fun to research but also gain a stockpile of new and interesting information. Your topic might even influence the direction of your life, as this example shows:

> In a freshman public-speaking class at Humboldt State University in California, Jonathan Castro chose a topic that he had always wanted to investigate—volcanoes. Preparing and delivering the speech ignited a passionate interest that led Castro to choose volcanology as his life's work. After graduating from Humboldt, he earned a Ph.D. in geology at the University of Oregon, and today he is a volcano specialist at Oberlin College.[2]

A college classroom speech on volcanoes changed the course of Jonathan Castro's life.

Even if it doesn't change the course of your life, an intriguing topic can yield benefits. One student had always wanted to know the safest options for investing in the stock market. She researched and gave a speech on the subject, and a year later, she used the information to make her own investments.

Brainstorming

If the suggestions already discussed don't yield a topic, try **brainstorming** (so called because it is supposed to create intellectual thunder and lightning). In brainstorming, you write down whatever pops into your mind. For example, if you start off with the word *helicopter*, the next word that floats into your mind might be *rescue* and then the

brainstorming
generating many ideas quickly and uncritically

Figure 5.1
A personal inventory, as filled in by one student.

Name: ___Rachel Zamora___

Personal Inventory

Jot down as much information about yourself
as you can in the categories below.

Work experience (past and present)
    Radiology intern, St. Francis Hospital
    Volunteer assistant, children's cancer ward
    Part-time server, Thai restaurant

Special skills or knowledge
    Managing money (I'm paying my way through college)
    Making hospital patients feel relaxed and comfortable

Pastimes (hobbies, sports, recreation)
    Swimming
    Chatting on Facebook
    Watching movies

Travel
    New York City
    Grand Canyon
    Yosemite
    Yellowstone

Unusual experiences
    Encountering a black bear in Yosemite
    Helping to build a house for Habitat for Humanity

School interests (academic and extracurricular)
    Magnetic Resonance Imaging (MRI)
    Hanging out with International Club students

Concerns or beliefs (politics, society, family, etc.)
    Society must stop cutting funds for elementary schools
    We need to find a cure for multiple sclerosis
    More money shoud be spent on solar energy research

next word might be *emergencies,* and so on. Don't censor any words. Don't apply any critical evaluation. Simply write whatever comes into your mind. Nothing is too silly or bizarre to put down.

Using a sheet of paper (with categories such as those in Figure 5.2), jot down words as they come to your mind. When you finish brainstorming, analyze your list for possible topics. Don't discard any possibility until you have chosen a topic.

One student's brainstorming notes are shown in Figure 5.2. Let's examine one category, Social Problems, in which the student started with traffic accidents, a serious problem in society today. This led him to jot down "distractions," perhaps because distracted drivers cause a large number of accidents. This prompted him to think of

Brainstorming Guide

People
  comedians
  Tracy Morgan
  Stephen Colbert
  talk show hosts
  Oprah Winfrey

Places
  Washington, D.C.
  Smithsonian
  Jefferson Memorial
  Tidal Basin
  FDR Memorial

Things
  e-book reader
  Kindle
  Nook
  tablet
  iPad

Health
  healthy food
  dried cranberries
  pomegranate seeds
  blueberries
  apricots
  sunflower seeds

Music
  Lady Gaga
  Adele
  Rihanna
  Black Eyed Peas
  Modest Mouse

Sports
  pitchers
  lefthanders
  knuckleball
  no-hitter
  perfect game

Current Events
  depletion of fish in oceans
  mercury in tuna
  farm fish
  tilapia
  salmon

Social Problems
  traffic accidents
  distractions
  smartphones
  texting
  teenage drivers
  driver education

Figure 5.2
One student's entries on a brainstorming guide.

"smartphones," followed by "texting"—two big factors in driver distraction. This led him to think of teenage drivers, who cause the majority of driving-while-texting mishaps. Finally, his brainstorm produced the idea of "driver education." Later, as he analyzed the list, he chose to speak on the need for classes to warn teens of the dangers of texting.

You may be wondering why you should put all this down on paper. Why not just let all your ideas float around in your mind? The advantage of writing your thoughts down is that you end up with a document that can be analyzed. Seeing words on a page helps you focus your thinking.

Exploring the Internet

An enjoyable way to find topics is to travel around the Internet. Here are some sample approaches:

- For current events, you can visit news media sites, such as the *New York Times* (www. nytimes.com), ABC News (abcnews.go.com), and MSNBC News (www.msnbc.msn .com), and then browse through various sections (Health, Technology, Business, etc.).
- For general-interest articles, look through the websites of National Public Radio (www.npr.org), *Psychology Today* (www.psychologytoday.com), and *National Geographic* (ngm.nationalgeographic.com).

- Social media outlets and web databases can be helpful tools for finding inspiration. If you are stumped, try browsing Twitter, YouTube, Wikipedia, the Internet Movie Database, the Urban Dictionary, Craigslist or another informational hub that you are familiar with. Make notes about what catches your attention. Most of these sites are not adequate bibliographic sources on their own, but they can help you cycle through lots of ideas quickly and give you a jumpstart.

Your Thoughts

If handled poorly, "painting a room" could be a boring topic. How would you make it interesting to an audience of college students?

Choose a Topic That Will Interest the Audience

To engage your audience, choose a topic that is timely, worthwhile, and interesting. A talk on why people decide to take vacations would be dull and obvious—everyone already knows that people take vacations to get away and experience something new, different, and fun. Instead, give a lively presentation on sightseeing in Boston or backpacking in the Rockies.

"I'm excited about my topic," some students say, "but I'm afraid the audience will be bored. How can I know?" Most listeners are bored by speeches that give them no personal enrichment. Their attitude is "What's in it for me?" To see things from their perspective, imagine a typical listener approaching you five minutes before your presentation and saying, "I'm trying to decide whether to stay for your talk. What do I stand to gain by listening to you?" If you realize that you couldn't make a compelling case, change your topic.

This doesn't mean that you must show listeners a dollar-and-cents gain, such as how to make money on the stock market. Perhaps their payoff is simply the pleasure of learning something new and fascinating. For example, you could explain why scientists anticipate that by the year 2100, extinct animals could be brought back to life and displayed in zoos.[3]

Two other ways to determine whether a topic is boring or interesting: (1) Ask your instructor. (2) Several weeks before your talk, survey classmates by asking them to rate several potential speech topics as "very interesting," "moderately interesting," or "not very interesting."

Narrow the Topic

Once you find a topic, you often need to narrow it. Suppose that you want to give a speech on weather; 5 minutes—or 20—is not enough time to adequately cover such a broad topic. How about limiting yourself to just storms? Again, 5 minutes would be too short to do justice to the topic. How about one type of storm—thunderstorms? This subject perhaps could be handled in a 5-minute speech, but it would be advisable to narrow the topic down even more—to one aspect of the subject: "how to avoid being struck by lightning."

Narrowing a topic helps you control your material. It prevents you from wandering in a huge territory: you are able to focus on one small piece of ground. Instead of talking on the vast subject of elections, you might limit yourself to explaining how some states conduct voting via the Internet.

Ask yourself this question: Is my topic one that can be adequately and comfortably discussed in 5 minutes (or whatever your time limit is)? If the honest answer is no, you can keep the topic, but you must narrow the focus.

Here are some examples of broad topics that can be narrowed:

Too broad: Native Americans

Narrowed: Shapes, colors, and legends in Pueblo pottery

Too broad: Prisons

Narrowed: Gangs in federal and state prisons

Too broad: Birds

Narrowed: How migrating birds navigate

An important way to narrow your topic is to formulate a specific purpose, which will be discussed later in this chapter. First, let's take a look at your general purpose.

The General Purpose

Establishing a **general purpose** for your speech will help you bring your topic under control. Most speeches have one of the following purposes:

general purpose
the broad objective of a speech

- To inform
- To persuade
- To entertain

Other purposes, such as to inspire, to pay tribute, and to introduce, will be discussed in Chapter 18 ("Special Types of Speeches").

To Inform

In an informative speech, your goal is to give new information to your listeners. You can define a concept (such as cyberhearts); explain a situation (why honeybees are essential for agriculture); demonstrate a process (how earthquakes occur); or describe a person, place, or event.

Your main concern in this kind of speech is to have your audience understand and remember new information. You are in effect a teacher—not a preacher, a salesperson, or a debater. Here is a sampling of topics for informative speeches:

- The pros and cons of Internet dating sites
- Bullies in the workplace
- How your credit score is figured

To Persuade

Your aim in a persuasive speech is to win your listeners to your point of view. You want to either influence their thinking (for example, convince them that humans can live on Mars someday) or prompt them to take action (for instance, persuade them to buy and drive an all-electric car).

As examples, in this kind of speech, you can try to persuade people to:

- walk or jog one hour per day.
- vote for your candidate for a public office.
- donate money for autism research.

To Entertain

An entertaining speech is aimed at amusing or diverting your audience. It is light, fun, relaxing.

Some students mistakenly think that an entertaining speech is a series of jokes. Although jokes are an obvious component of many entertaining speeches, you can amuse or divert your audience just as easily with other types of material: stories, anecdotes, quotations, examples, and descriptions. (For more details, see Chapter 18.)

Here are some examples of topics for entertaining speeches:

- My life with a parrot named Alex
- The five most outrageous excuses for absenteeism at work
- Being an "extra" in a Hollywood movie

Tips for Your Career

Examine Your Hidden Purposes

In an essay in *Harper's* magazine, Professor Jane Tompkins confesses that earlier in her career, while teaching at Columbia University, she was more concerned about making a good impression than meeting students' needs. "I was . . . focused on: (a) showing the students how smart I was; (b) showing them how knowledgeable I was; and (c) showing them how well prepared I was for class. I had been putting on a performance whose true goal was not to help the students learn but to act in such a way that they would have a good opinion of me."

If other speakers were as candid as Professor Tompkins, they would admit that they, too, often have hidden, unstated objectives that are far afield from listener-focused purposes such as "to inform" or "to persuade." If their purposes were written out, they might look like this:

- To dazzle my boss with my presentation skills
- To get listeners to like me and consider me smart and funny

Hidden objectives are not necessarily bad. All of us have unstated goals such as looking our best and delivering a polished speech. But we should watch for ulterior purposes that make us self-centered and insensitive to our listeners' needs.

The Specific Purpose

specific purpose
the precise goal that a speaker wants to achieve

After you have chosen a topic and determined your general purpose, your next step is to formulate a **specific purpose,** stating exactly what you want to accomplish in your speech. Here is an example:

> *Topic:* Health websites
>
> *General Purpose:* To inform
>
> *Specific Purpose:* To tell my listeners how to find reliable health information on the Internet

The specific purpose is an important planning tool because it can help you to bring your ideas into sharp focus so that you don't wander aimlessly in your speech and lose your audience.

Let's say you choose "protection of the environment" as a topic for a speech. Good topic, but much too broad—you might make the mistake of cramming too many different issues into the speech. How about "protecting national parks"? Now your topic is more manageable, especially if you devise a specific purpose that focuses on just one park:

> *Topic:* Preserving Yosemite National Park
>
> *General Purpose:* To persuade
>
> *Specific Purpose:* To persuade my audience to support steps to reverse overcrowding and neglect in Yosemite National Park

Now you have a sharp focus for your speech. You have limited yourself to a topic that can be covered adequately in a short speech.

Here are some guidelines for formulating a specific purpose statement.

Begin the Statement with an Infinitive

An **infinitive** is a verb preceded by *to*—for example, *to write, to read.* By beginning your purpose statement with an infinitive, you clearly state your intent.

> *Poor:*   Pyramids in Egypt
>
> *Better:* To explain to my audience how the pyramids in Egypt were constructed

For informative speeches, your purpose statement can start with such infinitives as "to explain," "to show," and "to demonstrate." For persuasive speeches, your purpose statement can start with infinitives such as "to convince," "to prove," and "to get the audience to believe."

infinitive
a verb form beginning with "to"

Include a Reference to Your Audience

Your specific purpose statement should refer to your audience. For instance, "To convince my listeners that . . ." This may seem like a minor matter, but it serves to remind you that your goal is not just to stand up and talk but also to communicate your ideas to real flesh-and-blood human beings.

> *Poor:*   To explain how some employers are using psychological tests to determine whether prospective employees are honest
>
> *Better:* To explain to my listeners how some employers are using psychological tests to determine whether prospective employees are honest

Limit the Statement to One Major Idea

Resist the temptation to cover several big ideas in a single speech. Limit your specific purpose statement to only one idea.

> *Poor:*   To persuade the audience to support efforts to halt the destruction of rain forests in Central and South America, and to demand higher standards of water purity in the United States
>
> *Better:* To persuade the audience to support efforts to halt the destruction of rain forests in Central and South America

In the first example, the speaker tries to cover two major ideas in one speech. Although it is true that both themes pertain to the environment, they are not closely related and should be handled in separate speeches.

Make Your Statement as Precise as Possible

Strive to formulate a statement that is clear and precise.

> *Poor:*   To help my audience brighten their relationships
>
> *Better:* To explain to my listeners three techniques people can use to communicate more effectively with loved ones

The first statement is fuzzy and unfocused. What is meant by "to help"? What is meant by "brighten"? And what kind of relationships are to be discussed: marital, social, business? The second statement is one possible improvement.

Your Thoughts

"Telling about white collar crime." How could you improve this statement of specific purpose?

Make Sure You Can Achieve Your Objective in the Time Allotted

Don't try to cover too much in one speech. It is better to choose a small area of knowledge that can be tightly focused than to select a huge area that can be covered only sketchily.

Poor: To tell my audience about endangered species

Better: To convince my audience that international action should be taken to prevent poachers from slaughtering elephants

The first statement is much too broad for a speech; you would need several hours to cover the subject. The second statement narrows the topic so that it can be covered easily in a short speech.

Don't Be Too Technical

You have probably sat through a speech or lecture that was too technical or complicated for you to understand. Don't repeat this mistake when you stand at the lectern.

Poor: To explain to my listeners the chemical composition of vegetable oils

Better: To explain to my audience how to choose the right vegetable oil for cooking different kinds of food

The first statement is too technical for the average audience. Many listeners would find the explanation tedious and over their heads. The second statement focuses on valuable information that people can use in their own kitchens.

The Central Idea

In a college class, a counselor from an alcohol rehabilitation center spoke on alcoholism, giving many statistics, anecdotes, and research findings. I did not hear the speech, but afterward, I overheard some of the listeners arguing about it. Several contended that the speaker's message was "Drink moderately—don't abuse alcohol," while others thought the speaker was saying, "Abstain from alcohol completely." Still others said they were confused—they didn't know what the speaker was driving at.

If this happens to you—if you give a speech and people later wonder or debate exactly what point you were trying to make—you have failed to accomplish your most important task: to communicate your **central idea.**

central idea
the key concept of a speech

The central idea is the core message of your speech expressed in one sentence. It is the same as the *thesis sentence, controlling statement,* or *core idea*—terms you may have encountered in English courses. If you were forced to boil your entire speech down to one sentence, what would you say? *That* is your central idea. If, one month after you have given your speech, the audience remembers only one thing, what should it be? *That* is your central idea.

As we will see in later chapters, the central idea is a vital ingredient in your outline for a speech. In fact, it *controls* your entire speech: everything you say in your speech should develop, explain, illustrate, or prove the central idea. Everything? Yes, everything—all your facts, anecdotes, statistics, and quotations.

If you are unclear in your own mind about your central idea, you will be like the counselor who caused such confusion: Listeners will leave your speech wondering, "What in the world was that speaker driving at?"

Devising the Central Idea

Let's imagine that you decide to give a speech on why governments should spend money to send powerful radio signals into outer space. The specific purpose statement of your speech might look like this:

Specific Purpose: To persuade my listeners to support government funding of radio transmissions into outer space

How are you going to persuade your audience? Can you simply say, "Folks, please support radio transmissions into outer space"? No, because merely stating your position won't sway your listeners. To convince them, you need to sell the audience on a central idea that, if believed, might cause them to support your position:

Central Idea: Most scientists agree that radio transmissions are the best means for making contact with extraterrestrial civilizations (if any exist).

If you can sell this idea, you will probably succeed in your specific purpose: To persuade the listeners to support public funding of radio transmissions. They will be persuaded because the central idea is so intriguing: Most people like the notion of communication with aliens from faraway planets, and if most scientists back the idea, it cannot be considered far-out and impractical. "Yes," the listeners will say, "let's spend some of our tax dollars to find other life."

After you decide upon a central idea, your task in preparing the rest of the speech is to find materials—such as examples, statistics, and quotations—to explain and prove the central idea. In this case, you would need to explain the technology and cite the testimony of eminent scientists who support radio transmissions into space.

Some students have trouble distinguishing between the specific purpose and the central idea. Is there any significant difference? Yes. The specific purpose is written from your point of view—it is what *you* set out to accomplish. The central idea is written entirely from the listeners' point of view—it is the message *they* go away with.

To learn to distinguish between the specific purpose and the central idea, study the examples in Table 5.1.

Your Thoughts

If the central idea of a speech is "People who take many different kinds of pills risk dangerous interactions," what do you think the specific purpose is?

Table 5.1 **How Topics Can Be Developed**

Topic	General Purpose	Specific Purpose	Central Idea
Space junk	To inform	To inform my audience about the dangers of "space junk" (dead satellites and bits of expended rocket stages) that orbits the earth	More than 9,000 pieces of debris orbit the earth, threatening commercial and scientific satellites.
Buying a car	To persuade	To persuade my audience to avoid high-pressure sales tactics when buying a car	By comparing prices and using reputable car guides, consumers can avoid being "taken for a ride" by car salespeople.
Driving tests	To entertain	To amuse my audience with the true story of my abysmal failure to pass my first driving test	Taking the test for a driver's license is a scary and sometimes disastrous event.

Central Idea for a persuasive speech: Sugar consumption by children should be limited.

In planning your speech, write the specific purpose statement first—before you start gathering material. In many cases, you will be able to write the central idea immediately afterward. Sometimes, however, you may need to postpone the central idea until you have completed your research. For example, let's say you are planning a speech on the use of steroids by athletes and bodybuilders. Here is your goal:

Specific Purpose: To convince my audience not to use steroids for building muscle

You haven't done any research yet, so you can't really write a central idea. But after you spend a few days studying articles on steroids, you are able to create your central idea:

Central Idea: Individuals who chronically use steroids risk kidney and liver damage.

Guidelines for the Central Idea

1. **Every speech should have only one central idea.** Why not two? Or three? Because you will be doing well if you can fully illuminate just one big idea in a speech. If you try to handle more than one, you run the risk of overwhelming the listeners with more information than they can absorb.

2. **Put the central idea on paper.** Writing it down gives you a clear sense of the direction your speech will take.

3. **Limit the central idea to a single sentence.** Whenever theatrical producer David Belasco was approached by people with an idea for a play, he would hand them his business card and ask them to write their concept on the back. If they protested that they needed more space, he would say, "Then you don't have a clear idea."[4]

4. **Make an assertion rather than an announcement or a statement of fact.** A common mistake is to formulate the central idea as a mere announcement:

    Ineffective: I will discuss robots as surgeons. *(This is a good topic, but what idea does the speaker want to communicate?)*

    Another mistake is to put forth nothing more than a statement of fact:

    Ineffective: Several operations at Johns Hopkins Medical Center have been performed by surgeons using robots. *(This is interesting, but it is just a fact—a piece of information that can be included in the speech but does not stand alone as an overarching theme.)*

    Now let's turn to a better version—one that makes an assertion:

    Effective: Robots are valuable assistants in surgery because they can work with great precision and no fatigue. *(This is a good central idea because it asserts a worthwhile point that can be developed in a speech.)*

5. **Let the central idea determine the content of the entire speech.** As you prepare your outline, evaluate every potential item in light of the central idea. Does Fact A help explain the central idea? If yes, keep it. If no, throw it out. Does Statistic B help prove the central idea? If yes, keep it. If no, throw it out.

Overview of Speech Design

How do the items discussed in this chapter fit into the overall design of a speech? If you look at Figure 5.3, which is an overview of a typical plan for a speech, you will see this chapter's items listed in the top ellipse, labeled "Objectives." These items—general purpose, specific purpose, and central idea—are planning tools to help you create a coherent speech. They are *not* the opening words of your speech. The bottom ellipse, "Documentation," is also a planning tool and does not represent the final words of a speech. The actual speech that you deliver is shown in the rectangles.

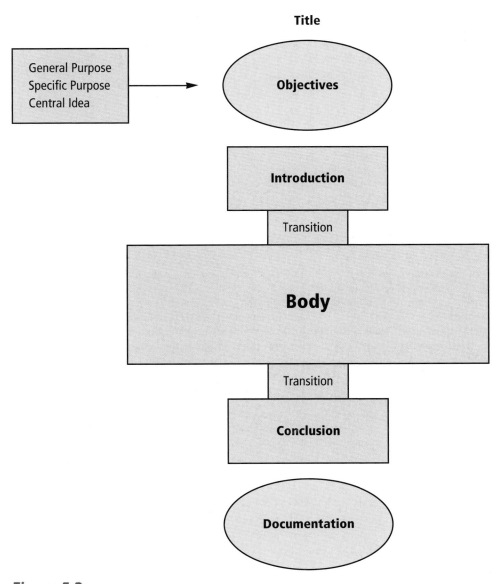

Figure 5.3

An overview of a typical plan for a speech. "Objectives" are explained in this chapter. The other terms will be covered in Chapters 6–12.

Don't make the mistake of assuming that a speaker should create the rectangles from top to bottom, in the order in which they appear. For reasons that will be obvious later, it makes sense to work on the body first, and then tackle the introduction and the conclusion.

Let's pause a moment to consider where we are headed. The next seven chapters will show you how to build a strong speech. First we will look at how to find good primary research materials and finesse them with raw materials (Chapters 6–9). Next we will examine how to develop the body of the speech (Chapter 10) and the introduction and conclusion (Chapter 11). Finally, we will discuss how to arrange all the parts in your outline and your speaking notes (Chapter 12).

All this work may seem wasteful of your time and energy, but in the long run, it pays rich dividends. It channels your thinking and prevents you from scattering your efforts across too wide a field. It helps you fashion an orderly, understandable speech, increasing the chances that you will enlighten, rather than confuse or bore, your listeners.

Resources for Review and Skill Building

Summary

In choosing a topic for your speech, think of subjects (1) about which you care a great deal, (2) about which you know a lot (either now or after you complete your research), and (3) that your audience will find interesting.

In looking for topics, start with yourself. What personal experiences might yield an interesting speech? If you want to go outside your own life, explore topics that intrigue you—subjects about which you have always wanted to know more.

Other methods for finding a topic include brainstorming (writing down ideas that come to your mind) and exploring Internet sites that list subjects for college papers and speeches.

After you choose a topic, decide upon your general purpose in speaking (such as to inform, to persuade, or to entertain) and then formulate your specific purpose—exactly what you hope to accomplish in the speech. Follow these guidelines: (1) Begin the statement with an infinitive. (2) Include a reference to your audience. (3) Limit the statement to one major idea. (4) Make your statement as precise as possible. (5) Make sure you can achieve your objective in the time allotted. (6) Don't be too technical.

Next, write out your central idea: the one key idea that you want your audience to remember even if they forget everything else in the speech. Make sure the central idea is phrased as an assertion rather than an announcement or a statement of fact.

In the long run, these preliminary steps will help you organize your ideas in a coherent, understandable form.

Key Terms

brainstorming, *75*

central idea, *82*

general purpose, *79*

infinitive, *81*

specific purpose, *80*

Review Questions

1. When a speaker is enthusiastic about his or her ideas, how do listeners usually react?

2. How does brainstorming work?

3. What are the characteristics of speeches that listeners find boring?

4. List three *general* purposes for speeches.

5. Are jokes required for an entertaining speech? Explain your answer.

6. List the six criteria discussed in this chapter for writing a specific purpose statement.

7. What is the central idea of a speech?

8. What is the difference between the specific purpose and the central idea?

9. Give an example of an infinitive.

10. What are hidden purposes, and how should you handle them?

Building Critical-Thinking Skills

1. Narrow down the following broad subjects to specific, manageable topics:

    a. Outdoor recreation
    b. Musical groups
    c. Illegal drugs
    d. Saving money
    e. Cloning

2. All but one of the specific purpose statements below are either inappropriate for a brief classroom speech or incorrectly written.

    Name the good one, and rewrite the bad ones so that they conform to the guidelines in this chapter:

    a. To inform my audience of the basics of quantum inelastic scattering and photodissociation code
    b. To inform my listeners about creativity on the job, getting raises, and being an effective manager
    c. To explain to my audience how to perform basic yoga exercises
    d. How persons with disabilities can fight back against job discrimination
    e. Immigration since 1800
    f. To persuade my audience to be careful

Building Teamwork Skills

1. Before you meet, each group member should list five potential speech topics. In your group, evaluate each topic: Is it interesting and appropriate for a classroom speech?

2. In a group, brainstorm topics that would be boring or inappropriate for speeches in your class. Choose one person to write down the topics. Remember that no one should criticize or analyze during the brainstorming session. Afterward, the group (or the class) can discuss each choice (Does everyone agree? Why is the topic inappropriate?).

3. Follow the instructions for item 2, except brainstorm topics that would be interesting and appropriate for speeches in your class.

Ethical Issues

Answer for p. 74: A. You should know—and respect—your instructor's policy. Some instructors may give permission, while others may prefer that you conduct fresh research.

Finding Information

OBJECTIVES

After studying this chapter, you should be able to:

1. Develop research strategies for finding materials quickly and efficiently.
2. Understand why the Internet is sometimes a less desirable source than traditional library materials.
3. Use electronic search techniques for finding books, articles, and websites.
4. Take advantage of the services and materials offered by librarians and libraries.
5. Locate useful materials on the Internet.
6. Recognize the value of deriving material from experiences, investigations, and surveys.
7. Conduct effective interviews with experts.
8. Take notes with precision, care, and thoroughness.

JENNIFER ZWILLING WAS KICKED OUT of her second-grade science class because her teacher failed to realize that she had a neurological disorder called Tourette Syndrome. People with TS symptoms sometimes make sudden, strange physical movements that they can't control, such as eye blinking, lip smacking, and nose wrinkling.

Her ejection from class, Zwilling says, occurred when "the teacher thought I was rolling my eyes over something she said." In other words, the teacher misinterpreted a TS eye movement as a smart-alecky gesture of contempt. This humiliation, says Zwilling, a Duke University student from Brookville, New York, motivated her to give speeches to schools in her area to inform students about Tourette Syndrome so that they would respect and help classmates who have TS symptoms. Her audiences praised her presentations for being both fascinating and educational.[1]

To gather information for her speeches, Zwilling drew upon her own experiences, and she also talked to other people with TS, including some who had symptoms and experiences different from her own. She interviewed educators at the Tourette Syndrome Association, and she read books, articles, and websites.

Zwilling's approach—gathering material from many different sources—is a good model for all public speakers. If you speak only from your own experience or from just one article, you risk having a speech that is erroneous, skimpy, and dull. But if you find a wide variety of information, you maximize your chances of being accurate, comprehensive, and interesting.

Figure 6.1 gives an overview of the major research options and a sampling of the resources that you can use. All these resources will be discussed in this chapter. The next chapter will cover how to evaluate the information that you find.

Duke University Student Jennifer Zwilling was motivated to give speeches because of a traumatic experience in second grade.

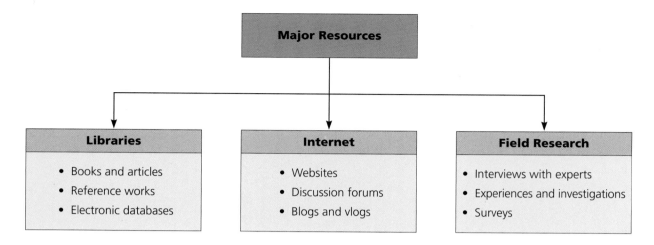

Figure 6.1
Research Options

The resources shown here sometimes overlap. For example, libraries provide access to the Internet, and the Internet provides access to traditional library materials such as magazine articles.

Finding Materials Efficiently

To avoid research that is unproductive and irrelevant, use these techniques.

Begin with Purpose Statement

Decide the specific purpose of your speech before you start your research. It will focus your efforts.

Some students find it helpful to turn the purpose statement into a question. For example, "To inform my listeners how they can determine if their drinking water is free of dangerous contamination" could be: "How can we know if our water is safe to drink?"

Whichever form you use, write it out and keep it in front of you at each step of your research. It will guide your efforts and prevent wasted time.

Plan Your Time

To give yourself ample time before the speech date, start your research far in advance. Determine the materials and resources you will need and create a time line. (See a sample in Figure 6.2.)

Call to arrange personal interviews early in the process so that the interviewees can fit you into their schedules.

Figure 6.2
Sample Time Line

Check off items as they are completed.

☑	Feb. 4	11 a.m.	Call to reserve Internet workstation in library for Feb. 8
☑	Feb. 4	2 p.m.	See reference librarian; explain my topic and get advice
☑	Feb. 5	3 – 5 p.m.	Library: look for info in books and encyclopedias
☐	Feb. 8	7 – 9 p.m.	Surf Internet for info; start with Google
☐	Feb. 9	7 – 9 p.m.	Library: look for full-text articles in electronic databases
☐	Feb. 11	4 – 5 p.m.	Review all notes in preparation for interview tomorrow
☐	Feb. 12	10 a.m.	Interview with Suzanne Ludtke at Pure Water Analysis office, 836 Broadway

Misconceptions about Research

Many people have two erroneous notions about research.

1. **Misconception:** Searching websites is always faster and more efficient than using traditional library resources such as books.

   Reality: Although using a search engine is quick and can lead you to multiple sites, it is sometimes more time-consuming than consulting a book. One of my students, Carole Campbell, who is a cabinetmaker, says that when she needs help on how to perform a complicated procedure, she can find information on the Internet, but it usually takes her 30 minutes to ferret out reliable advice. "I can find the same information in two minutes if I use a book on cabinetmaking," she says. "And the illustrations are more attractive and more helpful than anything I can find on the web."[2]

2. **Misconception:** For accurate information, websites are the best resource.

   Reality: Many websites contain inaccurate or misleading information, especially concerning controversial or disputed issues, so your best option in many cases is to consult books and articles by reputable experts.

Let's say you are trying to verify the healthiest foods for children, and you discover that some websites extol fruit drinks as ideal, while other websites criticize them. What should you do? For trustworthy advice, consult *Complete Food and Nutrition Guide,* a 676-page book (available in print or e-book format) sponsored by the American Dietetic Association, the largest group of food and nutrition professionals in the world. ADA experts recommend that children drink milk and water most of the time, with only occasional fruit drinks. They say that too many fruit drinks can add up to a lot of calories and crowd out nourishing foods like whole fruit and healthy beverages like milk.[3]

It is true that you might be able to get this information online, but there are pitfalls to depending on websites. Unless you have advanced training in nutrition, you would not know which websites are accurate and which are not. The *Guide*'s experts provide reliable conclusions, in contrast to the misinformation and crackpot theories that abound on the Internet. And in addition to the fruit drink issue, the experts have compiled the best information available on hundreds of nutrition topics—all gathered in one convenient volume.

For children, is milk better than fruit drinks?

Searching Electronically

Most research materials today are located by means of electronic searches:

- Books in a library catalog
- Articles in a periodicals database
- Information on the Internet

The starting point for most electronic search systems is a **keyword,** which can lead to relevant material. Follow these guidelines.

keyword
a word looked for in a search command

To narrow your search, use multiple keywords.   Imagine that you are planning a speech on steroids and the dangers they pose for athletes. If you search one of your library's databases of newspaper and magazine articles, using only one keyword—steroids—you may see 5,750 articles listed, but you obviously don't have time to wade through such a huge number. If you use two keywords—steroids sports—you may see 519 articles listed. Still too many. If you use three keywords—steroids sports danger—you may see 23 articles. Now the list is manageable, and the articles probably discuss your precise topic.

Use phrases whenever possible.   To narrow a search for information on the use of dogs in military operations, you can use the phrase "war dogs." (In most search systems, phrases must be placed in quotation marks.) One potential problem: a phrase might miss some good material. (For example, some articles on military dogs might not use the phrase "war dogs.") The solution is to make several searches, using a different phrase each time, such as "combat dogs" and "dogs in battle."

Learn how to use advanced techniques.   Most electronic search systems have a Help menu or Advanced Features, which you can consult to improve your chances of finding what you need. For instance, many systems permit you to specify "past month" or "past year," and some permit setting a range of dates. Also, you can use the sophisticated options like those shown in Table A.2 ("Electronic Search Options") in the appendix at the end of this chapter. For example, if you search on the Web for Madagascar (the country), you will get thousands of unrelated pages about a movie titled *Madagascar*. To exclude the unwanted pages, use a minus sign (Madagascar –movie).

Your Thoughts

For a speech on medieval armor, which would provide better information—books or websites? Defend your answer.

Use the "Find" feature.   Once you open a document, you can go straight to what you are looking for if you use the Find command—hold down the Control key as you press the letter F, and then enter a keyword.

Libraries

Libraries offer a treasury of resources for your speeches. Begin with your campus library, and also consider public libraries and specialized libraries maintained by museums and other organizations in your community. To verify that a library provides the services you need, call in advance or visit the library's website.

Getting Help from Librarians

Some people are reluctant to approach a librarian for help because they fear they will be bothersome. Nonsense. The main role of librarians is not to place books on shelves but to help patrons, so don't be shy about asking for help.

In most libraries, the person who is best able to help you with your research is called a **reference librarian.** This person is a specialist who has training and experience in tracking down information. Drop by, call for an appointment, or send in your query via the library's website.

"Don't spin your wheels and waste a lot of time if you get stuck or encounter something confusing," advises Kathy Herrlich, a librarian at Northeastern University. "A reference librarian can save you time and help you find better information, more efficiently. For example, we can suggest a couple of the best databases for your topic." Also, she says, if a library fails to have what you are looking for, a librarian can provide referrals to other sources and collections outside your campus—at another library, for example, or a community agency.[4]

reference librarian

a specialist in information retrieval

Books

Here are some tips on using books:

Use your library's catalog.   The catalog, an online compilation of all books owned by the library, permits you to make a quick search in at least three categories: (1) author's name, (2) title, and (3) subject.

Pay attention to the date of publication, because an old book may be useless for some research (such as current events). Another important item is the call number, which tells where a book is located in the library's stacks. If you have any problem finding a book, ask a librarian for help.

Some catalogs will indicate whether a book is already checked out and will permit you to place a "hold" on it. As soon as it is returned to the library, it will be reserved for you.

For tips on how to search electronically in a library catalog, see Table A.2 ("Electronic Search Options") in the appendix at the end of this chapter.

Consider using e-books.   Many books in electronic form are likely to be available at your library. E-books can be viewed on a computer screen or on a variety of devices (such as iPad, Kindle, Nook, and Sony Reader). A key advantage of e-books is that you can quickly search an entire book to find words or phrases.

Find previews.   Sometimes, when an entire book is not readily available, you can still find key information by searching online for previews. Let's say you are researching vegetarianism, and you would like to learn about Benjamin Franklin's famous decision to become a vegetarian. Go to a book site like Google Books (books.google.com), call up a biography of Franklin, and enter the keyword "vegetarianism." Figure 6.3 shows a preview from a biography of Franklin by Walter Isaacson.[5] The preview highlights the keyword and provides the paragraph in which the word appears. (Tip: you can also find previews by calling up a book on Amazon.com and clicking on "Search inside the book.")

For research, what is the main advantage of an e-book?

> As a young apprentice, Franklin had read a book extolling vegetarianism. He embraced the diet, but not just for moral and health reasons. His main motive was financial: it enabled him to take the money his brother allotted him for food and save half for books. While his coworkers went off for hearty meals, Franklin ate biscuits and raisins and used the time for study.

Figure 6.3
Book Preview

When an entire book is not readily available, an online preview may yield the desired information, as demonstrated by this excerpt from a biography of Benjamin Franklin.

Articles

Libraries provide access to articles in three types of periodicals: newspapers (such as *The Wall Street Journal*), popular magazines (such as *National Geographic* and *Time*), and scholarly journals (such as *African Studies Quarterly* and *Journal of Supercomputing*).
Articles are available in two formats:

1. *Print.* Libraries carry a wide variety of publications and keep past issues for at least one year.

2. *Electronic.* Most libraries have searchable databases (such as ProQuest and EBSCO) that are available to you but not to the general Internet user. Some of the databases can be accessed only on a campus computer. Some can be accessed off-campus if you use a password provided by your library.

Electronic databases provide information in three forms:

citation
basic facts about a source

1. *Citation.* A **citation** is a basic bibliographical reference that includes the title of the article, the name(s) of the author(s), the name of the magazine, the date, and page numbers.

abstract
summary of key information

2. *Abstract.* An **abstract,** or brief summary, of an article is designed to give you enough information to decide whether you want to see the complete text of that article. Sometimes the abstract itself gives you all the information you need.

full text
every word of a document

3. *Full text.* Some databases offer complete or **full-text** articles.

For tips on how to search electronic databases, see Table A.2 ("Electronic Search Options") in the appendix at the end of this chapter.

Reference Works

A library's reference materials—such as encyclopedias, dictionaries, and maps—are carefully researched and double-checked for accuracy. They are available in either print or electronic versions. For more information, see Table A.1 ("Where to Find Materials") in the appendix at the end of this chapter.

Interlibrary Loan

interlibrary loan
sharing of materials and
services among libraries

If your library does not have a book or an article that you want, librarians can seek help from other libraries, using **interlibrary loan.** A book can be borrowed, often at no cost to you, and an article can be photocopied (you pay only the copying fee).
Because a book or an article may take a few days or even weeks to arrive, make your request as far ahead of speech day as possible.

The Internet

The Internet is a set of interconnected networks that allow computers throughout the world to exchange information. It is best known for two of its components—the World Wide Web and e-mail. Let's look at Internet resources that are most useful for research.

Web Searches

The World Wide Web is a vast multimedia storehouse containing over 600 billion items—text pages, color pictures, video clips, and audio programs. To find websites (most of which contain more than one Web page), use search engines and subject directories.

Search Engines

A **search engine** (such as Google) finds documents on the Internet that match the keywords you have provided. Most search engines return results in order of relevance—the most relevant at the top, the least relevant at the bottom.

Because search engines usually return a staggering number of "hits," some people assume that they can find anything that is on the Web. This is not true. There are many valuable resources that cannot be reached by search engines. For example, some magazines and newspapers have large archives of articles that you can access only by going to the publication's website or by using a password supplied by your library.

For hard-to-find information, don't limit yourself to one search engine. Even relatively small search engines sometimes yield information that is unavailable through giants such as Google. For a list of search engines, see Table A.3 ("Internet Search Tools") in this chapter's appendix.

search engine
a service that lets you search for keywords on Web pages throughout the world

Subject Directories

An underrated (and often unknown) option for Internet research is a **subject directory,** a catalog that starts off with a broad subject area (such as animals), which is then subdivided into smaller categories (reptiles and then lizards and finally geckos). Subject directories have an advantage over search engines in that they direct you to the best websites on your topic, rather than giving you a multitude of URLs to wade through. For example, let's say you want to investigate websites offering movie reviews that reveal the entire plot of a movie. These reviews are called "spoilers," because if you haven't seen the movie yet, they "spoil the ending" for you. If you use a search engine and enter these keywords—spoiler AND movie—you will see a list of millions of documents, but you will have to sort through dozens of them to find what you want. A better approach is to go to the Yahoo Directory (dir.yahoo.com), click on "Entertainment," and then "Movies and Film," and finally "Spoilers." You will see a list of the eight or so websites that are devoted to providing spoilers. You can visit each site, read reviews, and compare how the sites go about their spoiling.

Note that the address for Yahoo Directory (dir.yahoo.com) is different from the address for the Yahoo search engine (yahoo.com). For a list of other subject directories, see Table A.3 ("Internet Search Tools") in the appendix at the end of this chapter.

subject directory
a list of websites categorized by subject

Online Communities and Individuals

In addition to consulting websites, you can tap the experiences and insights of people around the world who are eager and willing to share their knowledge and viewpoints. Here are three ways to find them.

Discussion Forums

Discussion forums (sometimes called discussion groups) are message centers where people who have similar interests can share ideas and observations. For a researcher, the vital part of a forum is its archives. Messages are organized by "threads"—that is, all the messages that deal with an original query can be viewed, one after another. For example, one person asked for comments about a company that was offering her a college scholarship. In response, over a dozen people from different geographic regions posted messages warning that they had been defrauded by the company's scholarship scam. All those messages, organized by thread, can be viewed sequentially in the archives.

discussion forum
a message center for people with a common interest

Tips for Your Career

Develop a Filing System for Important Ideas

Do you have a stockpile of key ideas that you will be able to use after you start your post-college career? If not, start building one today. To succeed in any career, you must have information available on short notice, so a bank of ideas will come in handy when it's time to write a report or prepare a presentation. Managers and colleagues will be impressed by the wealth of relevant information at your fingertips.

I recommend a two-part system:

1. *Computer files for materials you find online.* Keep computer files of Internet and other digitized documents, photos, and illustrations. Create a subdirectory for each broad category and give each file an obvious name (for example, TAXLAW for a file on tax laws in your field).

2. *File folders for clippings and photocopied articles.* For each folder, use a stick-on slip as a label (this makes it easier to discard a topic that is no longer of interest.)

Start with broad categories; later, when a folder starts overflowing, you can create subcategories.

Here are some guidelines about what types of materials to stockpile and how best to keep track of it all:

- Keep a pad or index cards handy so that you can jot down notes of important ideas that you encounter in articles, books, TV programs, speeches, workshops, and interviews.
- Since many of your instructors are experts in their fields, you may want to file lecture notes from some of your college classes.
- Take notes during presentations and interviews, and record the name of the speaker, date, place, and occasion. When you clip or photocopy an article, record the name of the publication, date, and page numbers.
- Don't worry about accumulating too many notes. You can go through your files once or twice a year and discard any deadwood.

Note of caution: Although it is acceptable to ask a discussion forum for help with small, specific items, don't ask the group to prepare a speech for you. Such a query is not only unethical but also unwise. People in forums are friendly and generous, but they get irritated when a lazy student writes, "I've got to give a speech next week on the death penalty, and I'd appreciate all the help I can get."

To access discussion forums, visit the addresses listed in Table A.3 ("Internet Search Tools") in this chapter's appendix.

Expert Sites

expert site
a website offering expertise on requested topics

Expert sites are question-and-answer services that sometimes provide information that you cannot get anywhere else on the Internet. But beware: the quality varies. Some sites have top people in a given field, but other sites have self-chosen experts whose expertise may be dubious.

To access expert sites, visit the addresses listed in Table A.3 ("Internet Search Tools") in this chapter's appendix.

Blogs and Vlogs

blog
frequently updated online log

A **blog**—a shortened term for Web log—is a website that posts material that the blogger (the person or organization that owns the site) wants to share with the world.

For researchers, the most useful blogs are those that give the latest news in a particular field and provide links to other sources. For example, The Health Care Blog (www.thehealthcareblog.com) reports on current developments in the health care system, with links to various websites.

In addition to text, a blog may contain images and videos. If its content is primarily in video format, it is sometimes called a **vlog** (short for video blog).

Increasingly, many blogs and vlogs permit readers to post responses or comments, thereby performing some of the same functions as discussion forums and expert sites.

vlog
frequently updated video log

field research
firsthand gathering of information

Field Research

Field research means gathering information firsthand by observing, surveying, interviewing, or being part of some activity.

Experiences and Investigations

As you gather materials for a speech, don't overlook your own personal experiences, which can bolster your key points. For example, if you escaped serious injury in a car accident because you were wearing a seat belt, you can use the story to supplement national statistics on the value of seat belts.

You can also undertake investigations. David Marcovitz, a medical student at Vanderbilt University, investigated what food stamp recipients can afford to eat. For five straight days, he spent only one dollar for each of his three meals—the amount of money the average food stamp recipient can spend in Nashville, Tennessee. For lunch one day, he had to limit himself to half an apple, a carrot, and a cold-cut sandwich built on day-old bread. (See Figure 6.4.) His investigation left him hungry and helped him "get into the shoes" of future low-income patients and have empathy for them.[6]

Figure 6.4
Medical student David Marcovitz found out what it's like to be a food stamp recipient. See text for details.

Surveys

Student speaker Kathleen Brady had heard a rumor that walk buttons at pedestrian crosswalks don't actually cause traffic lights to change. She tried a button in her neighborhood and it had no effect, but she wondered if the situation was the same throughout the country. So she conducted a survey by sending a query to her Facebook friends in different regions of the United States. She wrote:

> In your neighborhood, please test the button at the nearest crosswalk for pedestrians. How long does it take the traffic light to change if you push the button? And how long does it take if you don't push the button?

Brady received 37 responses from Facebook friends in many different locales. All but four reported that pushing the crosswalk button in their neighborhood had no effect.

In her speech, she said that traffic officials told her that walk buttons were deactivated years ago with the advent of computer-controlled traffic signals. The buttons are kept on the streets because (1) they give pedestrians a psychological sense of control, and (2) it would be too expensive to remove them.[7]

In addition to using Facebook, you can conduct surveys via e-mail, or you can distribute paper questionnaires in person. For more information, see the discussion of surveys in Chapter 4.

Chances are, this walk button doesn't work.

Ethical Issues Quiz

Jennifer conducts research as part of her plan to convince her audience that frequent use of cell phones can cause brain cancer. She interviews three different cancer specialists, all of whom say that her theory is possible but highly unlikely. In her speech, which approach should she take?

A. Quote the specialists as saying the theory is possible, but omit the "highly unlikely" qualifier.
B. Avoid any mention of the interviews and find specialists on the Web whose findings support the speaker's argument.
C. Report that all three specialists found the theory to be possible but highly unlikely.

For the answer, see the last page of this chapter.

Interviews with Experts

Interviews with people who are knowledgeable about your subject can yield valuable facts and insights. Often these individuals can provide up-to-date information not yet available in magazines or books.

Let's look at two avenues for interviews: electronic and face-to-face.

Electronic

Electronic communication via e-mail and social networks (such as Facebook and Google+) can be an excellent tool for interviewing experts. To find knowledgeable people on the Internet, visit websites or social networking sites on your topic and click on links that take you to the authors.

Bryant Wilson, a student at Grand Valley State University in Michigan, is a two-time NCAA national champion in pole vault. If you were preparing a speech on the sport of pole vaulting, you could interview vaulters like Wilson in person, by phone, or electronically (e-mail, Facebook, etc.). Interviews with experts are an effective way to gather up-to-date information.

If you already know the name of an expert, you can conduct a Google search to try to find his or her electronic address. Another option is to go to the website of the organization with which the expert is affiliated. For example, if a scholar teaches at a certain university, you can visit the school's website, click on the directory of faculty members, and then locate the professor's e-mail address.

Personal

For face-to-face interviews, where can you find experts? Start with faculty members at your own college; some of them may have special knowledge on your speech topic. Then look at the larger community beyond the campus. Are any businesses or agencies involved in your subject? If so, e-mail or phone them and ask for the appropriate expert. If you are speaking on snakebites, for example, call the nearest zoo and ask to speak to the chief herpetologist.

If you are lucky, there can sometimes be a wonderful bonus from an interview: you might develop a rewarding professional contact or personal friendship. Consuela Martinez, an accounting major in one of my classes several years ago, interviewed an official at a local bank to get information for a speech. The official was so impressed with Martinez that when she graduated and returned to the bank seeking a job, he hired her.

Don't let fear of rejection deter you. Some students have the idea that the knowledgeable people they want to interview are so important and so busy they will have no time for a "lowly" student. On the contrary, my students have found that everyone they approach loves to be interviewed. If this surprises you, think about yourself for a moment: when a friend asks you for advice, don't you enjoy holding forth as an "expert"? The same is true of knowledgeable people in your community: they are flattered to be interviewed by a student.

Here are some guidelines for planning and conducting interviews.

Preparing for an Interview

Before an interview, there are a few things you should do.

Make an appointment.   Never drop by and expect the person to agree to an interview on the spot. When you call or e-mail to line up the appointment, explain what you are trying to find out and how much time you are requesting.

Conduct research before the interview.   If you learn the basic facts about your subject beforehand, you can ask questions that will be right on target, yielding good information. Doing your homework can also help you avoid asking embarrassing questions. Suppose you are interviewing a neurologist about brain injuries suffered by Iraq War veterans, and you ask, "Where is Iraq?" The expert would resent your wasting her time as she spoon-feeds you elementary material you should already know.

Two other advantages of doing research before an interview: (1) If you are confused by something in your reading, the expert may be able to clarify. (2) If you are unable to find vital information in your library research, the expert can often supply it or tell you where to find it.

Prepare questions.   Decide ahead of time exactly what questions you want to ask, and write them down. Be sure to put the most important ones first—in case you run out of time.

If possible, send the most important questions ahead of time by letter or e-mail to help the interviewee prepare for the interview.

Your Thoughts

If you want a smartphone video of your interview with an expert, what would be the advantages and disadvantages of having a friend make the recording?

Decide how to record the interview.   Since human memory is highly fallible, you need a system for recording the interview. Most interviewers use either or both of the following methods:

1. *Writing down key ideas.* Jot down key ideas only. If you try to write down every word the person is saying, you will be completely absorbed in transcribing sentences instead of making sense out of what is being said.

2. *Using a recorder.* Smartphones (of the kind that are capable of recording audio or video) and camcorders are ideal when you want to get a word-for-word record of the interview. Sometimes you can even use part of the recording in your actual speech, as did one speaker who showed his audience excerpts of a smartphone video of a police officer demonstrating how to take a DNA sample from a suspect.

If you want to use a recorder, seek permission from the interviewee beforehand. Most people will permit recording, but a few will refuse (because it makes them feel uncomfortable or intimidated). You should, of course, respect their wishes. Using a hidden device is unethical.

Conducting an Interview

Here are some tips on how to conduct an interview.

Start in a friendly, relaxed manner.   Before you begin your questions, you need to establish rapport. You can express appreciation ("Thanks for letting me come by to talk to you today") and sincerely make complimentary remarks (about the pictures on the wall, the person's organization, etc.). Try to read the person's body language—does he or she seem relaxed and unrushed, or does he or she seem tense and hurried? Feedback will help you decide whether to plunge quickly into the subject of the interview.

Get biographical information.   Since the person you are interviewing is one of your sources, you need to be able to tell your audience later why he or she is an authority on your subject. If you have not been able to get background information in advance, the early part of the interview is a good time to get it because it continues the building of rapport. You could say, for example, "Where did you get your doctorate?" or "How long have you been working on this problem?"

Ask both prepared and spontaneous questions.   Earlier we noted that you should decide ahead of time exactly what questions you want to ask. There are two types of questions that can be prepared in advance.

closed question
a question requiring only a short, specific response

open-ended question
a question that permits a broad range of responses

Closed questions require only yes or no responses or short, factual answers. Examples: "Do Democrats outnumber Republicans in this state?" "What percentage of registered voters actually voted in the last presidential election?" Closed questions are effective in getting specific data.

Open-ended questions give the interviewee a wide latitude for responding. For example, "How do you feel about negative political ads?" The advantage of such a broad question is that the interviewee can choose the points he or she wishes to emphasize—points about which it may not have occurred to you to ask. The disadvantage is that such questions may allow an interviewee to wander off the subject into irrelevant side issues.

There are two other types of questions, which cannot be prepared in advance but may need to be asked spontaneously during the interview.

Clarifying questions are used when you are confused about what the person means. Ask a question like this: "Could you explain that a little more?" Or: "Correct me if I'm wrong, but I understand you to say that . . ." Don't shy away from asking clarifying questions because you are afraid of showing your ignorance. Remember that you are there to interview the person precisely because you are "ignorant" in his or her area of expertise. So ask about any point that you don't understand. The interviewee will appreciate it and respect you more.

Follow-up questions are designed to encourage the interviewee to elaborate on what he or she has been saying—to continue a story or to add to a comment. Here are some examples: "What happened next?" "Were you upset about what happened?" "Could you give me some examples of what you're talking about?"

Make the interview more like a relaxed chat than an interrogation. Be natural and spontaneous, and follow the flow of conversation. In other words, don't act as if you must plow through your list of questions item by item. Simply check off the questions as they are answered. Toward the end of the interview, ask those questions that still have not been covered. Also, the person may bring up surprising aspects of your topic that you have not thought about; this should inspire you to ask spontaneous follow-up questions.

Ask about other sources and visual aids.   Interviewees may be able to tell you about other people you can interview, and they may point you to promising books and websites that you were unaware of. They may even be willing to lend or give you visual aids that you can use in your speech.

Ask if you've omitted any questions.   When you have gone through all the prepared questions, ask the interviewee if there are any items that you have failed to ask about. You may find that you have inadvertently overlooked some important matters.

End the interview on time.   Respect the amount of time that was granted when you set up your appointment; if you were allotted 20 minutes, stay no more than 20 minutes—unless, of course, the interviewee invites you to stay longer. If you still have questions when the time is up, you can ask for permission to e-mail or phone with a few extra questions. As you leave, be sure to thank the person again.

Following Up

After you leave the interview, you have three important tasks.

Promptly expand your notes.   Immediately after the interview, go through your notes and expand them (by turning words and phrases into complete sentences) while the conversation is fresh in your mind. If you wait two weeks to go over your notes, they will be stale and you may have to puzzle over your scribbling or you may forget what a particular phrase means.

Evaluate your information.   Evaluate your notes to see if you got exactly what you were looking for. If you are confused on any points, or if you find that you need more information on a particular item, telephone or e-mail the interviewee and ask for help. This should not be a source of embarrassment for you—it shows that you care enough about the subject and the interviewee to get the information exactly right.

clarifying question
a question designed to clear up confusion

follow-up question
a question designed to stimulate elaboration

Write a thank-you note.   A brief note thanking the interviewee is a classy finale. If possible, mention some of the interviewee's points that you will probably use in your speech.

Your Thoughts

How do you save key information? What are the pros and cons of your method?

Saving Key Information

You should systematically save the key information that you find. There are many ways to accomplish this, and you may have already developed a system that works well for you. If not, consider this method, which many business and professional speakers use:

1. **Use file folders for subtopics.** Break your topic down into small segments and designate one folder for each subtopic. Don't write the subtopic name on the folder; instead, write it on a stick-on note, which can be placed on the folder tab. Using easily removable labels helps you to be flexible in reorganizing folders and eliminating and adding subtopics.

2. **Use stick-on notes for research findings.** While studying a book or an article, you can write down key information on stick-on notes, which can later be attached to the insides of the appropriate folder. (Instead of stick-on notes, some researchers prefer index cards.)

3. **Insert photocopies and printouts.** Place printed documents in the same folders you are using for stick-on notes.

Printouts and Photocopies

If you make printouts of Internet pages and photocopies of articles and book pages, analyze them carefully to extract the most important details and to plan any necessary follow-ups.

Use a color highlighter to spotlight certain items. On each separate document, be sure to identify author, publication or website, date, and page numbers.

Notes

There are two types of notations you should make: bibliography citations and notes of key ideas.

Bibliography Citations

As you gather materials, jot down the names of books and articles that seem promising. These citations will help you locate materials, and will come in handy later when you put together the bibliography for your speech. In addition, if you need to consult a book or an article again for clarification or amplification of facts, the data on your citation should help you find it quickly. Figure 6.5 shows two sample bibliography citations.

Make a bibliography notation for every book or article that you think might be helpful. You may end up with more sources than you have time to consult, but it is better to have too many sources than not enough. Leave space on each citation for personal comments, which can help you evaluate which sources are most likely to yield good information.

Table 6.1 shows how to format the most common citations, using the style guidelines of either the Modern Language Association (MLA) or the American Psychological Association (APA). Find out if your instructor has a preference.

Library call number	RJ506.H9
Author, title, place of publication, publisher, and date of publication	Kutscher, Martin L. ADHD – Living Without Brakes. London: Jessica Kingsley Publishers, 2008.
Personal comment	[see p. 150 on why people avoid ADHD patients]

Figure 6.5
Sample Bibliography Citations for a Book and a Newspaper Article

Author, title, publication, date, page numbers	Shellenbarger, Sue. "The Creative Energy Behind ADHD." Wall Street Journal 17 April 2008: D1.
Personal comment	[visit suggested link: SmartKidswithLD.org]

Table 6.1   How to Cite Sources

Book with one author	MLA	Kendall, Joshua. *The Man Who Made Lists*. New York: G. P. Putnam's Sons, 2008. Print.
	APA	Kendall, J. (2008). *The man who made lists*. New York: G. P. Putnam's Sons.
Book with two authors	MLA	Tapscott, Don, and Anthony D. Williams. *Wikinomics: How Mass Collaboration Changes Everything*. New York: Penguin Press, 2008. Print.
	APA	Tapscott, D., & Williams, A. D. (2008). *Wikinomics: How mass collaboration changes everything*. New York: Penguin Press.
E-book	MLA	Isaacson, Walter. *Steve Jobs*. New York: Simon & Schuster, 2011. *Kindle Fire*. Web. 25 Nov. 2011.
	APA	Isaacson, W. (2011). *Steve Jobs* [Kindle Fire version]. Retrieved from Amazon.com
Magazine article	MLA	McGrath, Ben. "Nails Never Fails." *The New Yorker* 24 Mar. 2008: 30–35. Print.
	APA	McGrath, B. (2008, March 24). Nails never fails. *The New Yorker*, 30–35.
Scholarly journal article	MLA	Grosse, Scott D., and Kakoli Roy. "Long-Term Economic Effect of Early Childhood Nutrition." *Lancet* 371 (2008): 365–366. Print.
	APA	Grosse, S. D., & Roy, K. (2008). Long-term economic effect of early childhood nutrition. *Lancet, 371*, 365–366.

Table 6.1   How to Cite Sources,   continued

Web document	MLA	Sohn, Emily. "Climate Change Could Drain Great Lakes." *Discovery Channel*. Discovery Communications, Inc., 29 Jan. 2009. Web. 3 Feb. 2009.
	APA	Sohn, E. (2009, January 29). Climate change could drain Great Lakes. *Discovery Channel*. Retrieved February 3, 2009, from http://dsc.discovery.com/news/2009/01/29/great-lakes-warming.html
E-mail	MLA	Ingle, Carole C. "Re: ITT Proposal Details." Message to Mary McClurkin. 1 Apr. 2008. E-mail.
	APA	Ingle, C. C. (personal communication, April 1, 2008).
Interview	MLA	Gillian, William, PharmD. Personal interview. 2 Sept. 2008.
	APA	Gillian, W., PharmD. (personal interview, September 2, 2008).
DVD, film, or video recording	MLA	HBO Miniseries. *John Adams*. Home Box Office, 2008. DVD.
	APA	HBO Miniseries. (2008). *John Adams* [DVD]. New York: Home Box Office.

For situations not covered here, you can visit MLA and APA style guides on the Internet.

Notes of Key Ideas

As you read through books and articles, make notes of key ideas. Put a subject heading at the top of each note, as shown in Figure 6.6. These headings will be valuable when you finish making your notes, because they will help you to group the notes into related batches. Identify each note with the author's name. There is no need to write down full bibliographical information, because those details are already on your bibliography citations.

In making notes, follow these steps:

- Quickly read through the material to see if there is anything worth noting.
- If there is, reread the material, this time very carefully.
- Try to summarize the key points in a few simple sentences. Your task is to interpret, evaluate, and boil down ideas, not convey a text verbatim.
- While striving for brevity, make sure that you put summarized information in a coherent form. If you jot down a phrase like "anorexia—Cheerios," and then wait five days before organizing your notes, you may forget the meaning of that note. Write out a coherent sentence such as this: "One anorexic woman bragged about eating nothing but Cheerios—one Cheerio a day."

Figure 6.6
Sample Note for an Article Summary

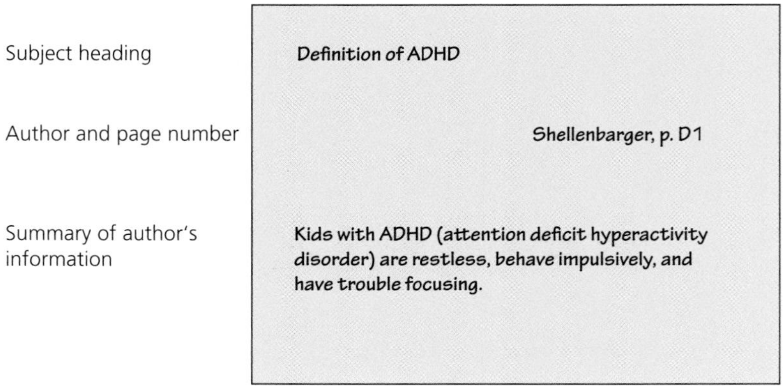

Subject heading	*Definition of ADHD*
Author and page number	*Shellenbarger, p. D1*
Summary of author's information	*Kids with ADHD (attention deficit hyperactivity disorder) are restless, behave impulsively, and have trouble focusing.*

- Occasionally, you will find an arresting phrase or a short, vivid sentence that you want to convey to your listeners in the form of a direct quotation. Be sure to put quotation marks around such passages in your notes. Don't use too many direct quotations in your notes, however, because you may end up copying large blocks of text without proper evaluation and condensation.

- Take more notes than you probably will need. It is better to have too much raw material than not enough.

- You can add personal comments at the end of a note to provide ideas on how to use the note or how to connect it to other notes. You also can express a personal reaction, such as, "Sounds implausible—check other sources." Use square brackets or some other device to distinguish your own comments from the text that you are summarizing.

- Use a separate note for each idea. This will make it easy to sort your notes by subject headings.

In the next chapter, we will turn our attention to how to evaluate the information that you have gathered.

Resources for Review and Skill Building

Summary

In finding materials for your speeches, you can draw from three major resources—libraries, the Internet, and field research. To begin the process, develop a specific purpose statement for your speech, and then devise a detailed research plan. Start early and follow your plan systematically.

As you research, it is important to know the limitations of Web searches. Contrary to popular misconceptions, using traditional library resources such as books is sometimes faster and more efficient than searching on the Web, and websites are not always the best resource for accurate information.

Use keywords when you search for books, articles, or information on the Web. To narrow a search, use multiple keywords or phrases.

Libraries are good resources because they often have material—in books, articles, and reference works—that is unavailable elsewhere. If you need help, talk to a reference librarian, who is a specialist in locating information. If your library doesn't have materials that you need, it might be able to get the items for you from another library through interlibrary loan.

The Internet can be a valuable resource for information and graphics. Although most people know how to use search engines such as Google, many people are unaware that subject directories such as Yahoo Directory are sometimes superior because they organize subjects in logical categories that are easy to scrutinize. Other little-known Internet options are online communities and individuals, who can be accessed via discussion forums, expert sites, blogs, and vlogs.

Field research—gathering information firsthand—can yield up-to-date information. You might rely upon your own observations and experiences, or you can interview knowledgeable people on your campus or in your community. To prepare for an interview, do extensive research on the topic and then draw up a list of questions to be asked. Conduct the interview in a relaxed, conversational manner. You also can conduct interviews electronically via e-mail or social networks like Facebook.

To save information, use stick-on slips, index cards, or a computer. On all notes of key ideas, put a subject heading at the top and have only one idea per note. These notes can later be arranged systematically as you organize and outline your material.

Key Terms

abstract, *94*

blog, *96*

citation, *94*

clarifying question, *101*

closed question, *100*

discussion forum, *95*

expert site, *96*

field research, *97*

follow-up question, *101*

full text, *94*

interlibrary loan, *94*

keyword, *91*

open-ended question, *100*

reference librarian, *92*

search engine, *95*

subject directory, *95*

vlog, *97*

Review Questions

1. What role should your specific purpose statement play in the research stage of preparation?

2. What is interlibrary loan and how can it help you?

3. In what ways are traditional library resources superior to websites?

4. Which Internet search option returns results in order of relevance, with the most relevant at the top?

5. Which Internet search option begins with broad subject areas that are subdivided into smaller categories?

6. Which kinds of blogs are most useful to a researcher?

7. Why should most of your research be done *before* you call someone for an interview?

8. What are the advantages and disadvantages of using a recorder in an interview?

9. What steps should you take after an interview is completed?

10. In your research, why should you take more notes than you probably will need?

Building Critical-Thinking Skills

1. Any person of any age can host a website on any subject and include anything he or she desires. From the viewpoint of a researcher, what are the advantages and disadvantages of this wide-open system?

2. If you use a search engine to find information on the Internet about a breed of dogs and you enter the keyword *bulldogs,* what kind of irrelevant websites are you likely to find in your list of results?

Building Teamwork Skills

1. In a group, choose a topic about which everyone would like to know more. Then brainstorm at least 15 questions that could be asked in an interview with an expert to elicit the most important information about the subject.

2. Working in a group, discuss which approach—Internet or traditional library resources (books, magazines, etc.) —

would be superior for finding answers to these research questions: (a) What are the causes of Arab–Israeli antagonism? (b) How many people were killed in house fires last year? (c) How effective are flu shots? (d) What was the impact of the Black Death on European civilization? (e) What are the title and cost of the latest Sarah Addison Allen novel?

Ethical Issues

Answer for p. 98: C. An ethical speaker will give a report that is fair and accurate, even if giving the specialists' assessment might seem to weaken her argument.

Appendix

Tips for Finding Materials

Table A.1   **Where to Find Materials**

Material Needed	Likely Sources
Background	• In a library, consult encyclopedias such as *The Harvard Guide to Women's Health* and *Encyclopedia of the American Military*. • On the Internet, the volunteer-maintained Wikipedia (en.wikipedia.org) can be a good starting point, but its information must always be double-checked against other sources.
Images & Video	• For photos, visit Google (images.google.com). Click "Advanced Image Search" to specify size and format. • For video clips, visit Bing (www.bing.com/videos), Hulu (www.hulu.com), Video Google (video.google.com), or Blinkx (www.blinkx.com).
Books	• Your library's electronic catalog lists the books it has on your topic. If it doesn't have a book that you want, it can probably borrow it from another library for you. • To view previews of pages in books, go to Google Books (books.google.com).
Articles	• For the full text of articles, the best selection is likely to be found on the electronic databases licensed by your college library. • For scholarly articles, visit Google Scholar (scholar.google.com). • Visit Internet Public Library (www.ipl.org) and select the type of publication that you want (magazine or newspaper).
Recent News	• Your library carries daily newspapers and weekly newsmagazines. • On the Internet, visit news media such as MSNBC (www.msnbc.msn.com) and *The New York Times* (www.nytimes.com). Links for local and regional publications can be found at RefDesk.com (www.refdesk.com/paper.html).
Media Reports	• For radio and TV reports, visit PBS (www.pbs.org) and NPR (www.npr.org). • For feature stories, see *Christian Science Monitor* (www.csmonitor.com), *Discovery News* (news.discovery.com), and *Psychology Today* (www.psychologytoday.com).
Definitions	• For word definitions, pronunciation, synonyms, and history, your campus library has dictionaries such as *Oxford English Dictionary*. • For definitions and synonyms online, visit TheFreeDictionary (www.thefreedictionary.com). To hear the correct pronunciation, click on the loudspeaker icon.
Government Information	• For government documents and handouts, visit the official Web portal of the U.S. government (www.usa.gov). • For laws and statistics, go to LibrarySpot (www.libraryspot.com). Under "Reference Desk," choose "Government." • For activities and laws of the U.S. Congress, visit THOMAS (thomas.loc.gov).
Organizations	• For listings of organizations dedicated to causes and issues, go to Yahoo Directory (dir.yahoo.com). Select "Society & Culture," and then "Issues and Causes." Choose a category, and you will find lists of organizations.
Cultures	• For information about cultures and ethnic groups, your library has reference works such as *Africana* and *The Encyclopedia of the Irish in America*. • On the Internet, visit Yahoo Directory (dir.yahoo.com). Select, in succession, "Society and Culture," "Cultures and Groups," "Cultures," and then a particular group.

Table A.1   Where to Find Materials,   continued

Material Needed	Likely Sources
Experts	• On your campus and in your community, interview local experts.
	• On the Internet, you can conduct e-mail interviews with experts. Some Web pages cite experts and give their e-mail addresses.
Colleges	• To enhance a speech with the experiences and observations of students on other campuses, browse online campus newspapers. For listings, visit Yahoo Directory (dir.yahoo.com) and follow this sequence: News and Media > College and University > Newspapers > By Region > U.S. States.
Almanacs & Maps	• Libraries have almanacs (containing statistical data) and atlases and gazetteers (containing maps and geographical information).
	• On the Internet, visit LibrarySpot (www.libraryspot.com) and choose an appropriate heading under "Reference Desk."
Biographies	• For information on the lives of famous people, your library has biographical dictionaries such as *Distinguished Asian Americans* and *Women in World History*.
	• On the Internet, visit LibrarySpot (www.libraryspot.com) and select "Biographies" for several good links.
Quotations	• Your library should have collections such as *The Beacon Book of Quotations by Women*.
	• For websites that specialize in quotations, visit Yahoo Directory (dir.yahoo.com) and select "Reference" and then "Quotations."

Table A.2   Electronic Search Options

Sample Research Question: "Why do some women stay in relationships in which they are physically abused?"

Option	Example	Discussion
Keywords	women abuse physical	If your research returns too many pages, add keywords. If you get too few pages, reduce the number of keywords.
Plus sign	+women +abuse +physical	A plus sign in front of a word means that all documents retrieved *must* contain that word. NOTE: Google no longer uses a plus sign; it now prefers quotation marks (for example, women "abuse").
Minus sign	+women +abuse +physical −war −prison −work	Minus signs exclude pages that contain these words. In this case, the researcher doesn't want information about violence against women in war, prison, and the workplace.
Phrase	"domestic violence against women"	Using double-quotation marks creates a searchable phrase. Although often highly fruitful, this option will omit relevant pages that don't use the exact phrase.
Wild card	+abus* +women +physical	A wild card (represented by a symbol such as an asterisk) finds words that start the same but end differently. In this example, abus* will yield documents that contain "abuse," "abusive," "abused," and "abuser."
AND, OR	violence AND (women OR wives)	These options permit fine-tuning. Note that parentheses allow the use of synonyms.
NOT	women AND violence NOT workplace NOT office	Excluding the words "workplace" and "office" would be useful if one did not want documents about violence at work.

Note: A few of the options may not be available in some programs.

Table A.3   Internet Search Tools

Search Engines	
Google www.google.com	A fast and comprehensive search engine, Google is the first option that many searchers try. Its "Advanced Search" feature is worth learning and using.
Yahoo or Bing www.yahoo.com www.bing.com	Use one or the other because both companies use the same search engine to find text, images, video, and audio.
Yippy search.yippy.com	Not as well known as Google, Yippy can sometimes find material that Google misses.

Subject Directories	
Yahoo Directory dir.yahoo.com	Select a broad category and "drill down" to narrower and narrower subcategories. For example, to find documents on CPR, select these headings in succession: Health > First Aid > CPR. You also can use the search box to look for directory categories.
About www.about.com	Click on the tab "Browse Categories."
Infomine infomine.ucr.edu	Good sites and reliable annotations are provided by librarians at several colleges.

Collections of Full-Text Articles	
Yahoo News Topics old.news.yahoo.com/topics	For current events, Yahoo News provides well-chosen packets of newspaper and magazine articles.
LibrarySpot www.libraryspot.com	Under Shortcuts, click on "Search full-text publications." Follow the links to the websites of many different publications.

Books and Book Pages	
Project Gutenberg www.gutenberg.org	Over 100,000 books are available online.
Google Book Search www.books.google.com	For some books, you are allowed to see a page or pages where your keywords appear.

Expert Sites	
Yahoo Directory dir.yahoo.com	For links to sites that feature advice and opinions of experts, select "Reference" and then "Ask an Expert."
Ask the Experts www.refdesk.com/expert.html	RefDesk.com gives links to experts in many different fields.

Discussion Forums	
Google Groups groups.google.com	On hundreds of different topics, people throughout the world everyday post messages on discussion forums. To find out what has been written on a given topic, use keywords to search the archives.
Yahoo! Groups groups.yahoo.com	These discussion forums are similar to the groups accessed by Google. You can search the archives of any group.
Facebook Groups and Forums www.facebook.com	If you are a registered member, you can access Facebook groups and forums.
Google+ Groups and Forums https://plus.google.com	If you are a registered member, you can access Google+ groups and forums.

Blogs and Vlogs	
Google Blog Search blogsearch.google.com	Blog Search finds keywords in blogs in the same way that the Google search engine finds keywords in websites.
Technorati technorati.com	This site not only permits searches of blogs—but also lists the most popular blogs and the most discussed news, books, and movies of the day.

Evaluating Information and Avoiding Plagiarism

OUTLINE

Being an Honest Investigator

Finding Trustworthy Information

Applying Critical-Thinking Skills

Analyzing Internet Sites

Avoiding Plagiarism

OBJECTIVES

After studying this chapter, you should be able to:

1. Explain the criteria for trustworthy information.
2. Reject claims based solely on anecdotes, testimonials, and opinions.
3. Recognize the fallibility of polls and experts.
4. Investigate impressive-sounding names of organizations.
5. Know how to scrutinize Internet sites for signs of bias and deception.
6. Avoid plagiarism.
7. Give proper credit to sources.
8. Avoid improper use of copyrighted materials.

DO WE HUMANS use only 10 percent of our brain? Student speaker Lauren Malone thought that the answer was yes as she prepared a speech on how we can make ourselves smarter.

She had read an article, "How to Train Your Brain," on the website of *Psychology Today* magazine. "Conventional wisdom holds that we use 10 percent of our brain cells," the article stated. "Why not put the rest of your head into gear?"[1] She had also seen TV commercials selling videos that promised to make you smarter by showing you how to take advantage of the unused 90 percent of the brain.

As Malone gathered more material, however, she discovered that the *Psychology Today* article and the TV commercials were repeating a widely believed myth that has been

In a U.S. Air Force study of brainwaves, a volunteer wearing an electrode cap verifies that humans use all parts of their brain.

around for over a century. All neuroscientists today say the notion that we use only 10 percent of our brain is nonsense, according to Dr. Barry L. Beyerstein of the Brain Behavior Laboratory at Simon Fraser University in Vancouver, Canada. Brain researchers using imaging technology have verified that we use 100 percent of our brain.[2]

Realizing that her original topic was based on a myth, Malone switched to a different topic.

In this chapter, we will look at how to evaluate information, so that you keep the reliable while eliminating the unreliable. Then we will discuss how to report information in an ethical manner.

Being an Honest Investigator

In the story on the preceding pages, Lauren Malone acted wisely and ethically. Unfortunately, some speakers would have acted differently. They would have clung to the original notion, not bothering to investigate whether it had the backing of reliable experts.

Conscientious, ethical speakers share two characteristics:

1. *They are willing to work hard.* Avoiding intellectual laziness, they dig for all relevant facts and refuse to rely on opinions, hearsay, and first impressions.

2. *They are intellectually honest.* Once they know the facts, they analyze them objectively and draw reasonable conclusions—even if it means admitting that their original idea is erroneous. They are more interested in finding and sharing truth than in clinging to a cherished cause or winning an argument.

In my classes, I have seen many students who embraced an idea but were willing to change their minds as they searched for truth. Here are some cases:

- Despite the popularity of the old saying, "blind as a bat," a student was surprised to learn that bats are not blind. Although they rely on sonar to track down prey, they have eyes and can see.

- One student believed that if a person gets drunk, coffee is an effective way to sober up. While doing research, however, he discovered that only time will sober up an intoxicated person. Coffee is deceptive. Because caffeine in coffee is a stimulant, it can make a person feel—mistakenly—as if he or she can perform dangerous activities like driving.

- Not being gifted in math, a student had always felt comfort in the belief that Albert Einstein failed math in school. But she researched the well-known "fact" and found it to be untrue.

Finding Trustworthy Information

As you examine information you have collected for a speech, your task is to determine which items are valuable and which are worthless. But how do you separate the accurate from the inaccurate? To be considered trustworthy, information should meet the following criteria:

1. *Factual.* Is the information based on facts—not on hearsay, distortions, or oversimplifications?

2. *Reliable.* Does the information come from sources that are honest and authoritative?

3. *Well-supported.* Do the sources provide strong evidence to prove a case?

4. *Current.* Is the information up-to-date?

5. *Verifiable.* Can the information be cross-checked against reliable sources?

6. *Fair.* Does the information come from unbiased and evenhanded sources? Is it presented in a spirit of fair play?

7. *Comprehensive.* Does the information include all relevant data?

To help you use these criteria in evaluating information, let's turn to a valuable set of skills.

Applying Critical-Thinking Skills

To be a savvy consumer of information, you must develop critical-thinking skills—the ability to evaluate evidence with fairness and intellectual rigor. You need *healthy* skepticism, which is not sour negativity that rejects everything, but open-minded inquiry that asks probing questions: "What is the source of this information?" "How do you know this is true?" "Why did this happen?"

Critical thinkers go beyond the obvious. They dive deep for underlying truth.

Here are some critical thinking techniques.

Recognize Dubious Claims

Some claims are compelling because they seem to be based on common sense. But look more closely and you will see major flaws.

Reject claims based solely on anecdotes.   Is the following statement true or false? "Super Bowl Sunday is the biggest day of the year for violence against women."

Although millions of Americans would say true, the statement is false. It is a myth that began in 1993 when rumors spread that the Super Bowl caused an upsurge in domestic violence. News media like CBS News labeled Super Bowl Sunday as a "day of dread," backing up the assertion by citing dozens of **anecdotes** from domestic abuse hotlines, battered women's shelters, and hospital emergency rooms throughout the United States.

The anecdotes proved nothing because, sadly, abuse occurs every single day in every town and city. The key question is: On Super Bowl Sunday, is there more violence than on other days? The answer is no, according to researchers at Indiana University.[3]

The Super Bowl myth illustrates the mistake of relying upon anecdotes alone as proof. This doesn't mean, however, that anecdotes are always bad. You can collect them in your research for possible use in a speech. Rightly used, they can add interest to your ideas (for example, anecdotes about thunderstorms can enrich a speech about protecting oneself from lightning). Just make sure that you never accept or make an assertion that is based exclusively on "anecdotal evidence."

Reject claims based solely on testimonials.   Like anecdotes, **testimonials** can be collected for possible use in a speech, but beware of claims based on nothing but personal recommendations.

Let's imagine a con artist who wants to make money fast by selling a cure for warts. In his basement lab, he mixes skin moisturizer, honey, and lemon juice, and then bottles the stuff with an attractive label, "Guaranteed Miracle Wart Remover." He sets up a website and sells the salve by mail. Before long, he is getting testimonials from people who are delighted and amazed. "This salve really is miraculous," says one enthusiastic user. "All my warts are gone."

Believe it or not, this scenario is not far-fetched, because his concoction really will remove warts. So will peanut butter or shoe polish or anything else lying around your home. In fact, anything under the sun will remove warts—or at least get credit for doing so. Here's why: Scientists have found that if warts are left untreated, 85 percent of them will disappear on their own.[4] This explains the popularity, for centuries, of such unlikely wart removers as pork fat and cow dung. No matter how weird,

To stop violence against women, should we worry about Super Bowl Sunday?

anecdote
a short account of an incident

testimonial
a statement supporting a benefit received

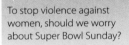

Your Thoughts

In a TV commercial, a tennis star claims that a certain herbal supplement increases one's stamina. Should consumers be skeptical? Defend your answer.

each cure "worked" for a large percentage of patients, and those grateful people gave enthusiastic testimonials to their friends and neighbors.

Testimonials can give us an indication of what might work, but they do not constitute proof. Be suspicious of claims that have no other substantiation.

Reject claims based solely on opinions.   Avoid being swayed by the strongly held **opinions** of your sources. Advocates who believe passionately in their ideas are often highly persuasive and charismatic, winning people over with their sincerity and burning conviction. But unless your sources' opinions are supported by solid evidence, they are worthless. Everyone is entitled to his or her opinion, but opinions are not facts.

opinion
a conclusion or judgment that remains open to dispute but seems true to one's own mind

Find More Than One Source

When my wife and I started lifting weights, we had a disagreement about the correct way to breathe. Based on a weightlifting book I had checked out of the library, I said that one should inhale when lifting; she argued that one should exhale.

To settle the argument, we searched the Internet for articles on the subject. The first article we found agreed with her: exhale. "It's a toss-up," I said. But then we looked at eight more articles. They all said the same thing: exhale.

I lost the argument but avoided an exercise mistake—thanks to our persistence in checking more than one source. (The book I used as a reference turned out to be 10 years old, advocating a method that fitness experts now agree is inferior.)

Never settle for just one source, because it might turn out to be wrong.

Examine Opposing Viewpoints

Imagine that you see an article about a husband and wife who are joint managers of a successful business. They love their company, they love each other, and they are having a wonderful time blending their marriage and their work.

So you decide to give a speech on the bliss that couples can achieve by working together as employees or as owners. In your research, you find dozens of other articles about happy work-together couples. So far, you are avoiding the mistake discussed previously (using just one source), but you are making a different mistake—compiling sources that all agree with one another. You need to investigate whether there are opposing viewpoints. If you do so, you will find articles such as one in *The Wall Street Journal* that is headlined "Despite Success Stories, Working with a Spouse Is Very Risky Business" and features an expert who says that only "about 5% of couples can pull it off."[5]

Finding this criticism doesn't mean you need to scrap your speech. You can still praise couples who are work partners, but—to give the audience a true and balanced picture—you should include information about the negative aspects. You could say, "Although a work partnership can be enjoyable and rewarding, it isn't a good choice for every couple. According to *The Wall Street Journal . . .*" and so on.

Evaluating all sides of an issue is especially important in persuasive speaking. If you are like many speakers, you become so devoted to your arguments that you find it hard to even look at opposing viewpoints. This attitude is unfortunate. You should want to find truth, even if it means you might need to revise your arguments or—in some cases—admit error and change your position.

In addition to ethical fairness, there is a practical value in examining what the opposition says: It enables you to anticipate objections and design your speech to overcome them. You can plan what you will say in the question-and-answer period if a listener challenges you.

Chapter 7   Evaluating Information and Avoiding Plagiarism   115

Be Cautious in Using Polls

Take care in interpreting data from polls and surveys. They have two frequent short-comings.

Some people do not respond honestly.   In surveys, more than 40 percent of Americans say that they go to church every week, but in reality only about 25 percent do so. After national elections, 70 percent of age-eligible Americans tell pollsters that they cast a ballot on election day, but the results show that only 40 to 55 percent actually vote.[6]

Why do some people lie to pollsters about voting?

Why the lies? Perhaps the less-than-candid participants like to think of themselves as the kind of people who go to church regularly and vote in national elections, and they don't want to admit their shortcomings to a pollster.

In another form of lying, some people will offer an opinion on an issue about which they know nothing. The American Jewish Committee once sponsored a survey of American attitudes toward various ethnic groups, and they included a nonexistent group called Wisians to see if some Americans tend to dislike all ethnic groups. A majority of the people who were surveyed responded with "no opinion" concerning Wisians, but 40 percent expressed a view—a dim view. They gave the Wisians a low favorability rating—4.12 on a scale of 0 to 9.0.[7]

Results often depend upon how a question is asked.   Marketing experts have learned that they can write questions for a poll in a way that will achieve the result they desire. For example, if they want to show that the public supports the Social Security system, they can use this question: "Do you favor employees paying money to Social Security out of each paycheck so that they can receive benefits when they retire?" Most people will say yes. But if the marketers want the public to say they disapprove of Social Security, they can ask, "Do you favor the government forcing employees to contribute to the Social Security system, which might be bankrupt by the time they retire?" The majority will say no.[8]

As you can see, polls can be slippery. Before using polling data in a speech, investigate these issues: What survey questions were asked? Were they free of bias? Did the respondents have any reason to answer untruthfully? Did the pollsters have a hidden agenda?

> **Your** Thoughts
>
> Imagine pollsters who want to survey public opinion on whether corporal punishment (spanking) should be permitted in elementary schools. If they wanted to make it appear that most people support spanking, what question could they ask?

Recognize the Fallibility of Experts

Experts can be a good source of information, but don't assume they are infallible. Every year experts are proven wrong in one way or another. For many years, for example, some experts on tornado safety have given this advice: if you are caught by a tornado, seek shelter under a highway overpass. But this advice is bad, and it has cost dozens of lives. The National Weather Service says that hiding under an overpass is one of the *worst* things you can do because the overpass becomes a dangerous wind tunnel.[9] (See Figure 7.1 on the next page.)

Some experts have a Ph.D. or an M.D. and are affiliated with a university or a medical facility, so they must be trustworthy, right? No. Unfortunately, there are unreliable, deceptive people in every field. Consider the M.D.'s who sponsor websites that sell worthless remedies—some of which are harmful. For example, the Food and Drug Administration has found over 800 cases in which a widely advertised herb

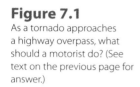

Figure 7.1
As a tornado approaches a highway overpass, what should a motorist do? (See text on the previous page for answer.)

called ephedra (or ma huang) caused adverse reactions, including strokes, seizures, and heart attacks. Three dozen people died after using dietary supplements that contained ephedra.[10]

What should be your attitude toward experts? Examine what they say because they often have valuable insights, but don't suspend your skepticism. Evaluate the comments of both their defenders and their critics.

Beware of Groups with Misleading Names

Research studies from worthy organizations can yield good information, but be careful. Some groups use impressive names to suggest that they are unbiased, neutral, and fair-minded when in reality they have backers with a hidden agenda. Consider these cases:

- Concerned that mercury-contaminated fish can harm babies, U.S. officials urge pregnant women and nursing mothers to limit their consumption of fish. But a group called *The National Healthy Mothers, Healthy Babies Coalition* counsels women to ignore the warning and eat more fish than the government recommends. What's going on here? It turns out that this group, with its noble-sounding name, is financed by the seafood industry.[11]

- *The National Wetlands Coalition* sounds like an environment-protection group, but *The Wall Street Journal* reports that it is financed by oil companies and real-estate developers whose goal is to reduce the amount of wetlands protected by federal law.[12]

Hundreds of groups like these—simply on the strength of their impressive names—arrange to have their spokespersons appear in TV interviews, and their news releases are often reprinted by unsuspecting newspapers and magazines. Their views and findings may have some merit, but these groups undermine their credibility when they use a misleading name and hide their backers.

To find out whether a group has hidden backers and undisclosed goals, use search engines to conduct keyword searches and evaluate what is being said by both friends and foes of the group.

Tips for Your Career

Be Willing to Challenge Reports in the Media

Television, magazines, websites, and Facebook pages frequently report amazing stories of people who come out of nowhere to achieve success overnight. Maybe they have a brilliant idea for a new product or a new business or a new blog. The reports often suggest that if you come up with a dazzling new concept, you, too, can find instant fame and fortune.

Skeptical of the stories, Alexandra Levit, a columnist for the *Wall Street Journal,* investigated and concluded that overnight success is the "number one myth" in the business world. "It's hugely misleading . . . and can be quite damaging for your career and life." In truth, "there are very few genuine cases of overnight success. The majority of successful people have dedicated themselves to a goal and persevered for a long time, experiencing several setbacks before reaching a high level of achievement that is finally noticed and talked about by others."

Why do some media reports foster the notion of overnight success? In most cases, the stories are inadequately researched, failing to give the full background of a successful person's long and bumpy road to achievement.

Some people are reluctant to challenge what is reported in the media because of the attitude "Who am I to question those bright writers and TV producers?" If this is your attitude, you need to trust your common sense when you encounter information that seems "too good to be true."

Analyzing Internet Sites

Because information on the Internet ranges from extremely useful to dangerously inaccurate, how can you sort out the good from the bad? Here are some suggestions.

Don't Be Swayed by Widespread Dissemination

When some people's "facts" are challenged, they defend themselves by saying, "It must be true—it's all over the Internet." But widespread appearance on the Internet is no proof of accuracy. Unfortunately, misinformation can be spread to all parts of the planet in the twinkling of an eye.

Millions of people, for example, have received an e-mail warning about kidney stealing. The message says that medically trained criminals are targeting healthy people—usually partygoers and business travelers—by drugging them and surgically removing a kidney and then selling it for $10,000 in an illegal market. The victims wake up in a bathtub of ice with a note telling them they need to call 911 for medical help. Although the message has been circulating for decades, no reliable news stories of any such attacks have ever been published. The National Kidney Foundation says the warning is totally based on fiction.[13]

Some widespread information on the Internet can be deadly. Many cancer patients, avoiding medical treatment that might save their lives, try (unsuccessfully) to cure themselves by using miracle cures that various Internet sites tout as guaranteed to eliminate cancer.[14]

Watch Out for Web Manipulation

When you watch TV, you can easily spot an infomercial—a show that tries to look like an informational report but really is a scripted commercial. For example, you see five people chatting about how the Fabulous Flat-Tummy Machine chiseled their torsos and made them highly attractive.

The Internet equivalent of infomercials is harder to detect. Let's say you are searching for information on how to take care of an automobile, and you come across a Web page with 12 tips on maintaining a car's exterior. The suggestions look like objective, reliable material. One of the tips ("Use high-quality wax") has a link that, when clicked, takes you to a page that is openly commercial—it sells exterior wax. Unknown to you, the original page and the wax page are operated by the same source—a company that sells wax. The company has done nothing illegal, but it has acted unethically in leaving you with the impression that the tips page was written by impartial researchers who are honestly recommending the best product. You have been manipulated.

To avoid being manipulated, weigh Web advice carefully and verify that the information is corroborated by independent sources that you know you can trust.

Don't Be Dazzled by High-Tech Design

News stories often tell of Internet users—including highly intelligent, college-educated men and women—who are lured into buying worthless merchandise or nonexistent services. How can so many bright people be fooled by con artists? One of the thieves' techniques is to create a website that has beautiful graphic design. The high-tech sparkle gives the website an aura of professionalism, wealth, and respectability.

A study by Stanford University psychologist B. J. Fogg found that people usually judge the reliability of a website by its appearance—not by an investigation into who sponsors it. Even the BBC (British Broadcasting Corporation) was duped by a handsome but fake website into broadcasting an interview with a man who claimed to represent Dow Chemical but really was an opponent who wanted to make Dow look bad.[15]

Look at the advertisement in Figure 7.2 on the next page, which purports to raise funds to fight a terrible childhood disease. Does it look legitimate to you? Some of my students—when shown this ad among a stack of both honest and dishonest Web ads—rate it as probably reliable. In fact, it is a fraud. I created it on my home computer to demonstrate how easy it is for Internet crooks to create impressive-looking graphics. Some students thought that the striking photo makes the ad look authentic. Don't be dazzled by photos. In this case, the picture was a royalty-free image on the Internet that cost only a few dollars. I imported it into my computer and added text. Total time: 10 minutes.

Although my experiment uses an ad that is fictional, it suggests how a con artist in the real world can quickly and inexpensively create a gorgeous website. As you search for information, remember that high-tech design is no indicator of honesty and reliability.

Investigate Sponsors and Authors

Who is behind a website? Are the owners and writers honest and unbiased? To help you evaluate a site, use these strategies.

Look for Author Credentials

Is the author of a Web page qualified to write authoritatively on the subject at hand? Look for some mention of his or her credentials or achievements. If none are listed, look

Childhood Leukemia
Help fight the disease. Click here to donate.

Figure 7.2
If you saw this advertisement on a website, would you assume that it is a legitimate appeal for funds?

for an e-mail link and send a message like this: "I am gathering materials for a speech, and I need to evaluate the credibility of your Web page. Could you please tell me about your qualifications and experience on this subject?"

Get Background Information on Sponsors

Who is funding or sponsoring a website? If the site does not display this information on the opening screen, sometimes you can get details by clicking on a button (such as "About Us"). Or, if there is an e-mail link, you can send a message requesting background information.

Try investigating the website by feeding the keywords of its name into a search engine such as Bing. Evaluate what supporters and opponents of the website are saying about it. You can also find details about any website at www.whois.net.

Examine Internet Domain Names

An Internet address is known as a domain name. The suffix at the end of the name signifies the "top-level domain," indicating whether the address belongs to a business, an educational institution, or one of the other broad categories shown in Table 7.1. These top-level domains can give you clues about a source's objectivity and motivations.

Commercial Web pages (.com) tend to be the least objective of all the domains. The website for Bayer aspirin (bayer.com) is obviously biased in favor of using aspirin for pain relief. You are more likely to find research that is objective and accurate if you visit an educational address (.edu)—for example, the Harvard Medical School (hms.harvard.edu).

Table 7.1
Top-Level Domains

Original	
.com	commercial (business)
.org	nonprofit organization
.net	networks
.gov	government nonmilitary organization
.mil	U.S. military branches
.edu	educational and research institutions
Additional	
.biz	businesses
.info	informational
.name	individuals

But don't jump to the conclusion that all ".com" addresses are untrustworthy. Many businesses offer excellent information. For example, the Mayo Clinic (www.mayoclinic.com) supplies valuable information about first aid. Some ".com" sites are operated by magazines and newspapers that provide reliable reporting. For example, the online *Christian Science Monitor* (www.csmonitor.com) is a business enterprise, but it has a reputation for honest, careful journalism.

Though ".edu" sites tend to be more objective and accurate than ".com" sites, this is not always the case. Some university research projects are funded by corporations that have a vested interest in a certain outcome. A professor at the University of Wisconsin recently announced on an ".edu" site that he had discovered that purple grape juice can help prevent heart attacks. A few days later, Reuters news agency revealed that the professor's study was funded by a juice manufacturer.[16] The professor's findings may prove accurate, but until they are confirmed by researchers who are not paid by juice companies, we should remain skeptical.

We also should be cautious when evaluating other noncommercial domains. For example, nonprofit organizations (.org) are often reliable sources, but they, too, have biases. The United Nations (www.un.org) can provide trustworthy international statistics, but it obviously has a bias in reporting UN peacekeeping operations.

The vast majority of sites on the Web are ".com," and they can create a lot of clutter when you are trying to find purely educational material. To overcome this problem, several search engines such as Google and Bing permit you to click on "Advanced" and then allow you to search by domain. In other words, you can specify that you want returns only from ".edu" sites.

Look for Country of Origin

Gathering information from throughout the world can be rewarding. If you are researching ways to combat soil erosion and you find a Web page on an innovative program in Costa Rica, you have broadened your knowledge base.

Beware, however, of using such material incorrectly. Suppose you come across an appealing website that lists major prescription drugs and the conditions they treat. If you notice that the page originates in another country, you would be wise to use the information carefully, if at all. Other countries have different trade names and different rules on which drugs are permissible. A prescription drug that is available in a developing nation may not be FDA-approved for the United States.

Most websites display an address or give some indication of the place of origin. For those that do not, you will have to look for clues:

1. **Investigate place names that do not sound familiar.** If you are looking for articles on criminal law and you find a website about legal cases in New South Wales, find out just where New South Wales is located. When you discover that it is a state in Australia, explore whether the information applies to your topic.

2. **Be aware of international country abbreviations.** Websites from many countries include two-letter abbreviations. For example, "www.cite-sciences.fr" is the address for a French science site.

You can find a list of international abbreviations at one of these sites:

- www.wap.org/info/techstuff/domains.html
- www.ics.uci.edu/pub/websoft/wwwstat/country-codes.txt

A few abbreviations that are sometimes misinterpeted:

- **ca** stands for Canada, not California (which is **ca.us**).
- **ch** stands for Confederation Helvetica (Switzerland), not China (which is **cn**).
- **co** stands for Colombia, not Colorado (which is **co.us**).
- **de** stands for Deutschland (Germany), not Denmark (which is **dn**).

Check the Date

Most websites will give the date on which the information was created or updated. Make sure you use recent sources.

Look for Verifications

To help find good information and avoid the bad, consult the websites listed in Table 7.2. Here is an example of a student who visited one of the sites:

> Daniel Opel had heard for years that a dog's mouth is cleaner than a human's. As he prepared a speech on animal-human interaction, he visited About.com and discovered that this "fact" is not true. A veterinarian, Dr. Gary Clemons, is quoted as saying, "A dog's mouth contains a lot of bacteria."[17]

Table 7.2   Internet Verifications

Evaluated Sites These directories provide links to websites that are considered ethical and reliable.	• Internet Public Library (www.ipl.org) selects reliable sites. Click on "Resources by Subject." • Infomine (infomine.ucr.edu/) features websites that have been evaluated by librarians at several top U.S. colleges.
Misinformation Alerts These services try to expose scams, quackery, and phony news—not only in websites, but in society at large.	• Snopes.com (http://snopes.com) is a leading source of corrections for myths and misconceptions on the Internet. • About.com (www.about.com) has many articles that can be retrieved for a specific topic (such as work-at-home scams) or a general term like "hoaxes" and "urban legends."

plagiarism

stealing the ideas or words of another and passing them off as one's own

Avoiding Plagiarism

To enrich a speech, you can use materials (such as examples, stories, and statistics) from many different sources. As you do, though, take care to avoid **plagiarism,** which means taking someone else's words, ideas, and images and pretending they are your own.

You will never be in danger of committing plagiarism if you do two things: (1) give credit to your sources and (2) use borrowed materials in an ethical, responsible way—not mindlessly copying or inappropriately paraphrasing, as explained below.[18]

Plagiarism is theft. It is unethical and in some cases illegal (if a copyright is infringed). It is a lazy avoidance of work. It plunders the hard work done by others, and it risks breaking a bond of trust that should exist between speakers and listeners.

Most listeners assume that a speech is the speaker's own creation, and when they find out otherwise, they feel deceived and angry. Here's an example:

In June 2011 Philip Baker resigned as dean of the University of Alberta's medical school after admitting that he had plagiarized large portions of a speech at a graduation banquet. He had appropriated a famous address by surgeon Atul Gawande—an address that had been delivered at Stanford University a year before and widely disseminated on the Internet.

As Baker delivered his speech, some students recognized the plagiarism, got out their smartphones, found the original speech online, and followed along as he gave Gawande's speech word-for-word.

One of the students who had used her smartphone to track the speech, medical school graduate Sarah Fung, told a newspaper later that the incident showed a profound lack of respect for the students and the university.[19] If caught, a plagiarist suffers humiliation and sometimes a penalty, such as failing a class or losing a job, as these speechmakers discovered:

- In recent years, over a dozen ministers—in places such as Providence, Rhode Island; Charlotte, North Carolina; and Clayton, Missouri—have resigned as pastors of churches after admitting that they took sermons from other ministers (often on the Internet) and passed them off as their own.[20]

- The presidents of three colleges (in New York state, Nebraska, and the Bahamas) resigned after being accused of giving speeches in which they copied large amounts of material and failed to give credit to their sources.[21]

Types of Plagiarism

Information Technology Services at Penn State University cites three major types of plagiarism.[22]

Wholesale Copying

If you copy an entire work or a section of a work, making no changes or just a few minor tweaks, you are guilty of blatant theft. But what if you give credit to the original source—does this make the copying acceptable? No, because you have stolen the author's manner of expressing herself, her choice of words, and her way of organizing the material.

Imagine a speaker who finds an article about the Galàpagos Islands on the Smithsonian Institution's website, downloads it, and uses virtually the entire article as her speech. Even if she gives credit by saying, "I derived my information from the Smithsonian Institution," she is still guilty of plagiarism.

Other examples of wholesale copying are (1) buying a speech from a website that sells papers and speeches to students, and (2) persuading a friend to create a speech for you. If you engage in these kinds of cheating, you are doing more than behaving unethically—you are cheating yourself of the learning experience that can be gained by preparing your own speech.

There is one exception to the no-copy rule. If you give credit, you may copy a brief quotation; for example, "In the words of humorist Erma Bombeck, 'Anybody who watches three games of football in a row should be declared brain dead.'"[23] This can enliven your presentation.

Cut and Paste

Samuel (we'll call him) is a lazy researcher. He sits in front of his computer and searches online to get material for his next speech. He snags a piece of information from one website and copies it into a document. Then, directly underneath, he pastes another snippet from another website, and so on, until he has "created" a speech. Samuel has done his work mechanically, with no real thinking, no synthesis of ideas, no creativity, and no originality.

This is an example of "cut and paste." If you copy bits and pieces of material from several sources and string them together to make a speech, you are committing plagiarism. Even though you are stealing fragments instead of a whole document, it is still wrong because you are passing off the work of others as your own.

"Cut and paste" is not only unethical—it is sometimes counterproductive. Listeners don't want a collection of miscellaneous fragments. They would prefer a summary and evaluation of what you have discovered.

Some students defend their "cut and paste" activities by pointing out that they give credit for each piece of information. That's a good thing, but they need to go further—they need to make the information their own.

Unacceptable Paraphrase

Paraphrasing—taking someone's material and restating it in your own words—is a legitimate way to report what others have said (if you give credit). But you must put the material into your own way of speaking. If you just replace a few words—for instance, "freedom" for "liberty"—this still constitutes plagiarism because you retain the overall organization of ideas and the basic sentence structure of the original. See Table 7.3 for an example of a bad paraphrase and a good one.

Giving Credit to Sources

Always tell your audience where you got your information. This is important for three reasons: (1) You protect yourself from accusations of plagiarism. (2) You satisfy listeners' curiosity about the origin of your material. (3) You demonstrate that you are an ethical researcher who wants to give credit where credit is due.

To look at the steps leading up to your speech, let's discuss a hypothetical scenario:

 Ethical Issues Quiz

Thad, an executive at an advertising agency, is preparing a presentation on how a client can sell more vacuum cleaners. While gathering ideas, he interviews a colleague named Bob, who suggests a brilliant strategy for boosting sales. Thad likes the strategy so much that he uses it in his presentation, leaving the impression that it was his own idea. He makes no mention of Bob. Which of the following statements is correct?

A. Thad should have given full credit to his colleague Bob in the presentation.

B. There was no need for Thad to reveal his source because the audience was interested in the idea itself, not the identity of the creator.

C. Thad had no obligation to reveal whose idea it was, since the idea came from a colleague working for the same company, and all ideas should be shared among colleagues.

For the answer, see the last page of this chapter.

Table 7.3   **How to Paraphrase without Plagiarizing**

ORIGINAL:

"Dogs catch our yawns. Just as happens between humans, dog subjects who saw someone yawning themselves began uncontrollably yawning in the next few minutes. Chimpanzees are the only other species we know of for whom yawning is contagious."

— Alexandra Horowitz, *Inside of a Dog: What Dogs See, Smell and Know* (New York: Scribner, 2010), p. 280.

UNACCEPTABLE PARAPHRASE:	**COMMENTS:**
"Dogs imitate our yawns. In the same way that humans yawn, dogs who see someone yawning will yawn uncontrollably very soon. Chimps are the only other type of animals that we know about who yawn contagiously."	This is too close to the original. The speaker fails to speak in his own language and style, and he fails to give credit to Alexandra Horowitz.
ACCEPTABLE PARAPHRASE:	**COMMENTS:**
"Alexandra Horowitz, in her book *Inside of a Dog*, says that humans, dogs, and chimpanzees are the only species that yawn after seeing someone else yawn. For example, if a dog sees you yawn, it will yawn within the next few minutes."	The speaker restates – in his own way of speaking — Horowitz's ideas, and he is careful to give her credit.

You are preparing a speech on how to invest money on the stock market. In your outline, you list all your sources. Here is an example of one entry:

Becket, Michael. *How the Stock Market Works*. London: Kogan Page, 2012. Print.

In the speech itself, you don't need to state the complete citation—in the format printed above. To do so would clutter your remarks with too many distracting details. Simply say, "In a book titled *How the Stock Market Works*, Michael Becket, the small-business editor of London's *Daily Telegraph*, says . . ."

Some students wonder: If you don't need to say the complete citation in the speech, why bother putting it in the outline? Three reasons: (1) Your instructor will want to see it. (2) You need it for yourself if you have to go back to your sources for further investigation. (3) At the end of your speech, some listeners may ask for the complete data so that they can pursue your topic further.

There are five ways to share your sources with an audience. For classroom speeches, consult your instructor for guidance on which method he or she prefers. For career and community speeches, you can use any of these techniques, or even combine them:

oral footnote

a spoken citation of the source of one's material

1. **Give credit as you go through your speech.** When citing a source, use an **oral footnote** (which is the equivalent of a footnote in a written document); for example, "According to the *CBS Evening News* of March 15th of this year . . ." and "In the words of Thomas Jefferson . . ." (For more examples, see Table 7.4.)

    Oral footnotes do more than just give credit: they also bolster your credibility. You are saying, in effect, "I didn't pull this information out of thin air; I derived it from someone who is an authority on the subject."

    When you are quoting verbatim, use "oral" quotation marks, such as "To quote Albert Einstein . . ." or "In the words of Jane Austen . . ." This is smoother than saying "Quote" at the beginning of a statement and "Unquote" at the end. Use a slight pause to signal that you have finished quoting.

Table 7.4
Sample Oral Footnotes

Interview	"Two weeks ago, when I interviewed Dr. Jennifer Wang, head of the pediatrics unit at Memorial Hospital, she emphasized that all children should be vaccinated for measles."
Website	"According to the Honeymoon section of About.com, the most popular honeymoon travel destination—by far—is Hawaii."
News media	"On NBC's *Today Show* in February of this year, career counselor Zack Manchester discussed two keys to a successful job interview: wear the right outfit and maintain good eye contact."
Book	"In his recent book, *Last of the Dinosaurs,* dinosaur expert Thom Holmes says that evidence has been mounting that the mass extinction of most species of dinosaurs was caused by the collision of a large asteroid with the Earth."

An effective technique is to hold up your note with the quotation so that listeners can see that you are reading word-for-word.

2. **Give global credit in the introduction.** After they grab their listeners' attention in the opening of a speech, some speakers like to provide an overview of all the resources they will be using in the body of the speech. For example, "All of my information in this speech comes from a book *Wind Power* by energy researcher Paul Gipe, an article in *National Geographic* published in April of this year, and a recent e-mail interview with Cristina Archer of Stanford University, one of the world's top experts in alternative energy."

3. **Display a slide or a poster listing your sources.** If you use this technique, you should not show complete citations (as you would in a handout, discussed below). Rather, you should have condensed versions of the bibliography information (to reduce text). Using the example we discussed earlier, you could condense book information like this:

> **How the Stock Market Works**
> by Michael Becket

Aneesh Chopra, Chief Technology Officer of the U.S. Government, explains a plan to put health records online (with the patient's permission), so that if a citizen is hurt in an accident, his or her medical history will be available in any emergency room in the nation. In his speeches and writings, Chopra is careful to give credit to his sources.

Tips for Your Career

Be Specific When Citing Internet Sources

"I got my information from the Internet."

That is a common statement by many speakers in business and professional settings. It is worthless—like saying, "I got my information from people."

Instead, when you speak to colleagues, say something like this "My information on TV's depiction of women comes from an article by Sue Naegle, president of the cable TV network HBO. The article was posted on HBO's website."

Another big mistake occurs when speechmakers cite a search engine (usually Google) as their source. Google is *not* a source—it's a delivery system. Giving credit to Google is like citing the U.S. Postal Service as the source of medical information mailed to you by the American Medical Association. Don't even mention Google. Instead say, "My information about cancer medications comes from Dr. Nancy H. Nielson, who provided a detailed report on the website of the American Medical Association."

---

4. **Provide listeners with a handout listing sources.** A complete list of your sources with full bibliography details can help listeners evaluate the credibility of your message. Your handout should be distributed at the end of a speech so that it does not distract the audience from focusing on your remarks.

5. **Display all books, articles, and materials.** During a speech on precious gems, one student showed photos and then invited classmates to visit a table in the back of the room at the end of class. On it were all her source materials—books and articles on gems, along with actual rubies, pearls, opals, and other gemstones that could be held and examined.

Using Copyrighted Material

Copyright is the ownership of intellectual property, such as songs, books, articles, photos, videos, websites, and computer software. A copyright can be held by the author or by the sponsoring company, and it is protected by U.S. and international laws. Except for some special situations (discussed below), it is illegal to use copyrighted material unless you get permission (and in some cases pay a fee).

copyright infringement
unauthorized use of legally protected material

Anyone who uses copyrighted material improperly can be charged with **copyright infringement.** If convicted, a person can be forced to pay a fine, and in some cases serve prison time.[24]

A copyright notice is usually attached to a product, but it is not required. In other words, an item such as a photo on the Internet is owned by the copyright holder *even if there is no copyright notice attached.*

How can you use copyrighted material and stay within the limits of law? The answer depends on the setting for your speech or presentation, as discussed below.

Classroom Speeches.   Good news for students: You don't need to worry about copyright in a classroom speech because you are engaged in a nonprofit, educational activity, which is exempt from legal restrictions. This means you can use anything—photo, video, music, poem, and so on—without worrying about whether you are violating the law.

Career and Community Speeches.   Outside of the classroom, different rules apply. Before you can use copyrighted materials in a presentation or in handouts, you must get permission to do so (and in some cases pay a fee)—unless an item falls under one of these three exceptions: public domain, fair use, and royalty-free. Let's look at each category.

Public Domain

Anything published or created before 1923 is no longer protected by copyright and is said to be "in the **public domain,**" which means you are free to use it however you please.[25] If, for example, you find a drawing of Niagara Falls in a 1920 encyclopedia, you can use it in a speech or publication without violating the law.

Any publication of the *federal* (not state) government is not copyrighted and can be used freely. Thus, a U.S. Department of Agriculture booklet on avoiding food poisoning can be reproduced and distributed without your needing to get permission or pay a fee.

Note of caution: In the realm of copyright, the U.S. Postal Service is not considered a part of the federal government; it is an incorporated business and therefore can copyright its postage stamp designs. You cannot copy stamp designs without getting permission.

public domain
what is owned by the community at large; unprotected by patent or copyright

Fair Use

A loophole in copyright laws—called the **fair use** doctrine—was created to enable scholars, writers, and public speakers to disseminate information without having to spend enormous amounts of time getting permission for every item used. The fair use doctrine allows you to use small amounts of material if you meet *all three* of the following tests.[26]

1. You use only a small and relatively insignificant portion of a copyrighted work.

2. Your purpose is primarily educational, rather than commercial.

3. You do not cause economic harm to the copyrighted work.

Two notes of caution: (1) Fair use does not remove the need to cite your sources. You still should give credit. (2) A common mistake is to think that if you take a copyrighted work and make some changes here and there, it is no longer protected by copyright law and becomes your property. That is wrong. If you take the transcript of a speech, change some words, rewrite some sentences, and modify the visual aids, the speech is still not yours. If you find a magazine photo of a movie star, scan it into your computer, and change the color of her hair and dress, the photo still does not belong to you. To think that manipulating a work makes it your property, says Steven Blaize, president of a multimedia production company, "is like saying as long as you paint flames on a stolen car before you display it in your collection, it's yours."[27]

fair use
allowable and reasonable exceptions to copyright rules

Royalty-Free Material

To avoid fees and legal uncertainties, many speakers, writers, and editors buy artwork (such as drawings and photos) and multimedia works (such as music, sound effects, and videos) that are **royalty-free**—that is, free of restrictions and fees. When you pay for a royalty-free product, you are buying the right to use it in a publication, speech, or video production without having to ask permission or pay anything extra.

royalty-free
devoid of restrictions or fees

Resources for Review and Skill Building

Summary

When you evaluate material, look for high-quality information that is factual, reliable, well-supported, current, verifiable, fair, and comprehensive.

Apply healthy skepticism, probing for erroneous or unreliable data. Reject claims that are based solely on anecdotes, testimonials, or opinions. Don't use just one source, because it might turn out to be wrong. Examine opposing viewpoints in an effort to find truth and to anticipate possible listener objections.

Be cautious in using polls, because some people don't respond honestly and results often depend upon how a question is asked.

Recognize the fallibility of experts. Don't assume that a Ph.D. or an M.D. is always trustworthy. Don't assume that affiliation with a prestigious university is assurance of credibility.

Watch out for groups with names that can mislead the public into thinking they are unbiased. Find out who is financially backing the group.

In analyzing Internet sites, watch out for subtle manipulation on Web pages. Examine domain names for clues on a source's objectivity and motivation. See if the material comes from a foreign country. If a website has a beautiful, sophisticated design, don't assume that it is reliable. Investigate its sponsors and authors to see if they are legitimate authorities on their subject matter.

In borrowing information for a speech, be careful to avoid plagiarism—taking someone else's words, images, or other content and using them as your own creation. Plagiarism is unethical, whether it involves wholesale copying of an entire work, patching together bits and pieces from several different sources, or inappropriate paraphrasing. You can avoid plagiarism if you are careful to summarize information, and if you give credit to your sources.

A related ethical and legal issue is copyright infringement. Don't use copyrighted material unless you get permission from the copyright holder or unless the material falls into one of three categories: public domain, fair use, and royalty-free.

Key Terms

anecdote, *113*

copyright infringement, *126*

fair use, *127*

opinion, *114*

oral footnote, *124*

plagiarism, *122*

public domain, *127*

royalty-free, *127*

testimonial, *113*

Review Questions

1. What are the characteristics of high-quality information?
2. What is anecdotal evidence? Why does it fail to prove an assertion?
3. How do opinions differ from facts?
4. Why should more than one source be consulted?
5. Why are polls often unreliable?
6. What are the domain names for commercial, nonprofit, and educational websites?
7. What is the meaning of the term *cut and paste plagiarism*?
8. What is an *inappropriate paraphrase*?
9. What is an *oral footnote*?
10. Define *fair use*.

Building Critical-Thinking Skills

1. Imagine a website called www.superamazingskin.com that touts a miracle drug that banishes acne. The drug is praised on the website by a man identified as Roger Taschereau, M.D. You are trying to decide whether to recommend the product in a speech you are preparing. What is your evaluation of the website up to this point? What additional steps should you take before recommending the drug?

2. Project Gutenberg (promo.net/pg) is a website with links to hundreds of books, poems, and plays that are in the public domain. If you want to copy a poem or a book chapter for distribution to listeners at a business presentation, must you get permission? Explain your answer.

Building Teamwork Skills

1. Can a person find relief from pain by attaching tiny magnets to an injured area? In a group, discuss how to find reliable information on "biomagnetic therapy," which has grown in popularity in recent years. Rank the sources below from (probably) most reliable to (probably) least reliable. Discuss why some of these sources are likely to be more reliable than others.

    a. A website devoted to debunking the claims of alternative medicine.
    b. A website that sells magnets and is operated by a self-styled "alternative healer," who claims that a magnetic mask placed on one's face can cure head colds.
    c. A brochure by a corporation that sells over $1.5 billion worth of magnetic materials each year.
    d. A recently published scholarly book, with reference notes, by a biology professor at the University of Washington.
    e. An endorsement of magnets by a professional baseball pitcher, who places them on his pitching arm.
    f. An e-mail interview this week with Edward McFarland, M.D., head of sports medicine at Johns Hopkins University, who has studied biomagnetics.

2. Working in a group, compile a list of current information sources used by you and other group members (for example, ABC News, *USA Today, The Tonight Show with Jay Leno*, e-mail from friends). Next, place these sources into three categories: very reliable, fairly reliable, and not reliable. Justify your evaluation.

Ethical Issues

Answer for p. 122: B. One offense is as serious as the other, as evidenced by the number of public speakers who lose their jobs for plagiarizing.

Answer for p. 123: A. An ethical researcher should always give credit where it is due. If you're not sure, ask yourself, "How would I feel if I came up with a great idea and someone else took credit for it?"

Supporting Your Ideas

OBJECTIVES

After studying this chapter, you should be able to:

1. Explain why support materials are needed in a speech.
2. Describe nine types of support materials: definitions, vivid images, examples, narratives, comparison, contrast, analogies, testimony, and statistics.
3. Discuss the use and abuse of statistics in speeches.

CAN FOOTBALL FANS literally cause the earth to shake? Yes, asserted student speaker Anthony Carino in an informative speech in his public speaking class.

At first his instructor was disbelieving—until Carino gave more details. On January 8, 2011, the Seattle Seahawks clinched a playoff victory over the New Orleans Saints when Marshawn Lynch ran 67 yards for a touchdown. This caused a crowd of 66,336 in Qwest Field to cheer, jump, and stomp so vigorously that the stands shook and the earth trembled.

John Vidale, a geophysicist at the University of Washington's Pacific Northwest Seismic Network, said that vibrations—the equivalent of a small earthquake (magnitude 1 or 2)—were detected by a nearby seismometer at 4:43 p.m., the precise moment when Lynch reached the end zone for his touchdown. For the next 30 seconds, the seismometer recorded "moderate shaking," said Vidale. No damages were reported.[1]

Carino's instructor abandoned his disbelief because Carino backed up his assertion with **support materials,** including testimony from a reputable expert (the geophysicist), statistics, and diagrams.

When you are a speaker, you can make assertions, but you can't expect your audience to believe you unless you back up your statements with solid, credible support. In this chapter we will look at nine popular types of support material.

Marshawn Lynch of the Seattle Seahawks escaped a tackle and ran 67 yards for a touchdown that became famous throughout the world.

support material
elements that illustrate or substantiate a point

Reasons for Using Support Materials

Support materials enable you to move from general and abstract concepts, which are often hard for audiences to understand and remember, to specific and concrete details, which are more easily grasped. Support materials add spice and flavor to a speech, but they are more than just seasonings. They are basic nourishment that is essential to the success of a speech. Let's look at five reasons why support materials are so important.

To Develop and Illustrate Ideas

In a speech on sharks, student speaker Austin Fitzgerald pointed out that, unlike most creatures of the sea, sharks behave unpredictably. To develop and illustrate his point, he said:

> In his book on sharks, Jacques-Yves Cousteau, the famous oceanographer, says that he has seen sharks flee from an almost naked, completely unarmed diver, but soon afterward hurl themselves against a steel diving cage and bite furiously at the bars. Sometimes a diver can scare off a shark by waving his or her flippers at it, while at other times sharks are so determined to attack that they are not deterred by the sight of five divers with spears. The terrifying thing, Cousteau says, is that sharks never give clues as to what kind of behavior they will exhibit.

Without these examples, Fitzgerald's contention that sharks behave unpredictably would have been weak. With the examples, the listeners got a clear picture of sharks' volatile nature. Notice, too, that Fitzgerald enhanced the credibility of his remarks by attributing his information to a well-known authority.

To Clarify Ideas

Helping the listener make sense out of your ideas is one of the main reasons for using support material. Student speaker Maria Burton gave a speech on pit-and-fissure sealants, which are used to cover the rough surfaces of teeth and prevent cavities.

"Sealants," Burton explained, "are thin, clear plastic coatings that are painted on the teeth, much like nail polish on fingernails."

With this analogy, the audience had a clear picture of what sealants are.

To Make a Speech More Interesting

In a speech on how explorers from Earth would experience life on Mars, student speaker Diane Weber said,

> Most of the time Mars is much colder than the coldest regions of earth, with summer temperatures dipping down as low as 126 degrees below zero and winter temperatures twice that cold. Sometimes, however, at the equator of Mars, the temperature does warm up to an earthly level of comfort. For a few minutes, the temperature can climb to a high of 68 degrees—sort of like a pleasant October afternoon in New England.

Instead of merely reciting statistics, which would have been boring, Weber made her subject interesting by comparing and contrasting the climate of the two planets, using images (such as the October afternoon in New England) that her listeners could appreciate.

To Help Listeners Remember Key Ideas

Jeffrey Scott, a high school English teacher, says that his students are more likely to remember the meaning of a word in a vocabulary lesson if they are told the story of the word's origin. For example, he tells his students that we get the word *tantalize* from a king called Tantalus in Greek mythology: "As punishment for betraying Zeus, Tantalus was sentenced to hang from the branch of a fruit tree that spread out over a pool of water. Whenever he got hungry and reached for fruit, the wind would blow it out of his reach. Whenever he got thirsty and leaned over to drink from the pool, the water would recede." This story, Scott says, helps his students to remember that when we tantalize people, we torment them by showing them something that is desirable but unattainable.

To Help Prove a Point

If you want to prove an assertion, you must have evidence. If, for example, you wanted to prove that more counterfeiters are being caught today than ever before, you could quote a Secret Service official who states that the number of counterfeiting convictions this year is 10 times that of any previous year. Such a statistic from a reliable source is solid proof of your statement.

Note of caution: You can't assume that any kind of support materials will prove any argument you make. To convince your audience, you must have credible information that is beyond doubt. Suppose a speaker is trying to prove that echinacea, an herbal remedy, is a cure for the common cold, and she gives stories of three friends who take echinacea daily and never get colds. These stories prove nothing. You probably could find three people who caught colds despite taking echinacea. To prove her point, the speaker would need indisputable research by reputable medical authorities, based upon long-term studies of thousands of people.

Types of Support Materials

In this chapter, we will look at *verbal* support materials, reserving *visual* supports for the next chapter. The cardinal rule in using verbal supports is that they must be relevant; they must develop, explain, illustrate, or reinforce your message. They should not be thrown in just to enliven a speech.

Let's look at nine popular types of verbal supports.

Definition

One of the biggest obstacles to successful communication is the assumption that your listeners define words and phrases the same way you do. If you are speaking on gun control, it is not enough to say, "I'm in favor of gun control." Exactly what does "gun control" mean? To some members of your audience, it may mean that citizens must surrender all their firearms. To some, it may mean that citizens must give up only their handguns. To others, it may mean that citizens can keep their guns if they register them with the authorities. If you say that you are in favor of gun control without giving your **definition** of the term, some listeners may misunderstand your position and angrily reject everything that you say on the subject. So define your terms at the outset; for example: "When I talk about gun control, I'm not talking about confiscation of all guns; I'm talking about citizens registering the serial numbers of their guns with the authorities." Now you and your audience have a common basis for an evaluation of your views.

Avoid using formal dictionary definitions. Instead, use informal definitions that can be easily understood by the audience. Here is an instructive case: *chutzpah,* a slang word that the English language has borrowed from Yiddish, is defined by the *Random House College Dictionary* as "unmitigated effrontery or impudence." I once heard a speaker give a humorous, informal definition of the word: "Chutzpah is the kind of audacity and gall that a youngster would show if he killed both of his parents and then demanded that the court be lenient to him because he was an orphan." This informal

If you speak of "sustainable agriculture," you need to define what you mean.

definition
a statement of the meaning of a word or phrase

definition drives home the point that chutzpah is more than ordinary gall; it is the *ultimate* form of gall. Such a definition does more than help the listeners understand the term—it also helps them remember it.

Vivid Image

Student speaker Rebecca Hale describes two earthly extremes:

> The deepest point in the ocean is 6.9 miles down, and if you went there, you would be crushed by the immense pressure of the water. The highest point on earth—Mount Everest—is 5.4 miles above sea level, and if you went there, you could stay only a few minutes, and you would need oxygen and heavy protection against bitter cold and raging wind. These two extremes—you would think—would be separated by a huge distance, but you would be wrong. From the lowest point on earth to the highest is just a little over a dozen miles.[2]

vivid image
a description that evokes a lifelike picture within the mind of the listener

This passage is an example of **vivid images**—word pictures that are created by describing objects, animals, people, places, or situations. To make your description come alive in the minds of your listeners, you must use *specific details*. Instead of merely saying, "The dessert tasted good," say, "The crunchy pretzels were coated with a soft, white yogurt icing, giving a delicious blend of sweetness and salt in each bite."

Example

example
an instance that serves to illustrate a point

An **example** is an instance or a fact that illustrates a statement or backs up a generalization. Student speaker Sharon King told her classmates that it is risky to rely too heavily upon spell-checkers, and she gave examples of mistakes that appeared in the yearbook at Middletown Area High School in Pennsylvania. Its publisher's spell-checker changed many students' names. For example, Max Zupanovic was listed as "Max Supernova," Kathy Carbaugh as "Kathy Airbag," and Alessandra Ippolito as "Alexandria Impolite."[3]

While these examples are short, you may want to give longer examples in some cases. In a speech on animal cleverness, student speaker Mark Dayton said:

> Animals can develop ingenious strategies. For example, at the Institute for Marine Mammals Studies in Mississippi, trainers had taught dolphins to clean their pool by giving a reward—a fish—every time a dolphin brought up trash. One female dolphin figured out a clever way to maximize her rewards. She would hide trash under a rock at the bottom of the pool and then bring up one small piece of trash at a time.[4]

How many examples do you need to develop a point? In some cases, one example is sufficient; other situations might require a series of examples. Ask yourself, "If I were those people sitting out there, how many examples would I need in order to understand, remember, or be convinced?"

Narrative

It's called "the Miracle of Paris." On November 1, 2010, an 18-month-old boy was playing on the balcony of an apartment building in Paris (see Figure 8.1) when he slipped through the railing and fell seven stories. He bounced off a café awning and into the arms of a physician, who was passing by and happened to see the fall and positioned himself to catch the boy.

The child was unharmed, thanks to the physician's alertness and another stroke of luck: The incident happened on a holiday, and the awning that cushioned the boy's fall normally would have been folded up. But the night before, it had jammed, so the café owner left it standing.

Figure 8.1
A toddler fell from the seventh floor of this apartment building in Paris.

Where were the boy's parents? They had gone shopping, leaving the toddler and his 4-year-old sister alone in the apartment for several hours.[5]

This story was related by a student in a speech on why small children should never be left unattended. The speaker was using one of the most powerful of all support materials—a **narrative,** which is a story that explains or illustrates a message. Narratives are audience favorites, lingering in the mind long after a speech has ended.

People *love* stories, and even a sleepy or distracted member of the audience finds it hard to resist listening. As with all support materials, narratives must be relevant to your message. Never tell a story, no matter how spellbinding, if it fails to develop, explain, illustrate, or reinforce your key ideas.

While the preceding story is factual, there are occasions when you may want to use a narrative that is **hypothetical,** that is, about an imaginary situation. Katrina Benjamin, a private investigator, wanted to explain how computers have invaded the average person's privacy:

> A company is trying to decide whether to hire you, and they ask me to investigate you. All I have is your name and address. I sit down in front of my computer and within five hours, I know a great deal about you: I know what jobs you have held and how much you got paid. I know the names of your parents, siblings, spouse, and children. I know what kind of car you drive and how much you paid for it.

narrative
a story that illustrates a point

hypothetical narrative
imaginary story related to help listeners visualize a potential situation

I know if you have ever been arrested or charged with a crime—even if it's just a ticket for speeding. I know the amount of the monthly payment on your home mortgage. I know what kinds of medical problems you have, and I know the names of all the prescribed medications you have taken in the past and are taking right now.[6]

This hypothetical scenario dramatically demonstrates the easy availability of personal information.

Comparison and Contrast

comparison

showing how two or more items are alike

Sometimes the best way to explain a thing or a concept is to make a **comparison**—that is, show how it resembles something else. In a lecture on the development of the English language, a speaker noted the following similarities:

The Frisian language, spoken by 300,000 Frisians in the marshy headlands of northern Holland, is more closely related to English than any other language. Our *glass of milk* is their *glass milk*, our *butter* is their *butter*, our *dream* is their *dream*, our *boat* is their *boat*, our *green* is their *grien*, our *house* is their *hus*, our *cow* is their *ko*, our *goose* is their *goes*, our *sunshine* is their *sinneskine . . .*

By giving many points of comparison, the speaker strongly illustrated how similar the two languages are.

contrast

showing how two or more items are different

While a comparison shows how things are similar, a **contrast** shows how they are different. To show a big shift in attitudes toward wind, one speaker said:

For hundreds of years, ranchers and farmers on the Great Plains of the United States cursed the wind. Fierce windstorms would knock down trees, topple houses, and kill livestock. Frigid, icy winds would make it too cold to work outdoors. Terrible dust storms would bring huge clouds of sand and dust, blotting out the sun. Today, by contrast, many ranchers and farmers view wind as a friend because they can make thousands of dollars a year just by letting energy companies use their land for giant windmills. Now the whipping wind is the sweet sound of money.[7]

Sometimes it is helpful to use both comparison and contrast. For example, comparing and contrasting movie DVDs and movie downloads can help listeners understand more fully the features of each.

analogy

resemblance in some respects between things that are otherwise dissimilar

Analogy

A special type of comparison is the **analogy,** which explains a concept or an object by likening it to something that is—at first glance—quite different. For example, security expert William Cheswick explained how easily criminals can breach security walls at Internet sites. "The Internet is like a vault with a screen door on the back. I don't need jackhammers and atom bombs to get in when I can walk in through the door."[8]

How do analogies differ from ordinary comparisons? While ordinary comparisons show similarities between two things of the same category (two cars), analogies show similarities between two things of different categories (punctuation marks work like road signs and traffic signals). Student speaker Cheryl Williams used an analogy to show the futility of worry:

Worrying is like sitting in a rocking chair and rocking furiously. There is a great deal of movement and agitation, but you don't go anywhere.

Your Thoughts

In a speech on weird stunts, a speaker paraphrased an analogy created by *New York Times* columnist Janet Maslin: "Texting with your toes is like climbing Mt. Everest in house slippers—impressive but not necessary." Why are these words considered an analogy instead of a comparison?

Figure 8.2
To calm fears, one speaker made a helpful analogy between planes and boats. (See text for details.)

An analogy tries to show that what is true in one case is true in another. Student speaker Lisa Rathbone used this analogy:

> Cramming for a test the night before is like baking a cake faster by raising the oven temperature from 350 to 550 degrees. It just won't work.

When an airliner travels through a turbulent storm, some inexperienced passengers fear that the plane might crash. One speaker tried to help his listeners avoid these fears by showing a photo (Figure 8.2) and making this analogy: "In a storm, a plane might shudder and shake and make sudden dips, but this doesn't mean it's about to crash. A plane flies through an ocean of air, and bumpiness in a storm is normal. It's like a boat pushing through choppy waters. The boat bobs up and down, but the turbulence doesn't mean it will sink."

Testimony

Suppose that one of your classmates gives a speech on the jury system in the United States, and she tells you that the method of selecting and using jurors in most communities is inefficient, overly expensive, and demoralizing to the jurors. Would you believe her? Probably not, if all she gave was her personal opinion—after all, she is not a lawyer or a judge. But what if she quoted the Chief Justice of the U.S. Supreme Court saying the exact same thing? Now would you believe her? You probably would, because the Chief Justice is one of the nation's experts on what happens in our courts.

When you use what knowledgeable people have to say on your subject, you are using **testimony** to back up your assertions. The main advantage of using testimony is that it gives you instant credibility. Quoting an expert is a way of saying, "I'm not the only one who has this idea; it has the backing of a leading authority on the subject."

How to Use Testimony

There are three ways of using testimony:

1. **Quote verbatim.** Sometimes it is effective to quote a source word for word. For example, Lorraine Vallejo made the following point in a speech on dreams:

   > For all of us, dreams are weird, chaotic, and crazy. An expert on dreams, Dr. William Dement, says: "Dreaming permits each and every one of us to be quietly and safely insane every night of our lives."

testimony
statement by a knowledgeable person, used by a speaker to explain or bolster a point

quote verbatim
to cite the exact words used by a source

Tips for Your Career

Give Listeners Bonus Material

Imagine that you have been assigned to try to sell your company's services to a client, and you put together a presentation that absolutely must not exceed 20 minutes. To reach your goal, you are forced to omit a couple of video clips from the TV series *The Office*. You hate to drop them because they illustrate—with delightful humor—some of your key points. What can you do?

Situations like this happen frequently. You have lots of good support materials but not enough time to fit them in. The solution is to provide bonus materials at the end of your presentation, so that participants can examine them later. The materials can be placed on handouts or electronic media (such as DVDs), or they can be provided via Internet links.

In *The Office* scenario, you could put the clips on DVDs or thumb drives, or you could send them as e-mail attachments.

One speaker gave a speech on restaurants in her community that provided tasty food at reasonable prices. At the end, she gave a bonus to each listener—an envelope containing the menus of all the restaurants she recommended.

Quoting the expert verbatim was very effective because the statement was phrased in a colorful way. Paraphrasing would have weakened it.

summarize
to give the substance of a statement in condensed form

2. **Summarize.** When a statement is long, quoting it verbatim can bore the audience. It may be best to summarize any quotation that is more than one or two sentences. In another part of Vallejo's speech, she boiled a long quotation into one brief sentence:

> Sigmund Freud believed that dreams reflect unconscious wishes and urges that we are afraid to think about during our daytime waking hours.

paraphrase
to restate material, using different words

3. **Paraphrase.** If a quotation has archaic or technical language or is laced with jargon, you should paraphrase it. If, for example, you want to quote an expert on espionage who says, "Aldrich Ames was a Russian-sponsored mole working at the CIA," you can paraphrase this jargon into plain English by saying, "Aldrich Ames was a CIA employee who was secretly working for the Russians."

Ethical Considerations

Here are some guidelines for using testimony in an ethical and responsible manner.

Be fair.   One speaker quoted a blogger as saying that a certain new smartphone was "glitzy and overpriced." This was unfair because the speaker failed to give the entire quotation—"glitzy and overpriced, but the best smartphone on the market today." To decide whether you are being fair, ask yourself if your listeners would admire you if they discovered your way of handling a quotation.

Use testimony from unbiased sources.   Ethical speakers avoid using sources that are biased. Suppose you are researching the question of whether polygraphs (lie detectors) are accurate, and you come across glowing pro-polygraph statements by two "experts" who are on the payroll of a firm that manufactures polygraph machines. Could you expect such sources to be unbiased? Of course not. Reject such "evidence" and look instead for statements by people who have no vested interest in the issue.

State the credentials of your source.   If you quote a famous person such as Abraham Lincoln, you don't need to give any background information about the person. But for authorities who are not well known, be sure to give some biographical data to establish their credibility. For example, "Jack Smithson, who spent 25 years as a research scientist for NASA, says that . . ."

Statistics

For a speech explaining the immense distances of space, Paula Schiller began with some mind-boggling facts:

> Proxima Centauri, the star that is closest to our solar system, is only 4.28 light years away. That doesn't sound like a very great distance, does it? Is there any chance that we can reach that star—or one of its planets—in our lifetime? Before you start fantasizing about being the first human to travel to our nearest star, consider this fact: if you traveled to Proxima Centauri in the fastest spacecraft now in existence, it would take you *40,000 years* to make the trip.

Schiller was using **statistics,** which are numerical ways of expressing information. As this example illustrates, statistics don't have to be dry and boring. They can be made interesting and even exciting.

Statistics can be especially effective in persuading an audience to accept a particular point. In our society, people put a lot of trust in statistics. If a television commercial says that 78 percent of physicians prefer Cure-All pain reliever over all competing brands, sales of the product will increase dramatically.

In a speech in which she tried to persuade her audience to drive their cars less and walk more, Carol Morris wanted to prove that Americans are less fit than they once were, in part, because of all the time they spend driving in their cars, when they could be walking instead. She could have made a vague statement such as "Because of the automobile, we Americans are getting soft and flabby." Instead, she gave a fascinating statistic to prove her point: "Since the advent of the auto, the average waistline of American adults has increased one inch every generation." That single statistic, short and surprising, was one of the most persuasive parts of her speech.

statistics
numerical facts assembled to present significant information about a subject

Ethical Issues Quiz

Fact 1: In contrast to the 1970s, Americans today consume 25 percent more vegetables and fruits.

Fact 2: Potatoes account for 30 percent of the vegetables, usually as chips or fries. Which one of the following is the best way to present these facts in a speech?

   A. Americans today eat 25 percent more vegetables and fruits than they did in the 1970s. Potatoes account for 30 percent of the vegetables.

   B. Americans eat 25 percent more vegetables and fruits than they did in the 1970s, but this is not as heartening as it sounds. Some 30 percent of the vegetables are potatoes, usually chips or fries, which of course are heavy in fat.

   C. Americans today eat 25 percent more vegetables and fruits than they did in the 1970s.

For the answer, see the last page of this chapter.

Race car driver Danica Patrick speaks at a congressional briefing in Washington, DC, to educate lawmakers about COPD (Chronic Obstructive Pulmonary Disease). In her talk, she used support materials, including a **narrative** (about her grandmother, who died from the disease) and **statistics** ("COPD is the fourth leading cause of death, after heart disease, cancer, and stroke").

Understanding Statistics

While statistics can provide powerful support for ideas, they also can be easily misused, either willfully or through carelessness or ignorance. Unfortunately, there is much truth in the old statement "You can prove anything with statistics." To understand how statistics are used (and abused), let's look at several of the more popular varieties.

average

a single value that represents the general significance of a set of unequal values

Averages.   The most popular kind of statistic is the **average.** It can provide interesting views of a subject, as when one speaker pointed out, "On an average day, 24 mail carriers in the United States receive animal bites." Giving the average in a case like this is much more compelling than simply stating the annual total.

Though averages seem like straightforward pieces of statistical data, there are pitfalls: most people are unaware that there are actually three kinds of averages: the mean, the median, and the mode. To understand these terms, consider Figure 8.3, which shows three ways for figuring the average age of recent winners of Oscars (Academy Awards) for Best Actress.

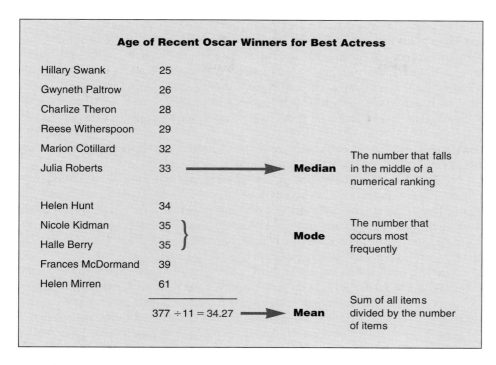

Age of Recent Oscar Winners for Best Actress

Hillary Swank	25	
Gwyneth Paltrow	26	
Charlize Theron	28	
Reese Witherspoon	29	
Marion Cotillard	32	
Julia Roberts	33	→ **Median** — The number that falls in the middle of a numerical ranking
Helen Hunt	34	
Nicole Kidman	35	} **Mode** — The number that occurs most frequently
Halle Berry	35	
Frances McDormand	39	
Helen Mirren	61	

377 ÷ 11 = 34.27 → **Mean** — Sum of all items divided by the number of items

Figure 8.3
Arranged from youngest to oldest, this list shows the ages of recent Best Actress Oscar winners at the time of receiving the award. The ages can be averaged in three ways (median, mode, and mean).

The **mean,** which is what most people use when they are asked to compute an average, is derived by adding all the ages (for a total of 377) and dividing by the number of actresses (11). This gives 34.27 as the mean.

The **median** is derived by listing the numerals, ranging from highest to lowest (or lowest to highest), and then locating the numeral that falls in the middle. (*Memory aid:* Just as the median is the strip in the *middle* of a highway, the median is the *middle* number.) In this case, 33 is precisely in the middle, so it is our median. Our example has an *odd* number of figures—this makes it easy to find the median; when you have an *even* number of figures, the median is defined as the number halfway between the median pair.

The **mode** is simply the number that occurs most frequently: in this case, 35.

As a researcher, you need to know the meanings of these three terms, but as an ethical speaker, you should restrict your use of the word *average* to the mean because that is what most people think of as the average. For the other two types of averages, simply explain them in context without using the word "average." Regarding Figure 8.3, for example, you could say, "The age that appears most often on this list is 35." For the median, it would help your audience if you said, "Ages range from 25 to 61, with 33 falling in the middle."

Percentages.   Giving a **percentage** (a portion of 100) can be a useful way to make a point. For example, suppose that you find that 2 percent of the employees in a company have physical disabilities, and yet only 1 percent of the parking spaces have been designated for employees with disabilities. With these figures, you can make a good argument for increasing the number of spaces for employees with disabilities.

Unfortunately, percentages can be misleading. A television commercial might say, "Eighty percent of the doctors interviewed said they recommend Feel Good pills for their patients." How many doctors were involved? If only 10 doctors were interviewed, and 8 of them gave the endorsement, the commercial is accurate (8 out of 10 amounts to 80 percent) but misleading.

mean
in a set of numbers, the sum of all figures divided by the number of figures

median
the number that falls in the middle of a numerical ranking

mode
the figure that appears most frequently in a set of figures

percentage
a rate or proportion per hundred

The following statement is true: In one recent year, Switzerland experienced a 50 percent jump in unemployment, causing that nation to rank number one in the world in the percentage increase of unemployed over the previous year. Sounds terrible, doesn't it? Is the prosperous little country sliding toward economic catastrophe? But here is another way of reporting the facts: In the year cited, there were 51 jobless persons in Switzerland as compared to 34 in the previous year. This represents a 50 percent increase, but when you look at the actual number of people involved, you find no reason for the Swiss to be alarmed.

correlation

the degree of relative correspondence between two sets of data

Correlations.   The term **correlation** refers to the degree of relationship between two sets of data.

Suppose I have the IQ scores and grade-point averages for you and 20 of your friends. When I compare the two sets of data, I find that for most of you, the higher the IQ, the higher the grade-point average. I can now state that there is a high correlation between the two sets of data. This should be no surprise: for most people in our society, the higher the IQ, the greater the level of academic achievement. Statisticians would say that IQ scores and grade-point averages are highly correlated.

Now let's suppose that I compare the IQ scores with the shoe sizes of you and your friends. Will I find that the larger the foot, the higher the IQ? No, of course not. There is absolutely no pattern to observe—no correspondence between foot size and intelligence. In the language of statisticians, there is no correlation at all.

Correlation is a handy statistical device because it can help us predict probable outcomes for individuals. For example, because a high correlation is known to exist between exercising regularly and longevity, medical experts can predict that a person who runs regularly is likely to live longer than someone who doesn't exercise.

However, while correlation can be a highly effective way to interpret data, it is often misunderstood and misused by people who think that it proves a cause-and-effect relationship. Just because two sets of data are correlated, we cannot conclude that one causes the other. For example, research in *Nature* magazine in 1999 found that young children who slept with a light on in their bedroom were more likely than those who slept in darkness to develop nearsightedness (myopia). Because this research established a definite correlation, many parents felt compelled to turn off all bedroom lights at night. By 2003, however, further research showed that lighting had nothing to do with children's vision. Nearsighted kids inherited their condition from their nearsighted parents, who were more likely to leave a light on in a child's room so that they themselves could see better. So a correlation between lights and nearsightedness did exist, but it was not the lights that caused the problem.[9]

Your Thoughts

Researchers at Ohio State University have found that college students who are heavy users of Facebook tend to have lower grades than students who are nonusers. Does this correlation prove that Facebook causes lower grades? How can the correlation be explained?

Guidelines for Using Statistics

Here are some guidelines to consider when you are evaluating statistics for possible use in a speech.

Use statistics fairly and honestly.   In one recent year, newspapers and TV stations reported some alarming news: four of America's largest cities—Los Angeles, San Diego, Dallas, and Phoenix—had experienced a record number of murders during the previous year. The story was true but misleading. All four of those cities had also reached new highs in population, with the per capita murder rates staying the same. In other words, there were more murders because there were more people.[10]

This case illustrates that even a true statistic can sometimes leave a false impression. An unethical speaker could cite the study and let the audience draw the wrong conclusion—that murder was becoming rampant in four big cities. An ethical speaker, in contrast, would analyze the statistics for their true significance and explain to the audience that the rate of murder—the only fair yardstick—had not increased.

Use statistics sparingly.   A long recital of statistics is hard for the audience to absorb:

> *Poor:* According to the U.S. Census Bureau, 222,600,798 Americans speak English at home; 38,844,979 speak a different language at home. Of the latter number, 19,339,172 speak Spanish; 2,189,253 speak Chinese; 2,102,176 speak French; 1,947,099 speak German; and 1,908,648 speak Italian. All other languages have under one million users.

> *Better:* According to the U.S. Census Bureau, 85 percent of Americans speak English at home. Of the 15 percent speaking other languages, one-half speak Spanish. Four languages—Chinese, French, German, and Italian—are each spoken by roughly 5 percent of the non-English group.

The statistics in the first version might work in a written essay, but in a speech they would be hard for the audience to follow. The second version, streamlined and simple, would be easier for the audience to hear and digest.

Round off long numbers.   In print, a long number is no problem, but in a speech, it is hard for the listener to absorb. A rounded-off number is easy to say and easy for the audience to grasp.

> *Poor:* In the last presidential election, 131,257,328 Americans voted.

> *Better:* In the last presidential election, over 131 million Americans voted.

Translate your statistics into vivid, meaningful language.   If you have a statistic that would be meaningless to most listeners or difficult for them to visualize, translate it into simple, down-to-earth language. To help her audience understand the dangers of pieces of debris in space, student speaker Melissa Pollard said:

> Right at this moment, there are about 2,000 tons of garbage sailing around earth. Most of the items are leftovers from previous space missions—fragments of spacecraft, rocket launchers, and dead satellites. To give you an idea of the danger that is caused by all this junk, consider this: If a fragment less than an inch wide were to hit a spaceship, the impact would be like being struck by a bowling ball that is traveling at 65 miles per hour.

Relate statistics to familiar objects.   One way to make statistics dramatic is to relate them to something familiar. In a speech on bats, student speaker Sally Ingle wanted to give the audience an idea of the incredibly small size of one variety of bat. Instead of giving its weight in grams, which would have meant little to most of the audience, she said, "One variety of bat is so tiny that when it is full-grown, it weighs less than a penny."

English astronomer Fred Hoyle once made the point that outer space isn't as remote as many people think. Instead of using dry statistics, he created a startling image that everyone could relate to: "It's only an hour's drive away if your car could go straight upwards."[11]

Sample Speech with Commentary

To see how support materials can be used, let's look at a speech by student speaker Brian Snowden. A commentary alongside the transcript points out the types of support materials that are used. (*Note:* The speaker delivered this speech in a conversational manner, looking at the audience most of the time and glancing occasionally at brief notes. What you see below is the transcript of what he said. In other words, he did *not* write out the speech and read it aloud—a method that would have been ineffective with his audience.)

No Laughing Matter

COMMENTARY

SPEECH

[The speaker displays the photo in Figure 8.4.]

I like clowns—I always have—so I was surprised when I heard a report on NBC TV news about several hospitals in the United States and Europe that have banned clowns from performing in children's wards. Their reason? They say that many kids are frightened by clowns—some of the kids have even developed a phobia.

Figure 8.4

To grab attention and set a mood, the speaker displays a photo, a type of support that will be discussed in Chapter 9 (Presentation Aids). For the benefit of any members of the audience who speak English as a second language, the photo quickly specifies which of several definitions of "clown" is being used.

This news was intriguing to me, so I decided to do some research. I discovered that the hospitals were right: there are many children and even some adults who are afraid of clowns. If the fear is extreme, it is called coulrophobia or clown phobia. Coulrophobia has been in existence for hundreds of years, but it was relatively rare until recent times. Now it is widespread among children throughout the world. What has caused this upsurge? How many people are affected? How are professional clowns coping with the problem? These are the questions I would like to answer today.

> Brian Snowden gives a **definition** of coulrophobia.

The number one reason for the upsurge in coulrophobia is the depiction of evil clowns in movies and TV shows. Most researchers say that the epidemic began in November 1990. That's when ABC aired Stephen King's *It* as a miniseries. I should say, in all fairness: there have been other movies that depict evil clowns, including *Killer Klowns from Outer Space, The Nightmare Before Christmas,* and *Clownhouse.* But Stephen King gets most of the blame because his clown, Pennywise, terrified millions of children.

> **Examples** of movies are given.

To describe Pennywise, I am going to paraphrase the words of Juliet Bennett-Rylah, who wrote an article in *Spry* magazine entitled "Stephen King Ruined the Circus." Pennywise, she says, is a clown with flashing zombie eyes and razor teeth. He is terrifying—white-faced and bald-headed except for two shocks of red hair. His makeup forms angry brows and a huge, red mouth. His voice is the deathbed mumblings of an old man with a throat full of tar. Worst of all, he murders children.

> A **vivid image** helps the audience grasp the full horror of the clown.

After seeing the show, Bennett-Rylah had nightmares for many weeks, and she had trouble sleeping. The phobia persisted for years. When her best friend gave her a tiny clown doll as a present three years later, she wanted to throw it away, but her father told her it would be rude to throw a gift into the garbage. So she buried it in the back yard. Whenever the circus came to town, she would be invited to attend, but she would vigorously shake her head. Whenever a show about a clown came on the TV in the living room, she would leave the room.

> A **narrative,** or story, shows how troubling the phobia can be.

To help you understand why clowns are so disturbing to some children, let me give you an analogy. Imagine how you would react if you were traveling in a rural area and you came across a village where all the inhabitants were extraterrestrial aliens with scaly green skin and gigantic eyes. In the minds of some children, clowns are strange, alien creatures.

> An **analogy** is useful to help listeners comprehend the mind of a child.

How widespread is the fear of clowns? Several researchers, including Dr. Penny Curtis of the University of Sheffield in England, have estimated that about 40 percent of children are afraid of clowns. Their fears range from mild to the extreme level, coulrophobia. What about adults? Some adults still have the coulrophobia that originated in childhood. *Psychology Today* magazine says that eight percent of adults suffer from a phobia, and coulrophobia is one of the most common phobias.

> **Statistics** show the extent of the problem.

(continued)

A **narrative** gives a good view of adult phobia.

A **comparison** is made to fear of snakes.

The speaker relates a **narrative** that also shows a **contrast** between being a clown before the Stephen King movie and being a clown today.

Citing **testimony** from a professional clown gives credibility to the speaker's remarks.

More **testimony** gives a **contrast** between the nineteenth century and today.

In his closing, Snowden makes a **contrast** between the present and the future.

Adults with coulrophobia get little sympathy from other adults, and sometimes they are made fun of. On an Internet discussion forum on phobias, a man in California wrote that in his office, his co-workers knew of his intense fear of clowns. One day they put a clown doll in a chair in his office. He was terrified, and he left work for the day. The next day he removed the chair, and replaced it with a new one. By the way, if you understand phobias, you will realize that what the co-workers did is not humorous—it's cruel. It's like tossing a snake into the lap of someone who is afraid of snakes.

Is coulrophobia having an impact on the world of clowns? I could not find any data on whether the number of clowns has decreased, but I did find some reports of clowns who are no longer finding any joy in clowning.

For the past 23 years, Jim Jelinske dressed as a clown whenever he gave anti-bullying presentations in schools in Dubuque, Iowa. He enjoyed being "Jelly the Clown." He enjoyed putting on full clown makeup and attaching a red nose. But he recently quit being a clown. He still makes his presentations, but he no longer appears as Jelly the Clown. He told a reporter for the *Dubuque Telegraph Herald* on January 29, 2008, that "it wasn't fun anymore" because of the "rising tide of clown fear." He said that Stephen King's horror movie caused a "whole different atmosphere for clowns over the past 10 years."

While Jelinske has put away his clown costume, many other clowns are continuing to perform, and some of them make an effort to avoid frightening children. Peggy Williams, a clown with the Barnum & Bailey circus, is quoted in the *Washington Post* as saying, "A child who is afraid of clowns has been introduced to them out of context too quickly." She says a clown needs to keep a respectful distance and not let parents force a child into "getting too close too soon."

Some clowns try to soften their faces and costumes. Beth Byrd, a professional clown, told the *Kansas City Star* that traditional clown makeup was created in response to the primitive lighting in three-ring circuses in the nineteenth century. The exaggerated features were necessary in order for the clown to be seen. Nowadays that is not necessary. She says she downplays makeup and costume. "My mouth is my real mouth," she says, "and I paint my own nose. Children must be able to see that you're human."

To summarize what we've covered, fear of clowns is no laughing matter, especially if it develops into clown phobia. An epidemic of clown phobia was ignited by movies and TV shows in the 1990s, and the effects are still being felt today.

We can only hope that in the future, instead of seeing horrible clown-monsters created by Stephen King and others, children will encounter happy, friendly clowns who will bring a smile to their faces and joy to their hearts.

Resources for Review and Skill Building

Summary

Verbal support materials are vital to the success of a speech. They develop, illustrate, and clarify ideas; they make a speech more interesting and meaningful; and they can help prove an assertion.

Some of the more popular types of verbal supports are (1) *definition,* which helps make sure that your listeners understand key terms as you intend them to be understood; (2) *vivid image,* which is a word picture that helps listeners visualize concepts; (3) *example,* which is an instance that illustrates a statement; (4) *narrative,* which is a story that amplifies your message; (5) *comparison,* which shows how two or more things are alike; (6) *contrast,* which shows how two or more things are different; (7) *analogy,* which explains a concept by likening it to something that seems different; (8) *testimony,* which provides input from experts; and (9) *statistics,* which are numerical ways of conveying information.

Of all these types, the narrative (or story) is the favorite of most audiences. People love to hear stories and are more likely to remember them than most other parts of your speech. As with all support materials, you must make sure that a narrative explains, illustrates, or reinforces the message of your speech. Telling a story that is irrelevant to the subject is not appropriate in informative and persuasive speaking.

Statistics such as averages, percentages, and correlations can be useful in a speech, but you must be careful to use them accurately and fairly. Make them as interesting and as meaningful as possible.

Key Terms

analogy, *136*

average, *140*

comparison, *136*

contrast, *136*

correlation, *142*

definition, *133*

example, *134*

hypothetical narrative, *135*

mean, *141*

median, *141*

mode, *141*

narrative, *135*

paraphrase, *138*

percentage, *141*

quote verbatim, *137*

statistics, *139*

summarize, *138*

support material, *131*

testimony, *137*

vivid image, *134*

Review Questions

1. List five reasons why support materials are important in a speech.

2. Why are informal definitions usually superior to dictionary definitions in a speech?

3. What must speakers use to make vivid images successful?

4. What is the main advantage of using testimony in a speech?

5. Why should statistics be used sparingly?

6. How many examples are needed to develop a point?

7. What term is used to refer to a story about an imaginary situation?

8. What is the difference between a comparison and a contrast?

9. A speaker who likens worrying to rocking in a rocking chair is using which kind of support material?

10. If we say that there is a positive relationship between height and landing a spot on a basketball team, we are using which type of statistics?

Building Critical-Thinking Skills

1. At a beach on the Atlantic Ocean, whenever ice cream sales increase, the number of drownings increases. In other words, there is a strong correlation between ice cream and drownings. Does the correlation prove that ice cream contributes to drownings? Explain your answer.

2. In three or four sentences, give an informal definition (not a dictionary definition) of one of these terms:

   a. Friendship
   b. Pizzazz
   c. Ideal pet

Building Teamwork Skills

1. In a group, choose several focal points (such as music and food preferences) and analyze how group members compare and contrast with one another. In what way are group members most alike and most unalike?

2. Working in a group, analyze these statistics, all of which are true. Discuss why they can be misleading.

   a. "Last year 37 people were killed by automobile airbags."
   b. "Three out of four doctors surveyed said that margarine is healthier for the heart than butter."
   c. "Studies show that children with longer arms are better at solving math problems than children with shorter arms."
   d. "College-educated people drink 90 percent of all bottled mineral water sold in the United States, so we can say that a high correlation exists between an advanced educational level and consumption of mineral water."
   e. "The average American parents last year named their daughter Isabella and their son Jacob."

Ethical Issues

Answer for p. 139: B. A speaker should present all of the facts and point out their significance. Answers A and C are accurate statements, but they fail to give the full picture, and therefore are misleading.

Presentation Aids

OUTLINE

OBJECTIVES

After studying this chapter, you should be able to:

1. Explain at least seven advantages of using visual aids in a speech.
2. Describe the types of visual aids.
3. Describe the media for visual aids.
4. Prepare appropriate visual aids.
5. Present visual aids effectively.
6. Communicate in channels other than visual.

WHEN PROFESSOR HIROSHI ISHIGURO of Osaka University in Japan gave a speech about a new female android robot, he had an ideal presentation aid—the robot herself, who is named Geminoid-F.

Dr. Ishiguro began his talk by demonstrating that Geminoid-F (on the left in the photo on the next page) can smile, frown, laugh, gesture, and talk. She costs $110,000 and can serve as a guide in institutions such as museums and hospitals. She is shown with the woman upon whom she was modeled.[1]

Geminoid-F is a good example of the power of presentation aids. Imagine how difficult it would have been for Dr. Ishiguro to describe how his robot looked and sounded without displaying her in action. Aids not only help an audience to understand key points, but they also make a speech more interesting and exciting.

A robot and a look-alike human are effective presentation aids.

Presentation aids can be conveyed in six channels of communication—vision, hearing, smell, taste, touch, and physical activity. We will cover all six in this chapter, but our primary focus will be on visual aids because they are the most widely used. The typical attitude of audiences is: "Don't just tell me—show me."

Advantages of Visual Aids

While *verbal* supports (discussed in the preceding chapter) are important for explaining and illustrating your ideas, you also should look for *visual* support. Let's examine some reasons for using visual aids.

1. **Visual aids can make ideas clear and understandable.** Your listeners can quickly grasp how to jump-start a car if you display a drawing that shows where to connect battery cables.

2. **Visual aids can make a speech more interesting.** In a speech on pollution, a chemist showed color slides of gargoyles and statues in Europe that had been eaten away by acid rain. The slides added a lively, provocative element to a technical subject.

3. **Visual aids can help an audience remember facts and details.** Research shows that oral information alone is not as effective as oral information coupled with visual aids.[2] Imagine that you give the same speech (on how to create a spreadsheet on a computer) to two different groups. To the first group, you use only words; to the second group, you use words plus visuals. If the audiences are tested a week later, the second group will score far higher in comprehension.[3]

4. **Visual aids can make long, complicated explanations unnecessary.** In medical schools, professors use close-up slides and videos to teach surgical procedures. The visuals show exactly where and how to make an incision, sparing the professor from having to give a tedious verbal explanation.

5. **Visual aids can help prove a point.** If a prosecutor shows the jury a surveillance video in which the defendant is seen robbing a store, the jury can be easily convinced of the defendant's guilt.

6. **Visual aids can add to your credibility.** Researchers have found that presenters who use good visual aids are rated by listeners as more persuasive and credible than presenters who use no visuals. *But a note of warning:* If listeners think that visual aids are poor, their confidence in the speaker declines. In other words, if you can't use a good visual, don't use any at all.[4]

7. **Visual aids enhance communication with people who speak English as a second language.** As more and more audiences include professionals and businesspeople from other countries, international students, immigrants, and others whose command of English is imperfect, visual aids have become a crucial way to overcome language limitations.

Types of Visual Aids

In this section, we will look at various types of visual aids. As you select aids for your speeches, be flexible. Public speaking instructor Linda Larson of Mesa Community College advises her students to think of "tools" instead of "visual aids." In various jobs, not every tool works. For example, not every job needs a hammer. In a particular speech, a PowerPoint slide may be the wrong tool, while a handout may be the perfect tool.[5]

Graphs

line graph

a visual consisting of lines (charted on a grid) that show trends

Graphs help audiences understand and retain statistical data. The **line graph,** which is widely used in textbooks, uses a horizontal and a vertical scale to show trends and the relationship between two variables, such as percent and years in Figure 9.1.

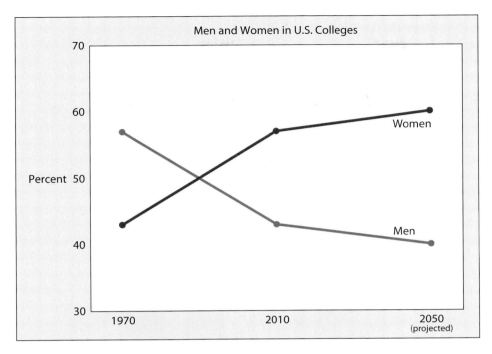

Figure 9.1
Sample Line Graph
In 1970 in the United States, 43 percent of college students were women. Today they have surpassed men and are expected to reach 60 percent by 2050.

A **bar graph** consists of horizontal or vertical bars that contrast two or more variables, as in Figure 9.2. A bar graph can effectively display a great deal of data in a clear, easily comprehended manner.

A **pie graph** is a circle representing 100 percent and divided into segments of various sizes (see Figure 9.3). A pie graph used in a speech should have no more than 7 or 8 wedges. (If necessary, several small segments can be lumped together into an "all others" category.) If you see a 20-piece pie graph in a book, resist the temptation to use it in a speech. While such a graph is fine in a book because readers can scrutinize it as long as they wish, it would be hard to decipher in a presentation.

Of all graphs, a **pictorial graph** is perhaps the easiest to read, because it visually translates information into a picture that can be grasped instantly. Figure 9.4 is an example of a pictorial graph.

bar graph
a visual that contrasts two or more sets of data by means of parallel rectangles of varying lengths

pie graph
a circle showing a given whole that is divided into component wedges

pictorial graph
a visual that dramatizes statistical data by means of pictorial forms

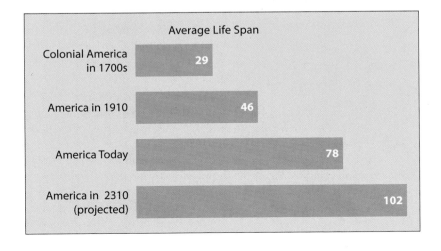

Figure 9.2
Sample Bar Graph
This bar graph shows that the life span of the average American has increased over the centuries and is expected to become even longer in future centuries, according to the U.S. Centers for Disease Control and Prevention.

Figure 9.3
Sample Pie Graph

Of the millions of dollars that retail stores lose each year from theft, employees account for 68 percent and shoplifters account for 32 percent.

Thefts from Stores

Figure 9.4
Sample Pictorial Graph

When the speaker explains that each image represents 400 wolves, the audience can quickly visualize the comeback of the gray wolf, an endangered species that had an estimated 400 survivors in 1965. Thanks to protection mandated by federal law, the gray wolf population has climbed to 3,200.

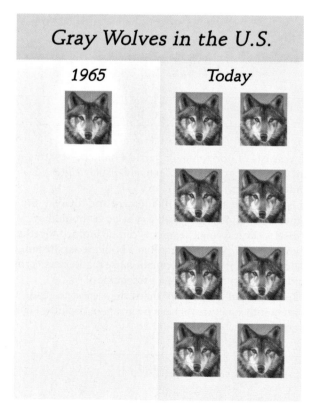

Charts

information chart

text material arranged as a series of key points

table

numbers or words arranged systematically in rows and columns

Charts provide information in a compact, easily digested form. An **information chart,** also called a *list of key ideas,* is a convenient way of presenting main points or steps in a process. Figure 9.5 shows a good format for presenting a list.

An information chart can sometimes take the form of a **table,** in which information is presented in rows and columns. Figure 9.6 shows how easy it can be to understand a table.

Note of caution: Most instructors dislike a speech that is nothing more than a recitation of a lengthy list. One student's entire speech was a list of 42 lucrative careers—a lazy way of doing a speech.

What to Wear for a Job Interview	1. Wear Dark Colors
2. Dress Up Rather Than Go Casual	3. Wear a Minimum of Accessories

Figure 9.5
Sample Information Chart
An information chart (or list of key ideas) can be presented on PowerPoint slides, posters, or transparencies. If possible, display only one item at a time so that listeners stay with you and don't read ahead.

Most Popular Baby Names, 2007–2011		
Rank	**Girl**	**Boy**
1	Isabella	Jacob
2	Emma	Ethan
3	Sophia	Michael
4	Olivia	Jayden
5	Emily	Joshua

Figure 9.6
Sample Table
A table is an effective type of information chart. This table shows the most popular names chosen for girls and boys in the United States in a recent five-year period.

Drawings and Photos

Drawings make good visual aids because they can illustrate points that would be hard to explain in words. One kind of drawing that is highly effective is a map. By sketching a map yourself, you can include only those features that are pertinent to your speech. If you were speaking about the major rivers of America, for example, you could outline the boundaries of the United States and then draw heavy blue lines for the rivers, leaving out extraneous details, such as cities. Figure 9.7 shows a map.

Because photographs have a high degree of realism, they are excellent for proving points. Lawyers, for example, often use photographs of the scene of an accident to argue a case. In a speech, you should not use a photograph unless it can be enlarged so that everyone can see it clearly.

Figure 9.7
Sample Map

This map illustrates that half of all Americans live in the nine most populous states. Here are the states in rank order:

1. California
2. Texas
3. New York
4. Florida
5. Illinois
6. Pennsylvania
7. Ohio
8. Michigan
9. Georgia

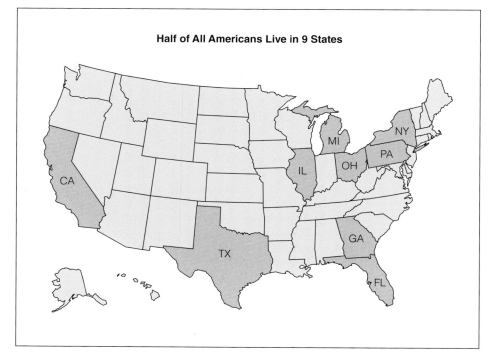

Video and Animation

With video, you can transport your audience to any corner of the world. To give listeners a glimpse of the rich spectacle of Mexican weddings, student speaker Victor Treviño showed a video of ritual, music, and dance at the wedding celebration of his sister in Guadalajara.

If you make a video of an interview as part of your research, you may be able to use some excerpts in your speech. Student speaker Adrienne Shields interviewed a bank official on how crooks steal from ATMs (automated teller machines). In her speech, Shields played video segments of the official as he demonstrated the machine's vulnerabilities. The video was much more effective than a verbal description alone would have been.

Animation—a sequence of drawings (such as diagrams or cartoons)—can be used in a PowerPoint presentation or video to clarify points. In courtroom trials, for example, lawyers often use animated drawings to re-create a car accident and help the jury understand what happened.

Audio and video gimmicks are incorporated into PowerPoint and can sometimes be used effectively, but Bill Howard, senior executive editor of *PC Magazine,* advises: "Go easy on the fly-in, swivel, wipe, zoom, laser text, and similar PowerPoint special effects. They get old in a hurry." For example, one presenter used the audio "gunshot" effect as each word was flashed in sequence on the screen. One irritated listener said later, "I felt like I was on a firing range."[6]

Objects and Models

Three-dimensional objects make good visual aids, provided they are large enough for everyone in the audience to see. You could display such things as a blood-pressure gauge, a hibachi, handmade pottery, mountain-climbing equipment, and musical instruments.

Tips for Your Career

Never Let Visuals Substitute for a Speech

Because visual aids are so powerful, some speakers let them dominate a speech. The visuals become the real show, with the speaker acting as a mere technician. It is easy for this to happen, especially if you have some dazzling slides or a spectacular video. The punch and glitz of the visuals make you feel inadequate, and you think you ought to step aside and let the graphics take command. This attitude is misguided, as shown by the experience of Preston Bradley, vice president of Graystone Corporation:

> Several years ago I made a presentation in which I used a commercially produced video. Thinking that the audience would prefer animated, full-color images to my words, I let the video take up most of the time; I merely added a few

comments at the end and fielded a few questions. Later, several listeners told me that the video had been far less helpful than my remarks, and they recommended that in the future I talk more and use video less. The reason: during my informal talk I was able to explain tough concepts and interact with the audience. The video, on the other hand, zipped along, incapable of sensing whether the audience was absorbing the information.

People can see jazzy video productions on TV at any hour of the day, but a speech has a dimension that TV lacks—a living, breathing human engaged in the stimulating act of direct communication.

A model is a representation of an object. One speaker used a model of the great pyramids to discuss how the ancient Egyptians probably built them. Another speaker used a homemade "lung," the interior of which consisted of clean cotton. When cigarette smoke was sucked through a tube, the lung turned from white to a sickening yellow-brown. One advantage of a model is that you can move it around. If you had a model airplane, for example, you could show principles of aerodynamics more easily than if you had only a drawing of a plane.

Yourself and Volunteers

Using yourself as a visual aid, you can demonstrate yoga positions, judo holds, karate chops, stretching exercises, relaxation techniques, ballet steps, and tennis strokes. You can don native attire, historical costumes, or scuba-diving equipment. One student came to class dressed and made up as a clown to give a speech on her part-time job as a clown for children's birthday parties.

Volunteers can enhance some speeches. You could use a friend, for example, to illustrate self-defense methods against an attacker. (For a classroom speech, be sure to get permission from your instructor before using a volunteer.)

Make sure you line up volunteers far in advance of speech day and, if necessary, practice with them to make sure they perform smoothly. Have substitutes lined up in case the scheduled volunteers fail to appear. Give instructions in advance so that volunteers know when to stand, when to sit, and so on. You don't want your volunteers to become a distraction by standing around when they are not needed.

PowerPoint Slides

Microsoft PowerPoint is a presentation program that permits you to create and show slides containing artwork, text information, animation, and audiovisuals.

Use a PowerPoint slide when you need to illustrate, explain, or enhance a key point in your speech. Make each slide attractive and simple. Choose graphics whenever possible, and use only small amounts of text.

connect
View speech videos that illustrate the wrong way and the right way to use PowerPoint slides. Look for "Failed to Get the Job?" in the Connect Media Library.

The Basic Steps

To get maximum benefit from PowerPoint, take these steps:

1. **Create your outline before you even think about using PowerPoint.** Your slides should *not* be your speech. In other words, don't collect a bunch of photos and then give a speech that just adds narration to the photos. PowerPoint slides should be aids—helpers—for the key ideas that you have already created in your outline.

2. **Look at your outline and ask, "Do I need visuals to highlight or explain any of my key points?"** Some points will not need visuals, but others may require them so that the audience will understand and remember what you are trying to say.

3. **For points that need visual support, decide which type of visual would be most effective.** Options include photos, drawings, graphs, charts, lists of key ideas, or other visuals discussed in this chapter.

4. **Create your slides.** Make them appealing and simple. (See the appendix at the end of this chapter for guidelines.)

5. **Practice in the room where you will be presenting.** Rehearse with all of the equipment several times so that you don't fumble during the actual speech. If possible, have a friend give a critique. Check your slides from the back row. If any words or graphics are hard to see, revise them before speech day.

6. **Give your speech, making sure that you—not the slides—are the dominant presence in the room.** Letting PowerPoint become the "star of the show," some speakers stand shyly in the shadows, stare at the screen, and narrate what appears on the slides. They are letting technology upstage a live, dynamic human being. You can avoid this mistake by boldly seizing your role as the primary communicator. Stand as close as possible to your listeners, and try to stay connected to them. Keep the room partially lit so that the audience can see your face. Focus all of your energy on reaching the listeners. Look at them—not the screen.

The Basic Steps in Action

Let's take another look at the steps we just discussed and use them in a scenario.

Step 1: Create your outline before you even think about using PowerPoint.

Your speech will be devoted to telling listeners how they can avoid becoming victims of identity theft, a crime in which personal information is stolen and used to defraud the victim. You create your outline, with carefully selected main points and support material.

Step 2: Look at your outline and ask, "Do I need visuals to highlight or explain any of my key points?"

You see three ideas that can use some visual support to help the audience remember them. For our scenario, let's focus on just one. You plan to warn listeners that they should *never* carry a social security card in their wallet because if the card is stolen, it can be used to buy a car or open a credit-card account at their expense. You decide that a dramatic visual would help drive home the point.

Figure 9.8
To avoid identity theft, keep your Social Security card in a safe place at home.

Step 3: For points that need visual support, decide which type of visual would be most effective.

To avoid overloading your slide, you decide to use just 9 words, emphasizing the words "Never Carry." (Additional words are unneeded because you will supply all the details orally.) Though not essential, a photo would brighten the slide and make it more interesting, so you search on the Internet and find a photo of a woman with a wallet.

Step 4: Create your slides.

In the PowerPoint program, you create a simple, readable slide with the photo and the key words. The result is Figure 9.8.

Step 5: Practice in the room where you will be presenting.

A week before your speech, you go to the classroom and run through several rehearsals, using all the equipment until you are proficient with it. A friend sits in the back row and gives you a critique. She suggests that one slide needs larger print for visibility. Later, you revise the slide.

A remote control lets you move away from a computer and advance slides from anywhere in the room.

Step 6: Give your speech, making sure that you—not the slides—are the dominant presence in the room.

You stay at center stage throughout your speech, focusing your attention and energy on the audience. Because you have only a few slides, the screen at the front of the room stays blank most of the time. When you display a slide, you continue to look at the audience. After discussing it, you blank the screen (press "B" on a keyboard or "A/V Mute" on a remote control) until you are ready to discuss the next slide.

For more information on how to use PowerPoint effectively, see the appendix "How to Avoid 'Death by PowerPoint' " at the end of this chapter.

Multimedia from the Internet

On the Internet, you can find photos, drawings, maps, charts, videos, and audio clips on a vast variety of subjects.

Is it legal to download these items without getting permission? For classroom speeches, yes. Copyright restrictions do not apply, because you are engaged in noncommercial, educational, one-time use of materials. For many business and professional presentations, however, you need to seek permission.

Many speakers use clips from commercial videos and online sources such as YouTube. A video clip should be brief, and it should contain no material that might offend any audience member. Avoid choosing a clip that has only a weak connection to your topic. (One student played an amusing YouTube clip on canine misadventures, but it was irrelevant to his topic—spaying and neutering pets.)

Media for Visual Aids

The types of visual aids we have just discussed—charts, graphs, and so on—can be conveyed to the audience through a variety of media.

Multimedia Projectors

Multimedia projectors can project a large array of audiovisuals—text slides, photos, drawings, animation, video clips, and DVD movies—onto a screen. They are usually linked to desktop or laptop computers, but some units need only a memory card or thumb drive.

Depending on the brightness of the screen and the strength of the machine's projection, you may need to dim the lights in a room, especially if you want to convey the full richness of a photo or a video.

Boards

Two types of presentation boards are whiteboards (well known for multicolored, "dry erase" pens) and chalkboards (less and less used because of chalk dust, which causes breathing problems for some people). Either type of board makes a good tool for visual aids if you have complex drawings that require constant insertions and erasures—for example, if you are diagramming plays for a soccer team.

Boards have some disadvantages. If you put your visual—a graph, say—on a board during your speech, you have to turn your back on the audience; while you're drawing, their attention drifts away from you, and you may find it hard to regain it. Would it be a good idea to put your graph on the board before the speech begins? No, because the audience would be distracted by it; they would scrutinize it before you are ready to talk about it. (It would do no good to say, "Don't pay any attention to this until I get to it." Such a request would make the graph all the more interesting—and therefore distracting.) There is one possible solution: cover the part of the board on which you have written. But this can be awkward. You would have to find something large enough to do the job without being distracting. Another problem is that speakers preceding you might also be planning to use the board, and they might have to erase your visual aid.

Because of the limitations of boards, some instructors forbid their use in a classroom speech, so be sure to find out your instructor's policy.

Posters

You can put many kinds of visual aids—such as graphs, drawings, and charts—on posters. Figure 9.9 shows the effective use of a poster.

Figure 9.9
In a speech on organ donation, Jessica Melore of Branchburg, NJ, says she would have died if she had not received a heart donation from the young woman pictured in the poster—Shannon Eckert of Mechanicsburg, PA—who lost her life in a car crash.

In the age of PowerPoint, posters are not outdated—they are widely used. In courtrooms, for example, many attorneys prefer posters to PowerPoint because posters can be placed on easels and kept on display for long periods, enabling jury members to glance at them whenever they need to refresh their memories. In some cases, jurors are allowed to take the posters into the deliberation room. (Normally you shouldn't keep posters on display after you've discussed them, but this situation is an exception to the rule.)

Make sure there is a reliable place to put your posters. If you prop them against a chalkboard or tape them on a wall, they may fall to the floor during the middle of the speech. Using thumbtacks might work if a corkboard or some other suitable place for tacking is available. One technique is to pile your posters on a desk and hold them up one at a time, being sure to hold them steady. Another method is to put your poster on an easel (which your school's audiovisual department may be able to provide). Even with an easel, however, some posters tend to curl and resist standing up straight. To prevent this, tape a second poster or a piece of cardboard to the back of your poster. (*Tip:* An even better solution to the problem of curling is to buy poster stocks that are sturdier than the standard stock sold at drugstores. Office-supply and craft stores have *foamboards.* Though more expensive than standard poster stock, these materials will not sag or curl.)

Flip Charts

A **flip chart** is a giant writing pad whose pages are glued or wired together at the top. It can be mounted on an easel. When you are through with each page, you can tear it off or flip it over the back of the easel.

You can prepare the visuals on each page in advance, or you can "halfway" prepare them—that is, lightly pencil in your sheets at home; then during the speech, with a heavy marker, trace over the lines. With some flip charts, the paper may be so thin that ink will seep to the next page, so you may need to leave a blank page between each two drawn-on sheets.

flip chart
a large book consisting of blank sheets (hinged at the top) that can be flipped over to present information sequentially

Be aware that some instructors disapprove of student speakers writing on a flip chart during a speech.

Handouts

handout

material distributed to an audience as part of a speaker's presentation

Despite the availability of high-tech tools, one of the most popular formats used in business and professional presentations is the paper **handout.** It is easy to explain the enduring popularity of handouts: they are easy to prepare, can be updated quickly at the last moment, and provide a permanent document that listeners can take with them when they leave a presentation.

Though handouts are popular, they are often misused. I have witnessed the following fiasco dozens of times: A presenter distributes stacks of handouts at the beginning of a talk. While he or she discusses each handout, the room is filled with the sound of rustling papers, as the listeners race ahead, reading material the presenter has not yet reached, ignoring or only half-listening to what he or she is saying. (Some speakers try to solve this problem by imploring the audience to stay with them and not read ahead, but this is futile; humans are naturally curious, and their eyes cannot resist reading.)

Because listeners study the pages instead of paying attention to the speaker, handouts are banned in some public speaking classes. Even if your instructor permits them, they are usually unsuitable during a classroom speech because distributing them eats up time and creates a distraction.

The best use of handouts—especially lengthy, complex documents—is to give them *after* the question-and-answer period so that listeners can take them to office or home for further study and review. (For classroom speeches, check with your instructor; he or she may prefer that you wait until the end of the class period; if you give out material at the end of your speech, students might read it instead of listening to the next speaker.)

One exception to the preceding advice: for informal presentations in career and community settings, it is permissible to distribute a handout during a presentation if it is short and simple—a one-page document with an easy-to-understand graphic or a *small* amount of text. In such situations, follow these guidelines: (1) Never distribute a handout until you are ready to talk about it—a premature handout grows stale. (2) Avoid talking about a handout while you are distributing copies. Wait until every listener has a copy before you start your explanation.

Giving listeners text-heavy handouts during a speech is a sure way to lose them.

Visual Presenters

visual presenter

a device capable of producing images of both two- and three-dimensional objects

A **visual presenter,** also known as a document camera or ELMO (the name of a leading manufacturer), is a camera mounted on a stand and pointed at a platform below. What the camera sees is shown on a TV or video monitor, or projected onto a screen by means of a digital projector. Visual presenters can show two-dimensional items such as photos and diagrams, and they also can show three-dimensional objects such as jewelry. A zoom feature permits very small items, such as a coin, to be enlarged for easy viewing.

Overhead Transparencies

transparency

clear sheets on which visuals are drawn or printed, and then viewed by light shining from an overhead projector

Overhead projectors are illuminated boxes that project images from **transparencies** (clear sheets of acetate) onto a screen. Transparencies are inexpensive and simple to produce.

To create a transparency, you can write directly on the acetate sheet with color pens (you must use a pen especially designed for overheads) or you can make a master copy on plain white paper and use an office copier or your own printer to make the transparency. Whether you use a copier or a printer, be aware that you need a special kind of acetate that won't melt inside the machine.

Preparing Visual Aids

Here are some guidelines for planning and creating your visual aids.

Choose Visuals That Truly Support Your Speech

Before using a visual, ask yourself: Will it help clarify or illustrate an important idea in my speech? If the honest answer is no, discard it. Your job is not to dazzle people with pretty colors on a screen or to impress them with your creative artwork. A beautiful drawing of an airplane in flight, for example, would not contribute much to a speech on touring the castles of Europe.

Prepare and Practice Far in Advance

Practice using your visuals as you rehearse your speech. If you will be using unfamiliar equipment, rehearsals will help prevent fumbling or faltering during your speech.

Don't create a visual—such as a diagram on a whiteboard—while you are actually giving your speech: few people can write or draw effectively while speaking to an audience. Make them far in advance so that they are not sloppy and unpolished.

Choose the Appropriate Number of Visuals

A common mistake is to display a large number of boring slides. For this reason, some speech coaches recommend that you use only three or four slides in a speech. Some supervisors forbid employees from using more than three. Although such rules might improve some speeches, they are too rigid to apply to all. The best rule is this: use a visual whenever it can make a key point more interesting, understandable, and memorable. Some speeches (such as a eulogy) may need no visuals at all. Some may need only one, while others may need more than a dozen.

Before speech day, practice in front of classmates or colleagues and ask their advice on which visuals, if any, should be eliminated.

While deciding how many visuals to use, here is an important consideration: When listeners complain about too many visuals, they are usually referring to slides or posters that are densely packed with text. They rarely complain about the number of visuals if all of them are exciting, easy-to-grasp photos and illustrations.

Make Visual Aids Simple and Clear

Make each visual aid so simple that your listeners can quickly grasp its meaning—either at a glance or after minimal explanation by you. Avoid complexity. Too much information can confuse or overwhelm the listeners.

A good model for a public speaker is an outdoor sign. As you walk or drive past it, the sign must snare your attention and convey a brief message—in just a few seconds. See Figure 9.10 on the next page for an example. A speech is a bit different because you have more than just a few seconds, but the key principles used by sign designers are worth applying to visuals in a speech:

1. Use graphics instead of words whenever possible.

2. If you must use words, use only a few.

Sometimes you might see a wonderful graphic in a book. Will it translate into a wonderful graphic in a speech? Not necessarily. Some visual aids in books are jam-packed with fascinating details; they are suitable in a book because the reader has ample time to analyze them, but they're too complex for a speech.

Tips for Your Career

With International Audiences, Avoid Informality

During a presentation to American audiences, you can write on boards, posters, flip charts, and overhead transparencies because spontaneity is considered appropriate. In some cultures, however, such informality is interpreted as a sign of unpreparedness and disrespect. Listeners may feel that the speaker did not value them highly enough to prepare proper visuals.

For an international audience, therefore, always use visuals that are created in advance.

Figure 9.10
An Iranian student in London holds a placard to protest the Iranian government's violence against pro-democracy citizens. Her sign is a good model for a visual aid in a speech—simple and easy to grasp, with good use of color.

In visuals such as graphs, make all labels horizontal. (In a textbook, many labels are vertical because readers of a book can turn the visual sideways, but listeners should not be forced to twist their necks to read vertical lettering.) You need not label every part of your visual, since you are there to explain the aid.

If you are displaying a multidimensional object, be sure to turn it during your talk so that everyone can see all sides of it.

Aim for Back-Row Comprehension

A common mistake is to use graphics that are difficult or impossible for everyone in the audience to see. The solution is to design every visual aid for the back row. *If all lettering and details cannot be seen easily and comfortably by a person in the rear of the room, don't use the visual.* Here are some guidelines:

Make letters, numbers, and graphics much larger than you think necessary. Be on the safe side. I've never heard anyone complain about visuals being too large.

Make enlargements. You can magnify a too-small visual by using video, visual presenters, PowerPoint slides, or posters. Here are some of the easiest options:

- A camcorder with a zoom lens can be used to make a close-up of a snapshot, a drawing, or a small object such as jewelry.
- To turn a photo or drawing into a PowerPoint slide, you can have the item scanned and converted into a digital file. Try the media center on your campus or visit a digital-imaging store in your community.

Test the visibility of your visuals. Before the day of your speech, go to the room where you will be speaking, display your visual aid in the front of the room, and sit in the back row to determine whether you can see it clearly. (Even better, have a friend sit in the back row to offer feedback.) If your visual cannot be seen with crystal clearness from the back row, discard it and create another (or simply don't use one).

Use Colors Carefully

To enliven visual aids, use color—but use it carefully. Here are two important issues, as illustrated in Figure 9.11.

Your Thoughts

A snapshot is too small for an audience to see clearly. How would you make this image large enough?

To help red-green color-blind people:

Don't use red and green together

Safe colors for everyone:

**Black on light color
with red for emphasis**

Figure 9.11
Color Combinations
The text in the top example will be difficult or impossible to read by people with red-green color-blindness, and jarring to everyone else. The bottom example shows a safe combination that should be readable and pleasant for all listeners.

The founder of Facebook, Mark Zuckerberg, who is red-green color-blind, chose blue and white for Facebook's icon because he can see those colors clearly.

1. Color-blindness is an inherited condition that makes it impossible to see colors the way most people do. Few women are color-blind, but about 8 percent of men have some degree of color-blindness. While there are several varieties of the condition, the most common is red-green, which means a difficulty or inability to distinguish red and green when they are next to each other. If you put red letters on a green background (or green on top of red), a person with red-green color-blindness probably could not read the text. The best advice: Don't place red and green close together.[7]

2. For all people, whether or not they have a color deficiency, the color combination that is clearest and most readable is dark text on a light-colored background. One of the safest choices is black on yellow, with red for emphasis. What about using white text on top of black or dark-blue backgrounds? Although this color scheme is dramatic, it can cause eye fatigue, so it's best to use it sparingly, perhaps only in headings.[8]

Presenting Visual Aids

Here are some tips for using visual aids effectively in your speeches.

Choose the Best Time to Show Visuals

Many speakers undermine their speech's effectiveness by showing visual aids at inappropriate times. Here are several guidelines.

Don't display a visual before your speech begins.   If visual aids are in plain sight before you start, you deprive your speech of an element of drama and freshness. There are exceptions, of course, as when you must set up items for a demonstration on a table in front of the room.

Display a visual whenever the audience needs help in understanding a point.   One speaker gave a talk on rock formations in caves but waited until the end to show photos illustrating his points. During the body of the speech, listeners were mystified and frustrated: What do these rock formations look like? Though he ultimately showed pictures, his listeners would have experienced a much greater understanding of the subject matter if he had displayed the images as he went along.

If listener comprehension is unharmed, it is acceptable to delay.   In some cases, you may want to withhold a visual or a demonstration to build suspense. In a speech on how to use Tae Kwon Do karate techniques to break objects, Lee Wentz stood in front of a cement block as he spoke, waiting until the end to demonstrate the actual breaking of the block with one hand. This built suspense—the audience wondered whether he would succeed. (He did, and the listeners applauded.)

Never Circulate Visual Aids among the Audience

Some people try to solve the problem of a too-small visual aid (such as a piece of jewelry) by passing it around the room, but this is a mistake. People will look at the visual instead of listening to the speaker. And there's likely to be distraction, perhaps even whispered comments, as it is being passed from one person to another. Some speakers walk from listener to listener to give each person a close-up view of the visual aid. This is also a poor technique; the listeners who are not seeing the visual may get bored or distracted, and they may start whispering comments to their friends. Moreover, the listeners who

Tips for Your Career

Ask a Friend to Assist You

For speeches that you give on the job or in the community, you may want to ask a friend to assist you. Here are some of the ways in which an assistant can be useful:

1. An assistant can help you set up and operate audiovisual equipment, turn lights off and on, or search for a missing extension cord. Such assistance will free you to concentrate on getting your message across to the audience.

2. If you are speaking to strangers, the presence of your friend can give you a psychological boost—you have an "ally" in the room.

3. An assistant may be able to handle any distractions or emergencies that arise. If, for example, a group of people start a loud conversation right outside the room in which you are speaking, the assistant can open the door and whisper a request for silence.

4. Your assistant can stand or sit in the back of the room while you are speaking and give you advice with hand signals on which the two of you have agreed in advance. For example:
   - "Slow down—you're talking too fast."
   - "Speak louder—I can barely hear you."
   - "You're looking at your notes too much."
   - "You've reached the time limit—wrap things up and sit down."

5. An assistant can give you a critique of your speech afterward so that you can learn from any mistakes you have made. Sometimes the assistant can mingle with the audience in the hall after your speech and find out how listeners responded to the presentation so that you can learn about your strengths and weaknesses.

are looking at the aid may ask questions that mean nothing to the rest of the audience. In a case like this, the speaker can easily lose the audience's attention and interest.

One way to solve the problem of a too-small object is to leave it in the front of the room and invite the audience to see it *after* the speech. This strategy is acceptable unless listeners need to see the aid during your speech to understand what you are talking about. In this case, the best solution is to create an enlarged image of the object, which you display during the speech, and then permit listeners to take a look at the real object after the speech.

When they need to show steps in a process, some speakers invite the audience to come to the front of the room and gather around a table. One speaker did this so that everyone could see him making garnishes out of vegetables (a tomato was transformed into a "rose"). If you are considering this approach, here are three guidelines: (1) Use the technique only with small audiences. (2) Make sure no disabled listeners are excluded from participating. (3) Get your instructor's permission before trying this in a classroom speech.

Remove Physical Barriers

Right before a speech, move any objects or furniture that might block the view of some listeners. If you're using equipment such as a projector, make sure it doesn't obstruct anyone's vision. If, despite your best efforts, some listeners will be blocked from seeing your visuals, ask them (before you start your introduction) to shift their chairs or move to a different part of the room.

Make Sure Listeners Get Maximum Benefit from Visuals

Don't rush through your visuals. A common mistake is for speakers to display a visual for a moment and then remove it from view. To these speakers, the visual is simple and obvious (they have seen it so many times, they are tired of it), but they should realize that it is brand-new to the listeners, who need time to study and absorb the contents.

Discuss each visual aid. But, you might say, can't listeners see and figure out for themselves? In some cases, yes, but by discussing each visual as you display it, you guarantee that listeners stay in step with you.

For a complex visual, don't wave your hand in the general direction of the aid and assume that the audience will know which feature you are pointing out. Be precise. Point to the specific part that you are discussing. For pointing, use a finger, a pen, or an extendable pointer. To avoid twisting your body, use the hand nearer the aid.

Don't Let Visuals Distract from Your Message

Visuals should never distract your audience from what you are saying. Here are some tips.

Show one visual at a time.   If you display five posters, neatly lined up on a chalk tray, your listeners will scrutinize the fourth poster while you are talking about the first. To keep the eyes and minds of your listeners focused on you and your remarks, show a visual, discuss it fully, put it away, and then display your next visual. There is one exception to this rule: if you have a visual aid that can provide a simple, undistracting backdrop or evoke a mood, you may leave it on display during the entire speech. One speaker kept a bouquet of flowers on the front table throughout her speech on gardening; the flowers provided a pleasing complement to her remarks.

Blank the screen.   If you have an interval between PowerPoint slides, blank the screen by pressing "B" on a keyboard or "A/V Mute" on a remote control.

Beware of using animals or children as visuals.   Exotic pets and cute kids can easily draw the attention of your listeners away from your ideas, so use them carefully, if at all. One speaker brought in a ferret to demonstrate what great pets they make. The only trouble was that the ferret acted up during the speech, causing the audience to laugh at its antics rather than listen to the speech. Some instructors disapprove of using animals in speeches, so be sure to get permission before bringing an animal into the classroom.

Don't Talk to Your Visual Aid

Many speakers are so intent on explaining a visual aid that they spend most of their time talking to it instead of to the audience. You should stand next to your aid and face the audience during most of your discussion. Look at the aid only in two situations: (1) When you introduce it, look at it for several seconds—this is long enough to draw the listeners' attention toward it. (2) Whenever you want to direct the audience's attention to a particular segment, look at the aid for one or two seconds as you point out the special feature.

Use Progressive Revelation

progressive revelation piece-by-piece unveiling of a visual

Whenever possible, use **progressive revelation**—that is, reveal only one part or item at a time. If, for example, you are discussing three sections of a sculpture, you can keep the entire piece covered at the beginning, and then unveil one section at a time. Progressive revelation creates suspense, making the listeners curious about what comes next, and it prevents them from reading or studying ahead of you. A variation of this technique, called the "build," is used in PowerPoint to reveal parts of a slide—for example, a pie chart can be shown one piece at a time. Likewise, bullet points can be displayed one point at a time.

Plan for Emergencies

With visual aids, there is always a chance of a foul-up, so you should plan carefully how you will handle any problems that might arise. Before you use any electronic media, talk with your instructor or the program chairperson to make arrangements (for darkening the room, getting an extension cord, and so on). Always check out the location of your speech in advance. Is there an electrical outlet nearby? If not, can you get an extension cord? Can the room be darkened for PowerPoint slides? Is there a place to put your posters? Is there a whiteboard or a chalkboard?

Be prepared for the unexpected, such as sudden malfunctioning of a computer or a multimedia projector. Some disasters can be mitigated by advance planning. For example, carry a backup CD of your PowerPoint presentation and have paper copies of your Power-Point slides for quick distribution. If equipment breaks down and cannot be fixed quickly, continue with your speech as best you can. Try to keep your poise and sense of humor.

Communicating in Other Channels

While the visual channel of communication is powerful, don't overlook other channels—hearing, taste, smell, touch, and physical activity—which can be effective avenues for reaching your audience.

A culinary class taught by a Nepalese chef involves seeing, hearing, smelling, tasting, touching, and physical activity.

Hearing

In almost all presentations, the sense of hearing is paramount, since you use your voice to convey words and meaning. (See Chapters 13 and 14 for tips on language and voice.) In addition, you can supply audio aids. For example, to accompany a visual presentation on dolphins, marine biologist Jennifer Novak played an audio clip of the clicks, whistles, and other sounds that dolphins use to communicate with one another.

The Internet has a rich variety of audio sources. For example, National Public Radio (npr.org) provides audio clips and podcasts that you can download to a desktop computer or MP3 device and then play during a presentation. (Some speakers insert their clips into PowerPoint presentations.) Here is a sampling of NPR downloads:

- Music and comments by the Latin jazz drummer Poncho Sanchez
- Interviews with ex-smokers who share their secrets for quitting the habit
- The lilting sounds of Irish accents in Dublin

Taste and Smell

Known as the chemical senses, taste and smell are closely related channels. Floral designer Charlene Worley gave a speech on how flowers provide not only messages of love and consolation but also medicine and food. At the end of her talk, she invited the audience to sniff a bouquet she had created. She also appealed to the sense of taste by serving crackers on which she had spread jam made from violets.

In culinary demonstrations, smelling a savory dish as it is prepared can stimulate appetite and interest, and tasting it can help the audience decide whether it is worthwhile.

Many business and professional presentations are held in rooms with a side table that provides beverages and snacks. This courtesy is more than simply satisfying people's hunger and thirst. Experienced presenters have discovered that the aroma of fresh coffee and the savor of tasty food can put an audience in a receptive mood and make it easier to inform or persuade. (Many real estate agents know that the smell of coffee evokes childhood memories of a pleasant home where breakfast is being prepared, so they arrange to have a pot of coffee brewing as they enter a house with a client to help make the house seem like a home.)

Touch and Physical Activity

Wishing to disprove the notion that snakes have slimy skin, herpetologist Jeanne Goldberg invited listeners to come forward and stroke the nonpoisonous king snake she was holding. Many listeners were surprised to find the skin dry and firm, with a texture like glass beads tightly strung together.

For learning new skills, the sense of touch is often coupled with physical activity. You need touch and muscular movement to apply first aid, draw a map, or perform a card trick. To persuade people to buy a product, some presenters give an audience hands-on experience. For example, one laptop computer sold well because sales representatives put laptops in front of listeners and invited them to try out the keyboard's pleasing responsiveness. In some situations, presenters provide physical activity by passing out pads and pens and inviting listeners to take notes during the presentation.

Using Multiple Channels

How many channels should you use? Some speeches (such as inspirational talks) do not require a variety of channels, but in many situations (such as teaching new material), the more you can use, the greater the likelihood that your listeners will understand and remember the information.[9]

In some cases, you can appeal to all the major channels in a single presentation. For example, in a culinary class, students can *see* the process as it is demonstrated, *hear* the explanations, *smell* the aromas, *taste* the delicacies, and use *touch* and *physical activity* as they practice making a dish.

Resources for Review and Skill Building

Summary

Presentation aids—which can involve vision, hearing, smell, taste, touch, and physical activity—enrich and enliven a speech. The most popular type, visual aids, can make your ideas clear and understandable; make your speech more interesting and memorable; help an audience remember facts and details; make long, complicated explanations unnecessary; help prove a point; add to your credibility; and enhance communication with people who speak English as a second language.

The major types of visual aids include graphs, charts, drawings, photos, videos, animations, objects, models, yourself, volunteers, PowerPoint slides, and multimedia from the Internet.

They can be conveyed to the audience through various media: multimedia projectors, boards, posters, flip charts, handouts, visual presenters, and overhead transparencies.

Guidelines for preparing visual aids: (1) Choose visual aids that truly support your speech. (2) Prepare and practice far in advance. (3) Choose the appropriate number of visuals. (4) Make your aids as simple and clear as possible. (5) Aim for comprehension by everyone, including the people in the back row.

Tips for presenting visual aids: (1) Decide on the best time to show visuals. (2) Never circulate a visual aid among the audience. (3) Remove physical barriers so that everyone has an unimpeded view. (4) Make sure listeners get the maximum benefit from each visual. (5) Make sure the aids don't distract from your message. (6) Don't talk to your aids. (7) Use progressive revelation. (8) Plan how you would handle equipment failure and other emergencies.

Although visuals are the most popular form of presentation aids, the other channels of communication—hearing, taste, smell, touch, and physical activity—can be quite effective. Whenever possible, use several channels to maximize listener understanding and retention.

Key Terms

bar graph, *153*

flip chart, *161*

handout, *162*

information chart, *154*

line graph, *152*

pictorial graph, *153*

pie graph, *153*

progressive revelation, *168*

table, *154*

transparency, *162*

visual presenter, *162*

Review Questions

1. List at least six types of visual aids.

2. List at least five media for presenting visual aids.

3. What is progressive revelation?

4. A *list of key ideas* is another name for which kind of chart?

5. Is it legal to use graphics from the Internet in a student speech in the classroom? Explain your answer.

6. The text recommends that you "aim for back-row comprehension." What does this mean and why is the advice necessary?

7. How can speakers test the visibility of their visuals?

8. Is it always a mistake for a speaker to wait until the conclusion of a presentation to show a visual or perform a demonstration? Explain your answer.

9. Why would it be a mistake to circulate a small photograph during your speech?

10. For the benefit of people with red-green color-blindness, which colors should never be placed next to each other?

Building Critical-Thinking Skills

1. "Some pictures may be worth a thousand words, but a picture of a thousand words isn't worth much," says corporate executive Don Keough. Explain what this means in terms of oral presentations.

2. At one website devoted to communication, public speakers are advised to distribute thought-provoking handouts at the beginning of a speech so that "if members of the audience get bored during the speech, they will have something interesting to read." Do you agree with this advice? Defend your position.

Building Teamwork Skills

1. Working in a group, create a scenario in which a sales representative gives a presentation that involves at least four of the six channels of communication.

2. In a group, create an outdoor sign that violates the guidelines of this chapter. Then create a new sign that corrects all the mistakes.

Appendix

How to Avoid "Death by PowerPoint"

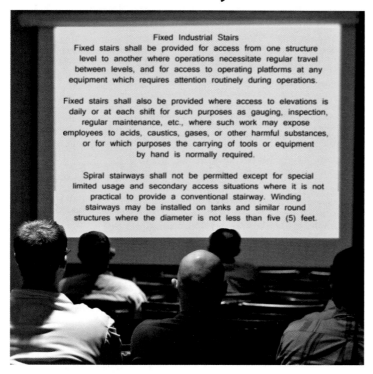

Imagine sitting in this audience as the speaker reads every word to you. Now imagine one hour of seeing 25 more slides just like this, all of them read to you. By the end of the presentation, you will be weary and bored.

This torment is known in the business and professional world as "Death by Power-Point."[1] According to *Industry Week,* "PowerPoint presentations have drugged more people than all the sleeping pills in history."[2]

Every day, in every part of the world, thousands of speakers display slides like the one above. The problem is not the PowerPoint software—it's the speakers. Why do they inflict so much misery? One reason is that they are self-centered instead of audience-centered.

If you focus primarily on yourself and your own convenience, PowerPoint seems like an easy way to create a speech. All you have to do is dump your information onto slides and read the material aloud. You don't even have to look at your audience.

If you are audience-centered, on the other hand, you will ask yourself, "How can I help my listeners understand and remember my key points?" If you decide that PowerPoint can help you to reach your goal, you will make sure that your slides are interesting and easy-to-grasp. During the presentation, instead of hiding behind the technology, you will occupy center stage. You will look directly at your listeners and stay connected to them.

On the following pages are six rules to help you avoid inflicting death by PowerPoint.

Rule 1: Don't assume you need PowerPoint

Problem

It is a mistake to think that every presentation should have Power-Point. Consider an Italian student who has compelling stories to tell about the Mafia, the Italian crime syndicate that murdered her father. If she uses a slide like this, she undermines the emotional intensity of her speech.

Solution

Speaking at a college in Italy, Rosanna Scopelliti urges students to work for the defeat of the Mafia, which murdered her father, a judge. She uses no PowerPoint. Instead, she paints pictures with words—vivid images more powerful than PowerPoint slides like the one above.

Rule 2: Choose images over text (when possible)

Favorite Color

• A survey throughout the world found that a majority of people picked blue as their favorite color.

• The earth is mostly blue, with the sky and the water, and the color blue goes well with anything.

Problem

Text is sometimes needed on a slide, but not in this case. When instructor Jan Caldwell sees a slide like this, she thinks, "I feel conflicted. Do you want me to read your slide or listen to you?"[3]

Solution

Display a photo while sharing your information orally. The slide makes your spoken words more engaging and memorable.

Using images also demonstrates to listeners that you care enough about them to do the extra work of locating interesting visuals.

Rule 3: Use text sparingly

Problem

While images are preferable to text, sometimes you may need to use words on the screen. But you make a mistake if you display large blocks of text, which are boring and fatiguing.

You make a second mistake if you read the text aloud—a common practice that one executive calls "a form of torture that should be banned by international law."

> You can avoid getting a cold if you exercise every day, make sure to wash your hands with soap and water many times a day, and don't touch your face because cold viruses enter the body through eyes, nose and mouth.

Solution

In this slide, text is okay because you want to help listeners remember the key points. Only a small amount of text is needed because you will elaborate with spoken words.

What about all the empty space on this slide? Is that bad? No, the space makes the key words stand out—and it makes the slide more inviting to the eye.

> **Prevent a cold**
>
> 1. Exercise regularly
>
> 2. Wash hands often
>
> 3. Don't touch face

Rule 4: Format text for easy reading

Bad Typography

- OVERUSE *of* fancy **fonts** *and* **different colors**
- Emphasizing with *italics* and <u>underlining</u>
- TOO MANY WORDS THAT USE ALL CAPITAL LETTERS

Problem

This slide hinders easy reading because (1) it uses too many different typefaces and colors, (2) it emphasizes with italics and underlining, and (3) it has too many words in all capital letters.

Good Typography

- Simple, readable font
- **Color** and **bold** for emphasis
- All capitals only for headings

Solution

Choose a typeface that is simple and easy to read, and avoid a lot of different colors. To emphasize a word or phrase, use a contrasting color or bold print, but avoid italics and underlining (which may be fine for printed material but impede readability on-screen). Use all capital words only for headings—excessive use is tiring to the eyes and hard to read.

Rule 5: Choose templates carefully

Problem

This template is busy and distracting. For a speech on cold-weather ailments, the green theme is inappropriate, evoking summer, not winter.

Other mistakes:
(1) Dull photo,
(2) More words than necessary, and (3) Text should never be super-imposed on an image if the words are hard to read.

Solution

You don't have to use templates, but if you decide to use one, make sure it has a simple, attractive design.

Instead of insert-ing a ho-hum photo, the speaker found an engaging image of a woman enjoying warmth and steam from a cup of hot tea. This helps to make the point that hot liquid promotes healing and is comforting.

Rule 6: Avoid visual clutter

Problem

This slide has too many small images. Your listeners might fail to follow what you are saying because their eyes are roving over the slide.

Some speakers try to solve the problem by using a "build"— displaying the first element, then adding the second, and so on. Though this is an improvement, you still end up with visual clutter.

Solution

Create six slides, one for each image. As a result, each image will be large, and it will be the focus of attention.

Does this approach add to the length of the presentation? No. Showing six simple slides should take no more time than showing one cluttered slide.

The Body of the Speech

OUTLINE

The Importance of Organization

Creating the Body

Devising Main Points

Organizing Main Points

Selecting Support Materials

Supplying Transitions

Simplifying the Process

OBJECTIVES

After studying this chapter, you should be able to:

1. Explain the importance of skillfully organizing the body of the speech.

2. Create the body of a speech by using a central idea to develop main points.

3. Identify and use five patterns of organization: chronological, spatial, cause–effect, problem–solution, and topical.

4. Identify and use four types of transitional devices: bridges, internal summaries, signposts, and spotlights.

5. Simplify the process of organizing speech material.

ASTRONAUT JOSÉ HERNÁNDEZ of Stockton, California, believes that when you make a presentation, it is a mistake to deliver a hodge-podge of unorganized information because listeners might get confused, and they might not understand and absorb key points. For this reason, he is careful to organize his material in a clear, logical manner.[1]

He shapes his material in several ways, most often using the *chronological* pattern (narrating a sequence of events from beginning to end) and the *spatial* (or physical space) pattern. For example, he explains the parts of his space suit from top to bottom. These two patterns are among the organizational techniques we will discuss in this chapter.

Before proceeding, let's look at where we stand in the speech-preparation process. In previous chapters, we discussed finding and developing materials such as statistics, examples, and visual aids. Now our task is to organize. We must take all our materials—our

bricks and mortar—and put them together to build a solid, coherent structure. This chapter will focus on organizing the body of a speech, Chapter 11 on creating introductions and conclusions, and Chapter 12 on putting all the parts together in an outline.

Astronaut José Hernández advises student speakers to organize their material in clear, logical patterns.

The Importance of Organization

A well-organized speech has vast advantages over a poorly organized one:

1. **A well-organized speech is easier to understand.** Wesley J. Smith, a former judge at a small-claims court in Los Angeles, says, "The most effective cases I heard involved people who presented their side of the issue as if they were telling a story. Their cases were organized logically, with a beginning, a middle, and an end. That not only kept my interest but helped me quickly understand the issues."[2]

2. **A well-organized speech is easier for the audience to remember.** In an experiment with a list of endangered species, one group of students memorized list A in Figure 10.1 and another group memorized list B. When tested two weeks later, the students who had learned list A recalled 56 percent of the terms, while the students who had learned list B recalled 81 percent.[3]

   List B is easier to remember because items are grouped in meaningful clusters. In a good speech, you should apply the same principle: Group your ideas in meaningful clusters that are easy to comprehend and recall.

3. **A well-organized speech is more likely to be believed.** Studies show that if you present a poorly organized speech, your listeners will find you less believable at the end than they did at the beginning of the speech.[4] If your speech is well-organized, however, you will come across as someone who is in full command of the facts, and therefore believable.

Creating the Body

A speech works best if it is divided into three well-developed sections: introduction, body, and conclusion. Does this mean that you should begin by working on the introduction? Not necessarily. Many experienced speakers find it easier to prepare the body first and then prepare the introduction. If you stop to think about it, this makes sense: How can you introduce the body until you know its full nature?

Figure 10.1

A list of endangered species is shown in two formats. Because it is organized in logical clusters, list B is easier to memorize and retain than list A.

List A	List B	
Indian python	**Mammals**	
Cheetah	Polar bear	Gorilla
Great white shark	Cheetah	Gray wolf
Gorilla		
Hawksbill turtle	**Birds**	
Hawaiian crow	California condor	Hawaiian crow
Gray wolf	Shore plover	Whooping crane
California condor		
Common sturgeon	**Reptiles**	
Polar bear	American crocodile	Indian python
Whooping crane	Hawksbill turtle	Painted terrapin
Giant catfish		
Shore plover	**Fish**	
Painted terrapin	Giant catfish	Cutthroat trout
Cutthroat trout	Great white shark	Common sturgeon
American crocodile		

Let's look at a good technique for creating the body.

Start with your *specific purpose,* which is the goal of your speech, and your *central idea,* which is the key concept that you want to get across to your audience. (If you are unsure about these terms, please review Chapter 5 before proceeding in this chapter.)

Suppose you hear a news report about a charity that has been ripping off donors, and you decide to devote your next speech to charity fraud. After reading articles and conducting interviews, you come up with the following purpose statement:

Specific Purpose: To persuade my audience to be cautious in donating to charity

Next, ask yourself, "What is my essential message? What big idea do I want to leave in the minds of my listeners?" The answer is your central idea. Here is one possibility:

Central Idea: Before donating to a charity, make sure it is honest.

This central idea is your speech boiled down to one sentence. It is what you want your listeners to remember if they forget everything else.

The next step is to ask yourself this question: "How can I get my audience to understand and accept my central idea?"

The best way to get the central idea across to your audience is to implant in their minds a few **main points** that are based on the central idea. In our charities example, here are three main points that could be made:

main points

key assertions made by a speaker to develop his or her central idea

I. Some charities give only a tiny sum to the needy.
II. These charities channel most of their money to salaries and gifts for staff members.
III. Potential donors should look for warnings posted on the Internet by watchdog groups that monitor charities.

The first and second main points focus on the problem (charity rip-offs), and the third main point provides a solution (investigation on the Internet).

By themselves the main points are not sufficient. Listeners would want more information, so you need to develop each main point with support materials such as narratives, examples, and statistics. For instance, if your listeners heard main point I, they would say, "Well, okay, can you give some examples?" Here are a couple of examples you could use:

- The *New York Times* reported that one man set up a charity to help wounded veterans, raising more than $168 million in two years. But he gave only 25 percent to help vets.[5]
- The *Knoxville News-Sentinel* revealed that a local charity called "A Child's Dream" raised $3 million to grant the wishes of sick and dying children, but only 3 percent of the funds were actually given to children.[6]

For the second main point, you could describe the lavish lifestyles of the owners of rip-off charities. For the third main point, you could discuss websites that post lists of fraudulent charities. At the end of your speech, you could give all listeners a handout containing the Web addresses so that they could pursue their own investigations later.

To see an overview of the process we have just discussed, take a look at Figure 10.2, which shows the key elements of a speech aimed at persuading listeners to eat fish frequently. The specific purpose leads to the central idea, which is sustained by two main points. The main points are not likely to be believed by the audience unless they are supported by solid information such as statistics and testimony from experts. For example, the speaker could cite clinical tests by reliable medical researchers that demonstrate the value of omega-3 acids (found in fish) for the brain and the heart.

Figure 10.2
Speech preparation should start with a specific purpose and a central idea. Then the central idea is developed by two or three (or occasionally four) main points, which in turn are strengthened by a variety of support materials, such as examples and statistics.

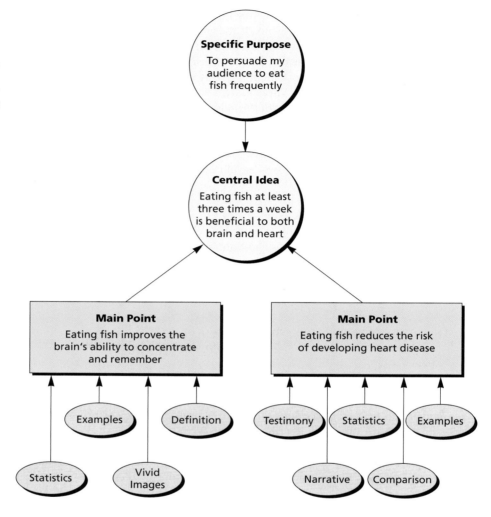

Devising Main Points

"Do I need more than one main point?" some students ask. Yes. If you have only one main point to develop your central idea, you have a weak structure, like a bridge that has only one pillar to hold it up. If you provide only one main point, your listeners have only *one* reason to believe your central idea. If you give them two or three main points, you multiply your chances of convincing them.

"How many main points should I have?" you may be asking. To answer this and other questions, let's examine some guidelines for refining main points.

Limit the Number of Main Points

A common mistake of public speakers is to cram too many points into a speech. They do this because they are approaching the speech from their own viewpoint and not from the viewpoint of the listeners. If you ask yourself, "How much information can

I squeeze into the five minutes allotted?" you are approaching the speech from your own viewpoint. To approach from the audience's viewpoint, you should ask, "How much information can the audience comfortably pay attention to, understand, and remember?" Audiences simply cannot absorb too much new information. You should know this from your own experience; you can probably recall many speakers (including some teachers) who overwhelmed you with a barrage of ideas, facts, and figures. Don't be reluctant to cut and trim your material.

Exactly how many main points should you have? In a short speech (5 to 10 minutes), you should limit yourself to two or three (or occasionally four) main points. That is as much as an audience can absorb. In a longer speech, you could have as many as five main points, but most experienced speakers cover only two or three, regardless of the length of their speech. It is a rare—and usually ineffective—veteran speaker who attempts six or more.

Having 3 main points is better than having 10.

Restrict Each Main Point to a Single Idea

Each main point should focus on just one idea. Consider the following:

> *Poor:*   I. Some employees who are diagnosed with cancer lose their jobs, and some of them lose their health-insurance coverage.

> *Better:*   I. Some employees who are diagnosed with cancer lose their jobs.
>
> II. Some lose their health-insurance coverage.

The first set makes the mistake of covering two issues; the second set splits the material into two distinct points.

Avoid Announcements

Rather than simply announcing a topic, each main point should make an assertion, a forthright declaration of the idea that you want to convey. Imagine that you create the following:

> *Poor:*   I'll talk about hot-dog headaches.

What about it? What's your point? You have done nothing but announce your topic.

> *Better:*   Sodium nitrites contained in hot dogs cause many people to suffer headaches.

Now you have made a point—a clear assertion of what you are driving at.

Your Thoughts

Most public speaking experts recommend that you use complete sentences to create your central idea and main points. Why do you think this advice is given?

Customize Points for Each Audience

As you play with ideas in your search for main points, ask yourself, "What main points would work best with this particular audience?" If you tailor your speech to each audience's needs and desires, you may end up using different main points with different audiences.

Let's say you plan to give speeches in your community aimed at persuading people to take up nature photography as a hobby. If you talk to a group of college students, you can anticipate that they will raise an objection: photography is too expensive. So you create a main point—"Photography is not out of reach for people with modest incomes"—and devote a good portion of your speech to giving specific examples and prices. If, however, you speak to an audience of wealthy individuals who could easily afford any kind of camera, this point may be unnecessary.

Another potential main point is that nature photography teaches a person to see the world with fresh eyes—to find "splendor in the grass," the visual glories that abound in nature for those who develop keen perception. This would be a good point to make with an audience of urban dwellers who rarely explore the outdoors. But if your audience is a birdwatchers' society, this point is probably unnecessary; these people have already trained their eyes to detect nature's nuances.

Use Parallel Language Whenever Possible

parallel language
equivalent grammatical forms to express equivalent ideas

Parallel language means that you use the same grammatical forms throughout a sentence or a paragraph. Read the following sentence aloud: "Joe enjoys hunting, fishing, and to camp." There is nothing wrong with the sentence grammatically, but it doesn't sound as pleasant to the ear as this version: "Joe enjoys hunting, fishing, and camping."

Rather than the discord of *-ing, -ing,* plus *to,* our ears prefer the rhythm of *-ing, -ing, -ing,* as in the second sentence.

Suppose that you started with the following:

Specific Purpose: To persuade my audience to swim for exercise

Central Idea: Swimming is an ideal exercise because it reduces nervous tension, avoids injuries, and builds endurance.

Now decide which of the following sets of main points would be more effective:

First Set: I. You can work off a lot of nervous tension while swimming.

II. Muscle and bone injuries, common with other sports, are not a problem with swimming.

III. Swimming builds endurance.

Second Set: I. Swimming reduces nervous tension.

II. Swimming avoids muscle and bone injuries.

III. Swimming builds endurance.

Just as parallel lines are pleasing to the eye, parallel language is pleasing to the ear.

The second set is preferable because it follows a parallel grammatical form throughout (the noun *swimming* followed by a verb). This consistent arrangement may not be practical in every speech, but you should strive for parallelism whenever possible.

Organizing Main Points

Main points should be organized in a logical, easy-to-follow pattern. Five of the most popular patterns used by speakers are chronological, spatial, cause–effect, problem–solution, and topical.

Chronological Pattern

chronological pattern
an arrangement of information in a time sequence

In the **chronological pattern,** you arrange your main points in a *time* sequence—what occurs first, what occurs second, and so on. If, for example, you are describing a process, you can use the chronological pattern to show the step-by-step progression. For an illustration, see Figure 10.3.

How to Treat a Bee Sting

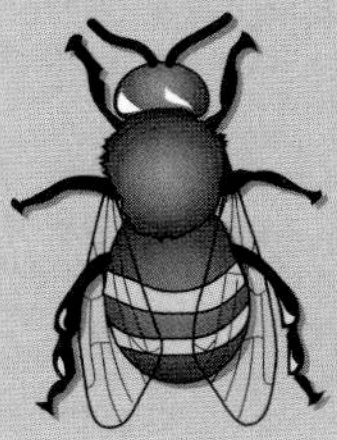

Step 1   Get the stinger out quickly.

Step 2   Wash sting area with soap and water.

Step 3   Apply ice pack for 15 minutes.

Figure 10.3
Chronological Pattern
The process of treating a bee sting is a chronological pattern (or time sequence)—what to do first, second, and third.

The chronological pattern is a logical choice for a speech dealing with periods of time in history. If, for example, you were speaking on the history of immigration in the United States, you could divide your subject into centuries, from the seventeenth to the twenty-first.

If you were speaking on the life of a person, you might divide your speech according to the stages of life, as in the following example:

Specific Purpose: To inform my listeners of the heroism of Harriet Tubman, a leading 19th-century abolitionist

Central Idea: Harriet Tubman was a courageous woman who escaped from slavery and then returned to the South to rescue others.

Main Points:

(*Childhood*)   I. Born a slave on a plantation in Maryland, Tubman suffered many whippings while growing up.

(*Youth*)   II. She escaped to freedom by using the Underground Railroad.

(*Adulthood*)   III. Wearing various disguises, Tubman smuggled over 300 slaves to safe havens from 1850 to 1860.

Spatial Pattern

In the **spatial pattern,** you organize items according to the way in which they relate to each other in *physical space*—top to bottom, left to right, north to south, inside to outside, and so on. If you were speaking on the solar system, for example, you could discuss the sun first, then move outward in space to Mercury, Venus, Earth, Mars, and so on. Here is an example in which the speaker divides a car into space-related sections:

spatial pattern
an arrangement of information in terms of physical space, such as top to bottom

Specific Purpose: To tell my audience how to inspect a used car before deciding whether to buy it

Central Idea: If you examine a used car carefully and critically, you can avoid buying a "lemon."

Main Points: I. Inspect the condition of the body of the car.

II. Inspect the condition of the motor.

III. Inspect the condition of the interior.

For an example of the spatial pattern as used from top to bottom, see Figure 10.4.

Figure 10.4
Spatial Pattern

For a discussion of the Eiffel Tower, a speaker could use the spatial (physical space) pattern, progressing from top to bottom. (Or the tower could be discussed from bottom to top.)

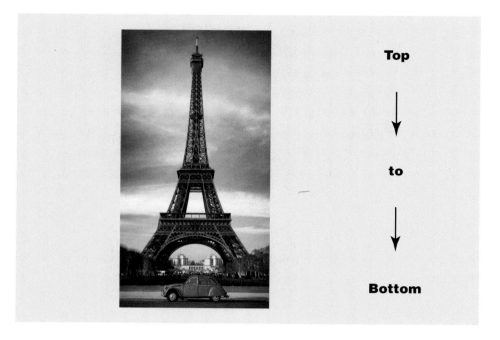

Cause–Effect Pattern

In some speeches, you are concerned with why something happens or happened—a cause-and-effect relationship. For example, some people refuse to ride in elevators because they have an inordinate fear of closed spaces. Their claustrophobia is the *cause* and their refusal to ride in elevators is the *effect*. For an illustration of a **cause–effect pattern** in a speech, see Figure 10.5.

Sometimes it is more effective to start with the effects and then analyze the causes, as in this case:

cause–effect pattern

a scheme that links outcomes (effects) and the reasons for them (causes)

Specific Purpose:	To explain to my listeners why many people are unable to get bank loans for a new car or house
Central Idea:	If you are denied a loan for a new car or house, it could be because you have been incorrectly branded as a poor credit risk by credit-rating companies.

Figure 10.5
Cause–Effect Pattern

For a speech about insufficient sleep, a speaker could show a cause-and-effect relationship.

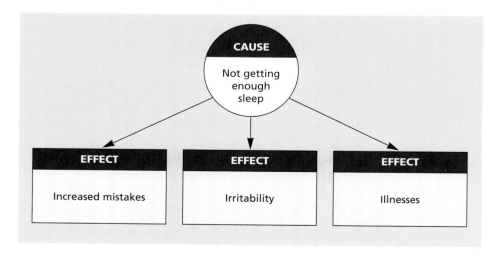

Main Points:

(*Effect*)   I. Many people are barred from getting loans for a new car or house without ever knowing the reason.

(*Cause*)   II. The credit-rating companies that keep computerized files on 90 percent of Americans frequently make mistakes without the consumer ever knowing.

In this case, putting the effect first is good strategy because it makes the listeners receptive to the rest of the speech—they are curious to know what caused the situation.

Problem–Solution Pattern

A much-used device for persuasive speeches is the **problem–solution pattern,** which divides a speech into two main sections: a problem and its solution. Here is an example:

Specific Purpose: To persuade my audience to support "pet therapy" for lonely elderly people in nursing homes

Central Idea: Contact with a pet can decrease the loneliness and improve the physical and emotional health of elderly people in nursing homes.

Main Points:

(*Problem*)   I. Many elderly people in nursing homes are lonely and depressed—emotional states that harm their physical health.

(*Solution*)   II. Researchers have discovered that contact with a pet improves the elderly person's physical and emotional health.

This pattern has the advantage of simplicity. You convince the listeners that a particular problem exists, and then you tell them how it can be solved. See Figure 10.6.

problem–solution pattern

an arrangement of information that explores a problem and then offers a solution

Figure 10.6
Problem–Solution Pattern

A speech on how to feel good mentally and physically could discuss a problem (depression and stress) and offer a solution (exercise).

Topical Pattern

In the **topical pattern,** you divide your central idea into components or categories, using logic and common sense as your guides.

Thus, a speech on the symphonic orchestra could be divided into three sections: string instruments, wind instruments, and percussion instruments. A speech on job interviews could be divided into three types of interviews: personal, video, and computer. See Figure 10.7 for another example.

Here is a portion of an outline that illustrates the topical pattern:

Specific Purpose: To inform my audience of the two kinds of sleep that all people experience

Central Idea: The two kinds of sleep that all people experience at alternating times during the night are NREM (non-rapid-eye-movement) sleep and REM (rapid-eye-movement) sleep.

Main Points: I. NREM (non-rapid-eye-movement) sleep is the period in which a person does very little dreaming.

II. REM (rapid-eye-movement) sleep is the period in which a person usually dreams.

A variation of the topical pattern is sometimes called the **statement-of-reasons pattern.** The speaker subdivides an idea by showing reasons for it, as in the following example:

Specific Purpose: To persuade my listeners that telephone companies should use alternatives to cellular phone towers

Central Idea: Telephone companies should be required to place their cellular antennas on buildings and trees rather than on freestanding towers.

Main Points:

(First reason)   I. Cellular phone towers are huge and ugly.

(Second reason)   II. Cellular telephone antennas work as effectively on church steeples, tall trees, and high buildings as they do on freestanding towers.

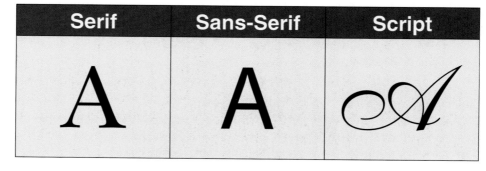

Figure 10.7
Topical Pattern

A speech on typefaces could be divided into three major styles. Serif letters have small embellishments, such as lines projecting from the main stroke of a letter, while sans-serif letters have no embellishments. Script letters simulate fancy handwriting.

(Third reason)   III. Steeples, trees, and buildings are easily available because many churches, landowners, and businesses desire the fees that telephone companies pay for antenna placement.

Note of caution: Some students make the mistake of thinking that the topical pattern is a formless bag into which anything can be dumped. Though you have a great deal of liberty to organize your points in whatever order you choose, you still must apply logic—by, for example, arranging your points from least important to most important, or separating your material into three major subdivisions.

Selecting Support Materials

In the preceding sections, we concentrated on main points, but main points by themselves are not enough for the body of a speech. You also need support materials—such as examples, narratives, testimony, and statistics—to develop and amplify your main points. As discussed in Chapter 8, support materials help your audience to understand and remember main points.

To see how support materials can be developed for main points, let's take a look at an outline of the body of a speech by student speaker Wendy Trujillo, who uses the statement-of-reasons pattern to give two reasons why cotton swabs should never be used for cleaning ears.[7] The introduction and the conclusion for this speech are printed in Chapter 11.

> *General Purpose:*   To persuade
>
> *Specific Purpose:*   To persuade my audience to avoid using cotton swabs in their ears
>
> *Central Idea:*   For cleaning ears, cotton swabs are dangerous and ineffective.

Your Thoughts

Which pattern would a speaker probably choose for a speech on how society's obsession with thinness has led to unhealthy weight-loss methods and eating disorders?

Are cotton swabs dangerous?

SPEECH	COMMENTARY

BODY

I. Cotton swabs can cause injury.
    A. Cotton swabs send more people to the hospital than razor blades or shavers.
        1. Over 400,000 Americans visit hospital emergency departments for ear injuries each year. (Centers for Disease Control and Prevention)
        2. Most of the injuries are caused by cotton swabs.
        3. These injuries can impair hearing.
    B. Some ear injuries are severe.
        1. New York Giants football player Chase Blackburn nearly ruptured his eardrum in the locker room while cleaning his ear with a cotton swab.
        2. He fell to the floor, bleeding, and lost his hearing for a few weeks.

The body has two main points, each giving a reason to avoid swabs.

Trujillo cites **statistics** from a trustworthy source.

A **narrative** (or story) helps the audience to visualize the risks involved.

(continued)

The speaker gives an **example** to support her point.

C. In a few cases, using cotton swabs leads to death.
   1. Daniel St. Pierre of Montreal, Canada, died in March, 2007.
   2. He suffered complications caused by the accidental piercing of his eardrum while he was using a cotton swab.

(*Transition:* Now let's turn to the second reason for not using swabs on your ears.)

II. Cotton swabs are ineffective.

An **analogy** between a swab and a broom helps to show the futility of using swabs to clean ears.

   A. Experts say that cleaning your ears with a cotton swab is like using a broom on a dirt floor.
      1. It just moves things around.
      2. It doesn't really get rid of most of the gunk.
      3. It pushes the gunk further down the ear canal, where it can create a problem.

An expert's **testimony** bolsters the speaker's argument.

   B. If you have a lot of earwax or some object lodged in your ear, a physician is far more effective than a swab. (Ear specialist Dr. Cynthia Steele)
      1. A physician has safe techniques, equipment, and liquids.
      2. Dr. Steele shows patients the warning label on every box of cotton swabs: "Do not insert into the ear canal."

If possible, distribute your supporting materials evenly. In other words, don't put all your support under point I and leave nothing to bolster point II. This does not mean, however, that you should mechanically place the same number of supporting points under every main point. You have to consider *quality* as well as *quantity*. A single powerful anecdote may be all that is required to illustrate one point, whereas five minor supports may be needed for another point.

When you are trying to decide how many supporting points to place underneath a main point, use this rule of thumb: Have enough supporting points to adequately explain or bolster the main point, but not so many that you become tedious and repetitious.

Supplying Transitions

transition

an expression that links ideas and shows the relationship between them

Words, phrases, or sentences that show logical connections between ideas or thoughts are called **transitions.** They help the listeners stay with you as you move from one part of your speech to the next. To get an idea of how transitions work, take a look at two paragraphs, the first of which has no transitions:

Poor: Olive oil is used extensively in Mediterranean cooking. It never became popular in Latin America. Olive trees can grow in Mexico and coastal regions of South America. The colonial rulers in Spain did not want anyone competing against Spain's farmers. They banned the production of olive oil in Latin America. The oil had to be imported. It was very expensive.

Now let's add transitions (shown in bold print):

Better: Olive oil is used extensively in Mediterranean cooking. **However,** it never became popular in Latin America. Olive trees can grow in Mexico and coastal regions of South America, **but**

the colonial rulers in Spain did not want anyone competing against Spain's farmers, **so** they banned the production of olive oil in Latin America. The oil had to be imported **and therefore** was very expensive.

The transitions obviously make the second paragraph superior.

In a speech, transitions clarify the relationship between your ideas, thereby making them easy to comprehend. They serve as signals to help the listeners follow your train of thought. Here is a sampling of the many transitional words or phrases in the English language:

- To signal addition: *and, also, furthermore, moreover, in addition*
- To signal time: *soon, then, later, afterward, meanwhile*
- To signal contrast: *however, but, yet, nevertheless, instead, meanwhile, although*
- To signal examples: *for example, to illustrate, for instance*
- To signal conclusions: *in summary, therefore, consequently, as a result*
- To signal concession: *although it is true that, of course, granted*

In public speaking, special types of transitions can be employed to help your listener follow your remarks. Let us look at four of them: bridges, internal summaries, signposts, and spotlights.

Your Thoughts

In a speech, transitions must be more prominent than they are in a book. Why?

Bridges

In crossing a bridge, a person goes from one piece of land to another. In giving a speech, the speaker can build **bridges** to tell the listeners of the terrain they are leaving behind and the terrain they are about to enter.

Imagine that you had the following as your first main point in a speech on workplace violence:

  I. Violence in the workplace has increased in recent years.

You give examples and statistics to back up this point, and now you are ready for your second main point:

 II. Workplace violence can be reduced if managers and employees are trained in conflict resolution.

How can you go from point I to point II? You could simply finish with point I and begin point II, but that would be too abrupt. It would fail to give the listeners time to change mental gears. A smoother way is to refer back to the first main point at the same time you are pointing forward to the second:

> Although workplace violence has increased dramatically, the situation is not hopeless. There is a way to reduce the number of incidents—a way that has proven successful in many companies throughout the world.

This is a successful bridge because it smoothly and gracefully takes your listeners from point I to point II. It also has the virtue of stimulating their curiosity about the next part of the speech.

bridge
a transitional device that links what went before with the next part of a speech

In a speech, a bridge takes listeners smoothly from one idea to another.

Tips for Your Career

Test and Verify Your Material

In 2010, NBC Today Show anchor Ann Curry gave a commencement address at Wheaton College in Norton, Massachusetts. She spent a lot of time preparing the speech, and "at the last moment," she says, "I decided to include a mention of all the great people who graduated from the school." So she used Google to find the names Dennis Hastert, Billy Graham, and Wes Craven. After she delivered her speech, she was told that she had made a blunder: none of those people had gone to the Wheaton College where she spoke. They had graduated from another Wheaton College—in Illinois. The next day, saying that she was "mortified," Curry apologized to the college and the graduating class.

To avoid mistakes like this, it's a good idea to test the strength and accuracy of your speech in advance. Here are three techniques:

- Do an "expert check." Discuss your material with someone who is knowledgeable about your subject, so that he or she can point out any errors or omissions. This is what Ann Curry should have done. She later acknowledged that she erred in failing to verify her information with school officials beforehand.
- Try out your material on friends or relatives. Victoria Vance, a hospital nutritionist who gives talks in her community on diet and nutrition, tests her ideas with her husband and teenage children at the dinner table. "I tell them, 'I'm going to give a speech at a high school next week. Here's what I plan to say.' Then I casually tell them the main points of my speech. Occasionally one of the kids will break in with something like, 'But, Mom, are you saying that *all* fast food is bad for you?' That tells me the places in the speech where I need to add some more explanations or examples."
- In regard to each main point, think of the typical people who will be in your audience and ask yourself, "How will they react to this?" Then shape your material accordingly. If your imaginary listeners say, "How do you know this is true?" give the name and credentials of the expert from whom you derived your material. If they ask, "What do you mean by that?" give them an explanation. If they say, "Who cares?" show them the importance of your subject.

Internal Summaries

At the end of a baseball game, announcers always give a summary of the game. But during the game itself, they occasionally give a summary of what has taken place up to the present moment ("We're in the middle of the fifth inning; Detroit is leading Milwaukee 4 to 3 on a grand-slam homer by . . ."). Though this summary is designed primarily for the viewers who have tuned in late, it is also appreciated by the fans who have been watching the entire game, because it gives them a feeling of security and confidence—a sense of knowing the "main facts." You can achieve the same effect in a speech. During the body of a speech, when you finish an important section, you may want to spend a few moments summarizing your ideas so that they are clear and understandable. This device, called an **internal summary,** is especially helpful if you have been discussing ideas that are complicated or abstract. An internal summary can be combined with a bridge to make an excellent transition, as follows:

internal summary
a concise review of material covered during the body of a speech

> [*Internal summary*] By now I hope I've convinced you that all animal bites should be reported to a doctor or health official immediately because of the possibility of rabies. [*bridge*] While you're waiting for an ambulance or for an examination by a doctor, there is one other important thing you should do.

Signposts

Just as signposts on a road tell motorists their location, **signposts** in a speech tell listeners where they are or where they are headed. If you gave a speech on how to treat a cold, you could say, "Here are three things you should do the next time you catch a cold." Then the audience would find it easy to follow your points if you said, "First, you should . . . Second, you should . . . Third, you should . . ." Using these signposts is much more effective than linking your points by saying, "Also . . ." or "Another point is . . ."

signpost
an explicit statement of the place that a speaker has reached

Spotlights

Spotlights are transitional devices that alert the listeners that something important will soon appear. Here are some examples:

spotlight
a device that alerts listeners to important points

- Now we come to the most important thing I have to tell you.
- What I'm going to explain now will help you understand the rest of the speech.
- If you take with you only one idea from this speech . . .

Spotlights can build up anticipation: "And now I come to an idea that can mean extra money in your pocket . . ." Or: "If you want to feel healthier and happier, listen to the advice of Dr. Julia Brunswick . . ."

When you choose transitional devices, remember that your listeners are totally unfamiliar with your speech, so try to put yourself in their shoes at each juncture. Ask yourself, "How can I lead the listener from one point to another in a way that is logical and smooth?"

Simplifying the Process

Organizing bits and pieces of material into a coherent, logical speech can be a difficult task, but it can be simplified if you use the following method:

1. **Survey all your material.** Bring together and examine your personal observations, interview notes, research notes, and visual aids.

2. **Choose an organizational method.** Three options are recommended:

   - **Computers.** Most word processing programs permit split screens, so that you can have notes in one window and an outline in another, making it easy to look over your notes and transform them into items for your outline.
   - **Stick-on slips.** This method uses file folders of different colors, with a different-colored folder for each major part of the speech. Stick-on slips (such as the 3M Post-it™ slips) are placed inside the folders.
   - **Cards.** This method is similar to the stick-on slips, except that index cards are used. The cards can be kept together by a rubber band or stored in a file folder.

   All three options give you flexibility. You can easily move items around, add extra material, and delete unimportant points. Items can be spread out—stick-on slips in file folders, computer entries on a screen, and cards on a tabletop. This procedure lets you see the "big picture"—the overall architecture of your speech.

3. **Limit each note to just one idea.** To make the method work effectively, *you must use a separate slip, card, or computer entry for each point.* This will make it easy to move items around.

4. **Experiment with different sequences.** Try several ways of arranging your material until you find a good sequence, a smooth flow that will be easy for the audience to follow. Marcia Yudkin, a business trainer from Boston, uses the card system, but her advice can be applied to stick-on slips and computer screens as well:

> Sit in a comfortable chair and shuffle those ideas, asking yourself questions like, "What if I start with this, and move on to this, then this . . . ?" You're looking for a smooth, natural flow from each point to the next. Some sort of sequence will eventually emerge from this exercise. Don't get perturbed if you end up with extra cards that refuse to fit in; any leftover material might be perfect for the question-and-answer period after your speech, or for another presentation.[8]

5. **Transfer your material to a formal outline.** Once you have your information arranged, it's a good idea to transfer it to a formal outline—as a way to gain control over it and to test its strength and continuity. Your instructor may have a required format for the outline. If not, I suggest you use the format shown in Chapter 12.

Resources for Review and Skill Building

Summary

A well-organized speech is more understandable, credible, and memorable than a poorly organized one.

The body of the speech should be organized with two or three (occasionally four) main points that develop the central idea of the speech. Some guidelines for main points: (1) Restrict each main point to a single idea. (2) Avoid announcements. (3) Customize points for each audience. (4) Use parallel language whenever possible.

Arrange the main points in a logical pattern, such as *chronological,* in which main points are placed in a time sequence; *spatial,* in which items are arranged in terms of physical space; *cause–effect,* in which causes and effects are juxtaposed; *problem–solution,* in which a problem is explained and a solution offered; or *topical,* in which a central idea is divided into components.

Next, select support materials to back up the main points, and then supply transitions to help the listeners stay with you as you move from one part of your speech to the next. Common types of transitions are bridges, internal summaries, signposts, and spotlights.

To simplify the task of organizing material, use one of these three options: stick-on slips, computers, or cards. Put one item on each slip, computer entry, or card so that you can easily add, delete, and rearrange your material.

Key Terms

bridge, *193*

cause–effect pattern, *188*

chronological pattern, *186*

internal summary, *194*

main points, *183*

parallel language, *186*

problem–solution pattern, *189*

signpost, *195*

spatial pattern, *187*

spotlight, *195*

statement-of-reasons pattern, *190*

topical pattern, *190*

transition, *192*

Review Questions

1. How many main points should you have in a speech?

2. How many ideas should be represented in each main point?

3. What is meant by the advice to "customize points for each audience"?

4. Which pattern of organization would be best suited for a speech on the solar system?

5. Which pattern of organization would be ideal for a speech on food contamination and how the problem can be corrected?

6. Which pattern of organization would be best suited for a speech on the three major reasons why businesses declare bankruptcy?

7. Why are transitions important in a speech?

8. In terms of speech organization, what is an internal summary?

9. Describe the transitional device called *bridge.*

10. Describe the transitional device called *spotlight.*

Building Critical-Thinking Skills

1. Which organizational pattern is used in the following:

   Specific Purpose: To inform my listeners how to soundproof a room

   Central Idea: A room can be insulated so that sounds do not penetrate.

   Main Points:

   (Top) I. The ceiling can be covered by acoustic tile and a tapestry to block sounds from above.

   (Middle) II. The walls can be covered with ceiling-to-floor tapestries (and heavy, lined drapes for windows) to block noise from outside.

   (Bottom) III. The floor can be covered with acoustic padding and wall-to-wall carpet to block sounds from below.

2. Which organizational pattern is used in the following:

   Specific Purpose: To tell my listeners how to revive a person who is in danger of drowning

   Central Idea: To revive a person who is in danger of drowning, you should follow three simple procedures.

   Main Points:

   (First) I. With the victim on his or her back, tilt the head back so that the chin juts upward.

   (Second) II. Give mouth-to-mouth resuscitation until the victim breathes regularly again.

   (Third) III. Place the victim on his or her stomach with the head facing sideways.

Building Teamwork Skills

1. Working in a group, examine the following scrambled statements and decide which is the central idea and which are the main points. (One item below is a central idea and the other two are main points to develop the central idea.) Discuss what kinds of support materials would be needed under each main point.

   a. Many U.S. companies that have instituted the 30-hour workweek report higher job satisfaction and performance with no loss of profits.

   b. A 6-hour day/30-hour workweek should be the standard for full-time employees in the United States.

   c. All Western European countries have fewer working hours than the United States.

2. In a group, discuss which organizational pattern would be most effective for the following speech topics.

   a. Why most fatal car accidents occur

   b. Three types of working dogs

   c. How to gift wrap a present

   d. Stalking—and what can be done to stop it

   e. The Amazon River

Introductions and Conclusions

OUTLINE

Introductions

Conclusions

Sample Introduction and Conclusion

OBJECTIVES

After studying this chapter, you should be able to:

1. Formulate effective attention material for the introductions of your speeches.

2. Formulate effective orienting material for the introductions of your speeches.

3. Create effective conclusions for your speeches.

COURTROOM BATTLES ARE LIKE DRAMAS, with three distinct parts:

- Beginning (opening statement)
- Middle (examination of evidence)
- End (closing argument)

While all three parts are important, most attorneys say that their opening and closing statements to the jury usually determine whether they win or lose a case.[1] "When you first talk to the jury, you've got to make a favorable impression and win their empathy immediately," says Michelle Roberts, a defense attorney in Washington, DC. Later, near the end of the trial, "your closing argument must be powerful and persuasive."[2]

In speeches outside the courtroom, the stakes are rarely so high: no one will be forced to go to prison or pay a million dollars in damages if the introduction and the conclusion are weak. Nevertheless, these two parts have great importance. If you don't have a lively introduction, you can lose your audience. "People have remote controls in their heads

today," says Myrna Marofsky, an Eden Prairie, Minnesota, business executive. "If you don't catch their interest, they just click you off."[3] And a conclusion that is weak or clumsy can mar the effectiveness of what otherwise might have been a good speech.

Prosecutor David Walgren presents arguments in a manslaughter trial in Los Angeles. For Walgren and other attorneys, their opening and closing remarks to a jury often determine whether they win or lose a case.

Ethical Issues Quiz

Bert is preparing a classroom speech about an urban street artist who is famous for his graffiti. To grab the audience's attention, he is thinking about using a shocking opener—a desecrated cross, which Bert thinks is a perfect example of the artist's innovative technique. Should Bert show the image?

A. No, he should choose an image that would be unlikely to offend the audience.
B. He should show the image without explanation and allow audience members to form their own opinions about the artist's work.
C. He should show the image, but warn listeners that it might be offensive to some people, and ask them to try to stay open-minded and focus on the artist's technique instead of the subject matter.

For the answer, see the last page of this chapter.

Introductions

The introduction to your speech has two main goals: first, to capture and hold your audience's attention and interest, and second, to prepare your audience intellectually and psychologically for the body of the speech. Let's examine each goal in greater detail.

Gain Attention and Interest

If you were sitting in an audience, would you want to listen to a speech that begins with: "I'd like to talk to you today about the fishing industry"?

The subject sounds dull. You might say to yourself, "Who cares?" and let your attention drift to something else.

Now imagine that you were sitting in the audience when student speaker Julie O'Mara began a speech with these words:

> Good news, bad news.
>> The good news: Scientists estimate that the oceans of the world contain as many as 30 million species of animals, and most of them have not yet been discovered.
>> Now the bad news: Half of these creatures may soon become extinct because of overfishing in the sea.[4]

Hearing this information about overfishing, you would have a hard time turning your attention away. O'Mara's technique was to use alarming statistics as an attention-grabber.

An attention-grabber is needed because of an unfortunate fact: audiences don't automatically give every speaker their full, respectful attention. As you begin a speech, you may find that some listeners are engaged in whispered conversations with their neighbors (and they don't necessarily stop in midsentence when you start speaking); some are looking at you but their minds are far away, floating in a daydream or enmeshed in a personal problem. So your task is clear: grab their attention when you start talking.

But grabbing their attention is not enough: your introduction must also make listeners want to hear the rest of your speech. Some speakers grab attention by telling a joke, but a joke creates no interest in the rest of the speech. In O'Mara's speech, her provocative opener made the typical listener want to learn more: "How can we stop mass extinction in the seas?"

attention material
the part of the introduction designed to capture audience interest

In this book, "grabbers" are called **attention material,** which should always be the first part of your introduction. Let's examine some of the more common varieties. Sometimes two or more grabbers can be combined.

Relate a Story

Telling a story is one of the most effective ways to begin a speech, because people love to listen to narrative accounts. Cynthia Wray of Western Carolina University began a speech with this story:

> A few years ago, over 100 third-graders were on a field trip at Chicago's O'Hare International Airport. Suddenly, an 87-year-old man lost control of his car and slammed into the group. One child was killed, and 67 children and 10 adults were injured.[5]

Wray went on to argue that older drivers should be tested frequently and denied a license if found to be impaired. As Wray demonstrates, a story should always provide an easy and natural entry into the rest of the speech.

Besides the real-life story, you can use a **hypothetical illustration,** as demonstrated by Jerome David Smith, an attorney, who used the following hypothetical illustration in a speech:

> One day you become angry over the nasty pollution of a river near your home, so you sit down and write a letter to the editor of your local newspaper. The letter is a scathing attack on a corporation that you believe is responsible for ruining the river. Two weeks later, you get a letter from the corporation's attorney informing you that you are being sued for $100,000 for "harming the reputation, prestige, and credibility of the corporation." Does this sound incredible? Can this happen in a country that celebrates freedom of speech? Yes, it can happen . . .

In the rest of his speech, he explained how lawsuits have become a way for companies and public officials to retaliate against criticism.

Ask a Question

Asking a question can be an effective way to intrigue your listeners and encourage them to think about your subject matter as you discuss it. There are two kinds of questions that you can use as attention material: the rhetorical question and the overt-response question.

With a **rhetorical question,** you don't want or expect the listeners to answer overtly by raising their hands or responding out loud. Instead, you want to trigger their curiosity by challenging them to think about your topic. For example:

> With powerful radio signals being beamed into outer space at this very moment, is there any realistic chance that during our lifetime we human beings will establish radio contact with other civilizations in the universe?

Not only does such a question catch the attention of the listeners, but it also makes them want to hear more. It entices them into listening to your speech for the answer to the question.

hypothetical illustration
an imaginary scenario that illuminates a point

rhetorical question
a question asked solely to stimulate interest and not to elicit a reply

Top Tourist Destination?
a. China
b. United States
c. France
d. Spain

This PowerPoint slide was used as an attention-getter. The correct answer is "c"—France is the world's most visited country, according to the U.N. World Tourism Organization. The U.S. is second, China is third, and Spain is fourth.

overt-response question

a question asked to elicit a
direct, immediate reply

With an **overt-response question**, you want the audience to reply by raising their hands or answering out loud. For example, student speaker Meredith Bollinger began a speech by asking:

> There is only one Olympic sport in which men and women compete against each other head to head in direct confrontation. Which sport am I talking about?

One listener guessed water polo—wrong. Another guessed softball—wrong. Another guessed synchronized swimming—wrong. Finally, Bollinger gave the correct answer: equestrian (horseback) competition.

Here are some pitfalls to avoid when asking questions.

Avoid questions that can fizzle.   One college student began a speech by asking, "How many of you are familiar with Future Farmers of America?" Everyone raised a hand, so the speaker looked foolish as he continued, "Today I'd like to inform you about what FFA is." Before you choose a question, imagine the answers you might get from the audience. Could they cause embarrassment or awkwardness?

When you ask questions, don't drag out the suspense.   If listeners are forced to guess and guess until the right answer is found, they may become exasperated, wishing that the speaker would get to the point.

Never ask embarrassing or personal questions.   Avoid such questions as "How many of you have ever tried cocaine?" or "How many of you use an underarm deodorant every day?" An audience would rightfully resent such questions as intrusions into their private lives.

Never divide your audience into opposing camps by asking "loaded" questions.   An example of a loaded question: "How many of you are smart enough to realize that capital punishment is an absolute necessity in a society based on law and order?" By phrasing your question in this way, you insult those who disagree with you.

When asking overt-response questions, don't expect universal participation.   With some overt-response questions, you can try to get every member of the audience to participate, but this can be very risky, especially if you poll the audience in this way: "How many of you favor the death penalty? Raise your hands. Okay . . . Now, how many of you are opposed to the death penalty? Okay, thanks . . . How many of you are undecided or unsure?" What if 3 people raised their hands for the first question, 5 for the second question, 10 for the third—but the remaining 67 people never raised their hands? When this happens, and it often does, it is a major embarrassment for the speaker. Sometimes audiences are in a passive or even grumpy mood; this is especially true with "captive" audiences—that is, audiences that are required (at work or at school) to listen to a speech. In such a case, refrain from asking questions that require the participation of the entire audience.

Make sure the audience understands whether you are asking a rhetorical question or an overt-response question.   If you ask, "How long will Americans continue to tolerate shoddy products?" the audience knows you are not expecting someone to answer, "Five years." It is clearly a rhetorical question. But suppose you ask a question like this: "How many of you have ever gone swimming in the ocean?" The listeners may be confused about whether you want them to raise their hands. Make it clear. If you want a show of hands, say so at the beginning: "I'd like to see a show of hands, please: How many of you have ever gone swimming in the ocean?" Alerting them in advance not only helps them know what you want but also makes them pay special attention to the question, since they know that you are expecting them to respond.

Make a Provocative Statement

An opening remark that shocks, surprises, or intrigues your listeners can certainly grab attention. (Just make sure the statement is not one that would offend or alienate the audience.) Student speaker Vanessa Sullivan began a speech on human cloning with this statement:

> I have seen a human clone with my own eyes. And so have you.

Then she explained:

> Richard Lewontin, professor of biology at Harvard University, says that about 30 human genetic clones appear every day in the United States. You and I know them as identical twins. Dr. Lewontin says that "identical twins are genetically more identical than a cloned organism is to its donor."[6]

Sullivan went on to argue that despite important ethical problems, cloning is not as far from human experience as many people think.

Cite a Quotation

A quotation can provide a lively beginning for a speech. In a speech on showing respect, student speaker Blake Painter began by saying:

> The American poet Maya Angelou once said, "If you have only one smile in you, give it to the people you love. Don't be surly at home, then go out in the street and start grinning 'Good morning' at total strangers."

Quotations usually work best when they are short. Don't use a quotation that is so long that the listeners lose track of where the quotation ends and your remarks begin. The best way to indicate that you have finished quoting is to pause at the end of the quotation. The pause acts as an oral punctuation device, signaling the end of one thought and the beginning of another.

Arouse Curiosity

An effective attention-getter is one that piques the curiosity of the audience. Brenda Johnson, a chef, began a speech by saying:

> I am addicted to a drug. I have been addicted to it for many years now. I feel like I need it to make it through the day. If I don't get this drug, my head aches. I'm nervous, irritable, and I begin to tremble. It's true—I am addicted.

Having aroused the curiosity of her listeners, Johnson continued:

> I am addicted to caffeine. Most people don't realize that caffeine is a drug—and that it is very addictive. It is present not only in coffee and tea and soft drinks but also in many legal drugs such as weight-control pills and pain relievers.

Johnson spent the rest of the speech giving details about caffeine and how listeners could reduce their intake.

Provide a Visual Aid or Demonstration

Any of the visual aids we discussed in Chapter 9 could be used to introduce a speech, but you must be sure that while the aids get the audience's attention, they also are relevant to the main points of your speech. One student showed slides of sunbathers on a beach to begin a talk on sharks. Though there was a logical link (sometimes sunbathers who go into the water must worry about sharks), the connection was too weak to justify using these particular slides. In a case like this, it would be better to show a slide of a ferocious shark while describing a shark attack.

A demonstration can make an effective opener. Working with a friend, one student gave a demonstration of how to fight off an attacker, and then talked on martial arts. If you want to give a demonstration, get permission from your instructor beforehand. *One note of caution:* Never do anything that might upset the listeners. For a speech on spiders, pulling tarantulas out of a box and letting them walk about would upset some people and put them out of a receptive mood.

Give an Incentive to Listen

At the beginning of a speech, many listeners have an attitude that can be summed up in these two questions: "What's in it for me? Why should I pay attention to this speech?" Such people need to be given an incentive to listen to the entire speech. So, whenever possible, state explicitly why the listeners will benefit by hearing you out. It is not enough to simply say, "My speech is very important." You must *show* them how your topic relates to their personal lives and their own best interests. If, for example, you were giving a talk on cardiopulmonary resuscitation (CPR), you could say, "All of you may someday have a friend or loved one collapse from a heart attack right in front of your eyes. If you know CPR, you might be able to save that person's life." Now each person in the audience sees clearly that your speech is important to his or her personal life.

If you tell listeners you will explain how to avoid food poisoning, they have an incentive to listen carefully.

Orient the Audience

Once you have won the interest of your listeners by means of the attention material, you should go into the second part of your introduction, the **orienting material,** which gives an orientation—a clear sense of what your speech is about, and any other information that the audience may need in order to understand and absorb your ideas. The orienting material is a road map that makes it easy for the listeners to stay with you on the journey of your speech and not get lost and confused.

orienting material
the part of the introduction that gives listeners the information they need to fully understand and believe the rest of the speech

The orienting material does more than prepare the listeners intellectually for your speech; it also prepares them psychologically. It reassures them that you are well-prepared, purposeful, and considerate of their needs and interests. It shows them you are someone they can trust.

The three most common ways to orient the audience are (1) give background information, (2) establish your credibility, and (3) preview the body of the speech. They are listed in this order because number 3 is usually delivered last, as a prelude to the body.

Do you need all three options in every speech? For classroom speeches, follow your instructor's guidelines. For some career speeches, you may not need the first two. The best advice is to use an option if it will promote audience understanding and acceptance.

Tips for Your Career

TIP 11.1

Use an "Icebreaker" to Start Off a Community Speech

Many speakers at business and professional meetings start off by saying something like this: "I'm glad to have a chance to speak to you today." They are giving an *icebreaker*—a polite little prologue to "break the ice" before getting into their speech.

In outline form, here is how an introduction with an ice-breaker would look:

I. Icebreaker
II. Attention Material
III. Orienting Material

When you give speeches in the community, an icebreaker is helpful because it eases your nervous tension and it lets the audience get accustomed to your voice. You don't need an icebreaker for classroom speeches because your audience has already settled down and is ready to listen. (Besides, most instructors would disapprove of using one.)

I don't like "Hello, how are you?" as an icebreaker. It sounds too breezy and flip. It leaves a question as to whether the speaker wants the audience to roar a response like "Fine, thank you!" It is much better to say, "I appreciate the opportunity to speak to you tonight." People use phrases like this so often that you might think they are meaningless. Yes, they are. They are clichés. Nevertheless, they are valuable aids to smooth social relationships. When you engage in small talk with your friends, you use sentences like "Hi, how are you?" Such expressions are trite, but they are necessary because they lubricate the wheels of human discourse.

In addition to expressing appreciation for the invitation to speak, you can include a thank-you to the person who introduced you or a reference to the occasion ("I'm delighted to take part in the celebration of Martin Luther King's birthday").

A note of caution: An icebreaker should be very brief—just a sentence or two. If you are too slow getting into the attention material of your introduction, you may cause some listeners to tune you out.

Give Background Information

Part of your orienting material can be devoted to giving background information—definitions, explanations, and so on—to help your listeners understand your speech. In a speech on the Boston-to-Washington megalopolis, Vandana Shastri used her orienting material to define the term:

> A megalopolis is a region made up of several cities and their suburbs which sprawl into each other. The biggest megalopolis in the United States is a densely populated, 500-mile-long corridor that starts in Boston and goes southward through Connecticut, New York City, northern New Jersey, Philadelphia, Wilmington (Delaware), Baltimore, and then ends in the Washington, DC, suburbs of northern Virginia.

Your Thoughts

If you are uncertain how much background information is needed by the audience, what is the best way to find out?

Sometimes it helps the audience if you explain the boundaries of your speech. For example, assume that you are giving a speech on the notion that criminals should make restitution to their victims. If you are not careful, many people in your audience will reject your argument immediately by saying to themselves, "Restitution, baloney! How can a murderer make restitution to his victim?" So in your orienting material, you head off such objections by saying, "In this speech, I will talk about criminals making restitution to their victims, but I'm only talking about nonviolent criminals such as swindlers, embezzlers, and bad-check writers. I'm not talking about rapists and murderers." By showing the boundaries of your subject, you increase the chances that the audience will listen with open minds.

Establish Your Credibility

No one expects you to be the world's authority on your subject, but you can increase your audience's chances of accepting your ideas if you establish your **credibility**—that

credibility
audience perception of a speaker as believable, trustworthy, and competent

In a speech on taking good photos, revealing your experience as a semi-pro photographer enhances your credibility.

is, give some credentials or reasons why you are qualified to speak on the subject. When student speaker Randy Stepp talked on how to escape a burning building, he enhanced his credibility by mentioning that he was a volunteer firefighter in a rural community and had fought many fires.

Some people shy away from giving their credentials or background because they think that doing so would make them seem boastful and arrogant. This concern is unfounded if you provide facts about yourself in a modest, tactful manner. In other words, if you are speaking on air pollution, say something like "I'm a chemist and I've analyzed in my lab the content of the air that we breathe in this community" instead of "I'm a professional chemist, so I know more about air pollution than anybody else in this room."

For information that does not come from your personal experience, you could cite your sources in the orienting material. For example, one speaker said, "The information I am giving you today comes from a book by David E. Hoffman entitled *The Oligarchs: Wealth & Power in the New Russia*."

Note: Mentioning your sources in the orienting material is just one of two options for citing sources. See Tip 12.2 in the next chapter. Before choosing an option, find out your instructor's preference.

In some speeches, you should tell the audience your connection to the topic—why you are speaking on that particular subject. For example, "I am speaking on defective automobile tires because my sister was seriously hurt in an accident that was caused by bad tires."

Confess any conflict of interest or bias. For example, "I am urging you to use Ask-an-Expert.com for Internet searches because I think it's the best expert site, but I should tell you that I get paid for being one of their experts."

Preview the Body of the Speech

Like a map on a smartphone, a preview in a speech gives a panoramic view of the subject and provides directions to the goal.

preview
a preliminary look at the highlights of a speech

Have you ever had trouble listening to a speech or lecture because the information seemed jumbled and disconnected and you couldn't grasp the significance of what was being said? An important way to avoid this problem is for the speaker to give the listeners a **preview** of the body of the speech. A preview is like a map that gives you the lay of the land as you travel. Arrows placed on top of the map can help you stay on course and not get lost. Your instructor may have specific requirements for what you must put in your preview. Unless he or she advises you otherwise, I recommend that you include your central idea or your main points or both.

1. **State the central idea.** Your audience can listen intelligently to your speech if you stress your central idea in the orienting material. For example, "Acid rain is killing all the trees on our highest peaks in the East. To prove this, I will give you evidence from leading scientists." (Occasionally, in special situations, it is best to withhold divulging your central idea until late in the speech; we will discuss this technique in Chapter 17.)

   In a speech on losing weight, Mary E. McNair, a nurse, stated her central idea in this way:

   Fad and crash diets can actually backfire, causing a person in the long run to gain more weight than was originally lost.

This helped the audience listen with "the right set of ears." They knew to pay attention to what she had to say about the counterproductive effects of fad and crash diets.

2. **State the main points.** In most speeches, listeners appreciate being given a brief preview of your main points. For example, Barbara LeBlanc said,

> I believe that passive-solar heating should be used in every home—for two reasons: First, it's easy to adapt your house to passive solar. Second, the energy from passive solar is absolutely free. Let me explain what I'm talking about.

By stating the main points, LeBlanc not only helped the audience listen intelligently but also gave them an incentive to listen: She mentioned the possibility of saving money.

Giving a preview by stating the central idea and the main points reassures the listeners that you are not going to ramble. In other words, you give the audience a message that says, loud and clear, "I'm well-prepared; I know exactly what I'm going to say; I'm not going to waste your time."

Guidelines for Introductions

Here are some points to keep in mind for introductions.

1. **Don't prepare your introduction first.** When you prepare a speech, what usually works best is to complete the body of the speech and *then* work on your introduction. Once you have developed your main points, you are in a stronger position to decide how to introduce them.

2. **Make your introduction simple and easy to follow, but avoid making it too brief.** Your audience needs time to get into the groove of your speech. If the introduction is too short, it may go by too fast for the listeners to absorb. That is why effective joke tellers stretch out their introduction to give the listeners time to get "into" the joke.

   If the idea of stretching out an introduction sounds wrong to you, it is probably because you have been taught in English classes to write concisely. While it is an error in a writing class to stretch out essays, it is a virtue to do so with a speech's introduction that might otherwise be too abrupt for an audience.

   A note of caution: Don't let this tip cause you to go to the opposite extreme—being tedious and long-winded. Be brief, but not too brief. If you are unsure about whether you have achieved a happy medium, deliver your speech to relatives or friends and then ask them if they thought your introduction was too long or too short.

3. **Make sure that your introduction has a direct and obvious tie-in with the body of the speech.** A common mistake is for speakers to give an introduction that has a weak or dubious link with the rest of the speech. This kind of introduction can be annoying and confusing to the listeners.

4. **Never apologize.** You weaken your speech and hurt your credibility if you say things like "I didn't have much time to prepare" or "This may be too technical for you" or "I'm sorry I didn't draw a diagram."

Conclusions

When movies are made, the producers spend a lot of time and energy on getting a "perfect" ending because they know that if the ending is unsatisfying, the viewers will tend to downgrade the film as a whole. As with the movies, the ending of a speech can either add to or subtract from the audience's opinion of the entire speech. So it is worthwhile to spend a lot of time working on your conclusion.

Your Thoughts

Although introductions and conclusions are both important, describe a situation where the introduction is more important than the conclusion. Then describe a situation where the conclusion is more important.

In your conclusion, you should do three important things: (1) signal the end of the speech to satisfy the audience's psychological need for a sense of completion, (2) summarize the key ideas of the speech, and (3) reinforce the central idea with a clincher. Let us discuss these points in greater detail.

Signal the End

Imagine that you are listening to your favorite song on the radio and letting your mind float freely with the music. Then suddenly, before the song is finished, the disc jockey cuts in with a commercial or a news bulletin. You missed only the last 10 seconds of the song, but you feel annoyed. Why? Because most people need to experience a sense of completion.

In listening to a speech, we have the same need for a sense of finality. We don't like an abrupt halt—we like to hear a conclusion that is psychologically satisfying.

To give listeners a satisfying finale, provide signals that the end is approaching. These signals can be verbal or nonverbal or both.

Verbal signals.   You can openly announce that you are coming to your conclusion by saying, "So, in conclusion, I'd like to say . . . ," or "Let me end by saying . . . ," or "Let me remind you of the three major points I've been trying to explain today."

Nonverbal signals.   Two nonverbal cues are subtle but important: (1) say your conclusion with a tone of dramatic finality and (2) subtly intensify your facial expression and gestures. These cues should come naturally to you, since you have seen numerous speakers use them in your lifetime. If you feel unsure of yourself, practice your conclusion in front of a mirror or, better yet, in front of a friend (who can give you feedback). You also can say it in front of a camcorder and play it back to check whether you have the appropriate tone of finality in your voice.

Summarize Key Ideas

Because listening is often a difficult mental task, some people in the audience might get drowsy or inattentive toward the end of your speech. But when you signal that you are about to finish, listeners usually perk up. If they know they can rest soon, they are better able to stay alert for a few more minutes. Like runners near the finish line, they can bring forth an extra burst of energy.

This mental alertness of your listeners gives you a good opportunity to drive home your message one more time. One of the best ways to do this is to summarize your key ideas. There is a formula for giving a speech that has been around for over 100 years. Sometimes it is attributed to a spellbinding country preacher, sometimes to a savvy Irish politician. The true originator will probably never be known, but the formula is worth heeding:

> Tell 'em what you're going to tell 'em.
> Tell 'em.
> Then tell 'em what you told 'em.

The first sentence refers to the introduction, the second to the body, and the third to a summary in the conclusion. The summary gives you a chance to restate the central idea or the main points or both.

If you are like a lot of people, you may say, "Why do I need to repeat my message? Isn't this overkill?" No, research shows that restating your main points increases the likelihood that the listeners will remember them.[7]

A summary should be brief, as in this recap of the body of a speech about preventing car theft:

> So remember, you can prevent your car from being stolen if you follow these guidelines: Always park in a well-lighted area. Always remove your key from the ignition. Always close all windows and lock all doors.

Listeners don't mind hearing this kind of information again; it helps them retain it.

Reinforce the Central Idea with a Clincher

In addition to providing a summary, close your speech with a **clincher** that reinforces the central idea—a finale that drives home the main theme of your entire speech.

Public speakers are like carpenters driving a nail into a floor, says Edward L. Friedman. They begin with a few preliminary taps in the introduction to get the speech started right. As they get into the body of the speech, they deliver one hammer blow after another to drive the nail into its proper place with carefully executed strokes. Then, in conclusion, they execute a powerful, clinching blow.[8]

Use a clincher that is memorable, that leaves a lasting impression with the listener. You can find clinchers by using some of the techniques mentioned earlier in this chapter for the introduction (such as a rhetorical question or a visual aid), or by using some of the following techniques.

clincher
a final statement in a speech that drives home the key concept of the speech

Cite a Quotation

A good quotation can dramatize and reinforce a speaker's central idea. After urging her audience always to buckle their seat belts, one speaker said,

> I would like to close with a quotation from Laura Valdez, an emergency medicine technician in California, who said, "I have driven my ambulance to hundreds of traffic accidents. I have found many people already dead, but I have yet to unbuckle the seat belt of a dead person."

At the end of a speech on why citizens should fight social ills rather than succumb to despair, Richard Kern said:

> Let me leave you with the words of Eleanor Roosevelt: "It is better to light one candle than to curse the darkness."

Eye contact is important at the end of your speech, so if you use a quotation, practice it so that you can say it while looking at the audience, with only occasional glances at your notes.

Issue an Appeal or a Challenge

In a persuasive speech, you can end by making an appeal or issuing a challenge to the audience. If you are trying to persuade the listeners to donate blood, you can end by saying:

> Next week the bloodmobile will be on campus. I call upon each of you to spend a few minutes donating your blood so that others may live.

One speaker tried to convince her audience to make out a will, and in her conclusion she issued a challenge:

> The simple task of writing a will can protect your family and give you peace of mind. It is a sad fact that three out of four Americans will die without a will. Are you going to be one of them? I hope not. Why don't you write your will before you go to bed tonight?

Give an Illustration

An illustration is a popular way to reinforce the central idea of a speech. In a speech urging classmates to avoid Internet gambling, one student speaker concluded with a true story:

> In his entire life, college senior Mark Scott had never gambled until one night, when he got an e-mail that said, "Congratulations, Mark, you won $100." Scott was intrigued, and he clicked on the gambling site and began playing blackjack. After an hour, $175 of his money was gone. Three months later, he had run up a $9,000 gambling debt on his credit card.

Refer to the Introduction

Using the conclusion to hearken back to something said in the introduction is an effective way to wrap up your speech.

In a speech on pet therapy, student speaker Jake Harland used the photo in Figure 11.1 in his introduction and again in his conclusion. He began by saying, "This puppy was one of 15 homeless dogs brought into George Mason University Law School to see if students would like to play with them to relieve stress during final exams. At the end of my speech, I'll tell you what happened to this puppy." During the body of the speech, he explained that the law school wanted to show students that playing with a pet was a better way to reduce stress and depression than overeating or drinking. At the end of the speech, Harland showed the photo again and said, "The student in this

Figure 11.1
Why did one speaker use this photo in both his introduction and conclusion? See text for the answer.

picture, Julie Dewberry, and her classmates ended up keeping all 15 dogs for a week, and later—after exams—they reported that the dogs had helped them to relax and take breaks from studying."

Guidelines for Conclusions

There are four pitfalls to avoid in conclusions.

1. **Don't drag out the ending.** Some speakers fail to prepare a conclusion in advance. When they reach what should be the end of their remarks, they cannot think of a graceful way to wrap things up, so they keep on talking. Other speakers signal the end of their speech (by saying something like "So, in closing, let me say . . ."), but then they drone on and on. This gives false hope to the listeners. When they see that the speaker is not keeping the promise, they feel deceived and become restless.

2. **Don't end weakly.** If you close with a statement such as "I guess that's about all I've got to say," and your voice is nonchalant and unenthusiastic, you encourage your listeners to downgrade your entire speech. End with confidence.

3. **Don't end apologetically.** There is no need to say: "That just about does it. I'm sorry I didn't have more time to prepare . . . ," or: "That's it, folks. I guess I should have looked up more facts on . . ." Apologies make you look incompetent. Besides, some people may not have noticed anything wrong with your speech or your delivery; you may have done better than you realized, so why apologize?

4. **Never bring in new main points.** It is okay to use fresh material in your conclusion; in fact, it is a good idea to do so, as long as the material does not constitute a new main point. Let's say you have given your audience three well-explained techniques for losing weight. It would be a mistake to end by saying, "Oh, yes, and another technique is . . ." This would drag out your speech. On the other hand, it would be acceptable to end with a brief comment about the 10 pounds you lost because you used the techniques discussed in the body of the speech.

Sample Introduction and Conclusion

In the previous chapter, we looked at the body of a speech on cotton swabs. Now let's see how Wendy Trujillo developed an introduction and a conclusion for her speech.

Danger in the Bathroom

COMMENTARY	SPEECH
	General Purpose: To persuade
	Specific Purpose: To persuade my audience to avoid using cotton swabs in their ears
	Central Idea: For cleaning ears, cotton swabs are dangerous and ineffective.

(continued)

INTRODUCTION

I. Attention Material

    A. Which item in a typical bathroom sends more people to the hospital emergency department than any other?

        1. Is it razor blades . . . scissors . . . hair dryers?

        2. No, none of these.

    B. The correct answer is cotton swabs, which many people use to clean their ears.

II. Orienting Material

    A. Today I would like to show you why you should never put cotton swabs into your ear.

    B. Reason number one: They are dangerous.

    C. Reason number two: They are ineffective.

[The body of the speech, which appears in Chapter 10, uses the statement-of-reasons pattern.]

CONCLUSION

I. Summary

    A. We have discussed two reasons why you should never use cotton swabs for cleaning your ears.

    B. First, you risk injury.

    C. Second, you are using a device that is worthless for truly cleaning ears.

II. Clincher

    A. Dr. George Alexiades of the New York Eye and Ear Infirmary has treated hundreds of people who punctured their eardrums with cotton swabs.

    B. He has some good advice: "Never put anything in your ear smaller than your elbow."

Trujillo opens with a question that is designed to capture the listeners' attention and interest.

To give listeners a clear road map of her speech, the speaker states her central idea and main points.

Trujillo gives a brief summary of the key information of the speech.

The speaker closes with a humorous quotation that underscores her central idea.

Resources for Review and Skill Building

Summary

Much of the success of a speech depends on how well the speaker handles the introduction and the conclusion. The introduction consists of two parts: attention material, which gains listeners' attention and interest, and orienting material, which gives the audience the information they need to listen intelligently to the rest of the speech.

For attention material, you can use one or more of the following techniques: tell a story, ask a question, make a provocative statement, cite a quotation, arouse curiosity, provide a visual aid or demonstration, and provide the audience with an incentive to listen.

For orienting material, you have three options: give background information, such as definitions; establish your credibility on your topic; and preview the body of the speech (by stating the central idea, the main points, or both).

The introduction should have a direct and obvious tie-in with the body of the speech. Avoid apologies and a too-brief introduction.

The conclusion of your speech should signal the end, summarize your key ideas, and reinforce the central idea with a clincher. A clincher may be an appeal or a challenge, an illustration, a reference to the introduction, or any of the techniques mentioned for attention material (such as a rhetorical question).

Avoid conclusions that are weak, apologetic, or drawn-out. While fresh material may be used, never bring in new main points.

Key Terms

attention material, *200*

clincher, *209*

credibility, *205*

hypothetical illustration, *201*

orienting material, *204*

overt-response question, *202*

preview, *206*

rhetorical question, *201*

Review Questions

1. Why is it necessary to have attention material at the beginning of a speech?

2. What is the purpose of the orienting material in the speech introduction?

3. What is a rhetorical question?

4. What is an overt-response question?

5. How can you give listeners an incentive to listen to a speech?

6. What is credibility?

7. In what way does a preview of main points reassure the audience?

8. Why is it a mistake to end a speech abruptly?

9. What is a clincher?

10. Why should you restate your main points in the conclusion?

Building Critical-Thinking Skills

1. What advice would you give a speaker who says, in the introduction, "This speech may be too technical for you."

2. Create a rhetorical question concerning the destruction of the Central American rain forest.

Building Teamwork Skills

1. In a group, brainstorm possible attention-getters to introduce speeches on

   a. world famine
   b. burglar alarm systems
   c. vacationing in Italy
   d. overcoming fatigue
   e. finding an honest car repair shop

2. Working in a group, discuss how listeners react when they hear speakers make these apologies:

   a. "I didn't have much time to prepare."
   b. "I'm not much of a speaker."
   c. "I know this is a boring topic."
   d. "I had wanted to show you some PowerPoint slides."
   e. "That last speech is a tough act to follow."
   f. "I hate public speaking."
   g. "I'm really nervous."

Ethical Issues

Answer for p. 200: A. While grabbing attention is a good technique, the speaker should choose a different image—one that does not shock and disrespect any listener. Showing a desecrated cross would put some listeners out of a receptive frame of mind.

Outlining the Speech

OBJECTIVES

After studying this chapter, you should be able to:

1. Understand the importance of developing an outline for a speech.
2. Create a coherent outline for a speech.
3. Create effective speaking notes based on your outline.

IMAGINE HIRING A BUILDER to construct a two-story house like the one on the opposite page. When you move in, you discover that he forgot to create a staircase between the first floor and the second floor.

Such a blunder might be hard to imagine, but it actually happened in 1926 in Palm Beach, Florida. A homebuilder named Addison Mizner forgot to include a staircase in a home built for George S. Rasmussen. Mizner tried to rectify his mistake by placing stairs on the outside of the house, but this forced the Rasmussen family to put on raincoats when they needed to go upstairs or downstairs on rainy days.[1]

If you build a two-story house like this, how can you avoid Addison Mizner's mistake of failing to include a staircase?

Mizner never would have made such a mistake had he created and adhered to a detailed architectural blueprint showing the exact placement and dimensions of all components of the house.

In public speaking, the equivalent of a blueprint is an outline, which can be used to make sure that all parts are included and that they fit together harmoniously. Many speakers say that an outline helps them to organize their thoughts into a logical sequence and to see which points are irrelevant, improperly placed, or poorly developed. It prevents them from rambling.[2]

Outlining is the culmination of the process we began describing many chapters ago—the process of gaining control of our subject matter. Up to this point, we have talked about formulating objectives (Chapter 5), gathering and developing materials (Chapters 6, 7, 8, and 9), and then organizing them in the body (Chapter 10) and the introduction and conclusion (Chapter 11). Now we will discuss how to put all these elements together in outline form.

Because some students have trouble understanding how an outline fits into the overall process of speechmaking, I created Figure 12.1 (on the next page). This flowchart shows your next three steps: First, create an outline; second, use the outline to prepare speaking notes; and third, use the speaking notes to deliver the speech. The first two steps will be covered in this chapter; the third step, delivering the speech, will be discussed in Chapter 14. (For classroom speeches, your instructor may have different guidelines. You should, of course, follow his or her rules.)

Step 1 Create an Outline

This is a slice from a student's outline. An outline is the basic structure of a speaker's ideas in streamlined form. It is not a word-for-word script. A detailed outline (like this one) is used only for preparation. It is not taken to the lectern.

Outline

I. Avoid choosing the wrong dog.
   A. Never buy on a whim.
   B. Research to find the right breed for you.
   C. Get to know a dog before adoption.

Step 2 Prepare Speaking Notes

The speaker prepares brief notes—derived from his outline—to be used in practicing and delivering the speech. These notes contain only a few key words—just enough to jog his memory. By using brief notes instead of his outline, he avoids the mistake of reading a speech.

Speaker's notes

I. Wrong dog
   A. Never – whim
   B. Research
   C. Get to know

Step 3 Deliver the Speech

When he delivers the speech, the speaker talks in a natural, conversational manner, glancing at his note cards occasionally to remind himself of his next point.

Speaker's actual words

Do you want to avoid choosing a dog that just isn't right for you? Never buy a dog on the spur of the moment because it's cute. Instead spend time researching the different breeds until you find the best match for your . . .

Figure 12.1
The outline-to-speech process has three steps.

Guidelines for Outlining

Instead of using an outline, why not just write out the entire speech? For one thing, a word-for-word script would create a sea of material that might overwhelm you. Even worse, you might be tempted to read the script, a method that could put the audience to sleep.

An outline is better than a script because it shows the basic structure of your ideas in a streamlined form. It also helps you to see the relationship between ideas.

In essence, outlining is a commonsense way of arranging information in a logical pattern. The Federal Bureau of Investigation's Crime Index, for example, can be broken down into two broad categories:

Your Thoughts

For an outline on the different breeds of dogs, which major headings would you create?

FBI Crime Index
  I. Violent crimes
 II. Property crimes

We could then break down each category into specific types of crimes:

  I. Violent crimes
      A. Murder
      B. Rape
      C. Robbery
      D. Aggravated assault
 II. Property crimes
      A. Burglary
      B. Larceny-theft
      C. Motor vehicle theft
      D. Arson

If we wanted to, we could divide items A, B, C, and D into subcategories. For example, we could break murder down into categories of weapons used, with one category for guns, one for knives, and so on.

The next section offers instructions for formatting your outlines.

Choose an Outline Format

The two most popular formats for outlines are the *topic outline* and the *complete-sentence outline.* Find out if your instructor prefers or requires one or the other. Some instructors and professional speakers recommend using both methods—the topic format in the early stages of preparation (when you are struggling to impose order on your material) and the complete-sentence format in the later stages (when you are refining and polishing your ideas).

Topic Outline

In a **topic outline,** you express your ideas in key words or phrases. The advantage of this format is that it is quicker and easier to prepare than a complete-sentence outline. The FBI Crime Index outline above is a topic outline. Also see the topic outline in Figure 12.2 on the next page.

topic outline
a systematic arrangement of ideas, using words and phrases for headings and subheadings

Figure 12.2
Some speakers use both forms of outlines: the topic outline for early drafts, the complete-sentence outline for refinements.

Topic Outline	Complete-Sentence Outline
Pre-employment Screening	Pre-employment Screening
I. Presenting self	I. Presenting yourself to a potential employer gives you a chance to highlight your qualifications for a job.
A. Job interview	A. A job interview can show your enthusiasm and commitment.
B. Résumé	B. A résumé summarizes your experience, education, and skills.
II. Testing	II. Testing is used by employers to eliminate unqualified or high-risk applicants.
A. Skills tests	A. Skills tests determine if you have the aptitudes and abilities needed for the job.
B. Physical exams	B. Physical exams determine whether your health will allow you to fulfill the duties of the job.
C. Drug tests	C. Drug tests screen for illegal substances such as cocaine and marijuana.

Complete-Sentence Outline

complete-sentence outline

a systematic arrangement of ideas, using complete sentences for headings and subheadings

In the **complete-sentence outline,** all your main points and subpoints are expressed in complete sentences (see Figure 12.2). Unless your instructor tells you otherwise, I recommend that you use complete sentences for your final outline. Here is why: (1) Writing complete sentences forces you to clarify and sharpen your thinking. You are able to go beyond fuzzy, generalized notions and create whole, fully developed ideas. (2) If another person (such as an instructor) helps you with your outline, complete sentences will be easier for him or her to understand than mere phrases, thus enabling that person to give you the best possible critique.

All the sample outlines in the rest of this book, including the one featured later in this chapter, use the complete-sentence format.

Note of caution: The complete-sentence outline is not your speech written out exactly as you will present it. Rather, it is a representation of your key ideas; the actual speech should elaborate on these ideas. This means that your actual speech will contain many more words than the outline. See Figure 12.1 for an example.

Use Standard Subdivisions

In the standard system of subdividing, you mark your main points with roman numerals (**I, II, III,** etc.); indent the next level of supporting materials underneath and mark with capital letters (**A, B, C,** etc.); then go to arabic numerals (1, 2, 3); then

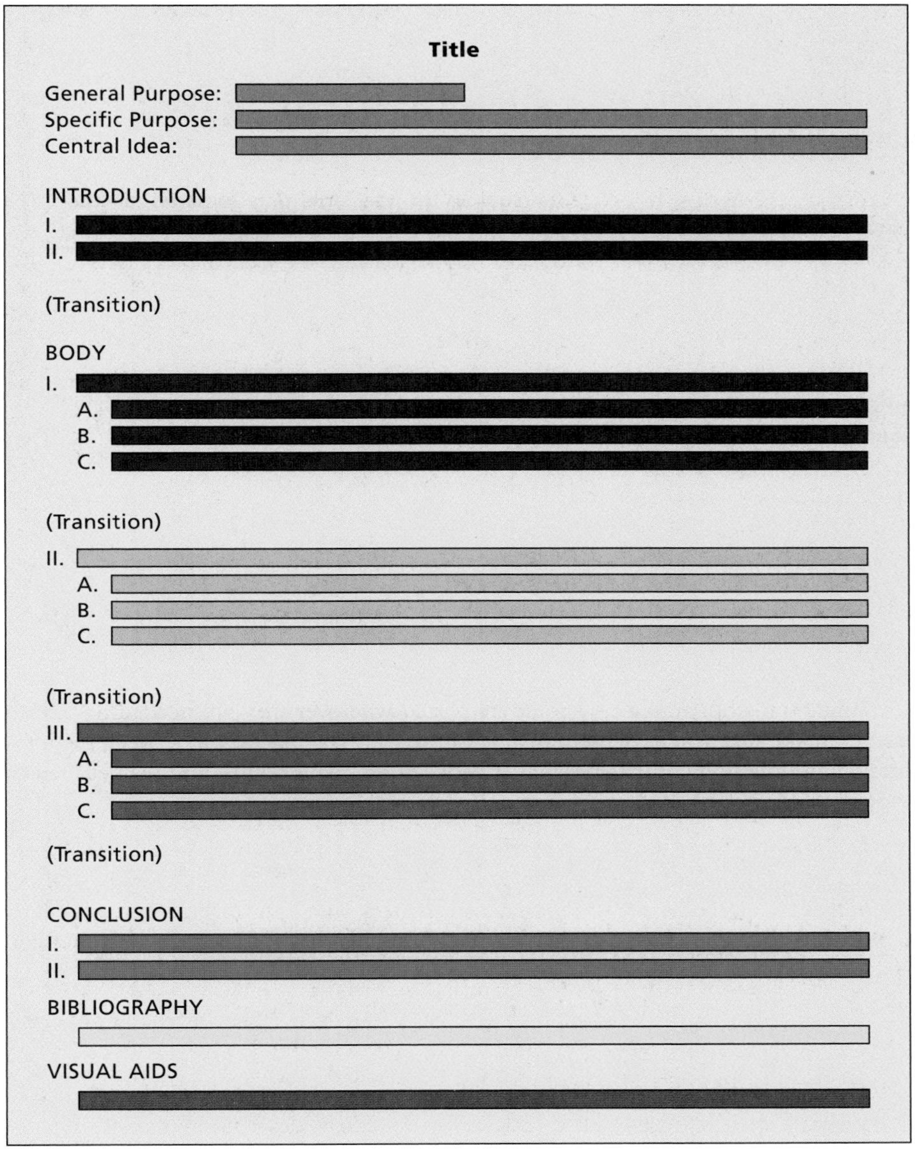

Title

General Purpose: ▭
Specific Purpose: ▭
Central Idea: ▭

INTRODUCTION
I. ▬
II. ▬

(Transition)

BODY
I. ▬
   A. ▬
   B. ▬
   C. ▬

(Transition)

II. ▭
   A. ▭
   B. ▭
   C. ▭

(Transition)

III. ▬
   A. ▬
   B. ▬
   C. ▬

(Transition)

CONCLUSION
I. ▬
II. ▬

BIBLIOGRAPHY
▭

VISUAL AIDS
▬

Figure 12.3
This is an overview of a typical outline. Although this outline shows three main points, a speech may have two or, occasionally, four.

Both sections should have their own numbering sequence, independent of the body of the speech.

4. **Body.** In the body of the outline, each main point should be identified by roman numerals. The body has its own numbering sequence, independent of the introduction and conclusion. In other words, the first main point of the body is given roman numeral I.

5. **Transitions.** The transitional devices we discussed in Chapter 10 should be inserted in the outline at appropriate places. They are labeled and placed in parentheses, but they are not included in the numbering system of the outline.

Tips for Your Career

Decide How You Will Reveal Your Sources

You strengthen your credibility with your listeners if you tell them where you got your information. But it would be boring if you read aloud your bibliography. How, then, can you cite sources without bogging down the speech?

Here are two options, which can be used singly or in combination. (For classroom speeches, seek your instructor's guidance on which option to use.)

1. Reveal the key data about your sources as you proceed through the body of your speech.

You could preface new points by saying something like "According to an article in the latest issue of *Communication Education* . . ." or "Writing in *The American Journal of Nursing*, Doctor Judith Fouladbakhsh says . . ."

2. Cite sources in the orienting material of the introduction.

For example, one speaker said, "The information I am giving you today comes from an article by Margaret Zackowitz entitled 'Royal City of the Maya' in *National Geographic* magazine, and from the website of the Mexico Tourism Board."

In some situations, you can list your sources on a handout that is provided to listeners at the end of a speech. For more information on this and other options, see the section "Giving Credit to Sources" in Chapter 7.

While transitional devices should be placed wherever they are needed to help the listener, make sure you have them in at least three crucial places: (1) between the introduction and the body of the speech, (2) between the main points, and (3) between the body of the speech and the conclusion.

6. **Bibliography.** At the end of the outline, place a list of the sources—such as books, magazines, and interviews—that you used in preparing the speech. Give standard bibliographical data in alphabetical order. Check with your instructor to see if he or she wants you to use a special format. Otherwise, see Table 6.1 in Chapter 6 for guidelines.

The bibliography is useful not only as a list of sources for your instructor but also as a record if you ever give the speech again and need to return to your sources to refresh your memory or to find additional information.

7. **Visual aids.** If you plan to use visual aids, give a brief description of them. This will enable the instructor to advise you on whether the visual aids are effective.

Sample Outline with Commentary

Below is an outline for a speech called "Not as Healthy as They Sound" by Jeffrey Omura. A transcript of the speech is printed at the end of this chapter.

Although the following outline uses the complete-sentence format, your instructor may prefer that you create a topic outline (which we discussed a few pages earlier). In this case, use the same system as here except write words or phrases instead of full sentences.

The speaker's outline uses the topical pattern, dividing the subject into two types of foods.

Not As Healthy As They Sound

SPEECH	COMMENTARY

General Purpose: To inform

Specific Purpose: To inform my audience of some foods that are not as healthy as they sound

Central Idea: Some healthy-sounding foods are not as high in nutritional value as you might think.

> Purposes and central idea should appear at the top of the outline to help the speaker stay on target.

INTRODUCTION

I. Attention Material
   A. At a coffee shop, you try to choose between a chocolate donut with sprinkles and a corn muffin. (Show photo.) [See Figure 12.4]
   B. You decide on the corn muffin because it's healthier, but is it?
   C. The donut has 270 calories, while the corn muffin has 510. (*Consumer Reports*)
      1. You need 2,000 calories per day, so the corn muffin provides about one-quarter of your daily needs.
      2. Also the corn muffin has a great deal more fat than the donut.
   D. Over 12 people who were interviewed said the corn muffin was healthier.

> The introduction has its own label and numbering sequence.

> The speaker grabs attention by describing an interesting choice.

II. Orienting Material
   A. Let's look at some other foods that are not as healthy as they sound.
   B. My goal is not to dictate a diet, but simply to inform you of some interesting facts.

(*Transition:* Let's start with vegetables.)

> A preview lets listeners know what the speech will cover.

> Transitions are placed in parentheses and are not part of the numbering system.

Figure 12.4
A corn muffin has far more calories than a chocolate donut.

270   510

(continued)

BODY

I. Vegetables can be nutritious, but often they are loaded with extra fat and calories.

> Roman numerals are used for main points.

    A. A salad with tomatoes, lettuce, cucumbers, and other veggies can be okay if you add a modest amount of low-fat dressing.

        1. But some people choose a salad at a fast-food restaurant because they think it's healthier than a burger. (Show slide.) [See Figure 12.5.]

        2. One fast-food chain sells a Spicy Chicken Caesar Salad with 750 calories, while its quarter-pound hamburger has 470 calories. (KGET-TV of Bakersfield, California)

        3. A salad becomes high in calories and fat if it's topped with cheese, bacon, croutons, spicy chicken strips, and a large quantity of high-fat dressing.

    B. Potato chips are high in fat, so veggie chips sound healthier.

> Under each main point, subpoints are marked with capital letters.

        1. Veggie chips are not more nutritious than potato chips, says Patricia Chuey of Vancouver, Canada, a nutritionist and author of *Simply Great Food.*

        2. They are high in fat and calories.

        3. They have almost none of the nutritional value of real vegetables.

> Sub-subpoints are marked with arabic numerals (1, 2, 3).

    C. A veggie sandwich sounds healthy, but beware.

        1. It's not all that healthy if you order the Veggie Supreme sub at one fast-food chain.

        2. The Veggie Supreme was rated as the Worst "Healthy" Sandwich in America. (*Eat This, Not That!*)

> Each level of subordination is shown by indention.

        3. It has 1,106 calories and 56 grams of fat, surpassing the calories and fat in two Big Macs from McDonald's.

        4. The sub is a foot long, contains three different kinds of cheese, and is covered in oil.

        5. Of course you can avoid the extra fat and calories if you ask the restaurant to skip the cheese and oil.

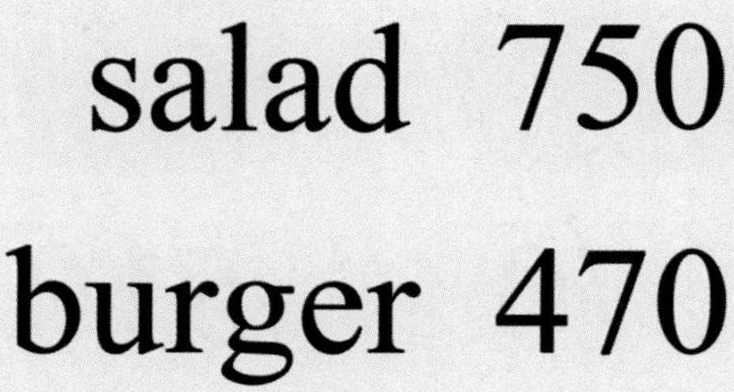

Figure 12.5
At a fast-food restaurant, a salad can have more calories than a hamburger.

salad 750

burger 470

Figure 12.6
Commercial granola bars are far different from homemade ones.

(*Transition:* Let's look at our second category of foods.

II. Nuts, fruits, and dairy products can be nutritious, but sometimes they have surprisingly high amounts of fat and calories.

    A. Granola bars would seem to be a super-healthy food. (Show photo.) [See Figure 12.6.]

        1. They contain nuts, dried fruits, and whole oats.

        2. They can be very healthy if you make your own granola bars at home.

        3. But commercial granola bars have lots of sugar and syrup.

        4. "They're basically cookies masquerading around as health food," says Jayne Hurley, a senior nutritionist with the Center for Science in the Public Interest.

    B. Yogurt-covered raisins sound like a healthy combination.

        1. By themselves, raisins and yogurt are good foods, says Rosie Schwartz, a dietitian in Toronto, Canada.

        2. But commercial yogurt-covered raisins are deceptive.

        3. The "yogurt" coating is not real yogurt, but a high-calorie combination of sugar, oil, and some dried milk.

        4. One cup of yogurt-covered raisins has 750 calories, more calories than in two slices of homemade chocolate cake with chocolate frosting.

    C. Combining two healthy foods—yogurt and fruit—sounds healthy.

        1. Yogurt is a nutritious food, and fruit contains essential vitamins and minerals.

        2. So wouldn't it be healthy to buy a container of yogurt that has fruit on the bottom?

        3. But Schwartz says it's not real fruit on the bottom.

           a. It's actually fruit jam loaded with sugar.

           b. One serving can contain as many as 28 grams of sugar.

           c. That's more sugar than in a cup of vanilla ice cream.

(*Transition:* Let's review.)

Transitions are needed between main points.

Audiences like to know the source of information—in this case, an expert.

Complete sentences are used to make sure all material is clear and well-developed.

Even though complete sentences are used, this outline is not a script to be read aloud. It is just a skeleton of key points. In the speech itself, the speaker expands on the points, using additional words in a conversational-style delivery.

The final transition prepares the audience for the conclusion.

(continued)

<table>
<tr><td>The conclusion has its own label and numbering system.</td><td>

CONCLUSION

I. Summary

    A. Some foods are not as healthy as they sound.

    B. They include corn muffins, some fast-food salads, veggie chips, the Veggie Supreme sub, granola bars, yogurt-covered raisins, and yogurt with fruit on the bottom.
</td></tr>
</table>

The conclusion has its own label and numbering system.

The speaker summarizes the main points.

CONCLUSION

I. Summary

    A. Some foods are not as healthy as they sound.

    B. They include corn muffins, some fast-food salads, veggie chips, the Veggie Supreme sub, granola bars, yogurt-covered raisins, and yogurt with fruit on the bottom.

A graceful ending is achieved by referring to the dramatic question asked at the beginning of the speech.

II. Clincher

    A. Rather than dictate, I have just given information.

    B. I'll bet all of you will remember that you don't save calories by choosing a corn muffin over a chocolate donut.

The bibliography lists all sources used to prepare the speech.

Sources are listed alphabetically.

The MLA format shown here is explained in Chapter 6, along with another format, APA.

BIBLIOGRAPHY

Chuey, Patricia, nutritionist, Vancouver, Canada. Message to Jeffrey Omura. 14 July 2011. E-mail.

"Food Fight." *Consumer Reports* March 2008: 7. Print.

Hurley, Jayne, nutritionist. "Granola Bars." Center for Science in the Public Interest Online, 21 Feb. 2011. Web. 14 July 2011.

"New Law Requires Big Restaurant Chains to Provide Nutritional Facts." KGET-TV, Bakersfield, California, 2010. Web. 14 July 2011.

Schwartz, Rosie, dietitian, Toronto, Canada. Message to Jeffrey Omura. 13 July 2011. E-mail.

Zinczenko, David. *Eat This, Not That!* New York: Rodale, 2012. Print.

Visual aids should be listed so that the instructor can give guidance.

VISUAL AIDS

    Two PowerPoint slides comparing calories.

    One photo of granola bars.

Speaking Notes

After you have devised an outline, what do you do with it? Do you use it to practice your speech? No. Do you take it with you to the lectern to assist you in the delivery of your speech? No. You use the outline only for *organizing* your ideas. When it comes to *practicing* and then *delivering* the speech, you should use brief **speaking notes** that are based on the outline.

speaking notes
brief reminders of the points a speaker plans to cover during a speech

Speaking from brief notes is a good technique because it enables you to look at your audience most of the time, occasionally glancing down to pick up your next point. It encourages you to speak naturally and conversationally.

How about using no notes at all? Would that be even better? No, without notes, you might forget important points, and you might fail to present your ideas in a logical, easy-to-follow sequence.

Notes bolster your sense of security. Even if you are in full command of the content of your speech, you feel more confident and self-assured knowing that you have notes as a safety net to rescue you if your mind goes blank and you fail to recall your next point.

By the way, some people have the idea that using notes is a sign of mental weakness or a lack of self-confidence, but this belief is unfounded. Most good speakers use them without losing the respect of an audience. After all, your notes represent a kind of compliment to your listeners. They show that you care enough about the occasion to spend time getting your best thoughts together in a coherent form. The kind of speaker that audiences *do* look down on is the windbag who stands up without notes and rambles on and on without tying things together.

Guidelines for Preparing Notes

As you read these guidelines, you may want to refer to the sample speaking notes in Figure 12.7.

- Make indentions in your speaking notes that correspond to those in your outline. This will reinforce the structure of the speech in your mind. Some speakers use checkboxes and dashes to signal points; others use the same numbering system that they used in their outline.

- Use only one side of a sheet of paper or note card because you might forget to turn the paper or card over.

- Write down only the minimum number of words or phrases necessary to trigger your memory. If you have too many words written down, you may overlook some key ideas, or you may spend too much time looking at the notes instead of at the audience. Exceptions to this rule are long quotations or statistics that you need to write out in full for the sake of accuracy.

Cues remind the speaker to look at the audience and speak slowly during the introduction.

For reminders, red ink is effective.

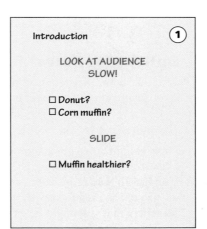

Figure 12.7
Here are samples of note cards for the speech about foods that sound healthy. Only the first two cards are shown.

Each card is numbered so that if the speaker accidentally drops or scrambles the cards, they can be put back into order very easily.

Only a few key words are used to jog the speaker's memory.

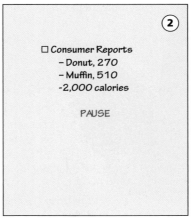

- Write words in large letters that are neat and legible so that you have no trouble seeing them when you glance down during a speech.
- Include cues for effective delivery, such as "SHOW SLIDE" and "PAUSE" (see the sample notes in Figure 12.7). Write them in a bright color so that they stand out. (By the way, some speakers find it helpful to use a variety of coded colors on their notes—for example, black for main points, green for support materials, blue for transitions, and red for delivery cues.)
- For speaking, use the same set of notes you used while rehearsing so that you will be thoroughly familiar with the location of items on your prompts. I once practiced with a set of notes on which I penciled in so many editing marks that I made a fresh set of notes right before I delivered the speech. This turned out to be a mistake because the notes were so new that some of the key words failed to trigger my memory quickly, causing me to falter at several points. I should have stayed with the original notes. Even though they were filled with arrows and insertions and deletions, I knew them intimately; I had a strong mental picture of where each point was located. The new notes, in contrast, had not yet "burned" their image in my brain.
- Don't put your notes on the lectern in advance of your speech. A janitor might think they are trash and toss them out, or a previous speaker might accidentally scoop them up and walk off with them.

Using one full sheet of paper for his notes, Canadian Member of Parliament Justin Trudeau makes a proposal to the House of Commons in Ottawa. By having notes that are brief, he can spend most of his time looking at the audience.

Options for Notes

Your instructor may require you to use one particular kind of note system, but if you have a choice, consider using one of these four popular methods.

Option 1: Use Note Cards

Your speaking notes can be put on note cards, as shown in Figure 12.7.

Note cards (especially the 3″ × 5″ size) are compact and rather inconspicuous, and they are easy to hold (especially if there is no lectern on which to place notes). The small size of the card forces you to write just a few key words rather than long sentences that you might be tempted to read aloud verbatim. If you use cards, be sure to number each one in case you drop or scramble them and need to reassemble them quickly.

Option 2: Use a Full Sheet of Paper

If you use a full sheet of paper, you can have the notes for your entire speech spread out in front of you. There are, however, several disadvantages: (1) Because a whole sheet of paper is a large writing surface, many speakers succumb to the temptation to put down copious notes. This hurts them in speechmaking because they end up spending too much time looking at their notes and too little time making eye contact with the audience. (2) A full sheet of paper can cause a speaker's eyes to glide over key points because the "map" is so large. (3) If a sheet is brought to the room rolled up, it can curl up on the lectern, much to the speaker's dismay.

(4) If a sheet is handheld because no lectern is available, it tends to shake and rustle, distracting listeners. (5) It is harder to make corrections on paper than on note cards. With paper, you may have to rewrite all your notes, whereas with note cards, you can simply delete the card containing the undesired section and write your corrected version on a fresh card.

If you have access to a lectern, you can use several 8.5″ × 11″ sheets in a clever way: put notes only on the top one-third of a sheet, leaving the bottom two-thirds blank. This will help your eye contact because you can glance at your notes without having to bow your head to see notes at the bottom of the page.

A final tip: To avoid the distraction of turning a page over when you have finished with it, simply slide it to the other side of the lectern.

Option 3: Use Visual Aids as Prompts

A popular technique is to use your visual aids (such as PowerPoint slides or posters) as the equivalent of note cards. The visuals jog your memory on what to say next, and they give you the freedom to walk around the room instead of staying behind a lectern.

If you use this strategy, avoid using a visual aid that is primarily a cue for yourself and has no value for the audience. In other words, design a visual aid for audience enlightenment, not for speaker convenience. Take a look at the notes in Figure 12.7. They are fine on note cards, but if they were displayed on a slide, they would be cryptic to the audience.

Option 4: Use Electronic Devices

If your instructor approves, you can put your notes on a smartphone or tablet. Just make sure that you limit yourself to brief notes, not a full text.

These options do not have to be used exclusively. They can be combined. For example, you could use note cards for part of a speech and visuals as prompts for another part.

Controlling Your Material

While preparing your outline, don't let your material become like an octopus whose tentacles ensnare you and tie you up. You must control your material, rather than letting your material control you. Here are four things you can do to make sure that you stay in control.

1. **Revise your outline and speaking notes whenever they need alterations.** Some students mistakenly view an outline as a device that plants their feet in concrete; once they have written an outline, they think that they are stuck with it—even if they want to make changes. An outline should be treated as a flexible aid that can be altered as you see fit.

2. **Test your outline.** One of the reasons for creating an outline is to *test* your material to see if it is well-organized, logical, and sufficient. Here are some questions that you should ask yourself as you analyze your outline (in your career, you can ask colleagues to critique your outline, using the same questions):

   • Does the introduction provoke interest and give sufficient orienting material?
   • Do I preview the central idea and/or main points?
   • Do the main points explain or prove my central idea?
   • Are the main points organized logically?

- Is there enough support material for each main point? Is there too much?
- Do I have smooth transitions between introduction and body, between main points, and between body and conclusion?
- Have I eliminated extraneous material that doesn't truly relate to my central idea?
- Does my conclusion summarize the main points and reinforce the central idea?
- Is my conclusion strong and effective?

3. **Revise for continuity.** Often an outline looks good on paper, but when you make your speaking notes and start practicing, you find that some parts are disharmonious, clumsy, or illogical. A speech needs a graceful flow, carrying the audience smoothly from one point to another. If your speech lacks this smooth flow, alter the outline and speaking notes until you achieve a continuity with which you are comfortable. (If you practice in front of friends, ask them to point out parts that are awkward or confusing.)

4. **Make deletions if you are in danger of exceeding your time limit.** After you make your speaking notes, practice delivering your speech while timing yourself. If the speech exceeds the time limit (set by your instructor or by the people who invited you to speak), go back to your outline and speaking notes and trim them. Deleting material can be painful, especially if you have worked hard to get a particular example or statistic. But it *must* be done, even if you exceed the limit by only five minutes.

Sample Speech as Presented

Earlier we examined the outline and sample notes for Jeffrey Omura's speech about foods that are not as healthy as they seem at first glance. A transcript of the speech as it was delivered is printed below. Notice that the wording of the actual speech is not identical to that of the outline. The reason is that Omura delivers the speech extemporaneously, guided by brief speaking notes.

Not as Healthy as They Sound

You go into a coffee shop, and you decide to buy a pastry to go with your coffee. [*Speaker shows the slide in Figure 12.4.*] At first you're attracted to the chocolate donut with sprinkles, but then you decide to go with the corn muffin because you figure it must be a lot healthier. But is it?

According to *Consumer Reports* magazine, the donut has 270 calories, while the corn muffin has almost twice as many—510. The average person needs about 2,000 calories per day, so the corn muffin gives you almost one-quarter of your daily allotment. The corn muffin also has a lot more fat than the donut.

I asked over a dozen people which they thought was healthier. Everyone said the corn muffin. It does sound healthy, doesn't it? Today I'd like to show you some other foods that aren't as healthy as you might think. By the way,

I'm not trying to tell you what you should eat. I just want to inform you about some surprising facts. Let's start with vegetables, which by themselves are very nutritious, but they're often served in ways that add a lot of extra fat and calories. Consider a salad with vegetables like tomatoes, lettuce, cucumbers. It can be healthy if you put a single serving of low-fat dressing on it. But the problem is, some people go into a fast-food restaurant and they order the salad because they think it's going to be healthier than the burger.

[*Speaker shows the slide in Figure 12.5.*]

A TV station in Bakersfield, California, KGET—they report that one fast-food chain sells a Spicy Chicken Caesar Salad with 750 calories, compared to the quarter-pound hamburger, which has 470 calories. What some people don't know is that a salad can become high in calories and fat if you add extra things like cheese, bacon, croutons, spicy chicken strips, and a large quantity of high-fat dressing.

You may have heard about potato chips being loaded with fat and contributing to the increased rate of obesity. So let's say you're in a grocery store and you see a bag of veggie chips. What could be unhealthy about that? Didn't your mother always say, Eat your veggies? Well, let's check with Patricia Chuey of Vancouver, Canada. She's a nutritionist and author of *Simply Great Food*. She says veggie chips are no more nutritious than potato chips. They're loaded with fat and they're high in calories. And they contain almost none of the nutritional value of real vegetables.

Well, how about a veggie sandwich? It can be healthy if you make it at home. But it's not as healthy if you get the Veggie Supreme sub at one national fast-food chain. A best-selling book *Eat This, Not That!* rated the Veggie Supreme as the Worst "Healthy" Sandwich in America. It has 1,106 calories and 56 grams of fat—more calories and more fat than you'd get in two Big Macs. The problem is, the foot-long sub comes with three different kinds of cheese, and it's covered in oil. By the way, in a case like this, you can avoid the extra fat and calories if you just ask the restaurant to skip the cheese and oil.

Now let's turn to nuts, fruits, and dairy products. As with vegetables, they can be very nutritious, but sometimes they, too, have unexpected high amounts of fat and calories.

Consider granola bars. [*Speaker shows the slide in Figure 12.6.*] They sound so wholesome and nutritious. They include nuts, dried fruits, and whole oats. Nutrition experts say that if you make your own granola bars, they can make a good healthy snack. But Jayne Hurley, a senior nutritionist with the Center for Science in the Public Interest, says that commercial granola bars you see in stores are loaded with sugar and syrup. She says, quote, "They're basically cookies masquerading around as health food."

Next we come to yogurt-covered raisins. What could be unhealthy about that combination? Rosie Schwartz, a dietitian in Toronto, Canada—she says that raisins by themselves are fine, and yogurt by itself is fine. But she says commercial yogurt-covered raisins—they're not what you think. The so-called yogurt coating is different from the yogurt you buy in the dairy section of your store. The coating is mostly sugar, oil, and some dried milk—and it's loaded with calories. One cup of yogurt-covered raisins has 750 calories—that's more calories than you'll find in two typical slices of homemade chocolate cake with chocolate frosting.

What would happen if you mixed two healthy foods together—like yogurt and fruit? Yogurt is a nutritious, calcium-rich snack. Fruit contains essential vitamins and minerals. So how about buying containers of yogurt that has fruit on the bottom? Sounds even better than the ordinary yogurt, doesn't it? But Schwartz says it's not real fruit on the bottom. It's fruit jam loaded with sugar. One serving can contain as many as 28 grams of sugar. That's more sugar than you'll find in a cup of vanilla ice cream.

Let's summarize. I've tried to show you that many foods are not as nutritious as you might think—corn muffins, some fast-food salads, veggie chips, the Veggie Supreme sub, granola bars, yogurt-covered raisins, and yogurt with fruit-on-the-bottom.

As I said in the beginning, I'm not trying to tell you what you should eat. But at least now you know you're not saving calories if you go with the corn muffin instead of the chocolate donut.

For three other complete outlines and transcripts of speeches, see the samples at the end of Chapters 15, 16, and 17.

Resources for Review and Skill Building

Summary

An outline is as important to a speechmaker as a blueprint is to a builder: the outline provides a detailed plan to help the speaker organize thoughts into a logical sequence and to make sure nothing important is left out.

Two popular types are the topic outline, which uses words and phrases for headings, and the complete-sentence outline, which uses entirely written-out headings. Some speakers use both forms: the topic outline for early drafts and the complete-sentence outline for refinements.

The parts of the outline include title, purposes, central idea, introduction, body, conclusion, transitions, bibliography, and visual aids.

After you complete your outline, prepare speaking notes based on it. You have four options: note cards, a full sheet of paper, speaking notes displayed as a visual aid, or an electronic device. Whichever you choose, avoid writing too many words because when you use notes in a speech, you want to be able to glance down quickly and retrieve just enough words to jog your memory.

Through all these stages, control your material by revising your outline and speaking notes whenever they need alterations. Test the strength of your outline, and revise for continuity—a smooth, logical flow from one part to another. Finally, make deletions if you are in danger of exceeding your time limit.

Key Terms

complete-sentence outline, *218*   speaking notes, *226*   topic outline, *217*

Review Questions

1. Why is an outline recommended for all speeches?

2. What is a topic outline?

3. What are the advantages of using complete sentences in an outline?

4. What are the parts of an outline?

5. The text says that the title of an outline should not be spoken in the speech. Why, then, should you have one?

6. Why should each subdivision of an outline have at least two parts?

7. What are the advantages of using cards for speaking notes?

8. What are the disadvantages of using a full sheet of paper for speaking notes?

9. You are advised to "revise for continuity." What does this mean?

10. What are the advantages of using visual aids as prompts?

Building Critical-Thinking Skills

1. Sort out the following items and place them into a coherent topic outline. In addition to a title, the scrambled list includes four major headings, with three subheadings under each. Scrabble, Cameras, Recipes, Ornamentals, Photography, Paintball, Gardening, Digital Imagery, Kitchenware, Annuals, Stoves, Hobbies & Interests, Cooking, Darkroom, Bingo, Perennials, Games

2. Transform the topic outline in the next column into a complete-sentence outline. Create a central idea for the outline.

Research
    I. Library
      A. Printed material
      B. Electronic databases
      C. Audiovisuals
   II. Personal
      A. Experiences
      B. Interviews
      C. Surveys

Building Teamwork Skills

1. Working in a group, create a central idea and a topic outline on one of the following topics. Put each item on a separate index card or slip of paper so that the group can experiment with different sequences. Your outline should have at least three major headings, each of which has at least three subheadings.

    a. automobile drivers
    b. fast food
    c. leisure-time activities
    d. good health

2. In a group, create a *complete-sentence outline* on how to study effectively. Include a central idea, at least three major headings, and at least four tips under each heading.

Wording the Speech

OBJECTIVES

After studying this chapter, you should be able to:

1. Explain the importance of choosing words that are appropriate for the audience and the occasion.
2. Use words that are clear, accurate, and vivid.
3. Describe the significant differences between oral and written language.

"GET TO KNOW YOUR WATER SOURCE" is the advice given by Alexandra Cousteau, an environmental scientist who is trying to educate the public on pollution in streams, lakes, and oceans. She says that we can begin our own understanding of water pollution in this way:

"Get acquainted with water as it runs through your life. I believe that everyone lives on a waterfront. Your waterfront can be the storm drain on your street, the creek in your backyard or the ocean that borders your town—our relationship with water in all of its

Alexandra Cousteau speaks at a World Water Day rally in Washington, DC.

forms is critical to the health and well-being of our families, our communities and the planet."[1] Cousteau's well-chosen words are a powerful force in her campaign to eliminate toxic chemicals from our water supply. In this chapter, we will look at how you, too, can use language to enhance the power of your speeches.

The Power of Words

If you witnessed a car crash, could you appear in court and give an accurate report of what you saw? Before you answer, consider this:

Courtroom lawyers have discovered that they can influence eyewitness testimony simply by choosing certain words when they ask questions. To demonstrate how this technique works, psychologist Elizabeth Loftus showed a group of people a video depicting a two-car accident. After the video, some of the viewers were asked, "About how fast were the cars going when they *smashed* into each other?" Other viewers were asked the same question except that the word *smashed* was replaced by the word *hit*. Viewers who were asked the *smashed* question, in contrast to the *hit* viewers, gave a much higher estimate of speed, and a week later, they were more likely to state that there was broken glass at the accident scene, even though no broken glass was shown in the videotape. Why? Because "smash" suggests higher speed and greater destruction than "hit." Thus, a single word can distort our memory of what we have seen with our own eyes.[2]

The power of words also is used by advertisers and retailers, as these research items show:

- Advertising agencies have learned that sales of a product can be increased if ads contain any of these words: *new, quick, easy, improved, now, suddenly, amazing,* and *introducing*.[3]

- Until a few decades ago, the toothfish was considered a "trash" fish—unfit for family meals. But when clever marketing people renamed it "Chilean sea bass," it became hugely popular, and is now one of the priciest items on restaurant menus.[4]

This little word has the power to boost sales significantly.

Can mere words have such power? Yes, but we shouldn't call words "mere." As writer C. J. Ducasse says, "To speak of 'mere words' is much like speaking of 'mere dynamite.'"[5] The comparison is apt. If dynamite is used responsibly, it can clear a rockslide on a highway; if used irresponsibly, it can maim and kill. In public speaking, if powerful "dynamite" words are used responsibly, they can keep listeners awake and interested, but if used irresponsibly, they can deceive audiences, distort facts, and dynamite the truth. Ethical speakers use words responsibly—not as clever devices of deception, but as vivid portraits of truth.

Finding the Right Words

The difference between the right word and the almost right word, Mark Twain once observed, is the difference between lightning . . . and the lightning bug. The truth of Twain's remark can be seen in the following historical vignette: One of President Franklin D. Roosevelt's most famous speeches was his address to Congress asking for a declaration of war against Japan in the aftermath of the Japanese attack on the American fleet at Pearl Harbor. As written by an assistant, the speech began this way:

December 7, 1941: A date which will live in world history.

Before speaking, Roosevelt crossed out the words *world history* and substituted the word *infamy*. Here is what he ended up saying:

December 7, 1941: A date which will live in infamy.

This has become one of the most famous sentences in American history, along with such memorable statements as "Give me liberty or give me death!" And yet, if Roosevelt had used the original sentence, it never would have become celebrated. Why? Because *infamy*—a pungent word tinged with evil and anger—was the right description for the occasion; *world history*—dull and unemotional—was merely "almost right." Lightning . . . and the lightning bug.

In choosing words for your speeches, your goal should not be to select the most beautiful or the most sophisticated but to use the *right* words for the *right* audience. As you analyze your audience before a speech, ask yourself, "How can I best express my ideas so that the audience will understand and accept them?" A word that may be ideal for one audience may be unsuitable for another.

Dr. Martin Luther King Jr., the leader of the civil rights movement of the 1960s, was a master at choosing the right words for each different audience. To a highly educated audience, for example, he would employ sophisticated language and abstract concepts, such as this sentence from his Nobel Peace Prize acceptance speech:

> Civilization and violence are antithetical concepts.

Such a sentence, appropriate for an erudite audience, would have been incomprehensible to most listeners if used in his speeches to sharecroppers in Mississippi who had been denied education. For them, he used down-to-earth illustrations. For example, in urging African Americans to struggle for their rights despite the fear of violence, Dr. King used a simple image that could be grasped by the least educated of his listeners:

> We must constantly build dikes of courage to hold back the flood of fear.

With either kind of audience, Dr. King was highly persuasive; but what did he do when he spoke to a group made up of both educated and uneducated people? He used inspirational messages designed to appeal to every listener. In his famous "I Have a Dream" speech, delivered to 200,000 people who had marched on Washington to demand equal rights for African Americans, Dr. King used stirring words that appealed to everyone:

> I have a dream that my four little children will one day live in a nation where they will not be judged by the color of their skin but by the content of their character.

There was nothing condescending about Dr. King's adaptation to his audiences. All good speakers choose the right words for each particular audience.

While considering your audience, you also should use words that are suitable for the *occasion*. If you speak at a fund-raiser, your words should be uplifting and encouraging; at a funeral, solemn and respectful; at a political rally, rousing and emotional.

Using Appropriate Words

Never make political, religious, racial, ethnic, or sexual references that might alienate anyone in your audience. Ask yourself, "Is there any chance at all that what I'm planning to say will offend someone in the audience?" If you have any doubt whether a word is appropriate, don't use it.

Tips for Your Career

Omit Crude Language

To many listeners, a speaker who uses profane, obscene, or explicit language comes across as insensitive, unprofessional, and uneducated. And yet some presenters use crude language because (they say) it adds spice and "most people don't mind." While it may be true that most people aren't upset, it is a mistake to ignore the feelings of those who are genuinely offended. (By the way, coarse language isn't an age-related issue, with the young unbothered and the old bothered. There are people of *all* ages who feel slapped in the face when they hear such words.) Consider this:

Advertising executive Ron Hoff tells of a business presentation in which the speaker was trying to sell his company's services to a public utility firm. The speaker liberally sprinkled his talk with four-letter words, plus some five-letter varieties not often heard in public.

There were 17 people in the audience, including one man "whose body actually convulsed a little every time he heard one of those words," says Hoff. "I watched him carefully. It was like somebody grazed him every few minutes with an electric prod. His body language attempted to cover these jolts he was receiving (he'd cross his legs, cover his face, slouch in his chair—nothing worked). He physically recoiled from the language he was hearing."

That man, it turned out, was the highest-ranking representative of the firm, so it came as no surprise when the firm declined to buy the services of the speaker's company.

Hoff later asked the speaker why he had used so much crude language.

"Oh, they love it," he said. "They talk just like that all the time."

"Yeah," Hoff said to himself. "All of them *except one*."

Avoid Stereotypical Words

sex-related stereotype
generalization that assigns roles or characteristics to people on the basis of gender

Stay away from language that reflects **Sex-related stereotypes,** such as *little old lady* and *typical male brutality.* Try to eliminate sexism from Sex-linked occupational terms. Here are some examples:

Original	Preferred Form
workman	worker
stewardess	flight attendant
fireman	firefighter
policeman	police officer
mailman	mail carrier
man-made	artificial
cleaning lady	housekeeper
foreman	supervisor

A speaker at an international electronics convention talked about *salesmen* who sell digital TVs at retail stores. To avoid excluding women, he should have talked about *salespeople, sales agents,* or *sales representatives.*[6]

Avoid Sexist Pronoun Usage

For centuries the masculine pronouns *he, his,* and *him* were used in the English language to designate an individual when gender was immaterial. In a sentence such as "Every driver should buckle *his* seat belt before *he* starts the engine," the pronouns *his* and *he* were understood to refer to drivers in general, both male and female. Today, however, such phrasing is undesirable because it excludes women.

To avoid offending anyone in your audience, you can handle this pronoun issue in one of three ways.

1. **Use masculine and feminine pronouns in tandem.** In other words, use *he or she* (or *she or he*) when referring to an indefinite person.

2. **Use plural pronouns.** Say simply, "All drivers should buckle *their* seat belts before *they* start the engine." This alternative has the advantage of being simple, while offending no one.

3. **Use the pronoun "you."** For example, "Whenever you get behind the wheel, *you* should buckle *your* seat belt before starting *your* engine." For speeches, this is almost always the best of the alternatives—it's simple and direct.

Using Words Accurately

To use words accurately, you need to be sensitive to two types of meanings—denotations and connotations—as well as to the use of correct grammar.

Use Precise Denotations

The **denotation** of a word is the thing or idea to which it refers—in other words, its dictionary definition. The denotation of *chair* is a piece of furniture on which one person may sit.

Try to use denotations precisely, bearing in mind the following cautions.

denotation
the thing or idea to which a word refers

Be aware that some words have more than one denotation.   The word *inflammable,* for example, is defined in dictionaries as "capable of burning quickly," but many people think that it means "not flammable." To be on the safe side (especially if matches are present), use a synonym such as "easily ignited."

Take care with words that have different denotations to different people.   What does "middle age" mean? Some people who are 30 say that it starts at 40, and some who are 40 say that it starts at 50. If middle age is an important concept in a speech, define the age span you mean by the term.

Avoid fancy words unless you are certain of their denotations.   Dennis Kessinger, a public speaker in Redding, California, once attended a retirement ceremony for a diligent worker whom one speaker fondly remembered as being a "superfluous" employee. Unfortunately, that word is an insult: It means nonessential, unneeded. Probably the speaker meant "superlative."[7]

Control Connotations

The **connotation** of a word is the emotional meaning that is associated with it. The words *slender, thin,* and *skinny* are synonyms; they have the same denotation, but the connotations are different: *slender* has a positive connotation, *thin* is neutral, and *skinny* has negative overtones.

connotation
the emotional overtones of a word that go beyond a dictionary definition

What are some connotations of the word "heart"?

As a listener and as a speaker, you should be aware of how connotations express the attitude of the person using the words. Let's say that some filmmakers produce a documentary on a Senator Dolores Perez. If they want to show that they are objective about the senator, they can describe her with a word that has a neutral connotation—*legislator*. If they want to convey approval, they can choose a term that has positive connotations—*national leader*. If they want to express disapproval, they can use a word that has negative connotations—*politician*. If they describe one of her campaign events, they could call it a *gathering* (neutral), a *rally* (positive), or a *mob* (negative). When she travels to Central America, the *trip* (neutral) could be called a *fact-finding mission* (positive) or a *junket* (negative).

Connotations can make a difference in persuasive campaigns. For years environmentalists tried to save swamps from being filled in and built on; they were often unsuccessful until they began to use the synonym *wetlands*.[8] *Swamp* evokes the image of a worthless quagmire filled with creepy, crawly creatures, while *wetland* suggests a watery wilderness of exotic birds and plants.

In exploring connotations, you don't have to rely solely on your own judgment. Many dictionaries have synonym notes, which are usually located after a word's definitions. On the Internet, you can use search engines to hunt for examples of how words and phrases are used by people throughout the English-speaking world. For example, if you want to explore the connotations of the word *maverick,* you can use it as a keyword in Bing (www.bing.com) and then scan articles for indications of how the word is currently used.

Use Correct Grammar

If you are like most people, you grew up speaking the way your family and friends did. But if that way of speaking is not considered standard English, it can hurt you in your career. Some business and professional people find "improper" English as offensive as body odor or food stains on the front of a shirt. For example:

- In North Carolina, a corporation executive said, "I just can't stand to be around people who use bad English. I would never hire a person who said things like 'I done it.'"

- In California, a man was passed over for a promotion (even though he was better qualified than the person who got the position) simply because he had the habit of saying "he don't" instead of "he doesn't."

- In New Jersey, the head of a company wanted to promote a deserving part-time worker to full-time secretary, "but I can't get her to stop saying 'youse' [as the plural of 'you']," he said. "My customers just won't accept that because they're used to dealing with educated people. They might think that the sloppiness in language carries over to the way we handle their accounts."[9]

Your Thoughts

A publishing company was embarrassed when a receptionist, responding to a request to speak to an executive, said, "He don't work here no more." Why do you think the company was embarrassed?

Are these people judging others unfairly? Of course! But many people associate poor grammar with lack of education and even low intelligence. They will seldom come right out and tell you that your grammar is incorrect. A boss, for example, may feel awkward about telling an employee his or her grammar is unacceptable; it is as embarrassing as telling friends that they have bad breath. So the employee is never told the real reason why he or she is being denied a promotion. Speaking at Dillard University, columnist William Raspberry told students, "Good English, well spoken and well written, will open more doors for you than

Incorrect	Correct
He (or she) don't	He (or she) doesn't
You was	You were
I done it.	I did it.
Between you and I	Between you and me
I had went.	I had gone.
She's (he's) already went.	She's (he's) already gone.
I been thinking.	I've been thinking.
I've already took algebra.	I've already taken algebra.
hisself	himself
theirself	themselves
We seen it.	We saw it.
Her (him) and me went.	She (he) and I went.
I come to see you yesterday.	I came to see you yesterday.
She ain't here.	She isn't here.
She don't love me no more.	She doesn't love me anymore.
He be late.	He is late.
I had wrote it.	I had written it.
Give me them apples.	Give me those apples.

Table 13.1
Common Grammar Mistakes

a college degree. . . . Bad English, poorly spoken and poorly written, will slam doors that you don't even know exist."[10]

In public speaking, errors in grammar cause you to lose credibility with your audience, according to business writers John V. Thill and Courtland L. Bovée, who add: "Even if an audience is broad-minded enough to withhold such a judgment, grammatical errors are distracting."[11]

From my observations, the mistakes in Table 13.1 seem to be the ones that are most likely to cause some people to downgrade you. If you commit any of these errors, I urge you to correct your usage, at least in professional settings.

Achieving Clarity

To be clear in the words you use, you must first be clear in your thinking. Think about a word before you use it. Ask yourself, will it be clear to someone who is new to my subject? In this section, we will examine how you can achieve clarity by using words that are simple, concrete, and precise.

Use Simple Words

A speechwriter for President Franklin D. Roosevelt once wrote, "We are endeavoring to construct a more inclusive society." President Roosevelt changed the wording to, "We're going to make a country in which no one is left out."[12] Roosevelt knew that although big words are sometimes needed to convey a precise meaning, a good communicator will choose simple words whenever possible.

But what if you want to convey a complex idea? Don't you need complex language—big words and weighty phrases? No. If you examine great works of literature, you will see that profound thoughts can be expressed easily and beautifully by simple words. Some of the greatest pieces of literature in the English language—the King James Bible and Shakespeare's works—use simple words to convey big ideas. For example, in Hamlet's famous soliloquy ("To be or not to be . . .") 205 of the 261 words are of one syllable. Citing an American literary classic, Abraham Lincoln's Second Inaugural Address ("With malice toward none . . ."), William Zinsser writes, "Of the 701 words in [the address], 505 are words of one syllable and 122 are words of two syllables."[13]

Big words are often used by pretentious speakers, who want to impress the audience with their intelligence, while simple words are preferred by audience-centered speakers, who want to make sure their ideas are clear. Here is an example of the contrasting styles:

Pretentious speaker:	From time immemorial, human beings have used their tongues to apply salivary secretions to heal a contusion, and medical researchers have ascertained that the procedure may indeed be efficacious.
Audience-centered speaker:	Licking a wound—a technique used by humans for centuries—may actually promote healing, according to medical researchers.

Use Concrete Words

concrete words
words that name persons and things that we can know by our five senses

abstract words
words that name qualities, concepts, relationships, acts, conditions, and ideas

Concrete words name or describe things that the listeners can see, smell, hear, taste, and touch—for example, *balloon, rose, gunblast, pizza,* and *chair.* They differ from **abstract words,** which refer to intangible ideas, qualities, or classes of things—for example, *democracy, mercy,* and *science.* While a certain amount of abstract language is necessary in a speech, you should try to keep it to a minimum. Whenever possible, choose concrete language, because it is more specific and vivid, and therefore more likely to be remembered by your audience. Concrete words help you create the mental images that you want to convey to your listeners. Here are some examples:

Abstract	Concrete
She is wealthy.	She makes $400,000 a year, has a winter home in San Diego and a summer home in Switzerland, and owns four sports cars.
It was a stormy day.	The sky was gray and gloomy, and the cold, moist wind stung my face.
Rattlesnakes are scary.	Its beady eyes staring at you without ever blinking, a rattlesnake can slither through the brush without making a sound—until it suddenly coils and makes its terrible buzzing rattle.

Use Precise Words

The most commonly quoted authority in America is "they," as in the following sentences:

They say that too much salt is bad for you.
They say that loud sound is not dangerous, as long as you don't feel any pain in your ears.

Instead of a vague "they," provide a precise source. For the first sentence above, find reliable sources: "Researchers at Johns Hopkins University have found that too much salt in one's diet can cause . . ." For the second sentence, if you try to find who "they" are, you may discover, as did one student speaker, that loud sound can cause permanent damage to one's hearing even if the noise is at a level that is not painful. The mysterious "they" can be wrong.

Two kinds of words—doublespeak and misused jargon—rob a speech of precision. Let us examine each.

Beware of Doublespeak

When some federal and state legislators raise taxes, they don't refer to their action as "raising taxes." To do so might anger taxpayers. No, instead they say they voted for "revenue enhancement."

"Revenue enhancement" is an example of **doublespeak,** language that is deliberately misleading, evasive, meaningless, or inflated.[14] Two of the most popular types of doublespeak are euphemisms and inflated language.

doublespeak
language that is designed to confuse or to be misunderstood

Euphemisms.   These are pleasant, mild, or inoffensive terms that are used to avoid expressing a harsh or unpleasant reality. If a public official talks about *regulated organic nutrients* and says that the stuff *exceeds the odor threshold*, would you know that he is talking about sewage sludge and admitting that it stinks?[15] Euphemisms are not always undesirable. Professor William Lutz of Rutgers University says:

euphemism
a mild, indirect, or vague word used in place of one that is harsh, blunt, or offensive

> When you use a euphemism because of your sensitivity for someone's feelings or out of concern for a recognized social or cultural taboo, it is not doublespeak. For example, you express your condolences that someone has "passed away" because you do not want to say to a grieving person, "I'm sorry your father is dead." When you use the euphemism "passed away," no one is misled. Moreover, the euphemism functions here not just to protect the feelings of another person, but to communicate also your concern for that person's feelings during a period of mourning.[16]

When a euphemism is used to deceive, it becomes doublespeak. Here are some examples:

- After one of its planes crashed, National Airlines described the event—in its annual report to stockholders—as an "involuntary conversion of a 727," a legal term designed to conceal the truth.[17]
- When politicians in Washington, DC, slashed funding for national parks in 2004, they asked park superintendents to call the budget cuts "service level adjustments."[18]

 Ethical Issues Quiz

In 2011, a United Airlines pilot spilled coffee all over his plane's communications equipment, causing navigation problems and forcing him to make an emergency landing in Toronto. An airline spokesperson referred to the incident as "a communications issue." Which of the following would have been the most ethical explanation by the airline?

A. "One of our pilots spilled coffee on equipment, causing navigation problems and forcing an emergency landing in Toronto."
B. "One of our pilots experienced issues with the airplane communications system and chose to make an emergency landing in Toronto."
C. "Because of an accident with onboard liquids, one of our pilots was forced to make an emergency landing in Toronto."

For the answer, see the last page of this chapter.

While some euphemisms can be deciphered, others are confusing. If a physician spoke of a *negative patient care outcome,* would you know that the term means death?[19]

Euphemisms become harmful when they mask a problem that should be dealt with. When homeless people are called "urban nomads," does this romantic euphemism cause the public to turn its eyes away from a problem that needs attention?

The best advice is this: Use euphemisms if tact and kindness require them; avoid them if they serve to deceive or confuse.

inflated language
words designed to puff up the importance of the person or thing being described

Inflated language.   This kind of doublespeak, says Lutz, "is designed to make the ordinary seem extraordinary; to make everyday things seem impressive; to give an air of importance to people, situations, or things that would not normally be considered important."[20] For example:

- A used car is advertised as a *pre-owned car* or *pre-enjoyed automobile.*
- A seafood restaurant calls its servers *seafood specialists.*
- A magazine refers to elderly people as *the chronologically gifted.*[21]
- A national pizza delivery chain announces that its drivers will henceforth be known as *delivery ambassadors.*[22]

Some inflated language seems harmless. If garbage collectors prefer to be called *sanitation engineers,* I may wince at the misuse of language, but I cannot criticize too strenuously. If they believe that the term dignifies their valuable but unglamorous work, why should I object to it? But the problem is that inflated language is spreading rapidly into all areas of life, causing misunderstanding and confusion. If you saw an advertisement for a *grief therapist,* wouldn't you envision a counselor for a mourning individual whose loved one has just died? If so, you'd be wrong, because *grief therapist* is an inflated term for an undertaker. How are we to know that an *excavation technician* is a ditch digger? That an *architect of time* is a watchmaker? That a *traffic expediter* is a shipping clerk? That a *customer engineer* is a salesperson? That a *corrosion control specialist* is the person who sends your car through a car wash?

One of my students once worked in a pet store as a cashier, but she was required to wear a badge that identified her as "Pet Counselor"—an inflated title that she resented because "it misled customers into thinking I was qualified to advise them on how to take care of their pets. All day long they would ask me questions that I couldn't answer. It was humiliating."

An inflated term may begin in kindness, but it often ends in confusion. Avoid it unless you know that it is clearly understood and preferred by your audience.

Your Thoughts

In referring to poor people, a government official once spoke of "fiscal underachievers." Why do you think he chose this term?

Don't Misuse Jargon

jargon
the technical language of a group or a profession

If a physician refers to a heart attack as an "acute myocardial infarction," she is using **jargon,** the specialized language of a group or a profession. Jargon is acceptable if all your listeners share your specialty. But if some listeners are outside your field, either avoid specialized terms or define them.

Some speakers use jargon unconsciously. Because they use certain words at work every day, they fail to realize that people outside their field may be unaware of the words' meanings. In a speech to a general audience, a mortgage broker talked about his involvement with "strippers." His listeners were startled and confused—they didn't know that "stripper" is finance jargon for someone who has stripped all the equity out of a home and spent the cash.[23]

Be careful with sports terms. After bicycle champion Lance Armstrong performed effectively during a day in the Tour de France competition, he told reporters, "There was no chain on the bike." Huh? It turns out that he didn't mean what he seemed to say. Unknown to most people outside cycling, the expression is used by riders to describe what it feels like when everything seems easy.[24]

Jargon is especially baffling to listeners who speak English as a second language. When you are speaking to these listeners, omit jargon or—if it is necessary to use a specialized term—explain it in concrete terms.

It's okay for this Indian film director to use movie jargon such as "Foley track" with film crews, but when he speaks to the general public, he should define such terms.

Using Vivid Language

"The best speaker," according to an Egyptian proverb, "is one who can turn the ear into an eye." How can one perform such magic? By using vivid language, such as imagery, metaphors, and similes.

Imagery

You can bring an abstract idea to life by using **imagery**—precise, descriptive words that create images. For example, E. Gordon Gee, president of Ohio State University, said in a speech at Vanderbilt University:

imagery
words that evoke mental pictures or images

> Our culture needs to discover this: that being angry all the time can dry out a person's heart. It can damage you, like stabbing yourself through the stomach to hurt someone standing behind you. The Buddha said, "If you knew what your anger was doing to you, you would shun it like the worst of poisons." Sustained animosity dries out and warps the soul. Please do not entertain it, because it gives no happiness.[25]

Gee's imagery of stabbing and poison and dried hearts is powerful and memorable. You can use imagery in your speeches by choosing details that paint a picture. For example, student speaker Juliann Martin describes her two-year-old son:

> Josh is a ball of energy. In everything he does, he has only one speed—high speed. He is very mobile, but he doesn't have the brains to put on the brakes. He would run right out into the street if you didn't watch him. His favorite word is "No!" But, to complicate matters, "no" sometimes means "yes." He is very rigid. He wants to wear the same clothes every day, and eat the same foods. Every night he wants the same story. Is Josh a mental case? No, he is a normal little boy who happens to be going through "the terrible twos."

By giving specific details, Martin paints a good portrait of what "the terrible twos" are all about.

Metaphors and Similes

Two devices that are especially effective for creating mental pictures are metaphors and similes. A **metaphor** is a figure of speech in which a word or a phrase that ordinarily describes one thing is used to describe another to suggest a resemblance. For example, "Enemy submarines were sharks that prowled the sea for prey." Comparing submarines and sharks creates a metaphor that is vivid and powerful. "The virtue of metaphor,"

metaphor
a comparison implying similarity between two things

Your Thoughts

What is the meaning of the metaphor "paint yourself into a corner"?

simile
a comparison, using *like* or *as,* of otherwise dissimilar things

mixed metaphor
incongruously combined metaphors

cliché
an overused word or phrase

alliteration
repetition of the beginning sounds of words

according to language scholars Bergen and Cornelia Evans, "is that it permits us to say a great deal in a few words."[26]

A **simile** is the same as a metaphor, except that the comparison between two things is made with the word "like" or "as." For example, "Langston Hughes says that a deferred dream dries up like a raisin in the sun."[27]

Here are some examples of the effective use of these devices:
Marriage is a cozy, calm harbor where you are protected from the storms of the outside world. (*Pamela Smith, student speaker*)

The snow covered up all the brown humps and furrows of the field, like white frosting on a chocolate cake. (*Joshua Burns, student speaker*)

Manic-depressives are like passengers on an emotional roller-coaster that goes up, up, up to a high of exhilaration and then down, down, down to a low of despair—without ever stopping to let them off. (*Sarah Gentry, student speaker*)

Beware of using a **mixed metaphor,** which occurs when a speaker combines two metaphors that don't logically go together. For example, if you say, "He stepped up to the plate and grabbed the bull by the horns," you are switching jarringly from a baseball image to a rodeo image. On a website, students at Calvin College in Michigan have collected mixed metaphors, including these:[28]

- "Once you open a can of worms, they always come home to roost." (*a Cincinnati radio announcer*)
- "I knew enough to realize that the alligators were in the swamp and that it was time to circle the wagons." (*a nationally syndicated radio host*)
- "Once again, the Achilles' heel of the Philadelphia Eagles' defense has reared its ugly head."(*a TV sports commentator*)

Avoid **clichés,** which are trite, worn-out words or phrases. Here are some examples: *better late than never, last but not least, raining cats and dogs, at the crack of dawn,* and *throw caution to the winds.* To eliminate clichés, try to find fresh, lively alternatives. Instead of saying, "His tie stuck out like a sore thumb," say something like "His tie was as out-of-place as a clown at a funeral."

Using Rhetorical Devices

Rhetorical devices are artful arrangements of words to make one's remarks more interesting and memorable. Here are four of the most popular devices.

Alliteration

Alliteration is the use of successive words that begin with the same consonant sound. We must love alliteration because our culture is filled with examples—in popular expressions (baby boomers), advertising slogans ("so soft and silky"), product names (Coca-Cola), TV shows (*Mad Men*), computer games (Leisure Suit Larry in the Land of the Lounge Lizards), sports events (Final Four), and people's names (Gail Gordon).

TIP 13.2

Tips for Your Career

Explore Rhetorical Devices

Have you ever used a polysyndeton in a speech?

A *polysyndeton* is the repetition, in quick succession, of several conjunctions (such as *and, or, nor, but*) that are unnecessary but give a dramatic rhythm to a spoken sentence. For example, an operations manager might assure her colleagues, "We will be even more efficient this year. That's because compared to other companies, we have better employees *and* faster software *and* a stronger infrastructure, *and* the largest warehouse in the business." You can say the sentence without all those conjunctions, but you would lose a great deal of power.

A polysyndeton is just one of the 40 rhetorical devices that are featured in over 200 audio (MP3) clips on the American Rhetoric website (www.americanrhetoric.com). Visit the site, click on "Rhetorical Figures in Sound," and explore clips taken from speeches, sermons, movies, songs, and so on.

Most of the devices were originally identified and labeled by teachers of rhetoric in ancient Greece and Rome. They have esoteric names such as *epanalepsis*, but don't be put off. If you listen to audio examples, you will realize that the techniques are easy to use and can enrich your own speeches.

Used sparingly, alliterative phrases can add sparkle to a speech. For example, "We need to help the hungry and homeless survivors of the tornado." But excessive use of alliteration can make you look silly: "I detest the puny political pygmies who pontificate piously about pure piffle."

Antithesis

An **antithesis** is a rhetorical device in which sharply contrasting ideas are juxtaposed in a balanced structure, as in "He has cold hands, but a warm heart." The balance and the contrast emphasize the ideas and make the sentence memorable.

antithesis
balanced juxtaposition of two contrasting ideas

The device has been used in great historical speeches, including President John F. Kennedy's famous words, "Ask not what your country can do for you—ask what you can do for your country." It also can be used in your speeches, with phrasing such as

- "We want action, but they give us words."
- "You call it a home—I call it a pigsty."
- "They don't care about people, but they do care about possessions."

Parallel Structure and Repetition

You can make your language memorable by taking advantage of rhythmic patterns. One such pattern is **parallel structure**—the repetition of a grammatical structure. Words, phrases, or clauses are arranged in parallel form, as in these examples:

parallel structure
equivalent grammatical forms used to express ideas of equal importance

We want a government . . . .   of the people,
                               by the people,
                               for the people.

We need parents who will . . . *praise honest efforts,*
                                punish bad behavior, and
                                ignore inconsequential acts.

repetition

repeating words or phrases
for emotional effect

Another effective rhythmic technique is **repetition** of words and phrases, as in the remark "This proposal is crazy, crazy, crazy."

When repetition and parallel structure are combined, the result can give emphasis to ideas while being pleasant to the ear. For example, student speaker Mei Zhang says:

> Who are the real heroes in society today? The famous and the powerful? Maybe so, but *we must not forget* the parents who work long hours in unglamorous jobs to help their kids succeed. *We must not forget* the kind souls who give loving care to the sick and dying. *We must not forget* the unselfish individuals who donate money to ease hunger and eradicate disease in countries they will never see.

Oral versus Written Language

One of the biggest mistakes some speakers make is to treat oral language in a speech as having the same requirements as written language. While the two forms of communication are similar, oral language requires more elaboration and repetition than written language. In an essay, you can write something like this:

> As an environmental prophet, Susan Jameson is a canary, not a cuckoo.

That terse sentence is excellent in an essay. The reader can study it at leisure if the meaning does not pop up immediately. But in a speech, a listener needs elaboration, such as this:

As an environmental prophet, Susan Jameson is a canary, not a cuckoo. We can trust her to be reliable. She's like the canaries that coal miners used to take into mines to detect poisonous gases. If the canaries died, the miners knew they needed to rush to safety. Like a canary, Jameson can reliably tell us when the environment is in danger. She is not a cuckoo—a bird that sings false warnings.

In addition to expanding material, a speaker must often use pauses and give vocal emphasis to certain words. For example, consider this concise sentence by author James Thurber: "Do not look back in anger, or forward in fear, but around in awareness." This sentence is perfectly written, but in oral communication, it is too compact to be easily retained. When I use it in a speech, I expand and dramatize it, giving emphasis to three key words: "To paraphrase James Thurber: [*pause*]

Do not look *back* in anger [*pause*] . . . Do not look *forward* in fear [*pause*] . . . Instead, look *around* in awareness." The pauses let the words sink in.

In oral communication, you need to repeat key ideas. You can use the exact same words, but if possible, change the wording—not only for the sake of variety, but also to increase your chances of reaching different segments of your audience. One set of words might work well for some listeners, while another set might be needed for other listeners. Dr. Rachel Marsella, an obstetrician who gives lectures to expectant parents going through Lamaze childbirth training, says of her talks:

> I try to use some medical language to reassure the better educated men and women that I'm a health professional and to show that I'm not talking down to them. But I have to keep in mind the less-well-educated people, too, so right after I use medical language, I'll say, "In other words . . ." For example, I might say, "About half of all mothers experience post-partum depression. In other words, they feel sad and blue and 'down in the dumps' after the child is born."

Dr. Marsella's technique permits her to repeat an idea, but with a fresh set of words.

Resources for Review and Skill Building

Summary

Because language has great power, the words that you use in a speech should be chosen with care and sensitivity. Always use language that is appropriate for your particular audience and occasion, avoiding words that might be over the heads of the listeners or that might offend any member of the audience.

To use words accurately, you must be sensitive to both denotation, which is a word's dictionary definition, and connotation, which is the emotional significance of the word.

Be careful to use correct grammar. In business and professional life today, "bad" English causes many listeners to lower their estimate of a speaker's intelligence and credibility.

You can achieve clarity in your language by choosing words that are simple, concrete, and precise. Beware of two types of doublespeak: euphemisms, which try to sugarcoat the unpleasant taste of reality, and inflated language, which exaggerates the importance of a person or a thing. Don't use jargon, the specialized language of a group or a profession, unless all listeners are certain to know the meanings of the words used.

You can make your language colorful and memorable by using imagery, metaphors, and similes, as well as rhetorical devices such as alliteration, antithesis, parallel structure, and repetition.

Oral language and written language are similar in many ways, but they should be treated differently in a speech. Oral language requires more elaboration than written language, and it needs repetition of key ideas.

Key Terms

abstract words, *242*

alliteration, *246*

antithesis, *247*

cliché, *246*

concrete words, *242*

connotation, *239*

denotation, *239*

doublespeak, *243*

euphemism, *243*

imagery, *245*

inflated language, *244*

jargon, *244*

metaphor, *245*

mixed metaphor, *246*

parallel structure, *247*

repetition, *248*

sex-related stereotype, *238*

simile, *246*

Review Questions

1. Why did Dr. Martin Luther King Jr. use different words with different audiences?

2. What is the difference between the denotation and the connotation of a word?

3. Why is incorrect grammar a handicap for a speaker?

4. What is a euphemism? Give an example.

5. What is inflated language? Give an example.

6. "Her life was a whirlwind of meetings, deadlines, and last minute decisions." Change this metaphor to a simile.

7. "My love," said poet Robert Burns, "is like a red, red rose." Change this simile to a metaphor.

8. This sentence commits a mistake: "Learning is a spark in a person's mind that must be watered constantly." What is the term used for this error?

9. "Louise languished in the land of lilies and lilacs." Which rhetorical device is used in this sentence?

10. In what way should oral language be treated differently from written language?

Building Critical-Thinking Skills

1. Some sports teams are named after birds—in football, Philadelphia Eagles, Atlanta Falcons, Seattle Seahawks, and Phoenix Cardinals; in baseball, Toronto Blue Jays, St. Louis Cardinals, and Baltimore Orioles. Why are teams named after these birds, and yet no teams are named after vultures, crows, or pigeons?

2. A book on automobile repair was once advertised under the headline "How to Repair Cars." When the advertising agency changed the headline to read, "How to Fix Cars," sales jumped by 20 percent. Why do you think sales increased?

Building Teamwork Skills

1. In restaurants, diners are more likely to select a dish if the menu describes it in appetizing terms, such as "topped with *zesty* garlic butter." In a group, create a list of at least 10 items for a menu. Pretending that you are managers of a restaurant, make the descriptions as tempting as possible.

2. A newspaper poll asked people to cite what they considered the most beautiful words in the English language.

Among the words mentioned were *lullaby, violet,* and *Chattanooga*. Working in a group, create a list of at least 10 words that group members think are especially beautiful. Discuss why the words are considered beautiful—is it the sounds of the words or the images the words evoke? If time permits, have group members who speak or have studied other languages contribute beautiful words from those languages.

Ethical Issues

Answer for p. 243: A. This is a straightforward, honest statement. The other two responses use euphemisms that are designed to mislead the public about what really happened.

Delivering the Speech

OUTLINE

The Key to Good Delivery

Methods of Speaking

Voice

Nonverbal Communication

The Question-and-Answer Period

Practice

OBJECTIVES

After studying this chapter, you should be able to:

1. Explain the four methods of delivery.
2. Practice and deliver an extemporaneous speech.
3. Use effective vocal techniques in a speech.
4. Demonstrate effective nonverbal communication in a speech.
5. Conduct a question-and-answer period in a manner that encourages audience participation.
6. Utilize productive methods in practicing a speech.

ALTHOUGH MICHELLE KWAN had skated in front of millions of people as a world champion figure skater, she was very nervous when she gave her first speech after being appointed by the U.S. State Department as a goodwill ambassador for the United States.

She began her talk in a choked, hesitant voice, she stumbled over her words a few times, she inserted a number of "uh's" into her remarks, her hands were fidgety and trembling, and she looked down at the lectern too often.

After a few minutes, however, a remarkable change occurred. She stopped shaking and stumbling. She looked straight at her audience. Her hands moved with strong gestures. She spoke smoothly and confidently.

After a shaky start, how did Michelle Kwan manage to achieve a polished delivery?

How did Kwan change from shaky to polished? "I learned in skating," she said, "if you fall, you quickly get up and keep going." She was determined to succeed, she said, because she wanted to reach every listener with her message—"All of us are alike, and we need to live in peace."

Since that first speech, she has taken her message to audiences in China, Russia, and many other countries, and she has gained a reputation as an effective speaker who creates a strong bond with her listeners.[1]

The Key to Good Delivery

The preceding story about Michelle Kwan exemplifies an important point: *The key to good delivery is a strong desire to communicate with the audience.* Though Kwan started out shaky, she had a burning desire to communicate with the audience, and before long she was effortlessly using good delivery techniques.

I have seen this phenomenon many times: Speakers who care deeply about conveying their ideas to the audience almost always do an adequate job with their delivery—even if they lack professional polish and training. R. T. Kingman, a General Motors executive, says that if you know what you want to say and if you want everybody in the room to understand your message, "all the other things like looking people in the eye and using good gestures will just come naturally."[2]

I am emphasizing the speaker's desire to communicate so that you can put the ideas of this chapter into proper perspective. The dozens of tips about delivery in the pages that follow are important, and you should study them carefully. But bear in mind that a strong desire to communicate with your audience gives you the power to deliver a speech with energy and effectiveness.

Methods of Speaking

Four basic speaking methods are used by public speakers today: memorization, manuscript, impromptu, and extemporaneous.

Memorization

Some speakers memorize an entire speech and then deliver it without a script or notes. Memorizing is a bad idea for most speakers, however, because of the following liabilities:

- You are forced to spend an enormous amount of time in committing the speech to memory.

- At some point in your speech, you might suddenly forget what comes next. This could cause you to panic. Once derailed, you might be unable to get back on track.

- Even if you remembered your entire speech, you would be speaking from your memory, not from your heart. This could cause you to sound remote and lifeless—more like a robot than a human being.

Memorizing does have one advantage: it lets you figure out your *exact* wording ahead of time. But this gain in precision fails to outweigh the disadvantages. I don't recommend this method.

> **Your** Thoughts
>
> While most instructors recommend against memorizing an entire speech, some suggest that you memorize short statements, such as a wedding toast or the last sentence of a speech. Do you think this is good advice? Defend your answer.

Manuscript

manuscript method
delivery of a speech by reading a script

Some speakers put their entire speech word for word on a **manuscript,** which they read aloud to the audience. In most cases, this is a poor method. Although a few people can read a text effectively, most speakers lack spontaneity and enthusiasm. They fail to look at the audience, do not speak with adequate expression, and often read too quickly.

There are some occasions, however, when reading a manuscript is appropriate. Here are two examples:

- In a highly emotional situation (such as delivering a eulogy at a funeral), having a script can give you stability and reassurance that you won't break down or ramble.

- Many government hearings and scientific conferences prefer manuscript delivery because each speaker's complete text is printed in a document or posted online.

Undesirable in most cases, reading a manuscript is appropriate in two situations. What are they?

If you use a manuscript, follow these guidelines: For ease of reading, print the document in large letters and leave generous spacing between lines. Print only on the top one-third of the page (so that you don't have to bob your head). Use a yellow highlighter to mark key words and phrases. Underline words that need to be spoken with extra emphasis. Insert slanting lines to indicate pauses. Practice reading the document many times, until you are thoroughly familiar with it.

If you are well-rehearsed, you should be able to look at your audience frequently and make gestures. Because you are using a method that is often boring, try to inject vigor and variety into your voice. Above all else, don't race through the manuscript.

Impromptu

Speaking **impromptu** means speaking on the spur of the moment—with no opportunity for extensive preparation. For example, without warning you are asked to give a talk to your fellow employees about your recent conference in Detroit. Or during a meeting, you are asked to explain a new procedure in your department.

impromptu method
speaking with little or no preparation

Because you have to respond immediately, impromptu speaking can be stressful. Just remind yourself that your listeners realize you are speaking off-the-cuff—they are not expecting a polished masterpiece. Here are some guidelines for impromptu success:

Decide your conclusion first.   Knowing how you will finish can prevent a long, drawn-out ending or a weak comment like "Well, I guess that's it."

Organize your speech.   You can use an organizational pattern from earlier chapters—for example, the problem-solution pattern—or you might consider one of the ready-made patterns shown in Table 14.1 on the next page. These patterns are used by experienced speakers to quickly structure impromptu speeches.

Let's explore one of the methods by imagining that you work for an accounting firm that has a standard 9-to-5 schedule, and you want to recommend staggered hours.

At a staff meeting, you are asked to make your case. Having only a few moments to prepare, you decide to use the PREP template (Table 14.1). Here is a streamlined version of your remarks:

> Position—"I believe that all employees will be happier and more productive if they are permitted to work 11-to-7 for one day a week."
>
> Reason—"With our present 9-to-5 system, many important services are unavailable to us."
>
> Example—"For example, we have no chance to renew a driver's license because the state license office is open only on weekdays, 9-to-5."
>
> Position—"Giving us one 11-to-7 day per week will improve morale because we will be able to meet both professional and personal responsibilities."

Don't rush.   Speak at a steady, calm rate. When beginning, and at various intervals, pause for a few seconds to collect your thoughts.

Whenever possible, link your remarks to those of other speakers.   When you take a statement made by a previous speaker and build upon it, you connect with your audience and hold their attention.

Don't feign knowledge.   If you are asked to comment on a matter about which you know nothing, simply say, "I don't know." Don't try to "wing it." Some speakers think that admitting ignorance will hurt their credibility, but the opposite is often true: if you fail to admit your ignorance and try to hide it behind a smokescreen of verbal ramblings, you can look insincere and foolish. In some situations you can say, "I don't know the answer to that, but I'll look into it and get back to you as soon as I can."

Be brief.   Some impromptu speakers talk too long, repeating the same ideas or dwelling on irrelevant matters. They usually do so because they are afraid they are omitting something important, or because they lack a graceful way of closing the speech. Rambling on and on is certain to weaken a speech.

Table 14.1
Patterns for Impromptu Speeches

Point-Support-Conclusion

- **Point** (State your point of view—that is, your key idea or objective.)
- **Support** (Give examples, stories, or other support material to explain or prove the point.)
- **Conclusion** (End with a restatement of the point and/or an appeal to action.)

PREP Method

- **Position** (State your position on the topic.)
- **Reason** (State your reason for taking the position.)
- **Example** (Give an example that helps to illuminate or explain your reasoning.)
- **Position** (Summarize and repeat your position.)

Past-Present-Future

- **Point** (State your key point.)
- **Past** (Discuss what happened in the past.)
- **Present** (Talk about what is occurring today.)
- **Future** (Predict what will or could happen in the future.)
- **Point** (Drive home your key point.)

Try to foresee situations where you are likely to be called upon to speak impromptu. Plan what you will say. For example, driving back from a workshop, rehearse in your mind what you will say if the boss asks you to make a little presentation to your colleagues about what you learned.

Extemporaneous

The **extemporaneous method** is the most popular style of speaking in the United States today. (Some people use the word extemporaneous as a synonym for impromptu, but most public speaking instructors make the distinction used in this book.) Your goal is to sound as if you are speaking spontaneously, but instead of giving the clumsy, faltering speech that many off-the-cuff speakers give, you present a beautifully organized, well-developed speech that you have spent many hours preparing and practicing.

In extemporaneous speaking, you speak from notes, but these notes are not a word-for-word script. Instead, they contain only your basic ideas, expressed in a few key words. When you speak, therefore, you make up the exact words as you go along. You glance at your notes occasionally to remind yourself of your next point, but most of the time you look at the listeners, speaking to them in a natural, conversational tone of voice.

This conversational tone is valued in a speech because it is the easiest kind for an audience to listen to, understand, and remember. When you speak conversationally, you are speaking directly, warmly, sincerely. Your manner is as close as possible to the way you talk to your best friends: Your voice is full of life and color; your words are fresh and vital.

Speaking extemporaneously permits flexibility because you can easily make adjustments to meet the needs of an audience. If, for example, you see that some listeners don't understand a point, you can restate your message in different words. If you are the last speaker of the evening at a banquet and you sense that your audience is about to go to sleep because of the long-winded speakers who preceded you, you can shorten your speech by cutting out minor points.

Despite its advantages, the extemporaneous method can be flawed if used incorrectly. Here are some common scenarios:

- In a three-point speech, Speaker A looks at his notes, states the first point, and then elaborates on it at great length. He loses track of time—until he finally notices a clock and gallops through the remaining points, confusing the audience.
- Speaker B has notes with key points, but she talks on and on about *all* the points. This causes her to go 20 minutes over her time limit, much to the annoyance of her listeners.
- Speaker C works from carefully crafted notes, but because he has not practiced the speech, his delivery is hesitant and ragged.

To avoid such mistakes, you must spend a lot of time preparing an outline and notes, and then rehearsing your speech, using a clock to make sure you are not ad-libbing too much.

Voice

Some people think that to be an excellent speaker, you must have a golden voice, rich and resonant, that enthralls listeners. This is not true. Some of the greatest orators in history had imperfect voices. Abraham Lincoln's voice was described by his

extemporaneous method

delivery of a speech from notes, following extensive preparation and rehearsal

How to Handle Tearful Situations

When one of my students, Sarah Mowery, was showing me her outline for a speech on drowsy driving, she told me that she planned to eliminate a photo and story about a close friend who had died after falling asleep at the wheel.

"But why?" I said. "That would be the most powerful part of your speech."

"I'm afraid I'd break down and cry," she replied.

I convinced her to keep the photo and story in the speech, and I told her a technique that I have used successfully when I deliver a eulogy at a funeral: As part of your preparation, accept the fact that you might be overcome with emotion. Have a handkerchief or tissue in your pocket or even in your hand. Tell yourself that tears are appropriate and that the audience will be sympathetic. Just making these preparations may be all that is necessary— I have never had to actually use my handkerchief.

In Mowery's situation (a classroom speech), the audience would not be expecting deep emotion, so I recommended that she hold a tissue in her hand and say, "Now I am going to tell you a sad story. I hope I can tell it without crying, but if I do cry, I am sure you will understand." Mowery followed this advice, and she ended up not crying at all.

But if she had cried, so what? The death of a close friend is a good reason to cry. Don't be afraid to show emotions. Listeners are very understanding, and some of them may join you in shedding tears.

One note of caution: Don't let tears cause you to end your speech prematurely. Pause, pull yourself together, and continue.

Jim Fordice, son of former Mississippi Governor Kirk Fordice, pauses in his eulogy to his father to wipe away tears. Fordice wisely kept a box of tissues nearby.

contemporaries as "thin, high-pitched, shrill, not musical, and . . . disagreeable,"[3] and Winston Churchill "stammered and even had a slight lisp."[4] It is nice to have a rich, resonant voice, but other characteristics of the human voice are more important—volume, clarity, and expressiveness. Let's examine all three.

Volume

The larger the room, the louder you have to speak. You can tell if your volume is loud enough by observing the people in the back. Are they leaning forward with quizzical expressions as they strain to hear your words? Then obviously you need to speak louder. You may have to raise your voice to overcome noises, such as the chatter of people in a hallway or the clatter of dishes during a banquet.

Speaking loudly enough for all to hear does not mean shouting. It means *projecting* your voice a bit beyond its normal range. If you have never spoken to a large group or if your instructor tells you that you have problems in projecting your voice, practice with a friend. Find an empty classroom, have your friend sit in the back row, and practice speaking with extra force—not shouting—so that your friend can hear you easily.

If you will be using a microphone, go to the meeting site early and spend a few minutes testing it. Adjust it to your height. If someone readjusts it during the ceremonies, spend a few moments getting it just right for you. Your audience will not mind the slight delay. Position it so that you can forget that it is there. This frees you to speak naturally, without having to bend over or lean forward.

When you speak into a mike, your voice will sound better if your mouth is 6 to 12 inches away. And remember this: You don't need to raise your voice. In fact, says professional speaker Arnold "Nick" Carter, "the invention of the microphone made it possible for me to speak to 18,000 people with a whisper."[5]

Your Thoughts

Will a microphone make a boring voice more interesting? Defend your answer.

Clarity

Spoken English is sometimes radically different from written English, as this news item demonstrates:

> One group of English-speaking Japanese who moved to the United States as employees of Toyota had to enroll in a special course to learn that "Jeat yet?" means "Did you eat yet?" and that "Cannahepya?" means "Can I help you?" Their English classes in Japan had failed to prepare them for "Waddayathink?" (What do you think?), "Watchadoin?" (What are you doing?), and "Dunno" (I don't know).[6]

For many speakers of English, **articulation**—the production of speech sounds by our vocal organs—is lazy and weak, especially in daily conversations. We slur sounds, drop syllables, and mumble words. While poor articulation may not hurt us in conversation as long as our friends understand what we are saying, it can hinder communication in a speech, especially if English is a second language for some of our listeners. We need to enunciate our words crisply and precisely to make sure that everything we say is intelligible.

articulation
the act of producing vocal sounds

If you tend to slur words, you can improve your speech by reading poems or essays aloud 15 minutes a day for three weeks. Say the words with exaggerated emphasis, and move your mouth and tongue vigorously. Enunciate consonants firmly and make vowel sounds last longer than normal. In real situations, you should not exaggerate in this way, but the practice will help you avoid the pitfalls of slurring and mumbling.

While poor articulation stems from sloppy habits, poor **pronunciation** is a matter of not knowing the correct way to say a word. Examine the common pronunciation mistakes listed in Table 14.2.[7]

pronunciation
correct way of speaking a word

Be careful using words that you have picked up from books but have never heard pronounced. One student had read about the Sioux Indians but had never heard the tribal name pronounced—he called them the *sigh-ox*. Another common slip is to confuse words that sound alike. For example, one student said that a man and woman contemplating marriage should make sure they are compatible before they say their *vowels*. (One listener couldn't resist asking, at the end of the speech, whether consonants were also important for marriage.) You can avoid such mistakes by practicing a speech in front of friends or colleagues and asking them to flag errors.

Expressiveness

A dynamic speaker has a voice that is warm and expressive, producing a rich variety of sounds. Let's examine five basic elements of expressiveness.

Table 14.2
Common Pronunciation Mistakes

	Incorrect	Correct
across	uh-crost	uh-cross
athlete	ath-uh-lete	ath-lete
burglar	burg-you-lur	burg-lur
chef	tchef	shef
chic	chick	sheek
drowned	drown-did	drownd
electoral	e-lec-tor-ee-al	e-lec-tur-al
environment	en-vire-uh-ment	en-vi-run-ment
et cetera	ek-cetera	et-cetera
evening	eve-uh-ning	eve-ning
grievous	greev-ee-us	greev-us
height	hithe	hite
hundred	hun-derd	hun-dred
library	li-berry	li-brar-y
mischievous	miss-chee-vee-us	miss-chuh-vus
nuclear	nu-cu-lar	nu-cle-ar
perspiration	press-pi-ra-tion	per-spi-ra-tion
picture	pitch-er	pick-shur
pretty	pur-tee	prit-ee
professor	pur-fess-ur	pruh-fess-ur
quiet	quite	kwy-it
realtor	reel-uh-tor	re-ul-tor
recognize	reck-uh-nize	rec-og-nize
relevant	rev-uh-lant	rel-uh-vant
strength	strenth	strength

Pitch and Intonation

pitch
the highness or lowness of a sound

intonation
the use of changing pitch to convey meaning

The highness or lowness of your voice is called **pitch.** The ups and downs of pitch—called **intonation** patterns—give our language its distinctive melody. Consider the following sentence: "I believe in love." Say it in a variety of ways—with sincerity, with sarcasm, with humor, with puzzlement. Each time you say it, you are using a different intonation pattern.

In conversation, almost everyone uses a variety of intonation patterns and emphasizes particular words, but in public speaking, some speakers fail to use any variety at all. Instead, they speak in a monotone—a dull, flat drone that will put many listeners to sleep. Even worse, they run the risk of appearing insincere. They may say something dramatic like "This crime is a terrible tragedy for America," but say it in such a flat way that the audience thinks they don't really mean it.

An absence of intonation also means that some words fail to receive the emphasis they deserve. For example, take a sentence like this: "Mr. Smith made $600,000 last year, while Mr. Jones made $6,000." A speaker who talks in a monotone will say the two figures as if there were no difference between $600,000 and $6,000. But to help listeners hear the disparity, the speaker should let his or her voice place heavy emphasis on the $600,000.

Loudness and Softness

Besides using the proper volume so that everyone in the audience can hear you, you can raise or lower your voice for dramatic effect or to emphasize a point. Try saying the following out loud:

> *(Soft:)* "Should we give in to the kidnappers' demands? *(Switch to loud:)* NEVER!"

Did you notice that raising your voice for the last word conveys that you truly mean what you say? Now try another selection out loud:

> *(Start softly and make your voice grow louder as you near the end of this sentence:)* "Edwin Arlington Robinson's character Richard Cory had everything that a man could want— good looks, lots of money, popularity." *(Now make your voice switch to soft:)* "But he went home one night and put a bullet through his head."

Changing from loud to soft helps the listeners *feel* the tragic discrepancy between Richard Cory's outward appearance and his inner reality.

Rate of Speaking

How quickly or slowly should you speak? It all depends on the situation. If you are describing a thrilling high-speed police chase, a rapid rate is appropriate, but if you are explaining a technical, hard-to-understand concept, a slow pace is preferred.

One of the biggest mistakes inexperienced speakers make is speaking too fast. It is especially important that you speak at a deliberate rate during your introduction. Have you ever noticed how TV dramas start? They don't divulge important details of the story until you are three or four minutes into the show. One obvious reason for this is to have mercy on late-arriving viewers, but the main reason is to give you a chance to "tune in" to the story and meet the characters. If too much action takes place in the first minute, you are unable to absorb the story. Likewise, when you are a speaker, you need to give your audience a chance to "tune in" to you, to get accustomed to your voice and subject matter. If you race through your introduction, they may become lost and confused.

Speaking at a deliberate, unhurried pace helps you come across as someone who is confident and in control, as someone who cares about whether the listeners understand.

Pauses

When you read printed material, you have punctuation marks to help you make sense out of your reading. In a speech, there are no punctuation marks, so listeners must rely on your oral cues to guide them. One of these cues is the pause, which lets your listeners know when you have finished one thought and are ready to go to the next. Audiences appreciate a pause; it gives them time to digest what you have said.

A pause before an important idea or the climax of a story can be effective in creating suspense. For example, student speaker Stephanie Johnson told of an adventure she had while camping:

> It was late at night when I finally crawled into my sleeping bag. The fire had died down, but the moon cast a faint, spooky light on our campsite. I must have been asleep a couple of hours when I suddenly woke up. Something was brushing up against my sleeping bag. My heart started pounding like crazy. I peeked out of the slit I had left for air. Do you know what I saw? *[pause]*

By pausing at this point, Johnson had the audience on the edge of their chairs. What was it? A bear? A human intruder? After a few moments of dramatic tension, she ended the suspense: "By the light of the moon, I could see a dark little animal with a distinctive white stripe. *[pause]* It was a skunk."

A pause also can be used to emphasize an important statement. It is a way of saying, "Let this sink in." Notice how Yvette Ortiz, a political science professor, used pauses in a speech on community service:

> When I am tempted to reject those ignorant fools who disagree with me, I remind myself of the words of novelist Peter De Vries: "We are not primarily put on this earth to see through one another, *[pause]* but to see one another through." *[pause]*[8]

In some speeches, you may find yourself pausing not because you want to but because you have forgotten what you were planning to say next and you need to glance at your notes. Or you may pause while searching your mind for the right word. Such a pause seems like an eternity, so you are tempted to use **verbal fillers** such as "uh," "er," or "um." Instead, remain silent, and don't worry that your silence is a "mistake." A few such pauses can show the audience that you are a conscientious speaker who is concerned about using the most precise words possible.

verbal fillers
vocalized pauses in which a speaker inserts sounds such as "uh"

Conversational Quality

Some inexperienced speakers give their speeches in a dull, plodding voice. Yet five minutes afterward, chatting with their friends in the hall, they speak with animation and warmth.

They need to bring that same conversational quality into their speeches. How can this be done? How can a person sound as lively and as "real" when talking to 30 people as when chatting with a friend? Here are two suggestions:

1. **Treat your audience not as a blur of faces but as a collection of individuals.** Here's a mental ploy you can use: at the beginning of a speech, look at one or two individuals in different parts of the room and act as if you are talking to them personally. You should avoid staring, of course, but looking at each face briefly will help you develop a conversational attitude. As the speech goes on, add other faces to your "conversation."

2. **Be yourself—but somewhat intensified.** To speak to an audience with the same natural, conversational tone you use with your friends, you must speak with greater energy and forcefulness. We are not talking now about projecting your voice so that the people can hear you but, rather, about *intensifying* the emotional tones and the vibrancy of your voice. How can you do this? Here are two ways:

First, let your natural enthusiasm show. If you have chosen a topic wisely, you are speaking on something you care about and want to communicate. When you stand in front of your audience, don't hold yourself back; let your voice convey all the enthusiasm that you feel inside. Many speakers are afraid they will look or sound ridiculous if they get involved with their subject. "I'll come on too strong," they say. But the truth is that your audience will appreciate your energy and zest. Think back to the speakers you have heard: Didn't you respond best to those who were alive and enthusiastic?

Second, practice loosening up. Some novice speakers sound and look stiff because they simply have had no practice in loosening up. Here is something you can try: Find a private location. For subject matter, you can practice a speech you are working on, recite poetry, read from a magazine, or simply ad-lib. Whatever words you use, say them dramatically. Ham it up. Be theatrical. Act as if you are running for president and you are trying to persuade an audience of 10,000 people to vote for you. Or pretend you are giving a poetry reading to 500 of your most enthusiastic fans. You will not speak so dramatically to a real audience, of course, but the practice in "letting go" will help you break out of your normal reserve. It will help you learn to be yourself, to convey your natural enthusiasm.

Nonverbal Communication

Nonverbal communication consists of the messages that you send without words— what you convey with your eyes, facial expression, posture, body movement, and the characteristics of your voice (as discussed in the preceding section).

nonverbal communication
transmission of messages without words

To be credible to your audience, your nonverbal communication must be synchronized with your words. If you say, "I'm very happy to be here," but your eyes are cast downward and your face is glum, your audience will think that you are not being honest. *Whenever there is a discrepancy between "body language" and words, listeners will believe the nonverbal signals instead of the verbal message.*[9]

To get your nonverbal signals synchronized with your words, show enthusiasm (with your eyes, facial expression, posture, and tone of voice) as you speak. However, you may be asking, "What if I don't really feel happy and confident? I can't lie with my body, can I?" This is a good question, because there are times when you don't want to speak or don't feel like standing up in front of a group. At times like these, what should you do?

Pretend. Yes, pretend to be confident in yourself and in your ideas. Pretend to be glad to appear before your audience. Pretend to be enthusiastic. But, you may ask, isn't this phony? Isn't this forcing the body to tell a lie? Yes, but we often must simulate cheerfulness and animation: a crucial job interview, a conference with the boss, an important date with someone we love. By *acting* as if we are confident, poised, and enthusiastic, we often find that after a few minutes, the pretense gives way to reality. We truly become confident, poised, and enthusiastic.

Consider the comedians and talk-show hosts who appear night after night on TV. Do you think they are always "up"? No. Like you and me, they have their bad days. Nevertheless, they force themselves to perform and pretend to be enthusiastic. After about 60 seconds, most of them report, the pretense gives way to reality and they truly *are* enthusiastic. (*A word of advice:* If this transformation fails to happen to you—if you don't feel enthusiastic after a few minutes—you should continue to pretend.)

This nonverbal signal is used throughout the world. What does it mean?

How can you make your body "lie" for you? By knowing and using the signals that the body sends out to show confidence and energy. The following discussion of the major nonverbal aspects of public speaking will help you become aware of these signals.

Personal Appearance

Your audience will size up your personal appearance and start forming opinions about you even before you open your mouth to begin your speech. You should be clean, well-groomed, and attractively dressed.

Janet Stone and Jane Bachner, who conduct workshops for women executives, have some good advice for both men and women:

> As a general rule of thumb, find out what the audience will be wearing and then wear something yourself that is just a trifle dressier than their clothes. The idea is to establish yourself as "The Speaker," to set yourself slightly apart from the crowd . . .[10]

Dressing up carefully is a compliment to the audience, sending a nonverbal message: You are important to me—so important that I dressed up a bit to show my respect for you.

Don't wear anything that distracts or diminishes communication. Baseball caps tend to hinder eye contact, and to some listeners, they suggest disrespect. A T-shirt with a ribald or controversial slogan printed on the front may direct attention away from the speech itself, and it may offend some members of the audience.

Some students have trouble accepting the idea of dressing up. Isn't it true, they say, that people should be judged by their character and not by their clothes? Yes, but in the real world, you *are* judged by what you wear. In the words of one magazine article title: "What You Wear Is Almost as Important as What You Say."[11] This is an exaggeration, of course, but the point is important: How you dress does make a difference.

Your Thoughts

What nonverbal message is given by a person who goes to a funeral dressed in a T-shirt and jeans?

Eye Contact

Look at your audience 95 percent of the time. Good eye contact is important because: (1) It creates an important bond of communication and rapport between you and your listeners. It is, in the words of Jack Valenti, former president of the Motion Picture Association

As Jason Terry of the Dallas Mavericks speaks at the American Airlines Center in Dallas, he demonstrates good delivery techniques by looking directly at his listeners and using gestures. Note that he has dressed up—an important way to show respect for the audience and the occasion.

of America, a "figurative handshake."[12] (2) It shows your sincerity. We distrust people who won't look at us openly and candidly. (3) It enables you to get audience feedback. For example, did a number of listeners look puzzled when you made your last statement? Then you obviously confused them; you need to explain your point in a different way.

The biggest spoiler of good eye contact is looking at your notes too much—a mistake that is usually made for these two reasons: (1) You are unprepared. This can be corrected by rehearsing your speech so many times that you need only glance at your notes to remind yourself of what comes next. (2) You are nervous. Some speakers are well-prepared and don't really need to look at their notes very often, but they are so nervous that they scrutinize their notes to gain security and avoid the audience. One way to correct this is to put reminders, in giant red letters, on your notes—LOOK AT AUDIENCE—to nudge you out of this habit.

Another killer of eye contact is handouts. As we discussed in Chapter 9, you should never distribute a handout during a speech unless it is simple and short. If you give listeners an eight-page packet during your speech, you will lose eye communication.

Eye contact is more than glancing at the audience from time to time. It is more than mechanically moving your head from side to side like an oscillating fan. For a large audience, the best technique is to have a "conversation" with three or four people in different parts of the room (so that you seem to be giving your attention to the entire audience). For a small audience, look at *every* listener. Professional speaker Danny Cox uses a technique called "locking" whenever he speaks to a small gathering:

> I learned something once from a piano player. I couldn't believe how she held an audience in a cocktail bar. It was so quiet in there you couldn't believe it. I realized one night what she was doing. She was looking at each person and as soon as she made eye contact with them, she smiled at them. And then moved on to the next one, and smiled. She was "locking" everybody in. This is a good technique in public speaking—very simple, too.[13]

Facial Expressions

Let your face express whatever emotion is appropriate during your speech. One student told me he was planning to speak on how to perform under pressure; his primary example was the thrilling moment in high school when he kicked the winning field goal in the final seconds of a championship football game. As he talked to me, his face was suffused with excitement. But when he got up in front of the class and told the same story, his face was blank. Gone was the joy; gone was the exhilaration. Without expression, he weakened the impact of the story.

Whatever your subject matter might be, your face should be animated. "Animation," says speech consultant Dorothy Sarnoff, "is the greatest cosmetic you can use, and it doesn't cost a cent. Animation is energy in the face . . . . It's action that comes not only through the eyes, but around the mouth and the whole face. It tells the listener you're glad to be right where you are—at the lectern, around a conference table or across a desk."[14] How can you make your face animated? By choosing a subject you care about, by having a strong desire to communicate your message to your listeners, and by delivering your speech with energy and enthusiasm.

Posture

Good **posture** conveys confidence. Stand up straight, with your weight equally distributed on your feet so that you appear stable and assured. Avoid two common pitfalls—slouching and drooping at one extreme, and being rigid and tense at the other extreme. Your goal should be relaxed alertness—in other words, be relaxed but not *too* relaxed.

posture
the position of your body as you sit or stand

Tips for Your Career

Decide Whether and How to Use a Lectern

Experienced speakers disagree about whether a lectern should be used for career and community speeches. Some say that a lectern gives the speaker dignity and is a convenient stand for notes, especially on formal occasions such as an awards ceremony or a funeral. Others object that a lectern creates a physical barrier. "I don't want anything coming between me and my audience," a politician told me. British speech consultant Cristina Stuart says, "I am 5′2″ and some lecterns are 4′0″ high, so how can I be a powerful speaker if my listeners can only see my head peeping over the edge?" Her advice: "Even if you are over six feet tall, try to stand to one side of the lectern so that you can refer to your notes and your listeners can see all of your body."

Here is a technique that has become popular: using the lectern as "home base," walk a few paces to the left or right of it each time you make a point. In other words, glance at the notes on the lectern to remind yourself of the point you want to make, move away from the lectern a few paces, make the point, then walk back to the lectern to pick up your next point.

If a lectern is movable, some speakers remove it and simply hold their note cards in one hand (leaving the other hand free for gesturing). For a large audience, if the lectern is unmovable and has a stationary microphone, says Stuart, "you have no choice but to stand behind it. Stand on a box if you are short so that your upper body can be seen."

With some audiences, you can arrange for a remote or mobile microphone so that you can move away from the lectern.

If you are speaking at a lectern, here are some things *not* to do: Don't lean on it. Don't slouch to one side of it. Don't prop your feet on its base. Don't rock back and forth with it.

Some speakers like to sit on the edge of a desk to deliver a speech. This posture is fine for one-hour classroom lectures because the speaker gets a chance to relax, and his or her body language conveys openness and informality. But for short speeches, especially the kind you are expected to deliver in a public speaking class, stand up. This will help to make you alert and enthusiastic.

Movement

You don't have to stand in one place throughout your speech. Movement gives your body a chance to dissipate nervous energy. It also can be used to recapture your listeners' attention if they are getting bored or tired; an animated speaker is easier to follow than an unanimated speaker who stays frozen in one spot.

You can use movement to emphasize a transition from one point to the next. (For example, walk a few steps to the left of the lectern as you say, "Now that we have examined the problem, let's discuss the solution.") You can move *toward* your listeners when you plead for an immediate response (for example, "Please donate five dollars to help find a cure for cystic fibrosis".)

Make sure that all movements are purposeful and confident—not random and nervous. If you pace like a tiger in a cage, your audience will be distracted and even annoyed. Don't sway back and forth; don't rock on your heels. In short, make your movements add to your speech, rather than subtract from it.

Using Notes

For classroom speeches, your instructor will tell you whether you may use notes. For speeches in your career, the note system that was explained in Chapter 12 is highly recommended.

Most professional speakers use cards or sheets of paper, and they have different ways of using them. Speakers who use a lectern place their notes in a stack on the lectern and consult one at a time, or they spread notes out so that several are visible at a time. Speakers who don't use a lectern prefer to hold their notes in one hand while gesturing with the other.

Whatever system you use, remember our earlier warning: *Use notes sparingly.* Look at your audience 95 percent of the time.

Gestures

Making gestures with your hands and arms can add power to your words, and cause you to look animated and engaged. Except in a few cases (discussed below), gestures should be natural and unplanned. They should occur spontaneously and be in harmony with what you are saying.

At all times, have at least one hand free to make gestures. To help yourself abide by this rule: (1) Don't grip the lectern with your hands. (2) Don't clutch your notes with both hands. (3) Don't stuff both hands into your pockets.

If you use a lectern, don't let it hide your gestures. Some speakers rest their hands on the lectern and make tiny, flickering gestures that can be sensed but not seen by the audience. This makes the speaker look tentative and unsure.

At a rally in Seoul, labor leader Kim Young-hoon campaigns for improved working conditions. His words are embellished by two elements of nonverbal communication—the speaker's assertive, confident arm gesture and the statue of a clenched fist, suggesting strength and determination.

When you make gestures, use all of your arm, advises British speech consultant Cristina Stuart:

> Don't tuck in your elbows to your waist or make jerky, half-hearted, meaningless gestures. I remember a tall woman in one of my courses who, through shyness, stood hunched up, making tiny movements with her hands. We advised her to stand tall, make eye contact, and use her arms to express her enthusiasm. The result was startling—she became regal and was very impressive. Without even opening her mouth, she looked like a self-confident, interesting speaker.[15]

Some speeches call for lots of gestures; some call for few or none. If you were describing your battle to catch a huge fish, you would find your hands and arms constantly in motion; if you were giving a funeral eulogy, you might not make any gestures at all.

While most gestures should occur naturally, there are a few occasions when it is appropriate to plan and rehearse them. If you have three major points to make, you can practice holding up the correct number of fingers. If you are discussing two contrasting ideas, you can hold up one hand when you say, "On the one hand . . ." and then hold up your other when you say, "On the other hand . . ."

The larger the audience, the more sweeping your gestures should be. Evangelists and political leaders who use broad, expansive arm movements in addressing multitudes in giant stadiums are doing so for a good reason: they are able to establish a bond with people who are hundreds of yards away. Small gestures would be lost in the vastness of the arena.

Some students worry too much about gestures. If you are the kind of person who simply does not gesture a great deal, don't be dismayed. Just be sure to keep at least one hand free so that if a gesture wells up, you will be able to make it naturally and forcefully.

One final note about your hands: make sure they do nothing to distract the audience. Don't let them jingle keys, riffle note cards, fiddle with jewelry, adjust clothes, smooth your hair, rub your chin, or scratch any part of your body.

Beginning and Ending

First impressions are important, especially in a speech, where "you have only one chance to make a first impression," as one IBM executive told me. You make this first impression as you walk to the front and as you say your first few words.

When you rise from your seat, avoid sighing or groaning. Walk forward with an air of confidence. Avoid the mistake of rushing forward and starting to speak even before you get to the front. Listeners need time to get settled for your speech, clear their minds of other things, and tune in to you.

When you face your audience, pause for a few seconds. Don't say a word—just stand in silence. Some inexperienced speakers are terrified by this silence; they think it makes them look too frozen with fear to speak. If you have this concern, relax. A brief period of silence is an effective technique that all good speakers use. It is a punctuation device, separating what went before from what is to come—your speech. It creates drama, giving the audience a sense of anticipation. In some cases, you may need to wait longer than a few seconds. If you are speaking at a community meeting, for example, and people are arriving late, it is best to wait until the noise created by the latecomers has settled down. Or if many members of the audience are chatting with one another, simply stand and wait until you have their attention.

During these opening moments of silence, you have a chance to make sure your notes are in order and to review once again what you will say in your introduction. The next step is very important. Before you say a word, give your audience a friendly,

Tips for Your Career

Deal with Distractions in a Direct but Good-Humored Manner

In classroom speeches, you should have an attentive, courteous audience, but at some point in your career, you may encounter an audience that contains listeners who chat among themselves while you are trying to speak, distracting other listeners.

Professional speakers stress that you should *not* ignore disturbances. Confront these listeners, but do so in a calm, friendly, good-humored manner.

One technique is to simply stop your speech and look directly at the rude listeners (try to look friendly and not irritated). This is often all it takes to get people to stop talking. Sometimes people sitting near the offenders will pick up on your cue and help you out by turning and saying, "shh."

Professional speaker Rosita Perez of Brandon, Florida, says that you may lose the respect of your entire audience if you ignore the talkative few. "Confront them *kindly*," she advises. "Say, 'It seems to me you must have a lot of catching up to do with your friends. I wonder if you would visit outside so I can continue?'" In most such cases, the listeners will stay in the room and give the speaker respectful silence for the rest of the speech.

Speech consultant Sandy Linver says that with a large audience,

> I take the trouble to gently zero in on . . . the chatterers and pull them back in. I say something like, "Are you with me?". . . If it's a small group, side conversations often are important to the subject at hand, so it is important not to ignore them. If I were speaking at a business meeting of 15 people or so, I might say to the 3 people talking among themselves, "That looks as if it might be important. Would you like to share it with the group?" Often they are discussing something I have said that needs clarification or elaboration, and the whole group benefits when they are encouraged to speak up.

Some speeches are marred by the incessant crying of a baby. Actor and orator Steve Allen once handled this situation by saying, "As the father of four sons I've more than once been in the position of the parents of that child. Personally I could go on even if there were several children crying at the same time, but I know that most

people are too distracted by that sort of thing to concentrate on what is being said. So if you wouldn't mind taking the child out—at least until he stops crying—I'm sure the rest of our audience would appreciate it." This remark, says Allen, prompted applause from the audience and "gracious cooperation from the parents."

Some speeches are marred by listeners with electronic devices. For advice on how to handle these situations, see Tip 3.3, "Confront Electronic Rudeness," in Chapter 3.

confident look (if possible and appropriate, smile) and then, continuing to look at your listeners instead of at your notes, say your first few sentences. You should have practiced your introduction thoroughly so that you can say it without looking down at your notes. It is important to establish eye contact at this point. By looking at the listeners directly, your body language is saying, "I'm talking to you—I'm not up here just going through the motions of making a speech. I want to communicate. I want to reach out to you."

If appropriate, a smile is a good way to begin a speech. Kimberly Oliver Burnim of Silver Spring, Maryland, the winner of the National Teacher of the Year Award in 2006, gives her audience a smile as she begins a speech at Wilmington University in Delaware.

While first impressions are vital, final impressions are also important. Your conclusion should be well-rehearsed (though not memorized) so that you can say it without looking at your notes. At the end of your speech, pause a few moments, look at your audience, and say, "I wonder what questions you have" or "I'll be happy to answer your questions now." Avoid gathering up your papers and leaning toward your seat—this sends a nonverbal message: "Please don't ask me any questions."

The Question-and-Answer Period

The question-and-answer period enables listeners to get clarification and further information about your topic. In classroom speeches, it usually involves only a small percentage of the total time spent in front of the audience, but in some career presentations—such as selling a product—it is the longest and most important part.

Many listeners are so accustomed to listener–speaker interaction that they will interrupt during a speech to ask questions. In some technical presentations or classroom lectures, such interruptions may be appropriate and acceptable, but in other speeches, they are a nuisance. The continuity of the speaker's remarks is broken because listeners are prematurely asking questions that will be answered later in the speech. If you feel that your speech would be marred by interruptions, you should announce (in the orienting material of your introduction), "I know many of you will have questions. I'd like to ask you to hold them until I finish my presentation and then I'll be happy to try to answer them."

Don't feel defeated if you are not asked any questions. It could mean that you have covered everything so well that the listeners truly have nothing to ask.

Why is the Q & A period considered vital in many presentations?

Here are some guidelines:

Planning

- Find out ahead of time if the person planning the program will want or permit a question-and-answer period, and, if so, how much time will be allotted.
- Plan for the question-and-answer period by jotting down all the questions that might come from the audience and decide how you would answer them. Also discuss your speech with a few friends or associates and ask them to prepare a list of possible questions.

Fielding Questions

- Give the audience time to ask their questions. Some speakers impatiently wait 3 seconds, and then dash back to their seats. They don't really give the audience a fair chance. When you ask for questions, pause for as long as 10 seconds. If you get the feeling that no questions at all will be asked, you can say, "Thank you," and then sit down. But if you sense that the audience is simply shy, you can break the ice by saying, "One question that I am often asked is . . ." In some community and career contexts, you may want to involve listeners by asking *them* a question; for example, "What do *you* think of my proposal?"

Ethical Issues Quiz

Suppose you are giving a speech on a controversial topic at a community meeting. Is it acceptable for you to invite a few friends to pose as community members and ask easy questions during the question-and-answer period?

A. Yes, having allies will bolster your confidence, and the audience will know that your ideas have support.
B. No, it is unethical to try to influence an audience by using devious techniques.

For the answer, see the last page of this chapter.

- While a person is asking a question, look directly at him or her, but as you give your answer, look at the entire audience.
- In a large room, when a question is asked, repeat it for the benefit of listeners who may not have been able to hear it. Repeating it also gives you time to frame your answer. If a question is unclear to you, ask the listener to clarify it.
- Be consistent in how you respond. If you reward some questions with "That's a good question" or "I'm glad you asked that," the listeners who receive no praise may feel as if their questions have been judged inferior. Reward all questions—or none.
- If you don't know the answer to a question, say so. Your listeners will not think less of you. They *will* think less of you if you try to fake expertise. In some cases, you can ask the audience for help: "I don't know the answer; can anyone help us out?"

Handling Problems

- If a listener points out an inaccuracy or an omission in your material, don't be defensive. If the listener's point seems to have merit, say so. You can say something like "You may be right—that statistic could be outdated. I'll have to check it. Thanks." Such an approach is not only honest—it gains respect from listeners.
- Don't let any listener hog the question-and-answer period. If a person persists in asking one question after another or launches into a long monologue, it is your responsibility to intervene. You can say something like "Let's give others a chance to ask questions; if we have time later, I'll get back to you" or "Why don't you and I talk about this in greater detail after the meeting?"
- Decline to answer questions that are not appropriate for a discussion in front of the entire audience—for example, questions that are too personal or that require a long, technical explanation that would bore most of the listeners. You can politely explain your reasons; for example, "That's a little too personal—I'd rather not go into that," or "I'm afraid it would take up too much time to go into the details right now." In some cases, you might tell the questioner to see you afterward for a one-on-one discussion.

Ending the Session

- Don't let the question-and-answer period drag on. If you have been allotted an hour, say, for both your speech and the Q & A period, end the session promptly at the end of an hour—even if some listeners still have questions. If you sense that some listeners would like to continue the session, you can say, "I'm stopping now because I promised I would take up only one hour of your time. However, if any of you would like to stay afterwards, you can move to the seats here at the front and we'll continue our discussion."
- At the end of the Q & A session, provide a conclusion. No, not the conclusion you have already given in your speech, but a brief wrap-up—to give a sense of closure and provide one last look at your message. For example: "Thank you for letting me talk to you today about the need to get a flu shot every year. With flu season approaching, I hope each of you will get a flu shot as soon as possible."

Practice

After you have written your outline and made notes based on it (as discussed in Chapter 12), you should spend a great deal of time rehearsing your speech. Practice, practice, practice—it's a crucial step that some inexperienced speakers leave out. Practice makes you look and sound fluent, smooth, and spontaneous. Practice bolsters your confidence, giving you a sense of mastery and competence.

McGraw-Hill **Speech Prep**
http://www.mhhe.com/ speechprep/

Here are some tips:

- Start early. If you wait until the eve of your speech, you will not have enough time to develop and polish your delivery.

- Practice going through your entire speech at least four times. Spread your practice sessions over several days, because having time intervals between sessions will cause you to make greater progress.

- "Practice ideas, not words" is a popular saying in Toastmasters clubs. In other words, learn your speech point by point, not word for word. Remember that your goal in extemporaneous speaking is not to memorize or read a speech. Every time you say your speech (whether in practice or in delivery to an audience), the wording should be a bit different. The ideas will be the same, but not the exact words.

- Time yourself. If your speech exceeds the time limit set by your instructor or by the group that invited you, go back to your outline and notes and trim them down.

- During most of your practice sessions, go all the way through the speech. Don't stop if you hit a problem; you can work it out later. Going all the way through helps you see whether your ideas fit together snugly, and whether your transitions from point to point are smooth.

- Some speakers find it helpful to practice in front of a mirror or to use a video camcorder or an audiotape recorder. Whether or not you use one of these techniques, you should practice at least once in front of a *live* audience—friends or relatives who can give you a candid appraisal. Don't say, "Tell me how I do on this," because your evaluators will probably say, "Good job—I liked the speech," to avoid hurting your feelings. Instead give them a specific assignment: "Please note at least three positive things and at least three things that need improvement." Now your listeners have an assignment that they know will not hurt your feelings, and you are likely to get some helpful feedback.

- Some speakers find it helpful to make a trial run in the very room in which they will give the speech. This would be an especially good idea if you have visual aids and equipment.

- In addition to practicing the entire speech, devote special practice time to your beginning and your ending—two parts that should be smooth and effective.

- Be sure that you don't put too many words on your notes. Have just the bare minimum necessary to jog your memory. Practice from the actual notes that you will use in the speech. Don't make a clean set right before the speech; the old, marked-up notes are more reliable because you're familiar with them from your practice sessions.

Time yourself in practice. If you are in danger of exceeding the time limit, trim your speech.

Resources for Review and Skill Building

Summary

The key to good delivery is a strong desire to communicate with the audience. Speakers who concentrate on getting their ideas across to their listeners usually find themselves using good delivery techniques.

There are four methods of delivering a speech: memorization, manuscript, impromptu, and extemporaneous. Of the four, extemporaneous is the most popular and usually the most effective, because the speaker delivers a well-prepared, well-rehearsed speech in a lively, conversational manner.

In delivering a speech, your voice should be loud enough for everyone to hear, your words should be spoken clearly so that they are easily understood, and your voice should be expressive so that you sound interesting and lively.

Nonverbal communication is the message you give with your body by means of personal appearance, eye contact, facial expressions, posture, movement, and gestures. All these elements should convey confidence and a positive regard for the audience. Of special importance is eye contact. You should look at your listeners during 95 percent of your speech to maintain a bond of communication and rapport with them and to monitor their feedback.

The question-and-answer period enables listeners to get clarification and further information. Anticipate what questions may be asked and prepare your answers accordingly. Try not to be defensive if you are challenged by a listener, and be prepared to say "I don't know" if you don't have an answer—in other words, don't try to fake expertise.

Practice is a vital part in the success of your speech. You should practice the entire speech over and over again—until you can deliver it with power and confidence.

Key Terms

articulation, *259*

extemporaneous method, *257*

impromptu method, *255*

intonation, *260*

manuscript method, *254*

nonverbal communication, *263*

pitch, *260*

posture, *265*

pronunciation, *259*

verbal fillers, *262*

Review Questions

1. What are the disadvantages of impromptu, manuscript, and memorized speeches?

2. What ingredient is essential for the success of an extemporaneous speech?

3. Why is it a serious mistake to speak too rapidly at the beginning of a speech?

4. What are the characteristics of good eye contact?

5. What can speakers do with their hands to make sure that they are free for gesturing?

6. Why should a speech be learned and practiced point by point, instead of word for word?

7. What form of visual aids can cause you to lose eye contact with your audience?

8. How many times should a speaker practice going through the entire speech?

9. How should you handle a listener who casts doubt on some of your facts and figures?

10. If there is a discrepancy between your words and your nonverbal behavior, which will the audience believe?

Building Critical-Thinking Skills

1. "If a man takes off his sunglasses, I can hear him better," says writer Hugh Prather. Explain the meaning of this statement in terms of public speaking.

2. Tennis coaches observe a phenomenon called "analysis equals paralysis." Players become so fixated on holding the racket correctly and swinging properly that they miss the ball. What lessons could public speakers draw from this phenomenon?

Building Teamwork Skills

1. In a group, create a list of six attributes of good delivery that are of utmost importance to group members when they are in an audience. Rank the attributes in order of importance. Then discuss why the top two attributes are more important than the others.

2. To practice impromptu speaking, members of a group should take turns playing the role of candidate in a job interview, while the rest of the group act as interviewers. Make the interview as realistic as possible, with serious questions and answers. After each candidate is interviewed, the group should give a brief critique of his or her verbal and nonverbal responses.

Ethical Issues

Answer for p. 271: B. An ethical speaker never uses deceit. Furthermore, if listeners learn about the ploy, the speaker's credibility is seriously damaged.

Speaking to Inform

OUTLINE

Goals of Informative Speaking

Types of Informative Speeches

Guidelines for Informative Speaking

Sample Informative Speech

OBJECTIVES

After studying this chapter, you should be able to:

1. Prepare an informative speech.
2. Identify four types of informative speeches.
3. Explain how to make information interesting.
4. Explain how to help listeners understand and remember key information.

CHILDREN CAN DROWN, says Olympic swimming champion Cullen Jones, if their swimming instructors do not teach the proper techniques for breathing and staying afloat. In the photo on the opposite page, Jones points to his nose as he teaches breathing skills to students in Houston, Texas.

When Jones teaches swimming, he demonstrates a procedure and then has each student try it out. When he is satisfied that the student is performing correctly, he asks him or her to practice. "Practice is the most important part," he says, "because it causes you to swim the right way without thinking."[1] Jones's approach is one of many techniques that you can use when you engage in informative speaking, a rewarding form of human communication. On topics such as "why some people become addicted to chocolate," you can enlighten your audience. On topics such as "how to improve photos with image-enhancing software," you can enrich the lives of your listeners. On topics such as "how to shut out distractions when you drive," you can even save lives.

In this chapter, we will look at four types of informative speeches and then discuss guidelines to help you create informative speeches that are clear, interesting, and memorable.

Olympic champion Cullen Jones feels strongly that every child should learn how to swim.

Goals of Informative Speaking

When you give an informative speech, your task is to be a teacher—not a persuader, or an advocate, or a salesperson. Think of yourself as a reporter who gives facts, instead of a debater who makes arguments or a pundit who offers opinions. You have three major objectives:

1. **Convey fresh information.** Provide as much new material as possible.

2. **Make your material interesting.** Use supports such as examples, stories, and visual aids.

3. **Help listeners remember important points.** Make your ideas clear and easily grasped. Repeat—in a graceful manner—key information.

Types of Informative Speeches

Informative speeches can be categorized in many ways, but in this chapter we will concentrate on four of the most popular types: definition, description, process, and explanation.

Definition Speech

Do you know what *synesthesia* is? Most people don't, so let me give you a dictionary definition: "a condition in which one type of stimulation evokes the sensation of another." Still not sure what I'm talking about? Here are some elaborations.[2]

- Neurologist Richard Cytowič says that two people out of every million experience a mingling of senses, so that they may taste a shape, hear a color, or see a sound. "Music, for example, is not just a sound and a melody, but it's like a visual fireworks that they see in front of them . . . rather than in the mind's eye."

- A woman named Kristen tastes words, and often the spelling affects the flavor. "Lori," for example, tastes like a pencil eraser, while "Laurie" tastes lemony.

- People who experience synesthesia, says Cytowič, are not crazy, but as children they often fear that they are, and they hide their sensitivity. Carol Steen, a New York artist, recalls, "When I was about 7, I was walking back from elementary school with a classmate, and we must have been learning how to write. I said that the letter 'A' was a wonderful shade of pink, and she was quiet, and then she looked at me and said, 'You're weird.' And I didn't say another word until I was 20."

These examples and quotations constitute an **extended definition,** one that is richer and more meaningful than a dictionary explanation. That is what a **definition speech** is all about—giving an extended definition of a concept so that the listeners get a full, richly detailed picture of its meaning. While a dictionary definition would settle lightly on the listeners' brains and probably vanish overnight, an extended definition is likely to stick firmly. Here are some sample specific purpose statements for definition speeches:

- To define for my audience "financial bubbles" in the world's economy
- To define for my listeners "trolls" who operate on the Internet
- To define for my audience a "Pyrrhic victory" in business and politics

Any of the support materials that we discussed in Chapter 8 (such as narratives, examples, vivid images, and statistics) can be applied to defining

Definition Speech topic: Gambling addiction.

extended definition
a rich, full elaboration of the meaning of a term

definition speech
an oral presentation that gives an extended definition of a concept

Your Thoughts

How can you avoid giving listeners information that all of them already know?

a topic. In a speech on iatrogenic injuries, Rosharna Hazel of Morgan State University in Maryland defined the term as "any injury caused by medical treatment" and then elaborated by giving two examples and some troubling statistics from a prestigious source.[3]

- Willie King of Baltimore was scheduled to have his right leg amputated below the knee, but during surgery, the surgeon incorrectly amputated his left leg instead.

- A woman named Martha entered a New York hospital to receive one of her last chemotherapy treatments in an apparently successful battle against cancer. She was given the wrong drug, however, and died a few days later.

- According to a study at Harvard University School of Public Health, "1.3 million Americans may suffer unexpected, disabling injuries in hospitals each year, and 198,000 may die as a result."

Sometimes the best way to define a topic is to compare or contrast it with a similar item. If you were trying to define what constitutes child abuse, for example, it would be helpful to contrast abuse with firm but loving discipline.

Description Speech

A **description speech** paints a vivid picture of a person, a place, an object, or an event. As with all speeches, a description speech should make a point—and not be merely a list of facts or observations. Here are some specific purpose statements for description speeches:

description speech
an oral presentation that describes a person, place, object, or event

- To describe to my listeners the Gulf Stream in the Atlantic Ocean

- To describe for my audience the "marijuana mansions" that drug dealers use in suburbs

- To describe to my audience the highlights of the life of civil rights leader Rosa Parks

If you were describing an object or a place, you might want to use the *spatial* pattern of organization. Here is an example of the spatial pattern as used in an outline describing New Zealand. The speaker travels from south to north.

Description Speech topic: Outdoor art

Specific Purpose:	To describe to my listeners the geographical variety of New Zealand
Central Idea:	The two-island nation of New Zealand has more scenic variety than any other country on earth.
Main Points:	I. The South Island—colder because it is closer to the South Pole—reminds visitors of Norway.

        A. The Southern Alps, with snowcapped peaks over 10,000 feet, extend the entire length of the island.

        B. Fjords, streams, and lakes are unspoiled and breathtakingly beautiful.

    II. The North Island is like a compact version of the best of Europe and Asia.

        A. The cities suggest the elegance of Italy.

        B. The mountains and vineyards remind one of France.

C.   Active volcanoes look like those found in the Philippines.
D.   In the northernmost parts, the beaches and lush, tropical forests seem like Hawaii.

Describing a person, living or dead, can make a fascinating speech. You might want to use the *chronological* pattern; in a speech on United Farm Workers co-founder Dolores Huerta, for example, you could discuss the major events of her life in the order in which they occurred. Or you might prefer to use the *topical* pattern, emphasizing three major features of Huerta's career:

Specific Purpose:	To describe to my audience the life and accomplishments of Dolores Huerta
Central Idea:	Dolores Huerta is one of the most influential labor leaders in United States history.
Main Points:	I. As co-founder of the United Farm Workers union, Huerta struggled to improve working conditions for migrant farmworkers.
	II. She is credited with introducing to the United States the idea of boycotting as a nonviolent tactic.
	III. Though Huerta practiced nonviolence, she endured much suffering.
	A. She was arrested more than 20 times.
	B. In 1988, she was nearly killed by baton-swinging police officers who smashed two ribs and ruptured her spleen.

Process Speech

process speech
an oral presentation that analyzes how to do something or how something works

A **process speech** covers the steps or stages by which something is done or made. There are two kinds of process speeches. In the first kind, you show the listeners how to *perform* a process so that they can actually use the skills later. (This is sometimes called a *demonstration* speech.) Here are some examples of specific purpose statements for this kind of speech:

- To demonstrate to my audience how to perform daily exercises to avoid and relieve back pain
- To show my listeners how to make low-fat pumpkin bread
- To teach my audience how to transform discarded CDs and DVDs into useful objects

In the second kind of process speech, you provide information on "how something is done" or "how something works." Your goal is to tell about a process—not so that listeners can perform it themselves, but so that they can understand it. For example, let's say that you outline the steps by which counterfeiters print bogus money. You are showing these steps to satisfy the listeners' intellectual curiosity and also to teach them how to spot a counterfeit bill, not so that they can perform the job themselves. Here are some samples of specific purpose statements for this kind of speech:

Ethical Issues Quiz

Which of these topics would be appropriate for an informative speech?

A. How to drive defensively so that you avoid a traffic accident.
B. How to call in sick when you just need a day off.
C. How to create fictitious credentials for your résumé that are certain to impress employers.

For the answer, see the last page of this chapter.

- To inform my audience of the process used to train horses to race in the Kentucky Derby
- To outline for my listeners the steps that astronomers take to find new stars in the universe
- To inform my audience of the process used by crime investigators to find and test DNA evidence

Here are some guidelines for preparing a process speech.

Process Speech topic: How pearls are formed

Use visual aids.   In some speeches, you can use a live demonstration. For instance, if you wanted to show how to treat a burn, you could use a volunteer and demonstrate the correct steps. In other speeches, PowerPoint slides and video are effective. For example, a student speaker told how to change a flat tire, using a video (with the sound off) to illustrate the steps in the process.

Involve the audience in physical activity whenever possible.   If you involve the audience in a physical activity, you capitalize on more than just the listeners' sense of hearing and seeing; you also bring in touch and movement. For an example, see Figure 15.1.

There is an ancient Chinese proverb that says:

- I hear—and I forget.
- I see—and I remember.
- I do—and I understand.

The wisdom of this saying has been confirmed by psychologists, who have found that of the three main channels for learning new information, the auditory is weakest, the visual is stronger, and physical action is strongest of all. The best approach is to bring all three together. For example, if you were telling how to do stretching exercises, you could discuss the techniques (auditory) as you give a demonstration (visual); then you

Figure 15.1
Aboriginal Australian Ron Murray (left) gives classes on how to throw a boomerang so that it returns to the thrower's hand. He lets each student practice until the technique is perfected.

could have each listener stand and perform the exercises (physical action). Some audience involvement can be accomplished while the listeners remain in their chairs; for example, if you are speaking on sign language, you can have the listeners practice the hand signals as you teach them.

Notes of caution: (1) Get your instructor's approval before you include physical activity in a speech. (2) Don't use an activity if it is likely to cause listeners to get so involved that they ignore you. (3) Don't ask listeners to do something that would be embarrassing or awkward for some of them.

Proceed slowly.   Always bear in mind that much of what you say may be new to the listeners. If you are giving instruction about how to make leather belts, for example, you may be describing activities that are so easy for you that you could perform them blindfolded, but they may be completely foreign to some members of the audience. That's why you should talk slowly and repeat key ideas if necessary. Give listeners ample time to absorb your points and form mental images.

Give warning of difficult steps.   When you are ready to discuss especially difficult steps, use transitions to give the listeners a warning. For example, "The next step is a little tricky." Or: "This next step is the hardest one of all." This alerts the listeners that they need to pay extra special attention.

Student speaker Garrett Roth presented a process speech on how to make a YouTube video. Using the chronological pattern, he displayed PowerPoint slides to illustrate the steps. Here is the outline for the body of the speech, with each main point devoted to a different step in the process:

Specific Purpose: To show my listeners how to make a video for YouTube

Central Idea: Making a YouTube video is easy if you follow three simple steps.

Main Points:

(1st Step)   I. Film your video.
     A. Use a camcorder or any other device that captures video.
     B. Make sure audio quality is high.
        1. Have participants speak up.
        2. They can raise their voices without shouting.

(2nd Step)   II. Edit the video.
     A. Download to your computer's video-editing program.
     B. Delete unwanted footage.
     C. Make the length less than 10 minutes.

(3rd Step)   III. Post the video on YouTube.
     A. Register for a free account.
     B. Click on "Upload Videos."
     C. Create a title and tags so that people can easily find the video.

If you look closely, you will see that Roth's outline really has more than three steps. There are a lot of minor steps underneath the three major steps. Did he make a mistake in not listing all these steps as main points? No, treating all steps as equal might have caused the audience to feel overwhelmed by technical details. By dividing his speech into three major sections, he makes the material more manageable—easier to grasp and remember.

Explanation Speech

An **explanation speech** (sometimes called an oral report or a lecture) involves explaining a concept or a situation to the audience. For this type of speech, you often must conduct in-depth research, using books, articles, and interviews, rather than relying on your own experiences.

explanation speech
an oral presentation that explains a concept or situation

Here are examples of specific purpose statements for explanation speeches:

- To explain to the audience why works of art are highly prized as financial investments
- To inform my listeners of the reasons for the near extinction of mountain gorillas
- To explain to the audience the pros and cons of the Electoral College

For organizing an explanation speech, you can use any of the popular patterns (topical, chronological, spatial). One arrangement that is especially effective is the *statement-of-reasons* pattern, which lists reasons for a situation or an event. Student speaker Melissa Greenbaum uses this pattern in a speech on stolen cars. Here is the essence of her outline:

Specific Purpose: To inform my listeners of the reasons why old cars are stolen more frequently than new cars

Central Idea: The most frequently stolen cars in North America are Toyotas and Hondas that are about 10 years old.

Main Points:
(1st Reason)   I. Stealing an old car is more profitable than stealing a new car because of the high demand for old-car parts.

(2nd Reason)   II. New cars are harder to break into because of sophisticated security devices.

(3rd Reason)   III. Old-car owners are less careful about locking up their vehicles.

In her speech, Greenbaum developed each reason with examples and statistics.

Another pattern is the *fallacy–fact* pattern, which also can be called *myth–reality*. In this pattern, the speaker cites popular fallacies and then presents facts that refute them. Student speaker Bob Metzger used this pattern to refute three popular misconceptions about nutrition:

Specific Purpose: To give my audience accurate information to overcome three common misconceptions about nutrition

Central Idea: Eggs, spicy foods, and frozen vegetables do not deserve their bad nutritional reputation.

Main Points:
(Fallacy)   I. "Eggs are bad for you" is a fallacy.
(Facts)   A. Eggs get a "bad rap" because they are high in cholesterol, but what's important is the level of cholesterol in the blood, not in the food.
                   B. Saturated fat is what causes high cholesterol levels in the blood.

Explanation Speech topic: Why most male birds are more colorful than females

C. Eggs are low in saturated fat, so they do not make a significant contribution to high cholesterol levels in the blood.

(Fallacy)   II. "Spicy food is bad for the stomach" is a fallacy.
(Facts)   A. Medical studies of healthy persons who eat spice-rich Mexican and Indian foods found no damage or irritation in the protective lining of the stomach.
           B. In a medical experiment in India, the stomach ulcers of patients who were fed spicy foods healed at the same rate as those of patients who were fed a bland diet.

(Fallacy)   III. "Frozen vegetables are not as nutritious as fresh" is a fallacy.
(Facts)   A. Quick freezing preserves all nutrients.
           B. In fact, if fresh vegetables have been sitting on the produce aisle too long, frozen vegetables are better.

Guidelines for Informative Speaking

In informative speaking, strive to make your message clear, interesting, and memorable. You can achieve this goal by applying the principles that we have covered so far in this book, plus the following guidelines.

Relate the Speech to the Listeners' Self-Interest

Many listeners approach a speech with an attitude of: "Why should I care? Why should I pay attention? What's in it for me?" The best motivator in a speech, therefore, is something that has an impact on their lives.[4]

Let's say you are planning to give a process speech showing listeners how to clean their computers. How do you think your listeners will react when they discover what your topic is?

"B-o-r-ing!" they will probably say to themselves. "Why should I pay attention to this stuff?"

Your best strategy, therefore, is to appeal to their self-interest:

> Imagine you sit at your computer all weekend working on a big research paper. You are almost through when suddenly your computer fails. Not only does it fail, but it deletes your entire report. To make matters worse, the technician who repairs your computer charges you $250.
>
> This could happen to you if you don't clean and maintain your computer. Today I'd like to show you some easy steps you can take to safeguard your computer files and avoid repair bills.

Now your listeners see that your information can have an impact on their own lives. They should perk up and listen carefully.

Make Information Interesting

The most important element in an effective speech, says nationally known TV and radio reporter Nina Totenberg, is "interesting information."[5]

Many speeches are boring because the speakers deal primarily with *generalities*, which tend to be dull and vague. To make a speech lively, use generalities sparingly, and each time a generality is offered, follow it with lots of *specifics*, such as examples and ancedotes.

Student speaker Catalina Garcia gave an informative speech on mystery shoppers—people who are hired to pose as customers to evaluate the quality of a company's service and products. She began by asking her audience to look at an ad for mystery shopping [Figure 15.2] and said, "Sounds like an exciting job, doesn't it?" Then she made this generalized statement:

> But as I read articles and interviewed people on the Internet, I discovered that for most mystery shoppers, the job is far from glamorous—it's a lot of hard work for low pay.

Garcia followed her generality with lots of specifics, including these:

- "Pamela Whitaker of Louisville, Kentucky, thought she would dine at fancy restaurants with her husband. Instead, she worked for a fast-food chain. She would visit one restaurant after another. First she would inspect the restroom. Then she would order food and take it out to her car. She would eat a few bites of a burger and fries and throw the food away. Then she would fill out her evaluation of cleanliness, friendliness, and the taste and temperature of the food. She said the job was boring, and she was paid only $7 per visit. She was reimbursed for the food she bought, but not for gas and car expenses."

- "Ed Mancini, who lives in New Jersey, worked as a mystery shopper for an office supply chain. The worst part of the job involved employees who ignored him because they were busy chatting with co-workers. He said, 'I would stand near them looking bewildered and clearly needing help.' He knew that when he filed his report, the employees would be fired. He said, 'I guess they deserved it, but I hated being a snitch.' Mancini also said he hated the tedious paperwork and the low pay. He got $18 per visit, but he traveled a lot—it turned out he was actually making only $5 per hour. After a few months, he quit."

Figure 15.2
Is mystery shopping a good job? A student speaker investigates. (See text for details.)

Tips for Your Career

For Long Presentations, Plan a Variety of Activities

Your boss asks you to conduct a three-hour workshop, scheduled for a Friday afternoon, to explain important procedures to a group of new employees. What do you do? Do you spend the entire three hours talking? No, not unless you want to put the group to sleep.

For long presentations, provide a variety of activities to keep your audience awake and attentive. Here are some suggested activities.

1. **INVITE AUDIENCE PARTICIPATION.** At various intervals, or even throughout the entire presentation, encourage listeners to ask questions or make comments. By letting them take an active role, instead of sitting passively for three hours, you invigorate them and prevent them from daydreaming.

2. **USE VISUAL AIDS WHENEVER POSSIBLE.** Visuals provide variety and sparkle, and they can clarify and reinforce key points.

3. **GIVE COFFEE OR "STRETCH" BREAKS AT VARIOUS INTERVALS.** A good rule of thumb for marathon sessions is to give a 15-minute break after every 45-minute period, even if the audience does not seem tired. In other words, don't wait until fatigue sets in. If you wait until the audience is nodding, you might lose their interest for the rest of the day. When you give a break, always announce the time for reassembly; when that time arrives, politely but firmly remind any stragglers that it is time to return to their seats. If you don't remind them, you will find that a 15-minute coffee break can stretch to 30 minutes.

4. **CALL ON PEOPLE AT RANDOM.** If your presentation is in the form of a lecture, you can use the teachers' technique of calling on people at random to answer questions. This causes every listener to perk up because he or she is thinking, "I'd better pay attention because my name might be called next, and I don't want to be caught daydreaming." Call the person's name *after* you ask the question. (If you call the name before the question, everyone in the audience except the designated person might breathe a sigh of relief and fail to pay close attention to the question.)

5. **ENCOURAGE LISTENERS TO TAKE NOTES.** Some speakers pass out complimentary pens and pads at the beginning of their presentations in the hope that the listeners will use them to write down key points. There is, of course, a side benefit: Taking notes helps the listeners to stay alert and listen intelligently.

Garcia's speech was interesting because she chose lively examples and stories. She also used a valuable strategy: before she delivered her speech, she tested her content with friends and relatives, asking them to tell her which items were interesting and which were boring. (For more on testing your material, see Tip 10.1 in Chapter 10.)

Avoid Information Overload

Give details, but not too many. You don't want to bore your audience with a tedious overload. "The secret of being tiresome," the French philosopher Voltaire said, "is in telling everything." Edit your material: instead of giving all 14 examples that you have compiled for a point, cite just 2 or 3.

When my students moan about all the wonderful material they must leave out, I offer a simple solution: put it on a handout or a DVD that listeners can pick up after the speech and take with them.

Tailor Information for Each Audience

A common mistake is to assume that your listeners possess the same knowledge that you possess. You may know that the Earth revolves around the sun, but one in five adult Americans thinks that the sun revolves around the Earth.[6] One in seven adults can't find the United States on a world map.[7] Many college students think that Islam is the dominant religion in South America.[8]

Even at elite universities, you can't make assumptions about listener knowledge. Michael Ranney, a cognitive scientist at the University of California, Berkeley, reports that students in one of his classes (who should have known that the U.S. population is about 308 million) estimated that California has 1 billion people (instead of 37.7 million).[9]

Find out in advance what your audience knows and doesn't know on your topic, and then adapt your information accordingly. Whenever necessary, define words, explain concepts, and give background information.

What should you do when your audience is mixed—that is, some know certain concepts already and some don't? How can you give explanations in a way that does not insult the intelligence of the listeners who already know the material? In some cases, you can give information in a casual, unobtrusive way. For example, let's say you are planning in your speech to cite a quotation by Adolf Hitler. Most college students know who Hitler was, but some do not. To inform the latter without insulting the intelligence of the former, you can say something like this: "In the 1920s, long before Adolf Hitler rose to power in Germany and long before he launched the German nation into World War II, he made the following prophetic statement . . ." An indirect approach like this permits you to sneak in a lot of background information.

In other cases, you may need to be straightforward in giving definitions or explanations. For example, if you need to define *recession* for a speech on economic cycles, do so directly and clearly. Knowledgeable listeners will not be offended by a quick definition as long as most of your speech supplies them with new material; in fact, they probably will welcome a chance to confirm the accuracy of their own understanding of the term.

Your Thoughts

In a National Geographic survey of American high school students, one-half could not find the United States on a globe unless it was labeled. Are these people stupid? Defend your answer.

Use the Familiar to Explain the Unfamiliar

Ozone is an air pollutant, often known as smog, that harms the health of millions of people. How can it hurt you? When you inhale ozone, says the American Lung Association, it reacts chemically with your body's internal tissues. Prolonged exposure causes the equivalent of sunburn to your lungs.[10]

The chemical complexities of pollutants in our lungs are unfamiliar to most people, but we are all familiar with what sunburn is.

When you want to explain or describe something that is unfamiliar to your audience, relate it to something that is familiar. Use comparisons, contrasts, and analogies. If, for example, you point out that divers in Acapulco, Mexico, astound tourists by diving into water from rocks 118 feet high, that statistic does not have much impact, unless you point out that a 118-foot plunge is equal to a dive from the roof of an 11-story building.

Similarly, to give listeners a mental picture of what the inside of a tornado is like, Dale Higgins said: "A tornado's funnel is like the vortex you see when you let water go down a drain." Since everyone has seen the swirling action of water going down a drain, the comparison helped the audience visualize a tornado's vortex.

Help Listeners Remember Key Information

To make sure that your audience retains important details, use the following techniques.

Repetition.   Present key ideas and words several times.

Presentation aids.   Use the sensory channels we discussed in Chapter 9—visual, hearing, taste, smell, touch, and physical activity.

Figure 15.3
This famous statue of a bull in New York City's financial district holds a key to remembering the meaning of the term "bull market." See text for details.

Memory aids.   Provide listeners with shortcuts to remembering. Here are some samples:

- In financial news reports, you often hear the terms "bull market" and "bear market." One term means that stock values are trending upward; the other means that values are trending downward. To help listeners distinguish between the two, you could tell them that "bull market" signifies an upward movement and ask them to visualize a bull's horns, which point upward. (See Figure 15.3.)
- In the United States, the color blue is often associated with one major political party and red with the other (red states vs. blue states). But which color goes with which party? The Republican party is red, so just remember that Republican starts with an "R," the same letter that starts red. That leaves blue for the Democratic party. (By the way, a purple state is one that is a combination of red and blue, sometimes voting Republican, sometimes voting Democratic.)
- Acronyms are handy. For years students have recalled the names of the Great Lakes by using the word HOMES, each letter of which stands for a lake: Huron, Ontario, Michigan, Erie, and Superior. If you are speaking on how to treat injuries such as ankle sprains, you can help listeners remember the four steps of first aid by providing the acronym RICE, which stands for rest, ice, compression, and elevation.

Your Thoughts

It is important to avoid overdosing on the fat-soluble vitamins A, D, K, and E. Create a memory aid to help an audience remember them.

connect

View a video of the speech "Gold Fever" in the online Media Library for Chapter 15.

Sample Informative Speech

Maria Romano delivered a speech on why gold is highly prized. Below is the outline, followed by a transcript of the actual speech. The speaker uses the statement-of-reasons pattern, giving three reasons why people love to possess gold.

The Outline with Commentary

Gold Fever

COMMENTARY	SPEECH

SPEECH

General Purpose: To inform

Specific Purpose: To explain to my audience why gold is highly prized

Central Idea: Gold is valuable because it is scarce, culturally appealing, and safe as an investment.

This speech covers a topic that is timely and interesting.

INTRODUCTION

I. Attention Material

    A. People have been obsessed with gold for 6,000 years.

        1. Exploration and warfare have resulted.

        2. Conquistadores destroyed civilizations to steal their gold.

Historical information and a photo are used to make the audience want to hear the rest of the speech.

    B. People today are seeking gold as an investment. (Show photo.) [See Figure 15.4]

        1. The market value recently reached $1,700 per ounce.

        2. This caused "gold fever." (CBS, NPR)

II. Orienting Material

    A. Why is gold valued so highly?

    B. My research uncovered 3 reasons for gold fever.

A preview shows the audience the terrain that the speaker will cover in the body of the speech.

        1. It is scarce.

        2. It has symbolic and cultural appeal.

        3. It is a safe investment.

(*Transition:* Let's begin with the first reason.)

Figure 15.4
Many investors are buying gold bars and coins.

(continued)

BODY

I. Gold has always been scarce.
  A. Very little gold exists.
    1. Only 161,000 tons have been mined in history. (*National Geographic*)
    2. That's only enough to fill 2 Olympic pools. (Show photo.) [See Figure 15.5]
    3. Some experts say 3 pools.
  B. Scarcity is a major impetus for finding gold.
    1. If gold were plentiful, people would still love it.
    2. But the price and hunger for gold would not be so high.

(Transition: Let's examine the second reason.)

II. Gold has symbolic and cultural appeal throughout the world.
  A. It has symbolized power and royalty for thousands of years. (Peter Bernstein, *The Power of Gold*)
    1. Pharaohs, kings, and queens wore gold crowns.
    2. (Show photo.) [See Figure 15.6] A princess in Ghana wears lots of gold.
  B. Gold symbolizes excellence and perfection.
    1. Gold surpasses silver and bronze as a prize.
    2. In the Olympics, gold is the ultimate honor.

(Transition: Let's turn to the third reason.)

III. Gold is considered a safe investment.
  A. India, which has 25 percent of the world's sales in gold every year, believes strongly in gold as an investment. (Christopher Corti, World Gold Council.)

> A photo of an Olympic pool helps listeners visualize the scarcity.

> Each main point gives a reason for gold's popularity.

> Quoting an expert adds to the speaker's credibility.

Figure 15.5
Experts say all the gold in the world could fit into two—maybe three—Olympic-size pools.

Figure 15.6
A princess in Ghana is adorned with gold.

1. Most gold in India is related to weddings. (Show photo.) [See Figure 15.7]
2. Brides receive gold throughout the process, from engagement to wedding night.
3. Gold is prized because it's like an insurance policy if the family ever gets into a financial crisis.

B. Gold will never burn up or wear out.
   1. It's a chemical element, so it can't be broken down into something else. (Dr. Elizabeth Raum, *The Story Behind Gold*)
   2. It will never tarnish or rust.
   3. It will remain bright and shiny even if you bury it underground or underwater.

C. In my research, most investment experts say a small amount of gold (10 percent) is okay in your portfolio, but don't put all of your money into gold.
   1. The price of gold goes up and down, and in a crisis, you don't want to be caught in a down moment.
   2. You will make more money with a diversified portfolio over 10 years than if you put all your money into gold.

(*Transition:* Let's summarize.)

> The speaker provides technical information in a way that is not too difficult for the audience to understand.

> Listeners appreciate hearing a tip that they can apply to their own lives.

(continued)

Figure 15.7
Gold is very important for brides in India.

CONCLUSION

I. Summary
   A. Gold is highly prized because there's not much of it in the world.
   B. It has enormous symbolic and cultural value.
   C. It is considered a safe haven during financial crises.

> The key reasons are given one more time to help the audience remember them.

II. Clincher
   A. In *The Power of Gold,* Peter Bernstein says gold has magical power, but one big question remains.
   B. Do we possess gold—or does gold possess us?

> The speaker ends with a provocative question.

BIBLIOGRAPHY

Bernstein, Peter. *The Power of Gold: The History of an Obsession.* New York: John Wiley & Sons, 2004. Print.

Burton, Jonathan. "Gold Is a Bet, Not an Investment." *The Week* 26 Nov. 2010: 50. Print.

Corti, Christopher, and Richard Holliday. *Gold: Science and Applications.* Boca Raton, Florida: Taylor & Francis Group, 2010. Print.

Larmer, Brook. "The Price of Gold." *National Geographic* Jan. 2009: 36–61. Print.

Raum, Elizabeth. *The Story Behind Gold.* Chicago: Heinemann Library, 2008. Print.

> High-quality sources are used.

VISUAL AIDS

Photo of gold coins and gold bar
Photo of Olympic pool
Photo of princess in Ghana
Photo of bride in India

PowerPoint slides help to illustrate and enliven the speech.

The Speech as Delivered

Here is a transcript of the speech as delivered by Maria Romano.

Gold Fever

For the past 6,000 years, men and women throughout the world have been obsessed with a beautiful, shiny metal called gold. The search for gold has led to world exploration as well as warfare. For example, the Spanish conquistadores destroyed the civilizations of the Aztecs and the Incas in order to steal their gold.

Today gold continues to be the most exciting of all the precious metals that come from the earth, and many people are trying to accumulate gold as an investment. *[Speaker shows photo in Figure 15.4.]* When the market value of gold recently hit seventeen hundred dollars per ounce, there was a huge rush of investors looking to buy gold coins and gold bars. News media such as CBS and NPR called it "gold fever."

Why do we humans prize gold so highly? To answer this question, I did some research, and I discovered that there are three reasons why gold is treasured: First, it is scarce. Second, it has tremendous symbolic and cultural appeal. And third, it is considered a safe investment during hard economic times.

Let's examine the first reason. Gold is scarce, and it always has been. There's just not that much gold in the world. *National Geographic* magazine says that in all of history, only 161,000 tons of gold have been extracted from the earth. *[Speaker shows photo in Figure 15.5.]* That's barely enough to fill up two Olympic-size swimming pools. Some experts say that a more accurate estimate would be *three* pools. Whether it's two or three, that's not much gold when you consider that gold mines have been in operation in mines all over the world for over 6,000 years.

You can see why scarcity is a big factor in the hunger for gold. If there were a lot of gold, people would still like it, but the price wouldn't be as high. And people would not be obsessed with finding it and hoarding it.

Now let's look at the second reason for gold's popularity. It has enormous symbolic and cultural value in all parts of the world. Peter Bernstein, the author of the book *The Power of Gold,* says that for thousands of years, gold has been a symbol of power and royalty. Pharaohs, kings and queens—they have all worn gold crowns. *[Speaker shows photo in Figure 15.6.]* This photo shows a princess from the West African nation of Ghana, who is adorned with lots of gold.

Gold is a symbol of excellence and perfection. In all kinds of competition, gold is offered as the ultimate prize, surpassing silver and bronze. For example, all Olympic athletes—in all events—want to win the highest honor of all, which, of course, is a gold medal.

Now let's examine the third reason why gold is so valuable. It is widely thought of as a safe haven for a person's wealth during tough economic times. This belief is strongest held in India, which is the world's largest consumer of gold. India accounts for 25 percent of global demand, according to Christopher Corti, who is an expert with the World Gold Council.

Almost all of the gold in India is used for events related to weddings. *[Speaker shows photo in Figure 15.7.]* A bride receives presents of gold at different stages, beginning with her engagement and ending with her wedding night. There is a reason why the bride receives a great deal of gold. If her family has a financial crisis someday, she can sell the gold to enable her loved ones to survive. It's kind of like an insurance policy.

(continued)

Gold is very stable—it won't burn up or wear out. In her book *The Story Behind Gold,* Dr. Elizabeth Raum says that gold is a chemical element, meaning that it cannot be broken down into anything else. It cannot tarnish or rust. It'll always be bright and shiny. You can bury gold underground or underwater and it remains unchanged.

I looked in financial magazines like Forbes, and I found about 20 recent articles on gold as an investment. The vast majority of investment experts say it would be okay to have a small amount of your wealth tied up in gold—say, 10 percent. But they recommend against putting *all* of your money into gold—for two reasons.

First, the price of gold goes up and down—if you ever need cash in a hurry, you don't want to be caught at a moment when the market is low. Secondly, if you put your money into a diversified portfolio of stocks and mutual funds, you're almost certain to make a lot more money over a 10-year period than you would make by having all of your money invested in gold.

Let's sum up what we've covered. Gold is valuable because it's scarce, it has great symbolic and cultural importance, and it's widely viewed as a hedge against hard times.

I would like to conclude with the paraphrasing of an observation made by Peter Bernstein in *The Power of Gold.* He says that gold has always had a magical power in the world, but one big question remains: Do we possess gold—or does gold possess us?

Resources for Review and Skill Building

Summary

The goals of informative speaking are to convey fresh information, make material interesting, and help listeners remember key points. Four types of informative speeches were discussed in this chapter:

- *Definition* speeches give an extended definition of a concept so that listeners get a full, richly detailed picture of its meaning.
- *Description* speeches paint a vivid picture of a person, a place, an object, or an event.
- *Process* speeches explain the steps or stages by which something is done or made.

- *Explanation* speeches involve explaining a concept or a situation to the audience.

In developing an informative speech, keep these guidelines in mind: (1) Relate the speech to the listeners' self-interest, if at all possible. Show them explicitly the connection between your material and their personal lives. (2) Make the information interesting by going beyond generalities to give lots of specifics, such as examples and anecdotes. (3) Avoid information overload. (4) Tailor information for each audience. (5) Use the familiar to explain the unfamiliar. (6) Help listeners remember key information.

Key Terms

definition speech, *278*

description speech, *279*

explanation speech, *283*

extended definition, *278*

process speech, *280*

Review Questions

1. What is an extended definition? Why is it preferable in a speech to a dictionary definition?

2. Which two organizational patterns would be most appropriate for a speech on the life and achievements of astronaut Sally Ride?

3. What are the two kinds of process speeches?

4. In a process speech, at what point should you give listeners a warning?

5. Which organizational pattern would be most appropriate for a speech aimed at dispelling misconceptions about wolves?

6. Why is it important to relate a speech, if possible, to the listeners' self-interest?

7. Why is the issue of generalities versus specifics an important matter in informative speaking?

8. What should you do if some members of an audience know the meaning of a term but others do not?

9. A speaker says, "The lungs of a heavy smoker look like charred meat." What principle of informative speaking is the speaker using?

10. "ASAP" is an example of what kind of memory aid?

Building Critical-Thinking Skills

1. A bad resume can prevent an applicant from getting a job. If you conducted a workshop on how to create effective resumes, what techniques would you use with your audience?

2. A handout from a dog-obedience class says, "Training a well-behaved dog takes time and practice. The more repetitions you do on a regular basis, the quicker your dog will understand. However, do not bore him. Keep your training sessions fun and interesting." Do you think this advice would apply to training humans? Justify your answer.

Building Teamwork Skills

1. If improperly developed, the topics below can be boring. In a group, brainstorm ways that each topic could be made interesting.

    a. Teaching methods
    b. Citizenship
    c. Transportation

2. The text advises that you relate a topic to listeners' self-interest. In a group, brainstorm how the following topics can be presented in a way that would satisfy a listener's attitude of "What's in it for me?"

    a. Social Security
    b. Rain forest destruction
    c. Secret video surveillance of employees
    d. Solar energy
    e. Homeless people

Ethical Issues

Answer for p. 280: A. This is a positive topic and a service to the audience. Topics B and C are unethical. A speaker should not give advice on how to cheat or defraud.

Speaking to Persuade

OUTLINE

Goals of Persuasive Speaking

Types of Persuasive Speeches

Patterns of Organization

Sample Persuasive Speech

OBJECTIVES

After studying this chapter, you should be able to:

1. Prepare a persuasive speech.
2. Identify two major types of persuasive speeches.
3. Identify four patterns for organizing a persuasive speech.

CAMILA VALLEJO, a student at the University of Chile, initiated a national campaign in 2011 to persuade the Chilean government to make high-quality university education available to low-income students.

Vallejo gave speeches, appeared on TV, and led peaceful marches through the streets of the capital city, Santiago. She succeeded in building widespread public support, and one year later, her campaign had achieved some of its major goals: The government granted a $350 million increase for higher education and promised to finance scholarships for low-income students.[1]

persuasion
the process of influencing, changing, or reinforcing listeners' ideas, attitudes, beliefs, or behaviors

The success of Camila Vallejo demonstrates the power of **persuasion**—influencing, changing, or reinforcing what people think, believe, or do. In a persuasive speech, you act as an advocate, a person who argues on behalf of an idea or a cause.

At first glance, persuasive speeches look like informative speeches, but that's because a persuasive speech must contain background information before it can make its case. The basic difference is that an informative speech is aimed at reporting, while a persuasive speech is aimed at winning audience assent.

To illustrate the two types of speeches, let's take the topic of solar-powered cars. For an informative speech, you would just give the facts—how the car works, how much the battery pack costs, and so on. For a persuasive speech, you would give some of the same facts, but you also would try to convince listeners that a solar-powered car is superior to a gasoline-powered vehicle and to persuade them to buy and drive a solar car.

In this chapter, we will examine types of persuasive speeches and how you can organize them. In the next chapter, we will look at persuasive strategies.

Camila Vallejo is highly successful in her persuasive campaign.

Goals of Persuasive Speaking

Three key goals in persuasive speaking are:

1. **Win over your listeners.** In some cases, your objective may be to convince your audience to adopt your view. For example, one student tried to convince her listeners that the moon will become a tourist destination within 50 years. In other cases, you may want to spur the audience to take action. For example, in a speech on contaminated food, a student asked his listeners to call federal lawmakers to urge them to increase the number of inspections of imported food.

2. **Know your subject thoroughly.** You will have little chance of persuading listeners if you are not perceived as knowledgeable and competent with regard to your topic. Develop as much expertise as possible by doing careful, extensive research.

3. **Maintain a high standard of ethical behavior.** Avoid any degree of manipulation and deceit. Use supports (such as examples and visual aids) that are accurate and truthful, and don't exaggerate or use half-truths. Be forthright in revealing to the audience your true goals and motives, and disclose any financial involvement you have in your subject matter (for example, let listeners know that you own stock in the company whose products you are recommending).

Ethical Issues Quiz

Wendy, a software developer for an accounting firm, gives speeches to high school students to persuade them to enroll in a certain four-year private college. She is a graduate of the college, and the college pays her to give her presentations. Which of the following would be most appropriate for her talks?

A. She makes no mention of being a graduate or being paid to speak.

B. She mentions being a graduate, but omits the fact that she is being paid to speak.

C. She mentions that she is a graduate and is being paid to speak.

For the answer, see the last page of this chapter.

Types of Persuasive Speeches

Persuasive speeches can be categorized according to two objectives: (1) to influence thinking and (2) to motivate action. Sometimes these categories overlap; for example, you often have to influence thinking before you can motivate action.

Speech to Influence Thinking

speech to influence thinking
an oral presentation aimed at winning intellectual assent for a concept or proposition

The **speech to influence thinking** is an effort to convince people to adopt your position on a particular subject. (If some listeners agree with your ideas even before you speak, your job is to reinforce what they already think.)

Here are some sample specific purpose statements for this kind of speech:

- To convince my audience that a paid sabbatical (extended time off) for employees is a good way for companies to avoid job burnout and low morale

- To convince my audience that child geniuses should be permitted to enroll in college classes

- To convince my listeners that immigrants continue to enrich American society and business life

A subcategory of the speech to influence thinking is the **speech of refutation**, in which your main goal is to knock down arguments or ideas that you believe are false. You may want to attack what another speaker has said, or you may want to refute popularly held ideas or beliefs that you think are false.

Here are some sample specific purpose statements for speeches of refutation:

- To persuade my audience to reject the widespread belief that everyone needs to consume eight glasses of water per day
- To convince listeners to reject the idea that tornadoes are incapable of striking large cities
- To persuade my audience to disbelieve claims by so-called psychics that they are able to predict future events

Refuting an argument is easier when you are dealing with facts than when you are dealing with deeply held beliefs. Suppose, for example, that you want to challenge the idea that brown sugar is more natural and therefore healthier than white sugar. You can refute this idea by citing nutrition experts who say that brown sugar offers no nutritional advantages because it is simply white sugar with small amounts of molasses or burnt sugar added for coloring. Since this assertion involves verifiable chemical facts, your persuasive task is easy. But suppose that you wanted to persuade an audience to reject the belief that children should be reared by their parents; instead, you argue, children should be reared by communes like the kibbutzim in Israel. Though you may win some respect for the value of your idea, you are highly unlikely to alter the deeply held belief that children should grow up under the wings of their parents. Such core beliefs are extremely difficult to change.

Speech to Influence Thinking: "To convince my audience that without trees, there would be no human life on earth"

speech of refutation
an oral counterargument against a concept or proposition put forth by others

speech to motivate action
an oral presentation that tries to impel listeners to take action

Speech to Motivate Action

Like the speech to influence thinking, the **speech to motivate action** tries to win people over to your way of thinking, but it also attempts one of the most challenging tasks of persuasion: getting people to take action. Your goal is to get listeners to respond in one or more of these ways: *start* a behavior (start taking first aid lessons), *continue* a behavior (continue donating blood), or *stop* a behavior (stop smoking).

Here are some sample specific purpose statements for speeches to motivate action:

- To persuade my listeners to sign a petition aimed at requiring drivers over 75 to be retested each year for their driver's license
- To persuade my audience to stop overspending on their credit card accounts
- To persuade my listeners to start a digital scrapbook of memories and images

Speech to Motivate Action: "To persuade my listeners to visit the Martin Luther King Monument in Washington or go to its website"

Sometimes you want prompt action from your listeners ("Please vote for my candidate in today's election"); at other times, you simply want them to respond at any appropriate point in the future ("Whenever you see a child riding a bike, please slow down and drive very cautiously").

Here are some suggestions for getting action.

Ask for the precise action that you want.   Don't just "give the facts" and assume that your listeners will know what action to take. Say *exactly* what you want them to do.

If you are speaking on the need for children in poor countries to have computers in their schools, don't be content to praise a nonprofit charity that is sending computers overseas and hope that your listeners will someday make a donation. Instead, urge them to donate at least $25 by the end of the day. (You can supply a Web address or a phone number for an easy credit card contribution.)

Late in his life, Henry Ford, founder of the Ford Motor Company, was chatting with an insurance agent whom he had known for many years. The agent, puzzled and hurt by the fact that Ford had never given him any business, finally asked, "Why didn't you ever buy insurance from me?"

Ford replied, "You never asked me."[2]

Countless speakers, says Dr. Jerry Tarver of the University of Richmond, "are reluctant to 'ask for the sale.' They appear to have a naive faith that if audiences are given some pertinent facts and a few exhortations, all will be well. These speakers fail to realize that when conditions are right, conviction can be turned into action."[3]

Whenever possible, get a response before listeners leave the room.   Often a speaker gets listeners fired up over an issue and asks them to go home and write an e-mail to the appropriate agencies. Listeners leave the room determined to write that e-mail, but unfortunately very few ever do. Everyone has good intentions, but life is busy and there are urgent personal matters to be taken care of. After a couple of weeks, the vows are forgotten.

To avoid this problem, try to get an immediate response. Even a small, token action is better than none at all. You can say, "On your way out, please sign the petition on the table at the rear of the room." Even better, if time permits, is to circulate the petition for them to sign before they stand up to leave.

Researchers have verified that if you persuade a person to take a positive step, you increase that person's commitment to your cause.[4] He or she now has made an investment of time and energy. If opponents try to persuade the person to believe the opposite of what you have espoused, he or she will be highly resistant to change (unless, of course, there is some compelling counterargument). Why? Because human beings feel a strong need to be consistent.[5] Going over to the other side would be inconsistent with an action such as signing your petition.

Let's examine some on-the-spot responses that can help strengthen your listeners' support of your position.

Your Thoughts

What are the pro's and con's of asking listeners to donate money at the end of a presentation?

- **Phone calls and social media.** Although cell phones and electronic devices should not be turned on during a speech, some speakers at the end of a presentation ask listeners to pull out their devices and take action on the spot. For example, listeners can be urged to call a hotline to offer help and donations to earthquake victims. Or they might be asked to use smartphones, tablets, or laptops to log onto Facebook or Twitter to join a national crusade against abuse of workers in an American corporation.

- **Petition.** Whether on paper or online, petitions are an effective way to get large numbers of people to demand action. In the last few years, online petitions have soared in popularity because thousands of names of supporters can be collected and sent to the recipient quickly. You can set up a laptop or other device in the back of your meeting room, and as people leave, they can type in their names and addresses at an online petition site (such as change.org). The power of online petitions was illustrated in 2011 when Molly Katchpole, 22, who was working two part-time jobs in Washington, DC, heard that Bank of America was planning to charge customers a $5 monthly fee for using their debit card. This made her angry, and she launched an online petition to urge the bank to cancel the fee. In just a few weeks, her petition received more than 300,000 signatures, causing Bank of America to cancel the fee.[6]

- **Show of hands.** "Studies show that something as simple as having people raise their hands is more likely to get long-range results than depending, as too many speakers do, on mere mental assent," says Dr. Jerry Tarver.[7] Ask for a show of hands only when you're sure that most listeners will be eager and unembarrassed to make a public commitment.

- **Sign-up sheet.** To garner commitment for some future activity such as volunteer work, you can ask people to write down their names and e-mail addresses. This strategy can be effective because even if their enthusiasm cools, most people will honor their promise to help when called upon later.

Don't pressure listeners.   No matter how much you want audience action, don't browbeat, manipulate, or beg. Don't single out and embarrass those listeners who decline to take action. Listeners who feel pressured might become so resentful that they will decline to support your cause simply out of spite.

Patterns of Organization

Organizing a speech effectively can enhance your persuasiveness. While any of the organizational patterns we studied in Chapter 10 can be used, four patterns are especially strong in persuasive speeches: the motivated sequence, the problem–solution pattern, the statement-of-reasons pattern, and the comparative-advantages pattern.

Motivated Sequence

The **motivated sequence** is an effective approach to persuasion that was developed by Professor Alan H. Monroe.[8] The pattern is especially useful when you want to sell a product or service, or when you want to mobilize listeners to take a specific action (vote for your candidate, pick up litter). It has the virtue of being suitable for any type of audience—unaware, hostile, apathetic, neutral, or favorable. There are five steps in this pattern:

motivated sequence
a series of steps designed to propel a listener toward accepting the speaker's proposition

1. **Attention.** Grab the audience's attention at the beginning of your introduction, as discussed in Chapter 11.

2. **Need.** Show your audience that there is a serious problem that needs action.

3. **Satisfaction.** Satisfy the need by presenting a solution, and show how your solution works.

Table 16.1   Example of the Motivated Sequence

1. Attention

(Grab the listeners' attention.)
"Sea turtles could become extinct within 15 years. This is not just an issue of losing a beautiful creature. Extinction would hurt humans, as well."

2. Need

(Describe a problem that needs action.)
"This photo shows a sea grass bed on the ocean floor—necessary for the survival of many species of fish. Sea turtles graze on sea grass, keeping the blades short (as shown here). If the turtles become extinct, the blades will grow tall, and sea grass beds will become a jungle that is unhealthy for fish. This will lead to the extinction of many types of fish that we eat."

3. Satisfaction

(Satisfy the need by presenting a solution.)
"Sea turtles spend most of their lives in the ocean, except when females go ashore to lay eggs on beaches. Sadly, the vast majority of eggs and hatchlings are eaten by animals or poached by humans. The solution is for volunteers to protect the turtles by patrolling assigned sections of beaches, nest-sitting at night, and carrying new hatchlings safely to the ocean."

4. Visualization

(Help the audience visualize the results.)

"If we get enough volunteers to protect them, sea turtles will survive and swim with fish in the ocean. The turtles will maintain the health of the sea grass beds, and the fish will provide sustenance for human beings."

5. Action

(Request audience action.) "In Florida, turtle patrol volunteer Pam Yates prepares to release a hatchling into the sea. I urge you to join Pam in helping to save turtles. You have two options: You can do volunteer work at beaches in America or in countries like Costa Rica. Or, if you can't travel, you can 'adopt a nest' and send money to help support the volunteers on the beaches. I will give you a list of volunteer websites."

4. **Visualization.** Paint a picture of results. Your scenario can be *positive:* help listeners visualize the good things that will happen when your solution is put into effect. Or it can be *negative:* show them the bad results if your solution is rejected.

5. **Action.** Request action from the listeners. Be specific: "Sign this petition" or "Write your legislators today—here are their addresses" or "You can volunteer in Room 211 this afternoon."

Table 16.1 gives an example of how the steps work.[9] While these steps seem simple enough, some students have trouble knowing how to fit the sequence into a speech outline. To clarify the matter, I have annotated the partial outline below to demonstrate how one speaker placed the steps of the motivated sequence at logical places.

COMMENTARY	SPEECH

INTRODUCTION

Attention
(Grab the listeners' attention.)

I. Did you know that you can experience eye problems if you stare too long at the screens of your electronic devices?

II. Text-messaging devices like smartphones are the worst, but you can also suffer from staring at a computer screen.

BODY

Need
(Describe a problem that needs action.)

I. "Computer vision syndrome" afflicts millions of Americans who stare at a screen for long periods of time.

A. Symptoms include dry, irritated eyes, headaches, sensitivity to light, and blurred vision, according to Dr. Kent Daum, associate professor of optometry at the University of Alabama–Birmingham.

B. The syndrome can cause long-term deterioration of visual acuity.

Satisfaction
(Satisfy the need by presenting a solution.)

II. Doctors recommend a simple solution—the 20/20/20 rule.

A. "Every 20 minutes, take a 20-second break and focus on something 20 feet away," says Dr. Jeffrey Anshel of Encinitas, California, who is a consultant on visual ergonomics for American Airlines.

B. The simple technique not only rests your eyes, but it also keeps them moist and prevents them from "locking into a close-up."

Visualization
(Help the audience visualize the results.)

III. The 20/20/20 rule is effective.

A. Dr. Amy Greer of Dallas, Texas, recommended the rule to patients who were suffering from headaches and eyestrain caused by staring at small screens.

B. All of the patients who tried the technique said that it eliminated their problems.

CONCLUSION

I. Prolonged staring at a screen can cause "computer vision syndrome," with symptoms such as blurred vision, dry and irritated eyes, and headaches.

II. The solution is simple: Every 20 minutes, take a 20-second break and focus on something 20 feet away.

A. I challenge all of you to follow the 20/20/20 rule.

B. Your eyes will thank you.

Action
(Request audience action.)

For another speech that uses the motivated sequence, see the sample outline and transcript at the end of this chapter.

TIP 16.1

Tips for Your Career

Use Role Play to Change Behavior

If you own a restaurant and you want to persuade your servers to respond in a friendly manner toward obnoxious customers, you can give them examples of how to treat diners, you can urge them to be friendly, you can show training films. But none of these techniques will be as effective as having your employees engage in role play. One person plays the role of the crabby complainer ("There's too much dressing on this salad!") while a server acts out the correct response (saying, with a smile, "I am so sorry—let me bring you another salad"). After each server's performance, give a critique and, if anything is wrong, ask him or her to try again.

According to research studies, role play is a powerful way to modify behavior. If possible, make a video of a session. All participants can view the video and discuss strengths they see, as well as areas that need improvement.

Problem–Solution Pattern

For many audiences, the most persuasive approach is the **problem–solution pattern**. You show that a problem exists, and then you present the solution. This pattern is especially effective when listeners either don't know about the problem or don't know how serious it is. Here is the partial outline of a student speech by Adam Cohen:

problem–solution pattern

an arrangement of material that explores a problem and then offers a solution

Specific Purpose:	To convince my audience to support tougher enforcement of child-labor laws
Central Idea:	Stronger enforcement of child-labor laws would reduce the number of deaths and injuries involving children and teenagers.
Main Points:	

(Problem)   I. Many children and teenagers are killed or maimed because they are illegally working at jobs that are supposed to be filled by adults.

    A. One child or teenager is killed on the job every five days in the United States.

> B. About 210,000 are injured annually, with 70,000 hurt badly enough to need emergency-room treatment.
>
> C. Some employers use underage workers for dangerous jobs such as roofing, mining, logging, meat slicing, and construction.

(Solution) II. The federal government should enforce the child-labor laws that already exist.

> A. Unlike the present situation, in which no one ever goes to jail for breaking child-labor laws, federal prosecuters should seek criminal indictments in cases involving serious danger.
>
> B. Unlike the present situation, in which the government routinely waives fines for violations, the government should assess a maximum fine of $40,000 for each violation.

In the speech itself, under the first main point, Cohen related news accounts of child-labor tragedies to show the audience that the problem was more serious than most people realized. Under the second main point, he gave specific examples of how enforcement should be carried out.

For a transcript of a speech that uses the problem–solution pattern, see Chapter 17.

Statement-of-Reasons Pattern

statement-of-reasons pattern
a variation of the topical pattern in which a speaker gives reasons for an idea

The **statement-of-reasons pattern**, a variation of the topical pattern (which we discussed in Chapter 10), gives reasons for the speaker's argument. It can be used for any persuasive speech, but it is especially useful when the audience leans toward your position but needs some justification for that leaning. In one community speech, Noah Brody, a paramedic, gave three reasons why people should donate blood:

Specific Purpose: To persuade my listeners to donate blood at a Red Cross center

Central Idea: Donating blood saves lives, is safe, and can improve your health.

Main Points:

(1st Reason)   I. You provide the gift of life for others.

(2nd Reason)   II. Donation is safe and easy.

(3rd Reason)   III. You improve your health because donating blood stimulates your bone marrow.

In his speech, Brody developed each reason with examples and expert testimony.

Comparative-Advantages Pattern

comparative-advantages pattern
an organizational scheme that shows the superiority of one concept or approach another

When listeners already agree with you that a problem exists but aren't sure which solution is best, you can use the **comparative-advantages pattern** to show that your recommended solution is superior to others. Let's say that your listeners agree with you that medicine is needed for alleviating the symptoms of the common cold, but they don't know whether herbal remedies or conventional medicines would be better. If you feel that the latter is the preferred option, you could use the comparative-advantages pattern:

Tips for Your Career

View Persuasion as a Long-Term Process

Persuasion is sometimes a one-shot event aimed at a quick decision, as when you urge listeners to vote for a certain candidate. But in your career, persuasion often takes a long time—weeks, months, or even years. You need to gently nudge people toward a goal, giving them time to trust you and evaluate your recommendations.

Imagine a real estate agent who meets a young couple who are in the market for a new house. Instead of pressing for a quick sale, she gets to know them and truly listens to their needs. She takes them to visit many different houses, making notes on which features the couple likes and dislikes. After a long process of friendly collaboration, she is able to match the couple with a house that truly satisfies their needs.

Whether you succeed or fail in persuasion often comes down to one key question: Are you trustworthy? Before people will buy your ideas, products, or services, they want to know whether they can trust you to guide them in the right direction. Proving your reliability may take time.

Specific Purpose:	To convince my audience that conventional medicines are superior to herbal remedies in treating a common cold
Central Idea:	Conventional medicines are more likely than herbal remedies to relieve symptoms of the common cold.
Main Points:	
(1st Advantage)	I. Unlike herbal remedies, conventional medicines are tested and given FDA assurance of safety and purity.
(2nd Advantage)	II. Unlike herbal remedies, conventional medicines are required to list possible side effects.
(3rd Advantage)	III. Conventional medicines act more quickly than herbal remedies to lessen discomfort.

Each main point shows the superiority of conventional medicines over herbal remedies.

Sample Persuasive Speech

Using the motivated sequence, Michael Liscio argues that some criminals should receive an alternative form of sentencing. Below is the outline of the speech, which is accompanied by a commentary. Note the discussion of the five steps of the motivated sequence. Following the outline is a transcript of the speech.

connect

View a video of the speech "House Arrest" in the online Media Library for Chapter 16.

The Outline with Commentary

House Arrest

COMMENTARY

SPEECH

General Purpose:	To persuade
Specific Purpose:	To persuade my listeners to petition lawmakers to authorize house arrest for nonviolent offenders
Central Idea:	House arrest and electronic monitoring for nonviolent offenders would relieve overcrowding in prisons and save taxpayers millions of dollars.

INTRODUCTION

In the **attention** step of the motivated sequence, the speaker tries to arouse curiosity.

I. Attention Material

    A. If you heard that most state prisons are greatly overcrowded, what would be your reaction?

    B. You might say, "So what? It doesn't matter to me."

II. Orienting Material

    A. What if states are forced to raise taxes to construct new prisons?

        1. The Supreme Court has ruled that all 33 prisons in California are overcrowded.

        2. California must release 34,000 inmates unless it can build more prisons.

        3. The state is considering raising taxes to build additional prisons.

        4. Other states are also thinking about tax hikes.

A preview of the central idea helps the audience follow the rest of the speech.

    B. There is an ideal solution.

        1. It can be done without raising taxes.

        2. Inmates can be confined in their own homes, not in prisons.

(*Transition:* Before looking at this idea, let's examine the problem more closely.)

BODY

For the **need** step, the speaker explains a problem.

I. Prisons are overcrowded because we lock up a huge number of nonviolent offenders. (Show slide.) [See Figure 16.1.]

    A. Last year 2.3 million men and women were incarcerated in the U.S. at a cost of $69 billion.

        1. 60 percent were nonviolent offenders.

        2. Their crimes were embezzlement, tax evasion, corruption, writing bad checks, failing to make child support payments, selling drugs, and driving while intoxicated.

In the outline, the names of sources are placed in parentheses, but in the actual ~ch, they will be woven into the fabric of ~aker's remarks.

    B. Today's prisons can't absorb 2.3 million prisoners. (Dr. Craig Haney, lawyer and psychology professor at University of California in Santa Cruz)

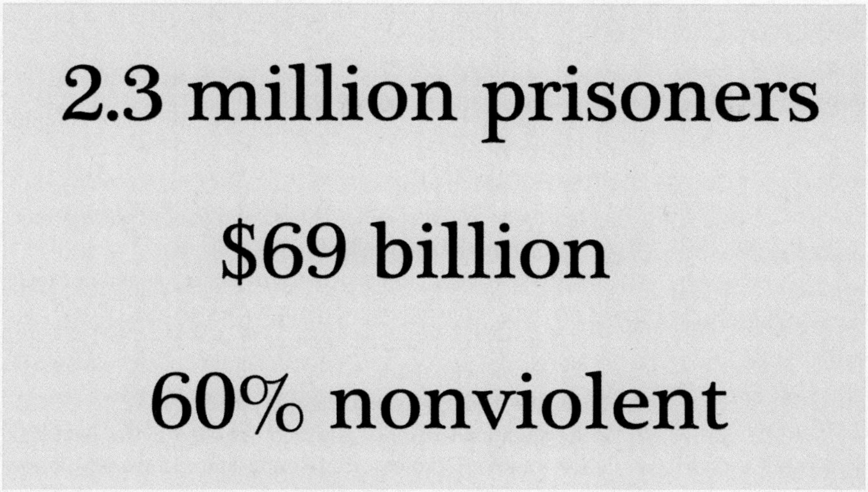

2.3 million prisoners

$69 billion

60% nonviolent

Figure 16.1
Most of the 2.3 million prisoners locked up at a cost of $69 billion a year are nonviolent offenders.

1. Prisoners live and sleep on bunks stacked 3 or 4 high in halls and auditoriums.
2. Crammed in, they have high levels of stress, illness, frustrations and fights.
3. They can't reduce stress by working out in gyms and recreational rooms because these facilities are unavailable—they have been transformed into dormitories.

(*Transition:* How can we solve the problem?)

II. The best way is house arrest with electronic monitoring.
   A. This keeps nonviolent offenders out of prison and doesn't cost society a lot of money.
      1. Most popular is an ankle bracelet, worn all the time. (Show photo.) [See Figure 16.2.]

> The **satisfaction** step presents a solution to the problem.

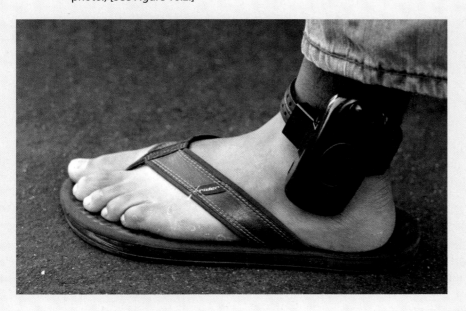

Figure 16.2
A popular type of house arrest uses an ankle bracelet for electronic monitoring.

(continued)

2. It sends a signal that is monitored by police or a private company.

3. If the prisoner goes out of range, police can act quickly.

B. House arrest is being used by only a few states and communities. (Dept. of Justice)

1. The reason is bad press.

2. News reports tell of convicts breaking out of their bracelets and committing another crime.

a. These events did occur, and may occur again, but technology is becoming more sophisticated. (Dr. Haney)

b. The newest bracelets alert police as soon as someone tampers with them.

C. House arrest costs less than prison.

1. The situation in Florida has been studied by Dr. Bill Bales, a criminology professor at Florida State University. (Show slide.) [See Figure 16.3.]

2. An offender under house arrest costs $1.97 per day, while a prisoner in a state prison costs $55.09 a day.

3. Some offenders must stay home 24 hours a day.

4. But most communities allow them to work, which helps avoid poverty and divorce.

(*Transition:* Has house arrest been successful anywhere?)

III. Some communities are saving millions of dollars by using house arrest.

A. Scottsdale, Arizona, started electronic monitoring of people convicted of drunk driving. (*Arizona Republic*)

1. In the first 5 weeks, the city saved more than $200,000.

2. Each offender is required to pay part of the cost—a $100 start fee and about $20 a day.

The speaker enhances his credibility by admitting that ankle bracelets have received bad publicity – at least in the past.

Citing an expert enhances credibility.

The **visualization** step reveals that the speaker's proposal has been tried—and has achieved success.

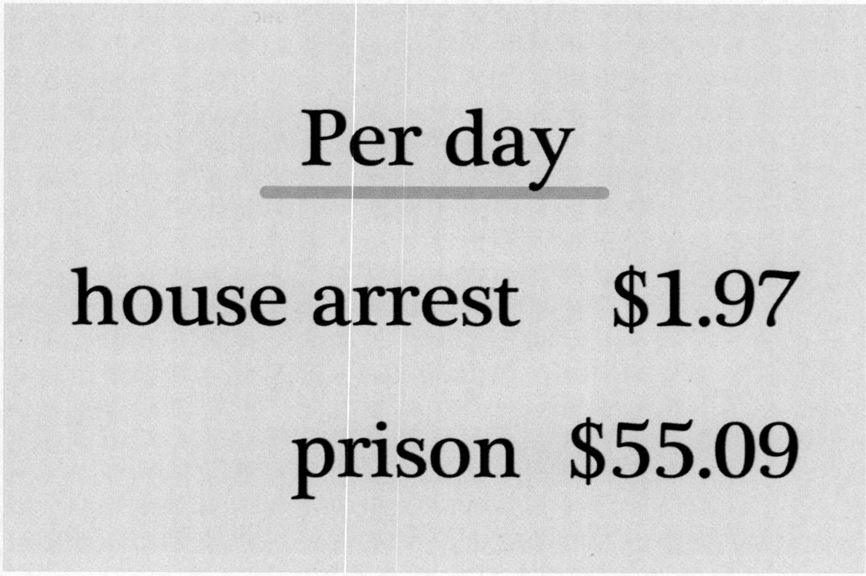

Figure 16.3
In Florida, far more money is spent per day on a prisoner in state prison than on an offender under house arrest.

Per day

house arrest $1.97

prison $55.09

B. Los Angeles County, California, has electronic monitoring of DWI offenders. (Judge Michael Barasse of Pennsylvania, who does studies for the U.S. government)
1. County saved $1 million in first year.
2. The average cost was $15 a day for each offender.
3. The offenders paid the costs themselves.

(*Transition:* What can you do?)

IV. Support house arrest and electronic monitoring in our state.
A. My petition asks our governor and legislators to authorize house arrest for nonviolent offenders.
B. As you leave today, please sign the petition.

(*Transition:* Here is how I see things.)

CONCLUSION

I. Summary
A. To solve overcrowding, we can use house arrest.
B. Or we can pay higher taxes to build new prisons.

II. Clincher
A. You have two options.
B. Which one do you choose?

BIBLIOGRAPHY

Bales, Bill, College of Criminology and Criminal Justice, Florida State University. "A Quantitative and Qualitative Assessment of Electronic Monitoring," paper presented at the National Law Enforcement and Corrections Technology Center's "Innovative Technologies for Corrections" Conference. 21 June 2010: 13-46. PDF file.

Barrasse, Michael (Judge). "Promising Sentencing Practice No. 6: Electronic Monitoring and SCRAM." National Highway Traffic Safety Administration website, 4 May 2010. Web. 14 Nov. 2010.

"Correctional Population in the United States." Bureau of Justice Statistics website (a branch of the U.S. Department of Justice), 5 April 2010. Web. 14 Nov. 2010.

Haney, Craig, professor of psychology, University of California, Santa Cruz. Telephone interview. 17 Nov 2010.

Madrid, Ofelia. "Scottsdale Saving Money with House Arrest in Some DUI Cases." *The Arizona Republic* 19 Nov. 2010: B1. Print.

Regoli, Robert M. and John D. Hewitt. *Exploring Criminal Justice: The Essentials.* Sudbury, MA: Jones and Bartlett, 2010. Print.

VISUAL AIDS

PowerPoint slide of key statistics
Photo of ankle bracelet
PowerPoint slide showing cost of house arrest vs. prison

In the **action** step, the speaker spells out exactly how listeners can help.

Because the body of the speech is necessarily long, it is appropriate to have a brief, to-the-point conclusion.

The speaker relies on highly credible sources.

The speaker uses three visuals that help the audience understand key points.

The Speech as Delivered

Here is a transcript of the speech by Michael Liscio. Notice that he uses the ideas of the outline without using the exact wording. In an extemporaneous speech, a speaker does not read or memorize a speech but speaks from brief notes.

House Arrest

What if I told you that state prisons throughout the United States are terribly overcrowded? If you're like most Americans, your reaction might be "So what? I'm not in prison, so it doesn't bother me."

But it *will* bother you if our state—and most other states—are forced to raise taxes to build new prisons. It's already happening in California. In 2011, the U.S. Supreme Court ruled that all of the 33 prisons in California are extremely overcrowded and that the state must release 34,000 inmates unless it can offer additional housing. So California state officials are thinking about raising taxes to build new prisons. And many other states are in a similar situation.

But raising taxes is never popular. Is there some way we can handle the problem without having to raise taxes? Yes, there is. We can confine a large number of inmates—not in prison, but in their own homes.

Before I explain my proposal, let's look at the problem in a little more detail. We have overcrowding in our prisons for one simple reason—we incarcerate a huge number of nonviolent offenders. *[Speaker shows slide in Figure 16.1]*

Special Techniques

How to Use Leave-Behinds

When you complete a persuasive speech in your career and you sit down, don't make the mistake of thinking that your persuasive task is finished.

"No matter how impressed and convinced the people in that room are when you're through," says computer consultant Jim Seymour of Austin, Texas, "your message hasn't finally clicked until they've taken it back to their staff, superiors, engineers, sales forces, or other constituencies. If you expect them to be even half as persuasive as you were—and to get it right when they retell your story for you!—you need to arm them with the tools they need to make your case persuasively."

These tools can be provided in "leave-behinds"—materials that are distributed at the end of your question-and-answer period. Make sure each listener receives a set. Leave-behinds may include:

1. *Summary.* A condensation of your key information will help listeners recall your points later, and it will provide a good abstract for those who could not attend. The summary must be brief—no more than one page.
2. *Memory aids.* A popular technique is to provide cards that can be slipped into a wallet or purse for future reference. Figure 16.A shows a sample card.
3. *Graphics.* Copies of key charts, diagrams, and tables provide visual support.
4. *New points.* If your time limit prevents you from covering all the points you want to discuss, you can focus on just a few points in the speech and cover the others on a leave-behind.
5. *Sources and Web links.* For listeners who want to pursue your subject further, provide a CD (or a piece of paper) giving your sources and relevant Web links.
6. *Samples and multimedia.* A sample product is a tangible reminder of your message. Videos on DVD or CD can provide bonus material in an enjoyable format.
7. *File folders.* Consider providing labeled file folders containing your materials. The folders help listeners keep material together, and make it easy to share with others.

For all important presentations, use leave-behinds. They enable your audience to take your message far beyond the meeting room to influence many people.

The U.S. Department of Justice says that last year, there were 2.3 million men and women locked up in prisons and jails throughout the United States at a cost of 69 billion dollars. Of all the prisoners, 60 percent were nonviolent. That means they were not guilty of crimes such as murder—they were guilty of crimes such as embezzlement, corruption, tax evasion, writing bad checks, selling drugs, driving while intoxicated, and failing to make child-support payments.

Let's go back a moment to the 2.3 million prisoners who are locked up. Our prisons today just aren't able to accommodate such a large number of people, according to Dr. Craig Haney, one of the nation's experts on prisons. Dr. Haney is a lawyer and a professor of psychology at the University of California in Santa Cruz, and he says that prisoners live and sleep on bunks stacked three to four high in hallways and auditoriums. The prisoners suffer high levels of stress and illness because they're crammed so close together. As you can imagine, there are many frustrations and fights.

Well, you might ask, why don't they work out in gyms or exercise rooms to reduce their stress level? That's a good idea, only that in many prisons, the gyms and recreational facilities aren't available anymore because they're being turned into dormitories.

So, what is the best way to solve the problem? I believe that house arrest with electronic monitoring is the best approach. It keeps nonviolent offenders out of prison without costing society a lot of money. There are many different kinds of electronic monitoring, but the most popular by far [Speaker shows photo in Figure 16.2] is the ankle bracelet, which offenders must wear at all times—even when taking a shower. The bracelet sends out a signal that is constantly being monitored by police or a private company. And if the offender goes out of a certain range, law enforcement can take prompt action.

Only a few states and communities are using house arrest, according to the Department of Justice. That's because house arrest has gotten a bad reputation in recent years. You may have seen news reports

(continued)

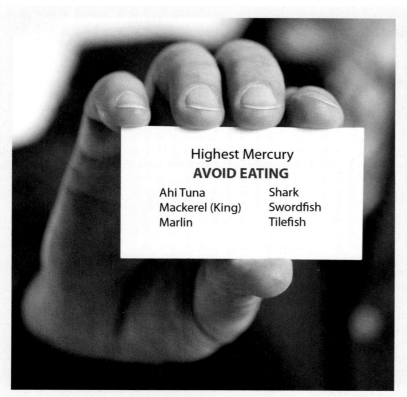

Figure 16.A
This memory aid was given to listeners by a student speaker at the end of a speech on dangerous mercury levels in fish. The card could be kept in a wallet or purse and pulled out at a restaurant or grocery store to help identify the types of fish containing high levels of mercury. (The student derived his information from the Natural Resources Defense Council.)

of convicted criminals breaking out of their brace-lets and committing another crime. These events did happen in the past, yes, and may happen again. But technology's becoming more and more sophisticated, according to Dr. Haney. The cases of breaking out of bracelets should diminish because the newest ankle monitors are able to alert the police as soon as they're tampered with.

House arrest is much less expensive than incar-ceration. Dr. Bill Bales, a criminology professor at Florida State University, has studied the situation in Florida. *[Speaker shows slide in Figure 16.3]* He found that an offender who is being monitored under house arrest costs $1.97 per day, while a prisoner in a state prison costs $55.09 a day.

In some cases, offenders are required to stay home 24 hours a day, but in most communities, they're allowed to go to work. This helps to avoid poverty and may prevent divorce or family problems.

Are there any success stories where house arrest is being used? Yes, there is. Communities that are using house arrest are saving millions of dollars. For example, Scottsdale, Arizona, has recently instituted house arrest with ankle monitoring for persons convicted of drunk driving, according to the *Arizona Republic*. City officials said they saved more than $200,000 in the first five weeks. Scottsdale requires the offender to help pay part of the cost—a $100 start fee and about $20 a day afterwards.

Michael Barrasse is a judge in Pennsylvania who studies electronic monitoring for the federal govern-ment. He points to a success story in Los Angeles County, California, which uses electronic monitoring for persons convicted of driving while intoxicated. In the first year alone, the county saved about $1 million in jail costs. The cost of electronic monitoring averaged about $15 a day per offender and that cost was paid off by the offenders themselves.

Now I would like to tell you what you can do about the situation. I urge you to support house arrest and electronic monitoring in our state. I have a petition that asks our governor and state legislators to authorize house arrest for nonviolent offenders. You can sign this petition in the back of the room as you leave today.

The way I see it, we have two choices for solving the problem of overcrowding. We can use house arrest, or we can pay higher taxes to build new prisons. Which do you choose?

For other persuasive speeches, see the sample speeches in Chapters 10, 11, and 17.

Resources for Review and Skill Building

Summary

Persuasion means influencing, changing, or reinforcing what people think, believe, or do. When you give a persuasive speech, you should have three key goals: (1) Win over your listeners so that they adopt your view or take a certain action. (2) Know your subject thoroughly. (3) Maintain a high stan-dard of ethical behavior.

There are two major types of persuasive speeches: the speech to influence thinking and the speech to motivate action.

In the speech to influence thinking, your primary goal is to convince people to adopt your position. A subcategory of this kind of speech is the speech of refutation, in which your aim is to knock down arguments or ideas that you believe are false.

In the speech to motivate action, you should tell the lis-teners exactly what action you want them to take. Whenever possible, encourage them to take some action—even if it's a small, token action—immediately.

Of the many patterns that can be used for the persuasive speech, four are especially effective: the motivated sequence, problem–solution pattern, statement-of-reasons pattern, and comparative-advantages pattern.

Key Terms

comparative-advantages pattern, *306*

motivated sequence, *301*

persuasion, *297*

problem–solution pattern, *305*

speech of refutation, *299*

speech to influence thinking, *298*

speech to motivate action, *299*

statement-of-reasons pattern, *306*

Review Questions

1. What is the goal of the speech of refutation?

2. In a speech to motivate action, why should you try to get listeners to take action immediately?

3. Give three examples of immediate, on-the-spot audience action.

4. What is the goal of the *need* step of the motivated sequence?

5. What is the goal of the *satisfaction* step of the motivated sequence?

6. What is the goal of the *visualization* step of the motivated sequence?

7. What is the goal of the *action* step of the motivated sequence?

8. Which organizational pattern is useful when listeners don't know how serious a problem is?

9. When is the statement-of-reasons pattern especially effective?

10. When is the comparative-advantages pattern most effective?

Building Critical-Thinking Skills

1. Charities often give instructions like these to their fundraisers: "If people decline to contribute, ask them to give just a token amount, such as a quarter or one dollar." These instructions are sometimes effective in building support for an organization because they follow one of the successful persuasive techniques discussed in this chapter. What is the technique?

2. Which organizational pattern would work best for a speech on why short résumés are better than long ones? Defend your answer.

Building Teamwork Skills

1. Working in a group, create a brief synopsis for a television commercial that uses the motivated sequence. Some possible topics:

   a. Buying a certain brand of toothpaste
   b. Exercising at a spa or gym
   c. Donating blood to the Red Cross
   d. Buying a cellular telephone

2. The text discusses the effectiveness of role play. In a group, brainstorm a list of distracting or disruptive behaviors that audience members sometimes exhibit. Then let each person take turns playing the role of a speaker, while the rest of the group members in sequence act out the bad behaviors. The speaker's job is to respond to each undesired behavior in a firm but friendly manner. After each speaker finishes responding to the disrupters, the group should discuss how the speaker fared both verbally and nonverbally.

Ethical Issues

Answer to quiz on p. 298: C. Wendy could say something like this: "I am a graduate of the college, and in the interest of full disclosure, I want you to know that I am being paid to give this presentation. However, let me add that even if I were not being paid, I would still recommend this college as an ideal school for you."

Persuasive Strategies

OBJECTIVES

After studying this chapter, you should be able to:

1. Describe how to analyze listeners, using a persuasion scale.
2. Explain how to build credibility with an audience in a persuasive speech.
3. Explain how to marshal convincing evidence in a persuasive speech.
4. Distinguish between deduction and induction as tools of reasoning in a persuasive speech.
5. Identify 10 fallacies in reasoning.
6. Select motivational appeals for a persuasive speech.
7. Explain how to arouse emotions in a persuasive speech.

JANUARY JONES is not scared OF sharks, but FOR sharks. The star of the TV show "Mad Men" is trying to persuade states and nations to ban shark finning, which is "the brutal practice of slicing off a shark's fin for use in shark fin soup. The shark—sometimes still alive—may be thrown back into the sea to bleed to death." Jones says that each year, more than 70 million sharks are killed worldwide—just for the fins.[1]

Jones and her fellow campaigners give speeches to the public and present testimony to legislators. By 2011, they had won some major battles, as California, Hawaii, Oregon, Washington, Guam, and the nation of Chile banned shark finning.[2] They gained their victories in large part because they used one of the key elements of persuasion—*knowing your audience*—which we will discuss shortly. Also in this chapter we will examine five other strategies that you can use in a persuasive speech.

JANURY JONES IS SCARED ^FOR SHARKS.

OCEANA

January Jones and her allies are successful in persuading people to protect sharks because they use the strategy of "know your audience." See the next page for details.

Knowing Your Audience

The first step in persuasion is to understand your listeners. To truly understand them, you must get inside their minds and see the world as they see it. In the case discussed in the preceding pages, Jones and other shark protectors know that they cannot persuade the public and legislators by focusing only on the cruelty of maiming and killing sharks. After all, sharks are widely feared and hated. ABC's Good Morning America anchor Josh Elliott recently referred to sharks as "nasty creatures."[3]

To win their case, the shark advocates have to show that finning drives sharks close to extinction, and if all sharks are gone, humans will be hurt. As science columnist Sandra Blakeslee put it, "As top predators, sharks help keep the marine ecosystem in balance." If they are eliminated, "food webs (who eats whom) unravel. Diseases emerge. Jellyfish populations explode. By slaughtering sharks, we degrade the sea itself."[4]

Here are some strategies for understanding your audience:

Analyze Listeners

How can you find out where listeners stand? Gather information about them in advance (see Chapter 4). For example, you can get the names of a few listeners and interview them (on the phone or via e-mail) to find out how much they know on your subject and what their beliefs and attitudes are. If time permits, use a questionnaire to poll all or most of the members of the audience.

Use a Persuasion Scale

For analyzing an audience, consider using the persuasion scale in Table 17.1.[5] On the scale, mark where the listeners are in relation to your specific purpose *before* you speak. Then mark where you hope they will be *after* you speak. Knowing a starting point and an ideal finishing point can help prevent you from giving a speech that fails to connect with your audience.

If your goal is to persuade your audience to switch from diet sodas to healthier beverages, it might be a mistake to assume that the audience is at Stage 5 (convinced of your view and wanting tips on how to find healthy substitutes). Perhaps they are really at Stage 1 (unaware of the long-term health hazards of diet sodas). In that case, you should start at Stage 1 and move toward Stage 5 and ultimately end up at Stage 6.

Set a realistic goal. You are not a failure if your listeners fall short of Stage 6. With some listeners, persuading them to move from Stage 2 to Stage 4 is a great triumph.

Plan Strategy

While some audiences may fit neatly into one category or another, many audiences are segmented—that is, you may find 16 listeners opposed to your view, 15 apathetic, 8 already convinced, and so on.

Table 17.1   Persuasion Scale

1	2	3	4	5	6
Unaware of the issue	Aware of the issue but opposed to your view	Aware of the issue but apathetic	Informed and interested but neutral on your view	Convinced of your view	Ready to take action

Tips for Your Career

Don't Expect Universal Success

One of the greatest orations in American history—the Gettysburg Address—was a failure, in the opinion of some of Abraham Lincoln's contemporaries. An editorial in the *Chicago Times* on the day after his speech said, "The cheek of every American must tingle with shame as he reads the silly, flat and dishwatery utterances of the man who has to be pointed out to intelligent foreigners as the President of the United States."

Career Track, a company that sponsors business speeches and seminars throughout the United States, asks listeners to evaluate each of its speakers. No speaker has ever received 100 percent satisfaction. No matter the speaker, no matter the subject matter, at least 2 percent of listeners are dissatisfied. Even popular spellbinders can please no more than 98 percent.

In your career, do your best, try to meet the needs of all listeners, but remember that you can give an oration equal in greatness to the Gettysburg Address and still fail to please that intractable 2 percent.

When you have several different segments, to which group should you devote your energies? An obvious answer is: Try to meet the needs of everyone. While this is an admirable goal, it cannot always be achieved. For example, if most listeners know a great deal about your topic but a few are totally uninformed, it would be foolish to spend almost all of your time focusing on the needs of a tiny minority.

The best approach: Try to meet the needs of all listeners, but when this is impossible, choose the group that is most important. If, for example, your pre-speech analysis shows that 21 listeners want guidance on how to deal with angry co-workers and 3 listeners don't think the issue is relevant to their lives, don't focus most of your time and energy on those 3.

Despite the difficulty of meeting the needs of several different segments, there are some strategies you can employ. Using our persuasion scale, let's examine how to reach listeners with *starting* points at each of the six stages. As we proceed, study Table 17.2, which shows an example of how to apply our strategies.

1. **Unaware of the issue.** For people in the dark on your topic, start by explaining the situation and showing why your ideas are important. Later in the speech, try to convince them to adopt your view.

2. **Aware of the issue but opposed to your view.** Find out the listeners' reasons for opposing your view and then aim at refuting them. When listeners are strongly skeptical or hostile to an idea, a smart plan often is to delay divulging your central idea until the end of your speech. (This idea will be discussed later in this chapter under inductive reasoning.)

Always show respect for opponents and their views. *Never* insult or belittle those who disagree; sarcastic or belligerent remarks make people defensive and all the more committed to their opinion. Try to persuade these people, but if that fails, be content if you can move them a few inches closer to your side. Sometimes the best you can hope for is to plant some seeds of doubt about their position that might someday sprout into full-blown conversion to your side.

3. **Aware of the issue but apathetic.** "Who cares?" is the attitude of listeners in this category. To break through their apathy, show how the issue affects their own lives.

Table 17.2   Using the Persuasion Scale

Situation: A speech aimed at persuading listeners to support curtailment of theft from hotel and motel rooms.

Position on Scale	Strategy	Example
1. Unaware of the issue	Explain the problem.	"Thefts from hotels and motels amount to more than $100 million each year. Items stolen are not just towels, but irons and ironing boards, hair dryers, bedspreads, blankets, pillows, wall-mounted telephones, coffee makers, lamps, mirrors, paintings, and TV remote controls."
2. Aware of the issue but opposed to your view	Refute opposing arguments or schemes.	"You may think that the solution is to seek police action, but this is not practical. The police don't have time to investigate and prosecute what they consider minor crimes."
3. Aware of the issue but apathetic	Show that the issue can affect listeners' lives.	"This kind of theft may seem inconsequential, but the American Hotel & Motel Association estimates that to make up for the thefts, hotels and motels have to price their rooms at 10 percent higher than they would otherwise. In other words, you and I must pay extra because of all this stealing."
4. Informed and interested but neutral on your view	Show that your proposal offers the best solution to the problem.	"I propose that hotels and motels require a $100 deposit when a person checks in. Then, when he or she is ready to check out, the room is quickly inspected and if nothing is missing, the $100 deposit is returned."
5. Convinced of your view	Reinforce existing beliefs and give new reasons for supporting your view.	"My proposal should not be an inconvenience for the honest person, and it can ensure that when we check into a room, we won't have to call the front desk and request a coffee maker to replace the one that the previous occupant of the room must have swiped."
6. Ready to take action	Show how, when, and where to take action.	"As you leave today, please sign the petition that details my proposal. I will make photocopies and send them to the headquarters of all the major hotel and motel chains."

4. **Informed and interested but neutral on your view.** People at this stage need little background information; you can plunge directly into convincing them that your position is correct or superior to other views.

5. **Convinced of your view.** For listeners who agree with you, try to reinforce their belief and, if possible, give them new reasons for supporting your position. Although they agree with your view, some listeners may not have considered or endorsed a plan of action; with them, your task is to demonstrate that your plan offers the best approach.

6. **Ready to take action.** For speeches aimed at motivating action, this is the stage you want all listeners to reach (although you may not be able to bring every listener this far). Show listeners how, when, and where to take action.

As we have already noted, it is difficult to meet the needs of all listeners when their starting points are at different stages on our scale. But sometimes you can do so. All the examples in Table 17.2 could be integrated into one speech, permitting you to meet the needs of listeners at all six stages.

Building Credibility

For years I had thought that mayonnaise is often the cause of food poisoning. But this is false, says Dr. Mildred Cody, head of the nutrition division of Georgia State University. "Commercially prepared mayonnaise is safe to use," she says. What causes problems at picnics and potlucks is contamination of foods that are often mixed with mayonnaise—such as pasta, potatoes, eggs, chicken, or tuna.[6]

I completely changed my mind about mayonnaise. Why? Because Dr. Cody is a leading authority on food poisoning, and she has investigated the issue thoroughly.

In other words, she has high **credibility**—a major source of persuasiveness in all human communication. Before listeners can accept your ideas, they want to know whether you are reliable, competent, and trustworthy.

In your career, when you want to persuade people who know you well, your credibility boils down to how they assess your ability and your character. If you are a person who is known for honesty, fairness, and competence, you enter the speech with a powerful asset. If you are known for dishonesty, unfairness, or incompetence, you enter with a heavy liability.

In the speech itself, credibility is enhanced if your delivery is enthusiastic and if your speech is clear, well-organized, and well-reasoned.[7] In addition, you can build credibility by adhering to the following guidelines.

Your Thoughts

Personal appearance and body language—what role do you think they play in a speaker's credibility with an audience?

credibility
degree to which a speaker is perceived to be believable, trustworthy, and competent

Explain Your Competence

If you have special expertise, let your audience know about it—modestly, of course. Don't boast; just give the facts. This enhances your credibility because it shows that you are speaking from personal experience. It says, "I've been there—I know what I'm talking about." Here is how student speaker Lauren Shriver bolstered her credibility during a speech:

> Deep-sea diving is not dangerous—if you follow all the safety rules. I've made over 50 dives myself, and I feel very safe because I'm very careful each time. I never allow myself to get slack and overconfident.

Shriver's information about her diving experience was necessary to give credibility to her remarks. Notice how she inserted her personal background in a modest way.

If you lack personal experience on your topic, you can still enhance your credibility by showing that you have chosen competent sources. For example, if you are speaking on asteroids that might strike the Earth, you can tell your audience that you derived material from two leading experts on asteroids, astronomers Bob Preston and Joán García-Sánchez of the Jet Propulsion Laboratory.

Be Accurate

Sloppiness with facts and figures can undermine your whole presentation. In a speech on child abuse, one student said that 55 percent of American parents abused their children—a statistic that listeners challenged during the question-and-answer period. (A few days later, the student admitted to the instructor that the original source estimated 5.5 percent rather than 55—the overlooked decimal point made a huge difference.) When listeners believe you are wrong on one point, even when it's a small matter, they tend to distrust everything else you say.

Tips for Your Career

In a Debate, Be Reasonable and Fair

Your boss knows that you strongly oppose a proposed policy, and she asks you to debate the issue with a colleague at the next staff meeting. What is your best approach? Should you demolish your foe with a slashing, take-no-prisoners assault? No, that approach is actually counterproductive.

"Victory is not won by bluster," says Professor Douglas Hunt. "Inexperienced arguers tend to enter the arena like gladiators ready for combat . . . They often allow their commitment to one side of an argument to blind them to the virtues of the other. They argue so aggressively that the audience dismisses them as cranks." Effective arguers, in contrast, "are usually cautious, courteous, and reasonable . . . They understand, anticipate, and even sympathize with the arguments of their opponents . . . They give the impression of being reasonable people whose judgment can be trusted."

Avoid cheap shots—personal abuse or ridicule. For example, a speaker at a public forum on air pollution ridiculed environmentalists as "mushroom pickers who weep at the thought of a butterfly dying." If you throw such poisoned barbs, listeners who agree with you may laugh and applaud your cleverness, but those who are neutral or opposed to your position (the very people you want to win over) may discount everything you say. In fact, your unfairness may elicit sympathy for the other side.

A scene from the TV show "Modern Family" depicts a debate in a race for a city council seat. Is Claire's finger-pointing an effective gesture?

Show Your Open-Mindedness

Showing confidence in your ideas is a good thing, of course, but some speakers go t[o] extreme—they become arrogant and inflexible, refusing to admit any possible prob[lem] with their argument.

Audiences distrust fanatical know-it-alls. They prefer a speaker who is open-minded and capable of admitting error or exceptions. In a speech that argued in favor of homeschooling, Patricia Caldwell gave glowing accounts of the success of homeschooled children when they went to college, and then she showed her open-mindedness by conceding that there are abuses:

> In one well-publicized case in Chicago a few months ago, the authorities brought legal action against a husband and wife for not sending their children to school. Their idea of a home school was to make the children—ages 7, 9, and 10—work all day instead of teaching them to read and write.[8]

Was it stupid for the speaker to relate an incident that seemed to negate her central idea (that some parents can do a better job of teaching than the public schools)? No, because she went on to say that bad parent-teachers are rare, and that periodic state inspections can weed them out. Rather than damaging her case, her concession strengthened it, for she showed herself to the audience as fair-minded. If you were a listener, wouldn't you trust her more than someone who asserted that *all* parents are good teachers?

It is especially important to be reasonable and open-minded during the question-and-answer period. I have seen some speakers do a good job in their speeches, but when they are asked questions, they become rigid and defensive. They refuse to admit error or to concede that a listener has a good point. These speakers severely damage their own credibility and undo much of the persuasiveness of their own speeches.

Show Common Ground with Your Audience

When you are introduced to someone at a party, you try to find things that you have in common. You ask each other questions ("What is your major?" "Where are you from?") until you hit upon some interest that you share. We try to find common ground because it not only helps us to make conversation but also helps us to feel comfortable with another person.

In a speech, listeners tend to respect and trust a speaker who is similar to themselves, so your job is to show how you are like your listeners. This does not mean compromising your beliefs; it means highlighting those characteristics you share with the audience. This is especially important if some of the listeners are hostile to your ideas. Imagine that you are speaking on gun control, and you know that half the listeners are already against your position. Here's what you can say:

> I'm talking on gun control today. I know that a lot of you are opposed to the position I'm going to take. I ask only that you hear me out and see if my arguments have any merit whatsoever. Though we may disagree on this subject, you and I have at least one thing in common: We want to see a reduction in the number of violent, gun-related crimes in our society.

With this kind of statement, you not only pinpoint common ground (opposition to crime) but also appeal to the audience's sense of fair play.

One of the best ways to build credibility is to show listeners that you share (or have shared) their experiences or feelings. Diana Fisher, manager of the bariatric surgery program at Mission Hospital in Asheville, North Carolina, went from 297 pounds to 125 pounds in just two years—thanks to the same surgical procedure that she now arranges for patients. As part of her job, she explains weight-reduction options to audiences of obese people.[9] (See Figure 17.1 on the next page.)

Her first presentation was nearly a failure. As she talked, she was dismayed to see that her listeners were unresponsive, with arms folded. When she asked for questions, there was silence. Then she realized that her listeners had no idea of her personal story. Perhaps they were looking at her and thinking that a thin woman could not know anything at all about the physical and emotional pain of being obese. So Fisher told the audience that she had once weighed almost 300 pounds and had suffered the same agony that they were experiencing. Suddenly, the audience came to life. Some people began crying, and there was a torrent of excited questions.

Now Fisher tells her story at the beginning of every presentation. When listeners see that she has walked the same path that they are treading, they are more inclined to trust her insights on overcoming obesity.[10]

Providing Evidence

evidence

the facts, examples, statistics, testimony, and other information that support an assertion

When you make an assertion in a speech, it is not enough to say, "Trust me on this" or "I know I'm right." The audience wants **evidence,** or proof. Evidence can be presented in the forms we discussed in Chapter 8, such as narratives, statistics, examples, and testimony. For each main point in your speech, choose the evidence that is most likely to prove your point with a particular audience. Ask yourself these questions:

1. Is the evidence *accurate?* Erroneous information would obviously undermine the credibility of your entire speech.

2. Is the evidence *up-to-date?* A research study conducted in the field of medicine in 1986 is almost certain to be outdated.

3. Is the evidence *typical?* An athlete may attribute his success to consuming five banana milkshakes a day, but is his diet common among athletes, or is he probably the only one in the world with such a diet?

Here are some tips on using evidence.

Choose evidence from credible sources.   While watching TV news one night, I was astounded by this story:

> A New York doctor reports that a patient experienced epileptic seizures whenever she heard the voice of Mary Hart, co-host of the TV show *Entertainment Tonight.* The seizures ceased when she stopped watching the show.

My immediate reaction was total disbelief. What nonsense! Hearing a person's voice cannot cause a seizure. But then the news anchor added:

> The woman was the subject of an article in the *New England Journal of Medicine* by Dr. Venkat Ramani, professor of neurology at Albany Medical College in New York.

Just as quickly as I had dismissed the story, I now believed it. Why? Because the *New England Journal of Medicine* is one of the mostly highly respected medical journals in the world.

Evidence—especially the hard-to-believe variety—becomes much more convincing to the audience if you cite a reliable source. Be sure to give specific details; instead of saying, "a judge," give her name and title: "Sharon Brown, Chief Justice of our state's Supreme Court."

Provide a variety of evidence.   In some cases, a single example or statistic may be sufficient to bolster an argument, but in most persuasive situations, a speaker needs multiple sources of support.

Use a vivid personal narrative whenever possible.   Imagine that you are planning a speech on drunk driving. If you want to convince your listeners that they could be victimized by a drunk driver, which of the following would be the more persuasive piece of evidence?

1. You tell about an automobile crash in which a drunk driver hit your car and killed one of your passengers.

2. You cite the fact that 25,000 people are killed in America each year in alcohol-related car crashes.

Though you would need to use both of these items in your speech, item 1 would be more persuasive for most listeners. But, you might ask, how can one solitary case be more persuasive than a statistic encompassing 25,000 people? Psychologists have conducted scores of experiments that indicate that one vivid narrative, told from the speaker's personal experience, is much more persuasive than its statistical status would imply.[11] "All other things being equal," writes social psychologist Elliot Aronson, "most people are more deeply influenced by one clear, vivid personal example than by an abundance of statistical data."[12]

The power of a personal narrative (preceding page) is demonstrated by Alison Conca-Cheng, a student at Tufts University, who tells a Congressional committee about the head concussion she suffered during a soccer match. Her testimony, which was part of an effort to persuade Congress to require greater protections for student athletes who suffer concussions, was eloquent and powerful.

Using Sound Reasoning

Reasoning, the act of reaching conclusions on the basis of logical thinking, is a part of everyday life. If you take an umbrella with you on a walk because you notice heavy clouds massing in the sky, you are using reasoning to prevent yourself from getting soaked by the rain that may soon fall. While it is true that people are not always logical and rational, it is also true that they frequently can be persuaded by a message that appeals to their powers of reasoning.[13]

Let's look at two popular types of reasoning and then examine some common fallacies of reasoning.

Deduction

Imagine that you are driving a car 15 miles per hour over the speed limit. Suddenly you see a police car parked behind a billboard, with a radar device protruding. You slow down, but you know it is too late. Sure enough, you glance in your rearview mirror and see a second police car with lights flashing.

How did you know that you were going to be stopped? By using **deduction**—a chain of reasoning that carries you from (1) a generalization to (2) a specific instance (of the generalization) to (3) a conclusion. In formal logic, this chain of reasoning is expressed in a form of argument known as a **syllogism:**

Major premise (generalization):   Motorists who are speeding when they pass a radar point are stopped by police.

Minor premise (specific instance):   I was speeding when I passed a radar point.

Conclusion: Therefore, I will be stopped.

Deductive reasoning with a syllogism is one of the most powerful tools of persuasion that a speaker can use. If you can convince your listeners to accept the major

reasoning

using logic to draw conclusions from evidence

deduction

reasoning from a generalization to a specific conclusion

syllogism

a deductive scheme consisting of a major premise, a minor premise, and a conclusion and minor premises, the conclusion is inescapable. The listeners are compelled by logic to accept it.

Until her death in 1906, Susan B. Anthony fought for the right of women to vote—a right that was not fully secured until 1920, when the Nineteenth Amendment to the Constitution granted nationwide suffrage to women. In speeches delivered throughout the United States, Anthony used deductive logic as her persuasive strategy. If we put the essence of her speeches in the form of a syllogism, it would look like this:

Major premise (generalization):   The Constitution guarantees all U.S. citizens the right to vote.

Minor premise (specific instance):   Women are U.S. citizens.

Conclusion: Therefore, women have the right to vote.

To us today, this syllogism looks simple and obvious: How could Anthony have failed to persuade every listener? But bear in mind that in the nineteenth century, many people viewed women as less than full-fledged citizens. In her speeches, Anthony had to convince her audience of both the major premise and the minor premise. Those listeners whom she won over were then obliged by force of logic to accept her conclusion.

In a speech, deductive reasoning is convincing *only if both premises are true and are accepted by the audience as true.*[14] Would an audience be likely to accept the following chain of reasoning?

Major premise: Cardiovascular exercise improves eyesight.

Minor premise: Jogging is a form of cardiovascular exercise.

Conclusion: Therefore, jogging improves eyesight.

The minor premise is true, but the major premise is false, so the entire syllogism is flawed. An audience would reject the conclusion.

Now let's turn to the correct use of deductive reasoning: Student speaker Stephanie Haas wanted to persuade her audience that some types of mushrooms and other fungi are in danger of becoming extinct. She realized that some listeners might think, "Well, no big deal. Why should I be concerned?" So Haas used a syllogism to construct her argument:

Major premise (generalization):   All plant species that contribute to public health should be preserved.

Minor premise (specific instance):   Endangered species of mushrooms and other fungi contribute to public health by removing toxins from contaminated soil.

Conclusion: Endangered species of mushrooms and other fungi should be preserved.

If listeners believed both the major premise and the minor premise, they were likely to accept her conclusion.

Induction

While deduction moves from the general to the specific, **induction** proceeds from the specific to the general. Imagine that you are a pediatrician seeing patients one January morning in your office:

- The first patient, age 9, complains of a runny nose, a sore throat, a headache, and muscle aches. She has a fever of 103°.

- The second patient, 7, has similar complaints and a fever of 102°.

What is the error in this syllogism? (1) All cats kill birds, (2) This is a cat, (3) Therefore, it kills birds.

induction

reasoning from specific evidence to a general conclusion

- Third patient—same symptoms, plus a fever of 101.5°.
- Fourth patient—similar complaints and a fever of 102.5°.
- Fifth patient—similar symptoms and a fever of 103°.

You know from your medical training that these complaints are classic symptoms of influenza (or flu). You know that influenza is a communicable disease, striking many people in a community, usually in winter. On the basis of what you have seen, you reason inductively that your community is experiencing an influenza outbreak. You use *specific* evidence (or isolated observations) to reach a *general* conclusion. In reaching this conclusion, however, you must take an *inductive leap*. You cannot prove that there is a flu outbreak simply because of your five patients. You are probably right, but your conclusion has to remain tentative (until further evidence is gathered and the county health department declares an outbreak), because there is always the chance that some other explanation can account for your five patients' illness. Perhaps they have nasty colds or suffer from some new virus; perhaps no other patients with those symptoms will show up at your office during the remainder of the week. The chances are overwhelming that an influenza outbreak *is* the explanation, of course; but the point is that induction, unlike deduction, never leads to a certain conclusion, only a *very likely* one.

The Usefulness of Induction

The inductive method is used frequently by scientists. They make isolated observations and then form a hypothesis. They may note, for instance, that the average temperature is rising each year in Sydney, Tokyo, Cairo, Rome, Copenhagen, Montreal, Lima, Mexico City, and Los Angeles. Therefore—now they take an inductive leap—the entire globe is warming up.

The inductive method has often led to useful discoveries. In World War II, British fighter planes had cockpit covers made of plastic. During combat a cover would sometimes shatter, causing pieces of plastic to become lodged in the pilots' eyes. In pilot after pilot, a British physician observed that the eyes were not damaged or infected by the plastic fragments. This observation led to the use of plastic to make artificial lenses, including contact lenses, for people's eyes.

If the first three crackers in a package are too salty for your taste, you can use inductive reasoning to conclude that all the crackers are too salty.

How to Construct an Inductive Argument

Some public speakers construct their inductive arguments by following three steps: (1) ask a question, (2) answer the question by collecting as much specific evidence as possible, and (3) reach a conclusion based on the evidence. Here is an example:

Question: Do some foods give the brain an energy boost?

Evidence:

   Item 1:   U.S. military researchers have found that turkey contains an amino acid that lifts energy levels and helps the brain to manage stress.

   Item 2:   U.S. Department of Agriculture scientists say that Brazil nuts can help make you feel more clearheaded and mentally confident.

   Item 3:   Researchers at Tufts University have concluded that brightly colored vegetables such as carrots and broccoli are "brain food," loaded with vitamins, minerals, and phytochemicals that maintain brain health and enhance mental performance.

Conclusion: Some foods energize the brain.

If you were using this material for a speech, you would need to flesh it out with additional facts, of course, but it gives you a framework, and it helps you think logically.

When you use inductive reasoning, you will convince an audience only if your evidence is strong. If you have weak evidence, your conclusion will be weak.

A Special Use for Inductive Reasoning

Earlier in this book, you were advised to state your central idea in the introduction of your speech; there is, however, an important exception to this guideline. If listeners are likely to have a negative reaction to your central idea, a wise strategy is to lead them through an inductive chain, saving the central idea for the latter part of the speech.

Student speaker Marilyn Zelinsky wanted to convince her audience that the United States should use punishments other than prison for people who are convicted of minor, nonviolent offenses such as writing bad checks and possessing marijuana. She feared, however, that if she stated her central idea in the introduction, her classmates would consider her a crackpot and fail to take her speech seriously. So she withheld her core concept, choosing to build her case with facts and figures like these:[15]

- "The United States has the largest prison population in the world—2.3 million. While the U.S. has five percent of the world's population, it has about 25 percent of the world's prisoners."
- "We are the only nation that imprisons people for long periods of time for minor crimes, such as passing bad checks and possessing marijuana. We have 700,000 of these offenders locked up right now."
- "To lock up a prisoner costs the taxpayers an average of $24,500 per year. If we didn't have the 700,000 nonviolent prisoners behind bars, we would have $17 billion to spend on more important things."
- "We can punish nonviolent offenders in other ways, such as house arrest, restitution, and community service."

Toward the end of the speech, she was ready to make her case for alternative sentencing. Her strategy must have worked, because many students, on their evaluation sheets, said they found her argument highly persuasive.

An inductive line of reasoning helps listeners keep an open mind. When they watch you build your case block by block, they are more respectful and appreciative of the central idea when it is finally presented to them. This doesn't mean they will always agree with you, of course, but it does mean that those who are opposed to your ideas will probably see more merit to your case than they would if you announced your central idea in the introduction.

Quick tip: If you have trouble remembering the difference between deduction and induction, keep in mind that they travel in opposite directions. Deduction (think of the word *deduct* in the sense of taking *away*) leads *away* from a generalization; it goes from general to specific, applying a general principle to a specific case. Induction (think of the first two letters *in*) leads *into,* or toward, a generalization; it goes from specific to general, accumulating specific instances that point toward a general idea.

Fallacies in Reasoning

A **fallacy** is an error in reasoning that renders an argument false or unreliable. You should become adept at recognizing fallacies so that (1) you can avoid using them in your own speeches—an ethical speaker would never knowingly mislead an audience—and (2) you can prevent yourself from being influenced by them when you listen to the speeches of others. Here are some common fallacies.

fallacy
an argument based on a false inference

Bandwagon

bandwagon fallacy
equating popularity with
truth and proof

"Most voters in our community are supporting Sandra Dawkins for mayor, so jump on our bandwagon as we roll to victory." This is an example of the **bandwagon fallacy,** an argument based on popularity rather than on evidence and reasoning.

Some speakers use public opinion polls to create a bandwagon effect for their argument: "Over 80 percent of Americans believe that beef is an important part of a healthy diet." Although poll results may be interesting, a poll number by itself does not prove the value of anything. A speaker arguing for beef should use nutritional data and other evidence.

This ad was created by the author to illustrate how a casino might use a band-wagon appeal to try to persuade people to come and gamble. Though the ad is fictitious, it is similar to the persuasion techniques that are widely used in advertising and politics.

*Everyone loves to win money
at Gran Dolina Casino*

Hasty Generalization

hasty generalization
a conclusion that is based on
inadequate evidence

A **hasty generalization** is a conclusion that is reached on the basis of insufficient evidence. In a speech on managing credit card debt, a student speaker said that "almost all students on this campus are deeply in debt because of credit cards." When he was challenged in the question-and-answer period by students who disbelieved him, he revealed that he had based his statement on interviews with four friends. If he had polled a larger number of students, he would have seen a different picture.

Red Herring

In seventeenth-century England, according to legend, if criminals were being pursued by bloodhounds, they would drag a red herring (smoked fish) across the trail, confusing the dogs and making them veer off into a new direction.

A **red herring** argument distracts listeners from the real issue and leads them toward an irrelevant issue. This trick is frequently used in political debates. One legislator, for example, may argue for laws protecting the California condor, and then an opponent counters, "How can we even think about birds when our most pressing problems deal with humans? Let's work on taking care of homeless people before we get all hot and bothered about animals."

The fallacy is also used in courtroom battles. If, say, a tobacco company is being sued by the government for endangering the health of citizens, a tobacco-company lawyer might try to divert the jury to a different subject: "Ladies and gentlemen of the jury, the government tells you that tobacco is poisonous, but they say nothing about alcohol. They say nothing about the 20,000 people killed each year by drunk drivers. I don't see the government suing whisky makers." Lawyers who employ this trick sometimes win their cases, but ethical speakers should never use it.

red herring
diverting listeners from the real issue to an irrelevant matter

Attack on a Person

Some speakers try to win an argument by attacking a person rather than the person's ideas. For example: "Fitzroy has lived in upper-class luxury all his life, so how can we believe anything he says about government assistance for the poor? He obviously knows nothing about poverty." This **attack on a person,** sometimes known as *argumentum ad hominem* (argument against the man), is unfair and unethical. Fitzroy's arguments should be judged on how sound his ideas are, not on any aspect of his personal life.

Attacks on a person are often used in the courtroom to discredit a witness ("Ladies and gentlemen of the jury, this witness admits that he's an atheist, so how can we trust him to tell us the truth?") and in politics to discredit a foe ("My opponent has gambled in Las Vegas at least five times. Do you want such a person to manage your tax dollars?"). Though this tactic may sometimes be effective, the ethical speaker never uses it, not only because it is dishonest and unfair, but also because it can backfire and cause careful listeners to lose respect for the speaker.

attack on a person
criticizing an opponent rather than the opponent's argument

False Cause

Beware of the fallacy of **false cause**—assuming that because events occur close together in time, they are necessarily related as cause and effect. A president takes office and four months later the unemployment rate goes up 1 percent. Can we say that the president's policies caused the rise in unemployment? It is possible that they did, but other factors may have caused the problem—for example, the economic policies of the previous administration.

The fallacy of false cause also can occur when a speaker oversimplifies the causes of complex problems. Take, for example, a speaker who says that *the* cause of cancer is negative thinking. That explanation is simple and understandable—and wrong. While negative thinking may be a contributing factor in cancer, medical researchers say that no one thing has been isolated as *the* cause of cancer. The disease is probably caused

false cause
assuming that because two events are related in time, the first caused the second

by an interaction of several factors, including genetic predisposition, susceptibility of the immune system, the presence of a carcinogenic virus, and environmental irritants. Cancer is too complex to be explained by a single cause.

Building on an Unproven Assumption

Some speakers act as if an assertion has been proved when in fact it has not. Suppose that a speaker tells an audience: "Since distance learning with a computer is more effective than traditional classroom education, all of you should take your college courses on your home computers." The speaker is acting as if the superiority of distance learning is an established fact, when in reality many people disagree. An ethical speaker would first try to prove the merits of distance learning and then urge the audience to support it.

The fallacy of **building on an unproven assumption** (which is also called "begging the question") makes careful listeners resentful. They feel as if they are being tricked into giving assent to a proposition that they don't believe.

False Analogy

When speakers use a **false analogy,** they make the mistake of assuming that because two things are alike in minor ways, they are also alike in major ways. Here is an example: "We can communicate effectively via satellite with people on the other side of the planet, so it should be easy for parents and children to communicate effectively within the intimate environment of their own homes." Upon close examination, this analogy falls apart. Satellite communication between nations is a purely technical matter of transmitting radio and television signals, whereas communication among family members is far more complex, involving psychological subtleties that are beyond the reach of technology.

Either-Or Reasoning

The **either-or fallacy** occurs when a speaker offers only two alternatives, when in fact there are many. For example: "Either we halt the world's population growth, or we face widespread starvation." Aren't there other options, such as improving agriculture and slowing down the rate of population growth?

Stating an argument in stark, either-or terms makes a speaker appear unreasonable and dogmatic. Most problems should be seen as a complex mosaic of many colors—not a simple choice between pure red and pure green.

Straw Man

To win arguments, some people create a **straw man,** a ridiculous caricature of what their opponents believe, and then beat it down with great ease. In a debate, imagine that you argue for standards that require cars to be more fuel-efficient so that less CO_2 is released into the atmosphere. Your opponent replies, "What you really want is to kill off the automobile industry. What you really want is for everybody to walk or ride bicycles." Then he spends the next 15 minutes attacking the notion of a world without automobiles. What he is saying about you is false, of course, but he is creating an easy target, made of straw. He can knock it down, smash it, and make himself look like a victor.

Slippery Slope

Imagine that you are standing at the top of a steep hill that is slippery with rain. You take a relatively small step downhill, but that step causes you to lose your footing and tumble to the bottom. This is an image of a **slippery slope,** the name for a fallacy that

---

building on an unproven assumption
treating an opinion that is open to question as if it were already proved

false analogy
creating a comparison that is exaggerated or erroneous

either-or fallacy
presenting only two alternatives when in fact more exist

straw man
a weak opponent or dubious argument set up so that it can be easily defeated

slippery slope
one action will initiate a chain of events that will result in a tragic ending

argues that if a certain event occurs, it will lead to a chain of events that ultimately end in tragedy. Consider the example of a toddler who keeps running from his yard into the street until a parent disciplines him with a swat on his bottom. Is the parent making a mistake? Those who use the slippery slope argument might argue yes. Their reasoning would be this: "Spanking can lead to severe child abuse, and everyone knows that child abuse is a frequent factor in the backgrounds of murderers. So, spanking can ultimately lead to murder." This chain of events *could* happen, but is it likely? Can the arguers prove that swatting a rambunctious toddler will lead to severe abuse and perhaps even murder?

Appealing to Motivations

Motivations are the needs, desires, or drives that impel a person toward a goal or away from some negative situation. People have hundreds of motivations, including love, happiness, and health.[16] If you show your listeners how your ideas can help them satisfy such needs and desires, you increase your chances of persuading them to adopt your point of view.[17] Here are some examples of how student speakers appealed to the motivations of their audiences:

- To raise money to buy food for starving people in Africa, LeeAnne Washington appealed to the motivation that most Americans have to help those less fortunate than themselves.
- To try to persuade listeners to use seat belts at all times in a car, Jason Bradley appealed to the strong drive that people have to protect themselves from harm.

motivations
the impulses and needs that stimulate a person to act in a certain way

> **Your** Thoughts
>
> At freshman orientation at some colleges, an administrator says something like this: "Look at the person seated next to you. One of you won't be here next year." Do you think this is an effective motivator to get students to study hard? Defend your answer.

Some Common Motivations

Here are some of the more common motivations that audiences have:

- Love and esteem
- Success
- Recreational pleasure
- Social acceptance
- Health
- Financial security
- Altruism
- Adventure
- Safety
- Self-improvement
- Curiosity
- Creativity

A popular model for analyzing motivations is **Maslow's hierarchy of needs,** created by the late Abraham Maslow, an American psychologist. As shown in Figure 17.2 on the next page, the hierarchy starts at the bottom with the most basic human needs and ranges upward to more and more sophisticated levels.[18]

At the top is **self-actualization,** where one realizes his or her full potential as a human. Maslow believed that when lower-level needs are present, they will usually take precedence. For example, if you are sleep-deprived and sick (lowest level), you probably will have no energy to engage in a creative activity such as violin playing (highest level).

Models such as Maslow's hierarchy can't cover all human needs, but they do remind us of the multiple motivations that can be found in our listeners.

Maslow's hierarchy of needs
a ranking of human needs from simple to complex

self-actualization
the need of humans to make the most of their abilities

Multiple Motivations

Whenever possible, appeal to more than one motivation. Listeners who are not reached by one appeal may be influenced by another. Suppose, for example, that you were trying to persuade your listeners to take up bicycling. Table 17.3 on the next page shows some of the motivations that you could identify, coupled with appropriate appeals.

Figure 17.2
Maslow's Hierarchy of Needs
Psychologist Abraham Maslow organized human motivations in a hierarchy that ranged from basic biological needs (at the bottom) to self-actualization needs (at the top).

Self-actualization needs
Fulfillment, creativity, self-acceptance, helping others

Esteem needs
Respect, recognition, success

Love and belonging needs
Friendship, family, being loved and accepted

Safety needs
Shelter, safety from violence, secure income, comfort, tranquility

Physiological needs
Water, food, sleep, clothing, medical care

Table 17.3   **Motivations and Appeals**

Motivation	Appeal
Feeling good	Bicycling works out tension and makes you feel energetic and happy.
Looking good	Bicycling burns lots of calories, so it's ideal for weight control. It also tones up leg muscles.
Long-term health	Bicycling is excellent exercise for heart and lungs, thus helping prevent cardiovascular disease.
Friendship	Being on a bicycle is an instant passport to the world of cyclists. It's easy to strike up conversations with other riders, and you can often make new friends. Cycling also provides an enjoyable activity to share with old friends.
Adventure	With a bicycle you can explore out-of-the-way places, travel long distances in a single day, and experience the thrill of flying down a steep mountain road.
Competition	If you enjoy competing, there are bike races in almost every city or town.

By appealing to more than one motivation, you increase your chances of persuading the audience. For example, the listener who is already in superb health may not be reached by any of the first three items but might be swayed by one of the last three.

Arousing Emotions

Emotions are spontaneous feelings that can be either positive (amusement, love, joy) or negative (fear, anger, sadness). You can use emotional appeals to stimulate listeners and rouse them to action.

How can emotions be evoked? By using support materials (such as provocative narratives) or powerful language (such as vivid metaphors).

As an example of how emotions can be used effectively, here is an excerpt from a speech by student speaker Ralph Barnes on how people with disabilities are sometimes victimized:

> Theresa Delzatto, 35, of Hartford, Connecticut, is paralyzed from the neck down. She survives on a Social Security check and lives in public housing. Just before Christmas last year, she went to Wal-Mart in her wheelchair to do some Christmas shopping. She went to the courtesy desk and explained that she could not use her arms, and she asked for assistance. An 18-year-old clerk was assigned to take items from the shelves and put them in her cart. When she was ready to pay, the clerk helped out by taking Delzatto's debit card from her purse and handing it to the cashier. But then—believe it or not—the clerk never returned the card! Instead she and a 17-year-old cousin went on a shopping spree with the card and racked up more than $400 worth of purchases. They were later arrested and charged with larceny, but the money was gone. The theft wiped out all of Delzatto's money. She told the *Hartford Courant*, "I'm at the point where I'm just ready to give in. It destroyed most of my independence." Can you believe that anyone could be so mean—especially at Christmas?[19]

This story was effective in eliciting anger—an appropriate emotion for listeners to experience as they learned of the outrages that are sometimes committed against people with disabilities.

Here are some tips on arousing emotions.

Always combine emotional appeals with rational appeals.   If you appeal only to emotions, you give the audience only one underpinning for a belief. Let's say you are arguing against the practice of keeping a dog chained up all day. If you focus on the suffering of the dog, you create an argument that appeals only to the heart. For a stronger case, add an appeal to the mind: Chaining a dog sometimes causes the animal to become aggressive. If it breaks free someday, it might attack a neighbor or passerby.

While people can be swayed by emotional appeals, they also need to think of themselves as rational. They need to have justification for the feelings and passions they embrace in their hearts. If you use logic and emotion together, you have a more powerful speech than if you use either one alone.[20]

Know how to use fear.   Over the years, communicators have wondered how much fear one should evoke in trying to persuade people. For example, if you want to convince an audience to avoid tailgating on the highway, would you be more successful with some low-fear visual aids, such as a chart on traffic fatalities, or with some high-fear graphics, such as a gory, full-color videotape of victims of a terrible car wreck? Research favors the latter. "The overwhelming weight of experimental data," writes psychologist Elliot Aronson, "suggests that . . . the more frightened a person is by a communication, the more likely he or she is to take positive preventive action."[21] Research also indicates that high-fear messages are most effective when they are coupled with specific instructions on how to take action. For example, a high-fear message on rabies would be more persuasive if it included instructions on how to avoid the disease than if it left out such instructions.[22]

Use emotional appeals ethically.   Any emotion can be exploited in the wrong way. Fear and loathing, desirable when targeted at an infectious disease, are repugnant when

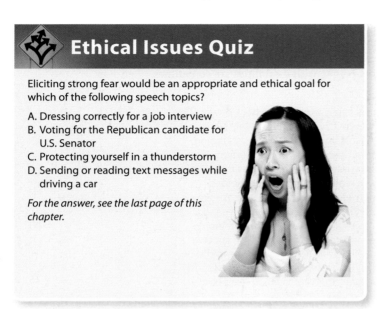

Ethical Issues Quiz

Eliciting strong fear would be an appropriate and ethical goal for which of the following speech topics?

A. Dressing correctly for a job interview
B. Voting for the Republican candidate for U.S. Senator
C. Protecting yourself in a thunderstorm
D. Sending or reading text messages while driving a car

For the answer, see the last page of this chapter.

aimed at a minority group. Unfortunately, some politicians have demonstrated that creating or exploiting fears and hatreds can win elections. If you are an ethical speaker, however, you will never let short-term gain entice you into using such tactics. If, for example, you are trying to mobilize public opinion to save an endangered species of bird, you will not demonize homebuilders who want to build on the bird's natural habitat; you will not incite hatred by falsely portraying them as merciless killers. Instead, you will channel emotional appeals in appropriate ways—by generating sadness over the possible disappearance of the bird or by appealing to the happiness listeners might feel over saving endangered creatures.

To determine whether you are acting ethically, identify each emotion you want to arouse and then answer the following questions.

- Do you avoid scapegoating any person or group?

- Does the emotion reinforce, rather than replace, solid evidence and sound logic? (If not, is it because your case is unsupportable and illogical?)

- In arousing this emotion, are you treating the issue and the opposing side with fairness? (Put yourself in the shoes of an opponent and see if your treatment looks fair from that perspective.)

If you cannot answer yes to all three, your ethical footing is shaky. You should omit the emotional appeal or alter the speech.

Develop the emotional appeals inherent in some pieces of evidence.   Often you don't need to hunt for emotional appeals to add to your accumulation of evidence. All you need to do is develop the evidence already collected so that it moves the listeners. Let's say that while preparing a speech on the appalling murder rate, you found this statistic: about 25,000 homicides occurred in the United States last year. You can state that figure in your speech and then develop it for emotional impact: "That means that every 22 minutes, another American is shot . . . stabbed . . . beaten . . . or strangled to death." By expressing a fact in this dramatic way, you help your listeners feel the magnitude of the problem. Note that vivid language ("stabbed," "beaten," and so on) enhances the emotional impact.

Sample Persuasive Speech

The following speech by Alexandra Morton uses the problem–solution pattern. The outline is presented first, with a commentary in the margin.

connect

View a video of the speech "Sleep Deficiency" in the online Media Library for Chapter 17.

The Outline with Commentary

Sleep Deficiency

SPEECH

COMMENTARY

General Purpose: To persuade

Specific Purpose: To persuade my audience to take necessary steps to achieve good sleep

Central Idea: Sleep deficiency is a major problem, but it can be overcome by changing priorities and strategies.

INTRODUCTION

I. Attention Material
   A. An air traffic controller is a vital person in your life if you are on a commercial airplane.
   B. The Federal Aviation Administration recently confirmed 7 cases of controllers sleeping on the job.
   C. In 3 of the cases, planes had to land without assistance.

> A disturbing news report makes an effective attention-grabber.

II. Orienting Material
   A. These reports illustrate a major problem—millions of Americans failing to get adequate sleep.
   B. We will look at the problem and then discuss the solution.

(*Transition:* Let's start with the problem.)

BODY

I. About two-thirds of Americans fail to get adequate sleep, causing health problems. (National Sleep Foundation)

> The speaker devotes the first half of the body to the problem.

   A. Adults need 7 to 8 hours of sleep each night. (Dr. Lawrence Epstein, Harvard Medical School)
      1. If you get only 4 to 6 hours for several nights in a row, you build up a sleep deficit.
      2. You will probably become irritable and groggy.
      3. You will have reduced energy and alertness.
   B. If you go for longer periods without enough sleep, you develop chronic sleep deprivation.
      1. You are more likely to overeat and gain weight. (Dr. Epstein)
      2. You are at higher risk for colds and infections.
      3. In some cases, you are at risk for depression, diabetes, heart disease, and obesity.

> A complete-sentence outline helps speakers organize material intelligently. For actual delivery, however, a speaker should not read the outline but, instead, use brief notes that are based on the outline.

   C. Insufficient sleep reduces alertness and can cause mistakes at work and accidents on the highway.
      1. Each year at least 100,000 car crashes are due to drowsy drivers. (National Highway Traffic Safety Administration)
      2. 40,000 drivers are seriously injured, 1,500 are killed.

(continued)

Statistics from a reputable source are effectively used.

D. Centers for Disease Control and Prevention says 60% of college students frequently have sleep disturbances.
  1. They don't sleep well or wake up feeling tired.
  2. Sleep-deprived students often have poor grades and stress-related illness.
  3. When stressed out, they avoid what they need the most—sleep.

(*Transition:* Now that we've looked at the problem, let's talk about the solution.)

The second half of the body is devoted to the solution.

II. People who have sleep problems need to change priorities or learn new strategies.
  A. Many of us have our priorities out of order because we consider sleep a waste of time. (Dr. Qanta Ahmed, Winthrop-Hospital Sleep Disorders Center in NYC)
    1. We consider sleep a necessary evil or nuisance—something that should be shortened.
    2. Instead, we should consider sleep "a fundamental biological need"—a top priority.
  B. Here are strategies recommended by the National Sleep Foundation.
    1. Each night, go to bed at the same time, and each morning, get up at the same time.
    2. Stop drinking caffeine and alcohol 5 hours before bedtime.

Listeners always appreciate tips that can help them improve their lives.

    3. Stop exercising at least 3 hours before bedtime.
    4. Don't eat large meals right before bedtime.
    5. Stop looking at screens (TV, tablet, computer) one hour before bedtime.

The speaker did more than just warn against looking at screens—she explained why.

      a. They contain "blue spectrum light."
      b. The light suppresses production of the brain hormone that helps us go to sleep.
    6. Before bedtime, wind down and relax—perhaps read in dim light or listen to music.
    7. If you're worried, imagine a calm and peaceful place or play comforting music.

(*Transition:* Let's sum up.)

CONCLUSION

I. Summary

A summary does not need to be long, but it should give the highlights of the speech.

  A. Lack of adequate sleep, a major problem in America, can lead to irritability, reduced energy, and less alertness.
  B. If chronic, a sleep deficit can result in traffic accidents, weight gain, and an increase in infections.
  C. The solution is to make sleep a priority and use strategies such as reducing caffeine late in the day and turning off screens one hour before bedtime.

II. Clincher
  A. If you or your friends or relatives are sleep-deprived, I want to give you hope.

The speech closes with a graceful finale—a memorable quotation.

  B. (Show poster.) [See Figure 17.3] In the words of Janet Kennedy, a sleep specialist: "A good night's sleep doesn't have to be a dream."

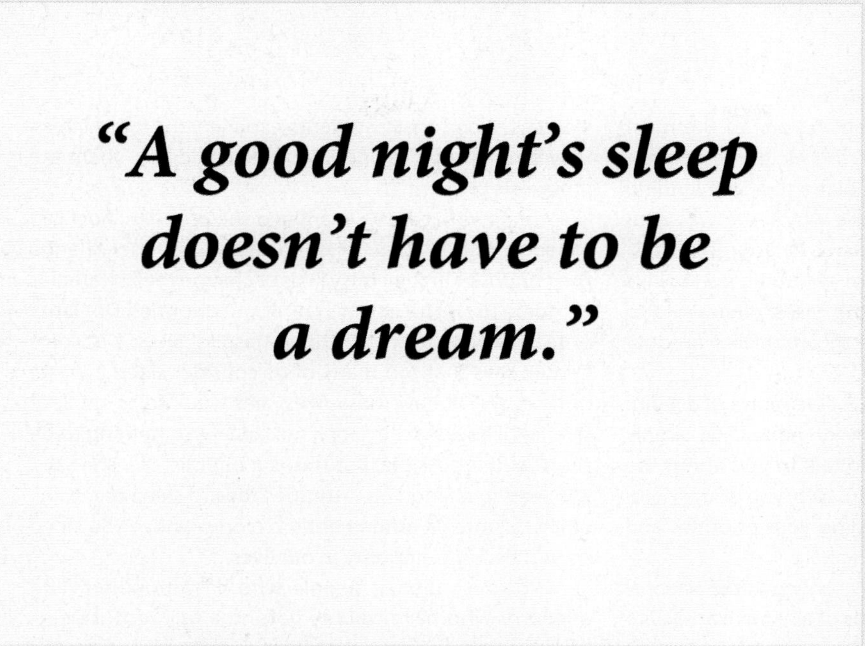

Figure 17.3
An interesting quotation makes a
good finale for the speech.

"A good night's sleep doesn't have to be a dream."

BIBLIOGRAPHY

Ahmed, Qanta, M.D., sleep disorders specialist, Winthrop-University
   Sleep Disorders Center, Garden City, NY. Message to Alexandra
   Morton. 4 July 2011. E-mail.
Epstein, Lawrence, M.D. *The Harvard Medical School Guide to a Good
   Night's Sleep.* New York: McGraw-Hill, 2006. Print.
"Research on Drowsy Driving." National Highway Traffic Safety
   Agency website, 16 April 2011. Web. 2 July 2011.
Rosenberg, Russell, Ph.D, Vice Chairman, National Sleep Founda-
   tion. "Annual Sleep in America Poll." Sleep Foundation website,
   Jan. 2011. Web. 5 July 2011.
"Sleep Deprivation." Centers for Disease Control and Prevention,
   Dec. 2010. Web. 4 July 2011.

See Chapter 6 for details on how to prepare
bibliographies.

VISUAL AIDS

Poster with Janet Kennedy quotation

The Speech as Delivered

Here is the transcript of Alexandra Morton's speech, which uses the problem–solution pattern. Notice that the speaker uses the ideas of the outline without using the exact wording. In an extemporaneous speech, a speaker does not read or memorize a speech but speaks from brief notes.

Sleep Deficiency

When you fly on a commercial airline, one of the most important people in your life is the air traffic controller, the person who guides your plane to a safe landing at the airport. So you can imagine why there was a lot of anger recently when the Federal Aviation Administration confirmed seven cases of air traffic controllers sleeping on the job. In three of the cases, planes had to land without assistance because the controller on duty was sleeping.

These reports are just the latest examples of a major problem in our society—millions of Americans simply don't get enough sleep. I'd like to talk to you about the extent of this problem, and then give you some solutions, which might involve changing your priorities and strategies.

Let's start with the problem. According to the National Sleep Foundation, about two-thirds of all Americans fail to get enough sleep, and this problem is hazardous to their health.

How much sleep does a person need? Dr. Lawrence Epstein of the Harvard Medical School says that adults need seven to eight hours of sleep every night. If you only get four to six hours for several nights in a row, you're building up a sleep deficit, he says, and you're likely to become irritable and groggy, and you'll have a reduction in energy and alertness.

If you go for even longer periods without adequate sleep, you develop what is known as chronic sleep deprivation. Dr. Epstein says you're more likely to overeat and gain weight, and you're more susceptible to colds and infections. In some cases, you're at risk for depression, diabetes, heart disease, and obesity.

When you don't get adequate sleep, your alertness is reduced, which can cause mistakes at work and at school, and can lead to traffic accidents. The National Highway Traffic Safety Administration says that every year there are at least 100,000 car crashes due to drowsy drivers—40,000 people get seriously injured and 1,500 are killed.

And how about college students? Studies reported by the CDC—Centers for Disease Control and Prevention—show that 60 percent of college students frequently experience disturbances during the night. That means they don't sleep well, and they wake up feeling tired instead of refreshed. The studies also show that students who have a high level of sleep deprivation often have poor grades and are more prone to suffering from stress-related illnesses. When these students experience a lot of stress, they often avoid the one thing that could help them the most—sleep.

So now that we've examined the problem, how can we solve it? The solution is for people to either change their priorities in their busy lives or change their strategies for going to sleep. First let's talk about priorities. Dr. Qanta Ahmed of New York's Winthrop-Hospital Sleep Disorders Center, says that too many of us consider sleep a waste of time. We all have busy lives, and we tend to think of sleep as a necessary evil or a nuisance—something to be shortened if possible. But this is a big mistake, she says. We need to change our attitudes toward sleep and think of it as, quote, "a fundamental biological need." So sleep should become a priority in our lives.

Now let's discuss people who have trouble falling asleep or who have trouble getting a full, restful sleep. I'd like to share some strategies recommended by the National Sleep Foundation.

- Go to bed at the same time each night, and get up at the same time each morning.
- At least 5 hours before bedtime, stop drinking caffeinated beverages and alcohol. Some people say that if they don't stop drinking coffee by noon, their sleep gets disrupted.
- Don't exercise within three hours of bedtime.
- Avoid large meals before bedtime.
- This next tip is very hard—for me and probably for a lot of you: About one hour before bedtime, stop looking at screens—TVs, tablets, computers, and so on. All these devices contain "blue spectrum light" and it suppresses the production of a hormone in our brains that helps us nod off at night.
- Allow time to wind down and relax before bed. Perhaps you can read in dim light or listen to music.
- If worries keep you from sleeping, relax your mind by imagining a calm and peaceful place. Or distract yourself from your troubles by playing comforting music.

Now let's summarize. We've seen that most Americans fail to get adequate sleep—a problem that leads to irritability, reduced energy, and less alertness. If a sleep deficit becomes chronic, it can lead to traffic accidents and increased risk of weight gain and infections. The solution to the problem is to make sleep a priority and use the recommended strategies, such as avoiding caffeine late in the day and cutting off electronic devices one hour before bedtime.

If you or the people you care about are among the ranks of the sleep-deprived, I'm here to give you hope.

[*The speaker displays the poster in Figure 17.3.*] In the words of Janet Kennedy, a sleep specialist:

"A good night's sleep
doesn't have to be
a dream."

Resources for Review and Skill Building

Summary

To be effective in persuasion, you must have a thorough *knowledge of the audience.* Find out exactly where your listeners stand concerning your view. Are they opposed, apathetic, neutral, or already convinced? Then plan a strategy to move them toward your position.

During a persuasive speech, enhance *credibility* with the audience by explaining your competence, by being honest and careful with speech material, by remaining open-minded, and by showing common ground with listeners.

Build your case by using strong *evidence* (such as statistics, examples, and testimony) that is accurate, up-to-date, and typical. Try to use a variety of sources, all of them reliable and reputable.

Use sound *reasoning* as a powerful tool of persuasion. Two popular forms are deductive reasoning, in which you take a generalization or a principle and apply it to a specific case, and inductive reasoning, in which you observe specific instances and then form a generalization. In using logic, avoid these fallacies: bandwagon, hasty generalization, red herring, attack on a person, false cause, building on an unproven assumption, false analogy, either-or reasoning, straw man attacks, or slippery slope arguments.

Whenever possible, appeal to listeners' *motivations*— their needs, desires, and drives that impel them toward a goal or away from some negative situation. Focus on the listeners' needs, not your own. If possible, appeal to more than one motivation, and anticipate conflicting needs.

Finally, try to arouse the listeners' *emotions,* making sure that you always combine emotional appeals with rational appeals, and that you always use emotions ethically.

Key Terms

attack on a person, *331*

bandwagon fallacy, *330*

building on an unproven assumption, *332*

credibility, *331*

deduction, *326*

either-or fallacy, *332*

evidence, *324*

fallacy, *329*

false analogy, *332*

false cause, *331*

hasty generalization, *330*

induction, *327*

Maslow's hierarchy of needs, *333*

motivations, *333*

reasoning, *326*

red herring, *331*

self-actualizations, *333*

slippery slope, *332*

straw man, *332*

syllogism, *326*

Review Questions

1. Why are sarcastic remarks inappropriate when directed toward listeners who are hostile to your view?

2. Why is it a good idea in many cases to tell the audience why you are competent to speak on your particular subject?

3. How is an audience likely to react if you are careless with your facts and ideas?

4. Which is more persuasive with the typical audience: one vivid personal narrative or a series of statistical data?

5. What is the difference between deduction and induction?

6. Why should a speaker never use the logical fallacy called "attack on a person"?

7. What is the "straw man" fallacy?

8. What is a "red herring" argument?

9. List at least five motivations that all listeners have.

10. Why should emotional appeals always be accompanied by rational appeals?

Building Critical-Thinking Skills

1. One of the most influential books in American history, *Silent Spring,* was published in 1962 as a warning against the health hazards of pesticides. Its author, Rachel Carson, had her credibility attacked by a scientist who questioned her concern for future generations because she was an unmarried woman with no children. What fallacy of reasoning was the scientist using? Why was the scientist's criticism invalid?

2. A TV commercial shows a video of an attractive young couple running barefoot on a beach while a voice says, "ABC multivitamin supplements—just one a day for the rest of your life." Identify the motivational appeals contained in the commercial.

Building Teamwork Skills

1. In a survey reported by *Health* magazine, 89 percent of adults said they know they should exercise three times a week for good health, but only 27 percent actually do. In a group, compile a list of excuses that people might use for not exercising. Then, for each excuse, brainstorm strategies that a speaker could use to discourage it.

2. Working in a group, list the motivations that students in a typical high school class are likely to have. Then brainstorm how an Army recruiter could appeal to each motivation in a speech aimed at persuading the students to join the military.

Ethical Issues

Answer to quiz on p. 336: C and D. These are life-or-death topics and eliciting strong fear could save a listener's life. For topics A and B, intense fear would be out of place.

Special Types of Speeches

OBJECTIVES

After studying this chapter, you should be able to:

1. Prepare an entertaining speech.
2. Prepare a speech of introduction.
3. Prepare a speech of presentation.
4. Prepare a speech of acceptance.
5. Prepare a speech of tribute.
6. Prepare an inspirational speech.
7. Identify potential pitfalls in using humor in a speech.

SPEAKING AT A FUND-RAISING EVENT in New York City, actress Jessica Biel paid tribute to a nine-year-old girl from Seattle, Rachel Beckwith, who died in a car accident in 2011. A few months before her death, Rachel (with help from her mother) had created a webpage requesting, in lieu of birthday gifts, donations for safe drinking water in villages in Africa. Her goal was to raise $300 by her birthday. The money would have brought clean water to 15 people in need. After her death, news of her wish spread across the nation, and more than $1.26 million was donated—enough to provide clean water for 60,000 villagers.[1]

Biel's tribute is an example of a special kind of speech that will be discussed in this chapter. Though most of the speeches you will give in your lifetime will probably be informative or persuasive, there are occasions when you may be called upon to give other kinds—an entertaining speech at a banquet, a brief speech introducing the main speaker

at a convention, a few words announcing the presentation of an award, a eulogy at a funeral to honor a close friend, an acceptance speech to thank an organization for giving you an award, or an inspirational speech to lift the morale of your subordinates or fellow employees.

Jessica Biel displays appropriate non-verbal communication for a speech of tribute—a warm smile, good eye contact, and an expansive gesture.

Entertaining Speech

An **entertaining speech** provides amusement or diversion for the audience. It can be given in any setting, from classroom to convention hall. It is sometimes referred to as an "after-dinner speech" because it is often given after a meal. People who have just eaten want to sit back, relax, and enjoy a talk. They don't want to work hard mentally. They don't want to hear anything heavy and negative.

An entertaining speech can contain a few elements of persuasion and information, but the primary goal is not to persuade or inform, but to create an interesting diversion—an enjoyable experience—for the audience.

Techniques for Entertaining

To entertain, do you have to tell jokes that elicit loud laughter? Not necessarily. Joke telling is just one option among many. (See the Special Techniques feature "How to Use Humor" below.) Here are some other devices you can use to entertain an audience.

Special Techniques

How to Use Humor

"Cats are smarter than dogs," says comedian Jeff Valdez. "You can't get eight cats to pull a sled through snow."

If used effectively, humor is a good way to keep an audience interested in your speech. It creates a bond of friendship between you and the listeners, and it puts them into a receptive, trusting mood. Here are some guidelines.

1. **Use humor only when it is appropriate.** A speech about a solemn subject such as euthanasia would not lend itself to an injection of humor.
2. **Tell jokes at your own risk.** A popular kind of humor is the joke—a funny story that depends on a punch line for its success. If you are an accomplished humorist, you may be able to use jokes effectively, but I don't recommend that any novice speaker use them, for these reasons:
   - Jokes usually don't tie in smoothly with the rest of the speech.
   - Few speakers (whether experienced or inexperienced) can tell jokes well.
   - A joke that is successful with your friends might bomb with a large audience.
   - The audience may have heard the joke already.
   - Listeners may not be in a receptive mood.

   I have seen speakers tell a joke that no one laughed at—not one single person. Maybe the audience had heard the joke before, or maybe it was too early in the morning or too late in the evening. Whatever the reason, a joke that fizzles can be devastating to the speaker's morale, and it can lessen the impact of the speech.

   "But it looks so easy on TV," some students say. It looks easy and *is* easy because TV joke tellers have advantages that most speakers lack: They have studio audiences that are predisposed to laugh at virtually any joke the comedians tell. (Your audiences will probably not be poised for laughter in this way.) They have gag writers who test the jokes out before they are used. Most important of all, they are talented performers who have years of joke-telling experience.

3. **Use low-key humor.** A mildly amusing story, quotation, or observation—although not as spectacular as a side-splitting joke—can be effective. The best thing about low-key humor is that it's safe. While the success of a joke depends on the audience laughing immediately after the punch line, the success of a light story or a witty observation does not depend on laughter—or even smiles. Sometimes the only audience response is an inner delight. In a speech on the elaborate cheating systems that some students use on tests, student speaker Henry Mandell said:

   There is one method of cheating that guarantees that you won't be caught. The night before a test, make a cheat sheet. Memorize it. Then tear it up to destroy the evidence. The next morning, you'll do well on the test.

Anecdotes, Examples, and Quotations

Using a single theme, some speakers string together anecdotes, examples, or quotations as if creating a string of pearls—one bright jewel after another. In a speech on the crackpot predictions that so-called experts have made over the centuries, Sarah Caldwell-Evans gave her audience one astonishing quotation after another. Here's an instance:

> When women began to enter all-male professions at the beginning of the 20th century, many prominent men warned that such work would be disastrous for women. Here's what a professor at Berlin University, Hans Friedenthal, said in 1904: "Brain work will cause the 'new woman' to become bald, while increasing masculinity and contempt for beauty will induce the growth of hair on the face. In the future, therefore, women will be bald and will wear long mustaches and patriarchal beards."

Mandell was using the kind of wry humor that does not depend on belly laughs. It was not a joke. If the listeners laughed or smiled, fine; if they didn't, no harm was done. It was still enjoyable.

4. **Always relate humor to the subject matter.** Never tell an amusing story about a farmer unless your speech is about farming and the story ties in with the rest of the speech.

5. **Never use humor that could possibly offend any person in the audience.** Avoid humor that is sexual. Avoid humor that targets members of any group in society (racial, ethnic, religious, political, gender, and so on). Even if the audience contains no members of a particular group, you are unwise to ridicule that group because you risk alienating listeners who dislike such humor.

6. **Never let your face show that you expect laughter or smiles.** If you say something that you think is hilarious, don't stand with an expectant grin on your face, waiting for a reaction. If no one smiles or laughs, you will feel very foolish. And remember, failure to get any smiles or laughs doesn't necessarily mean that the listeners did not appreciate your humor. As mentioned in guideline 3, many kinds of humor elicit only unexpressed amusement.

7. **Consider using self-deprecating humor in some situations.** Benjamin Franklin was a speaker who was willing to poke fun at himself in a speech. For example, he liked to tell audiences about an incident that occurred in Paris while he was attending a public gathering that featured many speeches. He spoke French, but he had trouble understanding the formal, rhetorical language of French orators. Wishing to appear polite, he decided that he would applaud whenever he noticed a distinguished woman, Mme. de Boufflers, express satisfaction. After the meeting, his grandson said to him, "But Grandpapa, you always applauded, and louder than anybody else, when they were praising you."

Many good speakers tell humorous anecdotes at their own expense because it's an effective way to build rapport with the audience—to create a bond of warmth, trust, and acceptance. Franklin's listeners must have been delighted to learn that the Great Man was capable of committing a faux pas, just like everyone else, and they loved him all the more.

Self-deprecating humor has two bonuses: (1) When you tell about something you did or said, there is no danger that the audience has heard it before. (2) You don't risk offending anyone—your target is yourself, not some group.

Two notes of caution:

- Poke fun at any aspect of yourself except your nervousness. (In Chapter 2 we discussed why you should never call attention to your jitters.)
- Don't use self-deprecating humor if you have not yet established your expertise or authority. For example, if you are a new employee who is making a presentation to the board of directors of a corporation, self-effacing humor could weaken your credibility. By contrast, if you are a manager whose confidence and power are well-known to your audience of subordinates, laughing at yourself can build rapport.

Narratives

An interesting journey, an exciting adventure, or a comical sequence of events can make an enjoyable speech, even if the story is serious. For example:

- A speaker related her encounter with a grizzly bear while backpacking in the Rocky Mountains.
- A police officer gave an hour-by-hour account of the extraordinary security measures taken by the Secret Service when a presidential candidate made a campaign stop in one city.
- One speaker told of the mishaps and misunderstandings that caused her to arrive late and frazzled at her wedding.

Descriptions

You can entertain with vivid descriptions of fascinating places, interesting people, or intriguing objects. For example:

- To give her audience an impression of the bright colors and exotic varieties of birds in the Amazonian rain forest, one speaker showed color slides she had taken of birds in a Brazilian zoo.
- At the meeting of a culinary club, the chef of a gourmet restaurant gave an after-dinner talk in which he described various French pastries. As the chef discussed each type of pastry, a sample was served to each listener.

An entertaining speech does not need to be as elaborately structured as an informative or persuasive speech, but it should have a unifying theme—in other words, all your material should tie together—and it should have the standard three parts of a speech: (1) an introduction to gain the attention and interest of the audience, (2) a body that develops the theme in satisfying detail, and (3) a conclusion that provides a graceful finale.

Choose a topic that you find enjoyable, and as you deliver your speech, try to share your enjoyment with the audience. Be light and good-natured. Have fun along with your listeners.

Tips for Your Career

Move Listeners Together

If your listeners are spread apart in a large room or an auditorium, try to move them together if possible. Let's say you have 15 people scattered about in a large hall. It will be easier to make contact with them if you ask them to move to seats at the front and center.

Moving them together is especially important for entertaining talks. Nightclub comedians make sure tables are pushed close together because they know that patrons are more likely to laugh if they are jammed together in warm coziness. Some comedians are reluctant to tell jokes to an audience widely scattered in a large room. People feel isolated, and they are afraid that if they laugh, they will be conspicuous. Have you ever noticed that funny movies are funnier if you see them in a packed theater than if you see them in a sparsely attended theater?

Sample Entertaining Speech

Below is a sample entertaining speech, delivered by student speaker Terry Triplett.[2]

The Names Are Real

This is no joke. At Texas Tech University, the director of the Water Resource Center is Dr. Ken Rainwater.

Dr. Rainwater is an example of a person whose last name suits his or her profession. I want to share some other examples with you.

According to a recent article in *The Chronicle of Higher Education,* there are a number of professors who have apt names: Michael Greenwood is professor of forest-ecosystem science at the University of Maine, David Music is professor of church music at Baylor University, Stephen Pope is associate professor of theology at Boston College, Randall Toothaker (pronounced "toothacher") teaches dentistry at the University of Nebraska's College of Dentistry, and Ernest Fish is director of the Texas Tech Wildlife and Fisheries Management Institute.

In the world beyond college campuses, the *New York Times* lists some well-suited names—a lawyer in Bellevue, Washington, named David J. Lawyer; a famous Detroit Tigers first baseman named Cecil Fielder; a poet named William Wordsworth; a novelist named Francine Prose; and a TV weather reporter named Storm Field.

All of the names I am giving you today are real names—not stage names or made-up names. When I heard that a national poker champion is named Chris Moneymaker, I was suspicious, but he swears that Moneymaker is his real name. He explains that his ancestors came from Germany, where some people were named for their professions. His family made silver and gold coins. When they came to America, their name was translated into the English word "Moneymaker."

Are all these names and professions just a coincidence? Some people think so, but others think that a person's name influences his or her decisions about a career. Did their names nudge Paul Horn to become a career musician and Robert Bugg to conduct insect research at the University of California?

The *Journal of the American Medical Association* reports that in the United States there is a doctor named Rash, who is a dermatologist, and one named Bone, who is an orthopedic surgeon. There are 10 physicians named Blood and 22 named Needle. Did their names inspire them to enter medicine?

Whether it's a matter of coincidence or destiny, these connections are intriguing. Here are some examples from a list compiled by the advice columnist "Dear Abby": The manager of a sleep disorder clinic in Jonesboro, Arkansas—Joe Yawn. A psychiatrist in Texas—Paul Looney. An undertaker in Missouri—Richard Dye.

And my favorite of all the names I came across—a liquor store owner in Hereford, Texas, who is named Joe Boozer.

Your Thoughts

Psychologists have discovered that humor can improve a person's problem-solving abilities. Why do you think this happens?

Speech of Introduction

speech of introduction
a brief talk that introduces a
speaker to an audience

The **speech of introduction** is designed for one speaker to introduce another to an audience. For example:

- At a meeting of her civic club, Paula Moreno spoke briefly on why she was supporting a particular candidate for Congress and then turned the lectern over to the candidate.
- Theodore Lansing, a university librarian, stood up in front of 1,500 delegates at a national librarians' convention and introduced the keynote speaker, a renowned writer of science fiction.

When you introduce one friend to another, you want them to get interested in each other and to like each other. When you introduce a speaker to an audience, you want to achieve the same goal. You want speaker and audience to be interested in each other and to feel warmth and friendliness.

An introduction should mention the speaker's name several times (so that everyone can catch it), and it should give background information to enhance the speaker's credibility with the audience. Your tone of voice and facial expression should convey enthusiasm for the speech to come.

Here are some guidelines for speeches of introduction.

Interview the speaker in advance.   Ask him or her exactly what should be covered in the introduction. For example, should you discuss the significance of the topic (to help prepare the audience for the speech)? Should you tell the audience to hold questions until the end of the presentation?

Verify name and pronunciation.   Ask the speaker these questions:

- "What name do you want me to use?" If you are introducing Dr. Elizabeth Wilson, don't assume that she prefers to be called "Dr. Wilson." Perhaps she prefers the informality of "Elizabeth" or even her nickname, "Liz."
- "How do you pronounce your name?" If the speaker has a name like Neophetos Apostolopoulos, you obviously need help. Practice saying it in advance so that you don't stumble during the introduction. For easier names, don't always assume you know the correct pronunciation. A speaker named Mia may pronounce her name ME-UH, or she may prefer MY-UH. Eva can be EE-VUH or AYE-VUH. Common names like Megan and Ralph have at least two different pronunciations.

Tell the speaker what you plan to say.   By doing so, you can avoid this nightmare: a speaker is about to talk to an audience of 1,000 people, and suddenly she realizes that the person introducing her is telling the very anecdote that she had carefully planned as the opener of her speech. Such nightmares actually happen, say experienced speakers, but they won't happen to you if you reveal your plans to the speaker, and then omit duplications.

Set the proper tone.   When you introduce someone, you help set the tone for the speech to follow. Be careful to set the right tone—a humorous tone for a humorous speech, a serious tone for a serious speech.

Keep it short.   A good rule of thumb is to keep an introduction under three minutes. After all, an audience wants to hear the speaker, not the introducer.

Avoid exaggeration.   If you exaggerate the speaker's abilities or credentials, you build up unrealistic expectations in the audience. Consider this kind of introduction: "Our speaker tonight is a funny person who will have you laughing so hard you'll be rolling in the aisles." Or: "The speaker will give us insights that are wise and brilliant." Such statements can cause speakers to become overly anxious because they feel pressure to live up to the excessive praise.

The following introduction of Joseph Conte was delivered at a meeting of a genealogical society; the introducer had consulted with Conte in advance to make sure that he did not steal any of the speaker's speech.

> Our speaker tonight, Joseph Conte, will talk to us about how to set up a computerized ancestry record. Mr. Conte brings a lot of personal experience to this subject. The great-grandson of immigrants from Italy, he has traced his own family roots back to Florence. He has put all of his genealogical records onto a computer, using a program that was created by a Mormon group in Salt Lake City. Mr. Conte has a background of expertise in scholarly detective work: For the past decade he has been a researcher for the National Archives in Washington, D.C., specializing in 19th and 20th century immigration. Mr. Conte, welcome to our society and thank you for taking the time to share your knowledge with us.

Speech of Presentation

Awards or honors are often bestowed upon individuals for their service to business, institution, community, church, or club. It is customary for a brief speech to be made before the award is presented.

The **speech of presentation** should include the following elements: (1) any background information that would help the audience understand the purpose of the award, (2) the criteria used for selecting the recipient, and (3) the achievements of the recipient.

In many cases, it is customary to withhold the name of the recipient until the very end of the speech, as a way of building suspense.

Humor is usually inappropriate. If you try to make a joke about the recipient, you may seem to be belittling him or her. At one company banquet, a department head gave an award for 10 years of service to a subordinate and used the occasion to tease him with a mock insult: "The only reason we keep him on the payroll is because his father worked here for 40 years." The "humor" was similar to the kind of bantering that the boss and the subordinate engaged in during a typical workday, but at the awards banquet, with his family present, the subordinate felt humiliated.

Here is a model speech of presentation delivered by Meredith Brody at the annual meeting of a community theater:

> The John Cleese Award is given each year to the top actor or actress in our theater. As most of you know, the award is given in honor of the British actor John Cleese of *Monty Python* and *Fawlty Towers* fame. The winner is selected by ballots circulated to all our members. Our winner this year is a seasoned veteran of our stage, a person who always performs with intelligence, audacity, and élan. I am pleased to announce that the winner of the third annual John Cleese Award is . . . James Colton!

speech of presentation
an address designed to formally present an award or honor

Speech of Acceptance

speech of acceptance
oral remarks made by the
recipient of an award or honor

If you are ever given an award, a promotion, or some other sort of public recognition, you may be called upon to "say a few words." Giving a **speech of acceptance** is difficult because you want to sound appreciative without being syrupy, and you want to sound deserving without being egotistical. Here are some guidelines.

Thank those who played a part in your achieving the honor.   If a few individuals made your recognition possible, mention them by name; if a lot of people did, mention the most important contributors to your success and say something like this, "There are many others but they are too numerous to name. Nevertheless, I am grateful to all of them."

Thank the organization giving you the award and recognize the work it is doing.   If, for example, you are cited by the United Way as top fund-raiser of the year, spend a few moments extolling its great work.

Be brief.   I have seen some ceremonies marred because an award recipient viewed the acceptance speech as a chance to expound on his or her pet ideas. If you deliver a lengthy oration, the people who are giving you the honor may regret their choice. Make a few sincere remarks—and then sit down.

Here is a sample acceptance speech, given by Rita Goldberg, who was honored by a chapter of the Lions Club for her work on behalf of people with disabilities.

> I want to thank you for choosing me to receive your Distinguished Service Award. In the past year I couldn't have accomplished half of what I did without the help of Henry and Judith Fletcher. I am grateful to them for their valuable assistance. And I am grateful to you Lions for setting up programs for the visually impaired. Because of your compassion and your work, you have made it easy for volunteers like me to help the disabled. Again, thank you for this honor.

Speech of Tribute

speech of tribute
an oration in praise of someone or something

A **speech of tribute** praises or celebrates a person, a group, an institution, or an event. It conveys gratitude, respect, or admiration. For example, the leader of a veterans' organization might pay tribute on Memorial Day to comrades who had died in combat. At a retirement banquet, you might give a brief talk lauding the work of a colleague who is stepping down after 25 years.

A speech of tribute should be completely positive. It is never appropriate to point out faults or dredge up old disputes.

Let's examine three popular types of tribute speeches—wedding speeches, toasts, and eulogies.

Wedding Speeches

Weddings are celebrated in many ways, depending upon religious, ethnic, and family traditions. Many of these traditions call for brief speeches of tribute at the rehearsal dinner and the wedding reception. The remarks may be delivered by members of the wedding party, parents, grandparents, siblings, and friends. Here are some guidelines.

Focus on the couple.   Instead of dwelling on your own experiences and emotions, talk mostly about the wedding couple and their love and future happiness.

Be brief, but not too brief.   If you speak for only 15 seconds, saying that the honorees are wonderful people whom everyone likes, you are not giving them the respect that they deserve. Say something specific and heartfelt, but keep your remarks under three minutes.

Don't say anything that could embarrass anyone in the room.   You've seen the movies in which a wedding celebration is marred when the best man reveals humiliating details about the groom or says something that is insulting to the bride. Such behavior is not limited to the movies. In real life, people make major blunders. Never mention ex-boyfriends or ex-girlfriends. Never tease about past misdeeds, goofy habits, or unfortunate shortcomings. For this occasion, focus entirely on the positive.

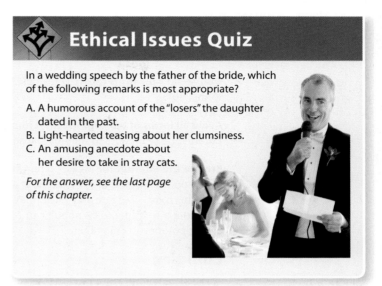

Ethical Issues Quiz

In a wedding speech by the father of the bride, which of the following remarks is most appropriate?

A. A humorous account of the "losers" the daughter dated in the past.
B. Light-hearted teasing about her clumsiness.
C. An amusing anecdote about her desire to take in stray cats.

For the answer, see the last page of this chapter.

Consider using an appropriate poem or quotation.   Anthologies and the Internet are full of apt quotations, such as this one by an ancient Chinese philosopher Lao Tzu: "To love someone deeply gives you strength. Being loved by someone deeply gives you courage."[3] Or you can use a lighter touch, like this poem by Ogden Nash:[4]

> *To keep your marriage brimming,*
> *With love in the wedding cup,*
> *Whenever you're wrong, admit it;*
> *Whenever you're right, shut up.*

If you create videos, make them short and tasteful.   A speech of tribute on a DVD, accompanied by photos and favorite pieces of music, can be a delightful part of the occasion if you keep it short, and if you avoid surprise photos that might embarrass someone. Concentrate on the couple, using upbeat, happy images.

End with a toast.   It's customary, and the perfect way to complete your speech. (In the next section, we will discuss the art of toasting.)

Toasts

I'd like to propose a toast to Miriam Steele, who has devoted 27 years to this company, giving us creativity, integrity, and a friendly ear to tell our troubles to. Miriam, we will miss you, and we hope your retirement years are filled with much happiness and abundant good health.

A toast is a short tribute spoken as glasses are raised to salute people, occasions, or things. Toasts are offered at graduation celebrations, family get-togethers, class reunions, retirement dinners, wedding celebrations, and many other events.

When is it a bad idea to use water for a toast?

Traditionally, the glasses contain wine, but at most events, any beverage is acceptable—even water. In other countries or with international guests, don't use water, because some cultures interpret it as disapproval of the toast.[5]

Announce a toast by raising your glass and saying, "I'd like to propose a toast." Participants show their agreement by raising their glasses and, at the end of the toast, lightly touching them against the glasses of those nearby. Then everyone takes a sip to "seal" the toast.

Here are some guidelines.

Strive for sincerity, warmth, and brevity.   At a party celebrating a college graduation, a classmate gave this toast: "Here's to Paul. May your future be filled with work that you enjoy and friends that bring you as much happiness as you have brought to us."

Don't read a toast.   Prepare your toast, practice it at home, but don't bring a manuscript to the table.

Avoid all forms of teasing.   A toast honoring a couple on their 35th anniversary should not include references to memory lapses, wrinkles, and weight gain.

Browse the Internet for ideas.   You can combine your own words with toasts that are found on the Internet. For example, at a wedding celebration, a friend of the newlyweds gave this toast: "Maggie and Zack, may your days be filled with wonder and grace, and (to quote a wedding toast popular in Mexico), I wish you health, love, happiness—and enough money to enjoy them."

Eulogies

eulogy

a laudatory oration in honor of someone who has died

An especially important kind of tribute speech you may be asked to make is a **eulogy**—a speech of praise for a friend, relative, or colleague who has died. A eulogy should be dignified, without exaggerated sentimentality. If it is appropriate, you may use humor, such

Carolyna De Laurentiis talks about her father (as her sister Dina listens) at the funeral of Italian filmmaker Dino De Laurentiis in Los Angeles. Sometimes joy and humor are appropriate at a funeral as loved ones share warm memories of the deceased.

as anecdotes about how a grandmother created elaborate and fun-filled surprises for her grandchildren.

A eulogy should focus on the *significance* of the person's life and deeds, rather than on a mere recital of biographical facts. In other words, how did this man or woman enrich our lives? What inspiration or lessons can we draw from this person's life?

As we discussed in Chapter 14, a script is usually not recommended for speeches, but an exception may be made for a eulogy. Because the death of a relative or friend often causes grief and disorientation, reading a script can give you stability and reassurance that you won't break down or ramble.

Your Thoughts

A new trend is to deliver a eulogy in the presence of an elderly person *before* he or she dies. Do you think this is a good idea? Explain your answer.

Inspirational Speech

The goal of the **inspirational speech** is to stir positive emotions—to help people feel excited, uplifted, encouraged. You may need to give inspirational speeches at various times in your life. Let's say, for example, that you are manager of an office or a department, and you give your staff an upbeat, "you-can-do-it" speech to motivate them to do their best work. Or you coach a children's soccer team and you give the boys and girls a "pep talk" before a game to encourage them to play well.

inspirational speech
an address that tries to stimulate listeners to a high level of feeling or activity

The inspirational speech is similar to the persuasive speech, with the two purposes often overlapping. The main difference is that in the inspirational speech, you devote yourself almost solely to stirring emotions, while in the persuasive speech, you use emotional appeals as just one of many techniques.

Delivery is an important dimension of inspirational speaking. To inspire other people, *you* must be inspired. Your facial expression, your posture, your tone of voice—everything about you must convey energy and enthusiasm.

An inspirational speech should tap the emotional power of vivid language. An example of effective use of language can be found in a speech delivered by Dan Crenshaw to a support group of parents of children with developmental disabilities. Here is a section from the speech:

> We must learn to live fully and joyfully in the here and now, setting aside all our pain from the past and all our worries about the future. Fulton Oursler said, "We crucify ourselves between two thieves: regret for yesterday and fear of tomorrow."
>
> If we live in the past or in the future, we miss what today has to offer.
> We miss the glistening beauty of a puddle of water.
> We miss the soothing melody of a love song.
> We miss the glint of wonder in a child's eyes.
> We miss the lingering aroma of fresh-baked cinnamon rolls.
> We miss the beautiful arrangement of clouds in the sky.
> We miss the satisfaction of rubbing a dog's fur.
>
> The past is over. Think of it as a bullet. Once it's fired, it's finished. The future is not yet here, and may never come for us. Today is all we have. Treasure *today,* celebrate *today,* live *today.*[6]

Crenshaw made effective use of the techniques of *repetition* and *parallel structure* (which we discussed in Chapter 13).

Resources for Review and Skill Building

Summary

While informative and persuasive speeches are the most frequent types, there are occasions when a speech must serve other purposes. When you need to entertain an audience, as in an after-dinner talk, your remarks should be light and diverting; any elements of information or persuasion should be gracefully woven into the fabric of entertainment. One device for an entertaining speech is to string together anecdotes, examples, or quotations on a single theme. Extended narratives or descriptions also can be entertaining.

Using humor in a speech is an effective way to create a bond of warmth and friendliness with an audience. Be cautious in telling jokes because they can be risky, and listeners may have heard the joke already. A safer type is low-key humor, such as a mildly amusing story, quotation, or observation. Whatever humor you use should relate to the topic and not be offensive to any person in the audience.

When you are asked to introduce a speaker, convey enthusiasm for the speaker and the topic, and give whatever background information is necessary to enhance the speaker's credibility.

When you make a speech of presentation, focus your remarks on the award and the recipient. When you are called upon to "say a few words" in acceptance of an award or a promotion, thank the people who gave you the honor and acknowledge the help of those who made your success possible.

When you give a speech of tribute, praise the person, group, institution, or event being honored, avoiding any negativity. Three types of tribute speeches are wedding speeches, toasts, and eulogies.

When you speak to inspire an audience, devote yourself to stirring emotions, using a dynamic delivery to convey your energy and enthusiasm.

Key Terms

entertaining speech, *352*

eulogy, *354*

inspirational speech, *355*

speech of acceptance, *352*

speech of introduction, *350*

speech of presentation, *351*

speech of tribute, *352*

Review Questions

1. Why would an informative speech on a difficult, highly technical subject usually be inappropriate for an after-dinner audience?

2. In what situation is self-deprecating humor inadvisable?

3. List three guidelines for the speech of acceptance.

4. What is the function of the speech of tribute?

5. What are the risks that a speaker takes when telling a joke?

6. If you are asked to introduce a speaker, why should you coordinate your remarks beforehand with those of the speaker?

7. When introducing a speaker, some introducers use the speaker's first name, others use the last name. What advice does the text give on this issue?

8. In which kind of special occasion speech does the speaker often withhold an honoree's name until the last sentence?

9. What should be the focus of a eulogy?

10. What is the main difference between an inspirational speech and a persuasive speech?

Building Critical-Thinking Skills

1. One speaker told his audience, "Before I left for this speech, my wife gave me some advice: 'Don't try to be charming, witty, or intellectual. Just be yourself.'" What kind of humor is the speaker using, and in what kind of situations do you think it is acceptable?

2. "Our speaker tonight," says the master of ceremonies, "will outline the five key steps in rescuing a person who is in danger of drowning. Let me give you a quick preview of these steps." What mistake is the master of ceremonies making? If you were the MC in this scenario, what would you say to introduce this speaker?

Building Teamwork Skills

1. Working in a group, decide on a topic and then prepare and deliver an entertaining talk, with each member of the group speaking in turn. Some possible topics:

   a. An embarrassing moment
   b. Good vacation spots
   c. The weird behavior of pets

2. In a group, choose a person (living or dead) whom everyone admires. Create a speech of tribute to that person.

Ethical Issues

Answer to quiz on p. 353: C. A story about stray cats could illustrate the daughter's compassion. Answers A and B would be embarrassing.

Speaking in Groups

OUTLINE

Meetings

Group Presentations

OBJECTIVES

After studying this chapter, you should be able to:

1. Serve as a leader or a participant in a small group meeting.
2. Describe the responsibilities of both leaders and participants in small groups.
3. Identify and explain the seven steps of the reflective-thinking method.
4. Prepare and deliver a presentation as a member of a team.
5. Participate in a symposium.
6. Serve as moderator or panelist in a panel discussion.

WHETHER YOU MEET IN A VIDEOCONFERENCE with colleagues based in Asia or meet with your co-workers in your hometown, you can bolster your career if you know how to work well in a group.[1] Here is what research shows:

- If you show that you have had experience in working on a team, you improve your chances of getting a job. "Experience on a team has become one of the top requests among recruiters looking over job candidates," says Dr. Mary Ellen Guffey of Los Angeles Pierce College.[2]

- Once employed, if you establish a reputation as an effective team member, you enhance your chances for promotion.[3]

Why is working on a team so important? Much of the work of society is done by small groups, such as a team of scientists who develop new medicines, a committee of educators who improve a curriculum, a group of neighbors who try to reduce crime, and a crew of workers who devise a labor-saving method of production.

An executive in Asia participates in a videoconference with colleagues in San Francisco.

Small groups have some advantages over the individual. Members of small groups can pool their resources, ideas, and labor. They can catch and correct errors that might slip past an individual. According to Yale psychologist Robert Sternberg, a group often has an IQ (or intelligence level) that is higher than the IQ of any individual in the group.[4]

In this chapter, we will look at working in groups and then discuss making presentations as a group.

Meetings

A meeting is often the best way for small groups to plan and carry out their collective work. Sounds simple, but there is a problem: the majority of business and professional people say (in surveys) that most meetings are unproductive and a waste of time.[5]

Fortunately, this problem can be solved. To have a productive meeting, group leaders and participants should follow well-established principles of effective group communication, as explained below. Let's start with the role of group leaders.

Responsibilities of Leaders

No matter what kind of group you are asked to lead—whether a committee to plan the office holiday party or a team to handle client complaints—your general responsibilities will be the same.

Make Sure You Need a Meeting

It is a mistake to hold a meeting just because "we always have a staff meeting every Friday afternoon." If there is nothing significant to discuss or act upon, a meeting is a waste of valuable time. If you simply need to share information, use e-mail or memos. But call a meeting when

- You need to develop ideas, gain consensus, plan, and follow up.
- You must share information that is sensitive, is emotionally charged, or could be misinterpreted.
- You need to build teamwork and cooperation.

Make Sure Group Members Know Purpose and Scope

In advance of the meeting, all participants should be clearly informed of the purpose of getting together. Otherwise, people will walk in saying "Why are we meeting?" Letting people know in advance gives them the opportunity to be thinking about the task.

Just as important, make sure group members know how their work will be used. Does the group have the authority to make and carry out a decision, or is it merely being asked to make a recommendation? Can the group's decisions be overruled by a higher authority?

When the meeting begins, you should quickly review the group's purpose and scope of power—to refresh everyone's memory.

agenda
document listing what is to be accomplished during a meeting

Set the Agenda and Length of Meeting

An **agenda** is a list of items that need to be covered in a meeting (see Table 19.1). When there is no agenda, groups are unfocused—they spend time and energy on minor items and never get around to the major issues. A study of meetings by the 3M Corporation found that "a written agenda, distributed in advance, is the single best predictor of a successful meeting."[6]

You don't need to set the agenda by yourself. Ask participants in advance to submit their ideas and concerns. You will not only get good ideas but also assure the participants that their input is valued and will be heard.

Arrange the agenda so the most important items are discussed first. Consider allocating an appropriate amount of time for each item.

Your Thoughts

Researchers at Stanford University estimate that in a typical meeting, an effective agenda prevents at least 20 minutes of wasted time. And yet most meetings use no agenda. Why do you think agendas are not used?

Table 19.1
Sample Agenda

AGENDA
Advertising Committee
September 5, 2012, 2:00–2:55 p.m.
Frazier Conference Room

Committee Chair: Janet Moore

Committee Members: Melissa Casey, Anne Hansen, Daniel Madden, Michael Pulaski, Luis Rodriguez, and Allison Schwartz.

Objective: To decide the best outlet for our spring advertising campaign

Agenda Items:

1. Welcome and call to order

2. Approval of last meeting's minutes

3. Approval of agenda

4. Discussion of TV advertising options (10 minutes)

5. Discussion of social networking opportunities (10 minutes)

6. Discussion of magazine options (10 minutes)

7. Vote on our recommendation to the company president

8. Suggestions for next meeting's agenda

9. Committee chair's summary

10. Adjournment

Early in the meeting, get the group's approval of the agenda in case new issues have come up that need to be addressed.

Many people automatically schedule meetings for one hour, perhaps because of the traditional 50-minute class length. Instead, estimate the time you really need. Holding quick meetings (sometimes with everyone standing up) can be an effective way to keep the group focused. (See Figure 19.1 on the next page)

While short meetings can be effective, they are not always ideal. When you have a long agenda, or complex issues, having one long session can be more effective than several meetings that break up your momentum.

Start on Time

Start your meetings on time and thank those who are there. When latecomers arrive, tell them where you are on the agenda and let them catch up. Waiting to start your meeting until everybody shows up is almost always a mistake.

- It rewards the latecomers, effectively "training" them—and those who arrived on time—to come later and later.

- It wastes the time of those who arrived on time and tells them you don't appreciate their punctuality.

Of course, there are sometimes valid reasons for starting late, such as a traffic tie-up or an office emergency. When this happens, make sure your group knows the reason for the delay and invite them to take a break and return at a specified time.

Figure 19.1
Some companies insist that all participants stand up during an entire meeting. "This ensures that our meetings are short," said one manager. "We get our work done quickly and efficiently because no one wants to dawdle or engage in idle chit-chat. Stand-up meetings boost our productivity."

Set the Tone

Greet people as they arrive. Set an appropriate tone. Usually it will be friendly and upbeat, but more serious if the purpose of the meeting is to share bad news. In any case, always thank your participants for coming.

If some of the participants are newcomers, make sure they are introduced to everyone else.

Make Sure Minutes Are Kept

minutes

written record of what occurred at a meeting

If the group is not a formal committee with a previously designated recorder, appoint someone to take notes and later prepare **minutes** of the meeting. Minutes are a record of what was discussed and accomplished during a meeting. They should be circulated to group members as soon after the meeting as possible. While minutes are obviously valuable for absentees, they are also important for people who were present—to remind them of their responsibilities for the next meeting. Minutes should consist of five elements: (1) agenda item, (2) decision reached, (3) action required, (4) person(s) responsible for taking action, and (5) target date for completion of action. At each meeting, the minutes of the previous session should be briefly reviewed to make sure that tasks have been completed.

Guide—Don't Dominate—the Discussion

Your challenge is to set the direction of the meeting while encouraging free and productive group participation. This is more than politeness; it's good strategy. Group members feel a commitment to the plans and decisions if they have helped to formulate them. Now it is *their* idea, *their* policy.

- Don't let anybody take over the conversation, including yourself. If any one person is doing most of the talking, you may have to gently but firmly intervene: "Those are excellent points . . . I'd like to hear how others are reacting to what you just said."

- Draw out participants who aren't speaking up—but don't put them on the spot. "Carlos, you've had experience with writing proposals. Are you seeing anything we're overlooking?"

- Encourage free discussion, but don't permit attacks on people or ideas.

- Address side conversations directly: "Brent and Ashley, it looks as if you've come up with something interesting. Could you share it with all of us?" They will either grin sheepishly and return to the group or share their thoughts—and they may be shy and welcome the invitation to give their input.

- Summarize periodically. Sum up what has and has not been decided, saying just enough to help the participants keep their bearings. "OK, we've decided to recommend A and B to the board for approval, but it looks like we're stuck on C until Jahquil gets numbers from Finance. Let's go on to item D."

- When you near the agreed-upon time to end the meeting, summarize what the group has accomplished, set the time and place for the next meeting, and make sure all participants know their assignments for the next meeting. Express appreciation for the work that the group has done.

- After the meeting, make sure that minutes are written and distributed to each participant and that all participants carry out their assignments.

Responsibilities of Participants

While leadership of a small group is important, the participants themselves play a vital role. People working together can combine their insights and energies to achieve goals that would be unattainable by a single person. The key is cooperation. "The secret of a successful team is not to assemble the largest team possible, but rather to assemble a team that can work well together," says Dean Kamen, founder of FIRST (For Inspiration and Recognition of Science and Technology).[7]

Here are guidelines to keep in mind.

Prepare for Every Meeting

Take time to review the agenda and the key players. Do whatever research, background reading, and interviewing you need to strengthen your position on issues to be discussed. Bring any documentation needed.

Arrive Early

Show up a few minutes before the meeting time. You'll look—and be—more in command, and you'll have a chance to touch base with others.

Participate

Join the discussion and contribute your ideas and opinions. It can be as simple as voicing agreement with a team member or asking a question. If you tend to be shy in group settings, speak up early. The longer you wait, the harder it will be.

Watch your body language. Nonverbal behaviors, such as facial expressions and posture, speak more powerfully than words. If you slump in your chair and don't make eye contact, people will assume you are bored or negative. Instead, sit in an alert but relaxed posture with an open, friendly expression. Make eye contact with those speaking. Smile and nod agreement when appropriate—everyone who speaks up appreciates positive feedback.

Ethical Issues Quiz

While at a meeting for your neighborhood block association, you find yourself disagreeing on an issue on which all of your neighbors agree. Which of the following would be an acceptable reason for you to concede and go along with the others?

A. Your block association's bylaws stipulate that decisions must be unanimous, and you don't want to stand in the way of a group decision.
B. You want to avoid conflict.
C. You want to see a quick decision reached so that the meeting doesn't drag on.
D. You know that standing in the way of a unanimous decision might cause your neighbors to be frustrated with you.

For the answer, see the last page of this chapter.

Have the Courage to Disagree

You've undoubtedly been part of a group in which everybody seemed to agree with an idea or an approach until one member expressed reservations—and then almost everybody jumped in to say they, too, had concerns. A good way to open the conversation to many points of view is to ask a question. Focus on the *issue*, not on people: "How can we be sure we draw a big enough audience to justify the expense?" As group members respond, they may realize that the idea *is* unworkable—or you may realize it has merit. You can help your group avoid making a decision in false unanimity.

Don't Work from a Hidden Agenda

hidden agenda
an ulterior motive

A group's work can be sabotaged if some members pretend to be committed to the goals of the group but in reality have **hidden agendas**—that is, unannounced private goals that conflict with the group's goals. One frequent hidden agenda is the desire to win the favor of a superior. One or more members of a committee will agree with the chairperson—the boss—even though they feel strongly that the boss's ideas are flawed. They would rather see the committee's efforts fail than go on record as disagreeing with their superior.

Don't Carry On Private Conversations

A whispered conversation by two or three participants is rude and insulting to the speaker; it is also damaging to the work of the group, since it cuts off teamwork and undermines cooperation.

The Reflective-Thinking Method

For every human problem, the American essayist H. L. Mencken said, "there is always an easy solution—neat, plausible, and wrong." Unfortunately, some business and professional groups leap at easy but wrong solutions. In the 1980s, when Coca-Cola was losing ground to Pepsi, the "neat, plausible" solution was to change the Coca-Cola formula and make it as sweet as Pepsi. The solution seemed reasonable, but it was a huge blunder. Sales plummeted because millions of Coca-Cola lovers disliked the new Coke. Soon the embarrassed company resumed making the original formula (which was sold as Coca-Cola Classic).

reflective-thinking method
a structured system for solving problems

An effective technique for avoiding mistakes like this is to use the **reflective-thinking method,** a step-by-step approach derived from the writings of the American philosopher John Dewey.[8] Follow the steps in this order:

1. **Define the problem.** Doing so clearly and precisely can save time and money. Here are some tips:

   • Phrase the problem in the form of a question. Instead of making a statement—"We have traffic jams on our campus"—ask, "How can we eliminate traffic jams after the 2 p.m. and 3 p.m. classes?"

- Avoid wording that suggests a solution. If you say, "How can we finance the hiring of more security officers to eliminate traffic jams on campus?" you are stating that you already know the best solution. You risk cutting off discussion that might lead to a different solution—one that is even better than hiring more security officers.
- Be specific about the problem. If it is litter, say so. Instead of "How can we improve our campus?" ask, "How can we discourage littering?"

2. **Analyze the problem.** You must get a clear picture of the full dimensions of a problem before the problem-solving process can continue. Ask these questions:

   - What are the causes of this problem?
   - What are the effects of this problem?
   - How severe is it? Are many people affected? Or just a few?

If you own a restaurant, and some of your customers have complained about slow service, your problem-solving team should focus on causes. Is slow service caused by the servers? If so, is it because they are careless and unprofessional, or is it because each of them is assigned too many tables? Or can the slow service be blamed solely on the cooks? If so, is it because they are lazy or inefficient? Or are they understaffed?

3. **Establish criteria for evaluating a solution.** Imagine you are employed by a company that assigns you and four others to work on a team to solve this problem: Many employees complain that the indoor air quality is very poor, causing headaches and fatigue. After hours of research and discussion, your team recommends installation of an air-filtration system costing $400,000. But the idea is quickly shot down by senior management. It's four times what the company can afford. Now it's back to the drawing board. Your team could have saved itself much time and effort if it had known that the spending ceiling was $100,000.

This scenario shows why a group should write down the criteria—the standards or conditions—by which to judge a solution. To establish criteria, a group should ask these key questions:

   - What must the proposed solution do?
   - What must it avoid?
   - What restrictions of time, money, and space must be considered?

4. **Generate possible solutions.** One of the best techniques for putting potential solutions on the table is **brainstorming**. People in the group throw out their ideas, which are captured—preferably on a visible board—and later discussed and analyzed. Many of the ingenious products that we use daily were invented or improved as a result of brainstorming. For example, consider the digital camera that we use to take photos. The image-capture chip in the camera was invented in a one-hour brainstorming session by two engineers who were under pressure to produce or lose their funding.[9]

brainstorming
generating many ideas quickly and uncritically

For brainstorming to work effectively, there must be an atmosphere of total acceptance—no one analyzes, judges, ridicules, or rejects any of the ideas as they are being generated. Nothing is too wild or crazy to be jotted down.

Total acceptance is vital because (1) it encourages the flow of creative thinking and (2) an idea that seems far-fetched and impractical at first glance might eventually prove to be a good idea.

In a brainstorming session, executives at a novelty company in Connecticut came up with the idea of putting pumpkin faces on leaf bags, transforming the bags from unsightly trash containers into autumn decorations. The company has sold millions of them. Brainstorming is one of the best ways for small groups to solve problems and create new ideas.

5. **Choose the best solution.** After the brainstorming session, a group should analyze, weigh, and discuss its ideas to come up with the best solution. It may be a combination of the ideas generated, or something new generated by the analysis and discussion. Regardless, the solution chosen must meet these standards:

   - The solution must satisfy the criteria previously established.
   - The group must have the authority to put the solution into effect—or recommend a way to do so.
   - A solution must not create a new problem.

6. **Implement the solution.** For this important step, decide how to put the solution into action. For example, if your committee has come up with a way to discourage

littering on campus, you should go to the appropriate administrators and give detailed instructions on exactly what needs to be done (such as installation of more conveniently located trash containers).

7. **Evaluate the solution.** Many groups hammer out a solution to a problem but never follow up to determine whether their solution really solved the problem. Make sure you design a way to evaluate your recommendation at the time you make it. For example, let's say your group recommends hiring more security officers to solve traffic jams on campus. You need set up an evaluation that will contrast *before* with *after*:

- What was happening *before* the solution was implemented: Student motorists required about 15 minutes to exit the campus after 2 p.m. classes let out.
- What must happen *after* the solution: The average exit time must be less than 7 minutes.

If the goal is not met, your group needs to go back to Step 4.

Group Presentations

In your classroom, career, or community life, you are likely to speak publicly as part of a group. Three popular ways of presenting are the team presentation, the symposium, and the panel discussion.

Team Presentation

Teams play an important role in the business and professional world, and sometimes they are called upon to deliver a presentation to an audience. A **team presentation** is like a speech given by an individual except that the content is divided, with each member delivering a different section. For effective team presentations, here are some guidelines.

team presentation
a well-coordinated presentation made by members of a group who focus on a common goal

Designate Roles

To keep the group on track, choose a project leader. He or she should conduct meetings (along the lines discussed earlier in this chapter) to determine key issues: Who will do the various research tasks? Who will deliver which section of the presentation? When will the assignment be due?

Prepare Content

Use all the steps you have learned for an individual speech. Analyze your audience, create a specific purpose and a central idea, develop an outline, and gather materials (especially visuals).

Plan Your Time

Going over your time limit can destroy your credibility and irritate your audience. Time every minute of your presentation. Leave plenty of time for questions and discussion—this is the most challenging part of your presentation, and the one most likely to win approval or lose it.

Practice, Practice, Practice

It is more important to rehearse when you do a group presentation than when you present alone. Practice many times, using all of the equipment and visual aids that you will be using on the big day. If you must travel to another city to give the presentation, take your own equipment—it can be risky to use unfamiliar equipment. In some situations, your team members may live in different parts of the globe, communicating by e-mail, telephone, or videoconference. To avoid being out of sync with one another, you and your teammates should come together several days before a presentation to practice together in the same room.

Get Feedback during a Practice Session

This is a critical—and commonly overlooked—key to success. Find at least one person who is typical of your audience and who has not heard your presentation so he or she can provide a fresh, unbiased viewpoint. Use the feedback to make necessary alterations.

Prepare for the Question-and-Answer Period

Compile a list of likely questions from the audience. For each question, decide the best answer and designate which team member will deliver it.

Plan for Emergencies

Identify potential problems such as equipment failure or a cancelled flight, and how you will manage them. For example, be ready to print hard copies of your PowerPoint slides in case the multimedia projector malfunctions.

Support One Another

Strive for harmony in the presentation. It looks bad if one team member contradicts or criticizes another in front of the audience. I once saw a team of architects give a presentation, at the end of which the senior architect on the team rose and apologized for the poor speaking skills of a young team member. His remarks were unnecessary—a gratuitous slap in the face—and they reflected poorly on him and the firm.

Listen to the Presentation Attentively

While your teammates are presenting, don't review your notes, check your BlackBerry, or whisper comments to others. These distractions signal to your audience that what's being said isn't important.

Symposium

symposium
a meeting featuring short addresses by different people on the same topic

A **symposium** is a series of brief speeches on a common topic, each usually discussing a different aspect of the topic. Every year, for example, Mt. Sinai School of Medicine in New York City holds a symposium on autism, with five to eight medical researchers speaking on various aspects of autism. One might discuss diagnosis, another might recommend a certain treatment, and another might explore possible cures.

Unlike the team presentation, the speakers in a symposium do not necessarily agree with one another. Sometimes they are not required to coordinate their remarks, although it is a good idea to do so, to avoid excessive duplication of material.

A symposium is conducted by a moderator, who gives a brief introduction of each speaker and manages a question-and-answer period after the speeches.

Symposium speeches are supposed to be brief, and each speaker should be careful to stay within time limits. If a speaker is long-winded, the moderator should intervene and politely ask him or her to yield to another speaker in the interest of fairness.

When you prepare and deliver a speech as part of a symposium, use the same skills and techniques as those of solo speechmaking, with an introduction, a body, and a conclusion.

American journalist Roxana Saberi, who was imprisoned for five months in Iran's notorious Evin Prison, speaks on a panel in New York City about human rights abuses in Iran.

Panel Discussion

In a **panel discussion,** a team converses on a topic in front of an audience. A panel is usually made up of three to eight team members and is led by a moderator. A common pattern is for panelists to give a brief opening statement and then discuss the subject among themselves, with the moderator guiding the flow. At the end of the discussion, the audience is usually invited to ask questions.

    Because of the variety of viewpoints and the liveliness of informed conversation, audiences enjoy a good panel discussion.

panel discussion
consideration of a topic by a small group in the presence of an audience

Guidelines for the Moderator

Much of the success (or failure) of a panel discussion is determined by the moderator. He or she must keep the discussion moving along smoothly, restrain the long-winded or domineering panelist from hogging the show, draw out the reticent panelist, and field questions from the audience. Here are some guidelines to follow when you are a moderator.

Arrange the setting.   You and the panelists can be seated at a table facing the audience. Or, even better, you can be seated in a semicircle so that all members of the panel can see one another while still remaining visible to the audience. A large name card should be placed in front of each panelist so that the audience will know the participants' names.

Brief panel members in advance.   Well before the meeting, give panel members clear instructions on exactly what they are expected to cover in their opening remarks.

Are they supposed to argue the "pro" or the "con" position? Are they supposed to speak on only one aspect of the topic? (For information-giving discussions, you may want to assign each panel member a subtopic, according to his or her area of expertise, so that there is not much overlap among speakers.) Instruct the panelists not to bring and read written statements, but tell them that they are free to bring notes.

Before the meeting, prepare a list of items that you think should be discussed.   This ensures that no important issues are inadvertently omitted. If the discussion begins to lag or go off into irrelevancies, you will have fresh questions ready.

Prepare and deliver an introduction.   At the beginning of the program, introduce the topic and the speakers, and explain the ground rules for the discussion; be sure to let listeners know if and when they will be permitted to ask questions.

Moderate the discussion.   Give each panelist a chance to make an opening statement (within the time constraints previously announced) and then encourage the panelists to question one another or comment upon one another's remarks. Be neutral in the discussion, but be prepared to ask questions if there is an awkward lull or if a panelist says something confusing or leaves out important information. Listen carefully to what each panelist says so that you don't embarrass yourself by asking questions on subjects that have already been discussed.

Maintain friendly, but firm, control.   Don't let a panelist dominate the discussion. During the question-and-answer session, don't let a member of the audience make a long-winded speech; interrupt kindly but firmly and say, "We need to give other people a chance to ask questions." If a panelist exceeds the time limit for opening remarks or monopolizes the discussion time, gently break in and say, "I'm sorry to interrupt, but let's hear from other members of the panel on their ideas concerning . . ." If a reticent panelist says very little, draw him or her out with specific, pertinent questions.

Be respectful of all panelists, including those with whom you disagree.   Think of yourself not as a district attorney who must interrogate and skewer criminal defendants but as a gracious host or hostess who stimulates guests to engage in lively conversation.

Ask open-ended questions.   For example, ask "How can we make sure our homes are safe from burglars?" rather than "Is burglary on the increase in our community?"

End the program at the agreed-upon time.   Wrap up the proceedings on time and in a prearranged way, perhaps by letting each panelist summarize briefly his or her position. You may want to summarize the key points made during the discussion. (To do this, you would need to take notes throughout the program.) Thank the panelists and the audience for their participation. If some members of the audience are still interested in continuing the discussion, you may want to invite them to talk to the panelists individually after the program is over.

Guidelines for Panelists

If you are a member of a panel, here are some guidelines to keep in mind.

Tips for Your Career

Strive to Improve Communication Skills

As you give speeches during your career, I hope that you will try to become better and better as a communicator. Here are three suggestions.

1. SEEK OPPORTUNITIES FOR SPEAKING.

The best way to improve your skills is to actually give speeches, so look for opportunities in your career and in your community. An excellent place to practice is in a Toastmasters club, where your speaking skills will be critiqued in a friendly, supportive atmosphere. For the name, Web address, and phone number of the club nearest you, visit www.toastmasters.org.

2. SEEK FEEDBACK.

See the guidelines in Tip 1.1 in Chapter 1.

3. BE A LIFETIME STUDENT OF PUBLIC SPEAKING.

You can improve your own speaking skills by studying the speechmaking of others. Whenever you listen to a speech, make notes on what does and doesn't work. Which delivery techniques were effective? Which were ineffective? What speech material seemed to please the listeners? What seemed to bore them? Keep your notes in a file for future reference, so that you can profit from both the successes and the failures of others.

Prepare for the discussion in the same way you prepare for a speech.   Find out all that you can about the audience and the occasion: On what particular aspect of the topic are you expected to speak? Who are the other panelists and what will they cover? Will there be questions from the audience? What are the time constraints?

Prepare notes for the panel, but not a written statement.   If you read your remarks, you will spoil the spontaneity that is desired in a panel discussion. In addition to notes, you may want to bring supporting data (such as bibliographical sources or statistics) from which to draw in case you are asked to document a point.

Respect the time limits set by the moderator.   If, for example, you are asked to keep your opening remarks under two minutes, be careful to do so.

In the give-and-take of the discussion, be brief.   If the other panelists or listeners want to hear more from you, they will ask.

Stay on the subject.   Resist the temptation to ramble.

Be respectful and considerate of your fellow panelists.   Don't squelch them with sarcasm, ridicule, or an overbearing attitude. Don't upstage them by trying to be the one to answer all the questions from the audience.

Listen carefully to the comments of other panelists and members of the audience.   If some people disagree with you, try to understand and appreciate their position instead of hastily launching a counterattack. Then be prepared to follow the next guideline.

Be willing to alter your position.   If you listen with an open mind, you may see merit in others' views, and you may decide that you need to modify your original position. Though such a shift may seem like an embarrassing loss of face, it actually causes the audience to have greater respect for you. It shows you are a person who possesses intellectual courage, flexibility, and integrity.

Resources for Review and Skill Building

Summary

Small groups are important elements in business and professional life, and much of the work of small groups is done in meetings. To lead a meeting, establish an agenda and make sure that it is followed; encourage all members to participate in group discussions; and guide the discussion to make sure that it stays on the subject. When you are a participant in a small group meeting, enter the discussion with a positive attitude and an open mind.

One of the most effective agendas for problem solving is known as the reflective-thinking method. It involves seven steps: defining the problem; analyzing it; establishing criteria for evaluating a solution; generating possible solutions; choosing the best solution; implementing the solution, and evaluating the solution.

Sometimes groups appear in public to discuss or debate an issue. Three popular formats are team presentations, the symposium (a series of brief speeches on a common topic), and the panel discussion (an informal presentation involving a moderator and panelists).

Key Terms

agenda, *360*

brainstorming, *365*

hidden agenda, *364*

minutes, *362*

panel discussion, *369*

reflective-thinking method, *364*

symposium, *368*

team presentation, *367*

Review Questions

1. Why is an agenda necessary for a meeting?

2. Why is nonverbal behavior important in a group meeting?

3. If you disagree with what everyone else in the group is saying, what should you do?

4. What does a group do when it brainstorms?

5. In what ways does a team presentation resemble an individual speech?

6. What is a hidden agenda?

7. What are the seven steps of the reflective-thinking method?

8. What should a group leader do after a meeting?

9. What are the duties of the moderator in a panel discussion?

10. What are the duties of panelists in a panel discussion?

Building Critical-Thinking Skills

1. A football huddle is a type of group meeting. Fran Tarkenton, former star quarterback for the Minnesota Vikings, says, "Many of my best plays were the result of input by other team members. For example, outside receivers often told me that they could run a specific pattern against the defense, and we adjusted to run those plays. I would guess that 50 percent of my touchdowns came about by my receivers suggesting pass patterns." How could Tarkenton's insights be applied to business meetings?

2. Some communication experts say that group meetings lose a great deal of their effectiveness when group members number more than 12. Assuming that this statement is true, what would account for a decline in effectiveness?

Building Teamwork Skills

1. In a group, use the steps of the reflective-thinking method (as shown in this chapter) to discuss how to solve a problem on your campus or in your community. Choose a leader to guide the discussion.

2. Using guidelines from your instructor, conduct either a symposium or a panel discussion to present the findings from the problem-solving assignment in item 1.

Ethical Issues

Answer to quiz on p. 364: A. Going along when unanimity is required is often a good choice so that the work of the group is not stymied by one person, although there may be cases when you should refuse to go along—for example, if you have good reason to believe that the group is about to make a terrible mistake. The other answers (B, C, and D) are weak reasons for capitulating.

Appendix

Sample Speeches

One Slip—and You're Dead
Natalia Payne

Most people who climb cliffs or mountains use ropes and safety gear, but there are some climbers who climb without any equipment and without any assistance from other people. *[Speaker shows photo in Figure A.1.]*   **1**

What they are doing is known as "free solo climbing." Of all the extreme sports, it is perhaps the most extreme, the most dangerous. One wrong move—and it's all over. There's no safety net. And for this reason, several free solo climbers have died over the last few years. Now I would like to give you a picture of what this sport is all about by discussing two famous climbers.   **2**

Let's look at our first climber. Steph Davis of Moab, Utah, is considered one of the most daring free solo climbers in the world. *[Speaker shows photo in Figure A.2.]* This is one of the scariest pictures I've ever seen. Steph Davis is 1,000 feet up the side of a sheer cliff known as the Diamond on Longs Peak in Colorado. She has no ropes, no safety gear. She is relying entirely on her climbing skills, her sticky shoes, and a container of chalk to keep her hands dry.   **3**

When Steph Davis is asked why she climbs, she says, "Because I love it." She loves the exhilaration, and she loves the freedom from everyday worries.   **4**

Growing up, she was not an athlete or an outdoors-type person. She spent all of her time practicing piano and flute, reading, and doing her homework. When she was a student at the University of Maryland, her life changed. One day she was sitting outside the cafeteria eating her lunch, and a guy started talking to her, and he invited her to go rock climbing. She says she had never even heard of rock climbing, but she agreed to skip her freshman calculus class and go with   **5**

Figure A.1
Free solo climbers use no ropes or safety gear.

Figure A.2
Steph Davis conquers a sheer cliff, relying only on her climbing skills, sticky shoes, and a bag of chalk to keep her hands dry.

him. And this first experience of climbing triggered an obsession. She decided to spend the rest of her life climbing, and she supported herself with jobs as a waitress.

6   Is Steph Davis crazy? I don't think so. I read her book *High Infatuation* and I exchanged e-mails with her a few weeks ago. She seems normal to me. I asked her if she has any fears. She said yes. In fact, believe it or not, she has public speaking fears. She gets very nervous when she has to show slides and video, and there's some kind of technical glitch. She says, "Technology is very scary."

7   Now let's turn to our second climber. Michael Reardon of Southern California is perhaps the greatest free solo climber of all time. [*Speaker shows photo in Figure A.3.*] Although he was actually afraid of heights as a child, he has climbed some of the most dangerous cliffs and mountains in the world.

8   He climbed with nothing but a bag of chalk and an iPod loaded with Kid Rock and Hank Williams Jr. Some climbers say that he had a death wish, but Michael would always laugh at that suggestion. He would say, "Nothing else makes me feel so alive."

Figure A.3
Michael Reardon always said he would never die while climbing.

He said that he put himself in a mental trance so that he saw only the 8 feet directly around **9** him. He said it was "like being in a giant, 8-foot eggshell. It's a way to zone out the rest of the world and put all your focus on the next move."

Michael claimed that free solo climbing was a lot easier than climbing with ropes and safety **10** gear because you're not weighted down and bothered by all that equipment. I can see his point, but a climber has no control over two factors—loose rocks and sudden rain, which can make it easy to slip and fall. These two factors are believed to be the causes of all the deaths of free solo climbers.

But Michael insisted that he was extremely careful. He said he felt no shame in walking away **11** from a climb—if dark clouds threatened rain, or if he felt that his mind wasn't in the right place.

And because he was so careful, Michael always said that he would never die climbing. He was **12** right. He died in a freak accident off the coast of Ireland in 2007. He had finished climbing up and down a cliff, and he was standing on a ledge at the bottom of the cliff, waiting for the tide to go out so that he could walk across to another piece of land, when a rogue wave hit him and swept him out to sea. His body was never found.

By the way, I could not find any statistics on how many solo climbers there are and how many **13** have died.

To sum up what we have covered: I've tried to show you what free solo climbing involves— **14** dangerous climbing without ropes and without safety gear. It is one of the most extreme of the extreme sports.

15   And Steph Davis and Michael Reardon are not people who most of us would want to imitate, but they do show us the incredible feats that some human beings are capable of achieving.

Speeches Online

To view 22 videos of full-length speeches, go to www.mcgrawhillconnect.com. Included are all the major speeches printed in this book, plus the speeches below:

● **Wedding Crashers**

Dave Reed

Can a Hollywood movie prompt thousands of people to crash real-life weddings? One speaker investigates.

● **Failed to Get the Job?**

Halle Morse

What are the major reasons for job applicants being rejected? While exploring these reasons, two speeches ("needs improvement" and "improved") illustrate the wrong way and the right way to use PowerPoint slides.

● **Do You Need Detox?**

Steven Kaplan

Is your body clogged with impurities? Do you need detoxification? Two speeches ("needs improvement" and "improved") show the wrong way and the right way to find reliable information on this issue.

● **Would You Vote for Aardvark?**

Turron Kofi Alleyne

Some candidates win an election simply because their name appears first on the ballot. What can be done to fix the unfairness?

● **The Four-Day Work Week – Pros and Cons**

Felipe Dieppa

What are the advantages and disadvantages of working four 10-hour days instead of the traditional five 8-hour days?

● **Humanoid Robots**

Joe Haupt

Are robots likely to equal human intelligence and capability in this century?

● How to Make Avocado Salsa
Nick Amick

Two contrasting speeches illustrate the wrong way and the right way to give a demonstration speech.

● Scars and Bruises
Christine Fowler

A self-introduction speech by a student who grew up with many scrapes and falls.

● Plus much more:

- 14 additional full-length speech videos
- 33 video clips showing elements of speeches (such as "conveying the central idea" and "providing transitions")

Glossary

A

abstract summary of key information.

abstract words words that name qualities, concepts, relationships, acts, conditions, and ideas.

adaptation adjusting one's material and delivery to meet listeners' needs.

adrenaline a hormone, triggered by stress, that stimulates heart, lungs, and muscles and prepares the body for "fright, flight, or fight."

agenda document listing what is to be accomplished during a meeting.

alliteration repetition of the beginning sounds of words.

analogy resemblance in some respects between things that are otherwise dissimilar.

anecdote a short account of an incident.

antithesis balanced juxtaposition of two contrasting ideas.

articulation the act of producing vocal sounds.

attack on a person criticizing an opponent rather than the opponent's argument.

attention material the part of the introduction designed to capture audience interest.

attitude a predisposition to respond favorably or unfavorably toward a person or an idea.

audience analysis collecting information about audience characteristics.

audience-centered speaker one who tries to establish a meaningful connection with listeners.

average a single value that represents the general significance of a set of unequal values.

B

bandwagon fallacy equating popularity with truth and proof.

bar graph a visual that contrasts two or more sets of data by means of parallel rectangles of varying lengths.

blog frequently updated online log.

brainstorming generating many ideas quickly and uncritically.

bridge a transitional device that links what went before with the next part of a speech.

building on an unproven assumption treating an opinion that is open to question as if it were already proved.

C

cause–effect pattern a scheme that links outcomes (effects) and the reasons for them (causes).

central idea the key concept of a speech.

channel the pathway used to transmit a message.

chronological pattern an arrangement of information in a time sequence.

citation basic facts about a source.

clarifying question a question designed to clear up confusion.

cliché an overused word or phrase.

clincher a final statement in a speech that drives home the key concept of the speech.

closed question a question requiring only a short, specific response.

comparative-advantages pattern an organizational scheme that shows the superiority of one concept or approach over another.

comparison showing how two or more items are alike.

complete-sentence outline a systematic arrangement of ideas, using complete sentences for headings and subheadings.

concrete words words that name persons and things that we can know by our five senses.

connotation the emotional overtones of a word that go beyond a dictionary definition.

contrast showing how two or more items are different.

copyright infringement unauthorized use of legally protected material.

correlation the degree of relative correspondence between two sets of data.

credibility audience perception of a speaker as believable, trustworthy, and competent.

customize to make or alter to a customer's specifications.

D

deduction reasoning from a generalization to a specific conclusion.

definition a statement of the meaning of a word or phrase.

definition speech an oral presentation that gives an extended definition of a concept.

denotation the thing or idea to which a word refers.

description speech an oral presentation that describes a person, place, object, or event.

discussion forum a message center for people with a common interest.

doublespeak language that is designed to confuse or to be misunderstood.

E

either-or fallacy presenting only two alternatives when in fact more exist.

entertaining speech an oral address designed to amuse or engage listeners.

ethnocentrism judging other cultures as inferior to one's own culture.

eulogy a laudatory oration in honor of someone who has died.

euphemism a mild, indirect, or vague word used in place of one that is harsh, blunt, or offensive.

evidence the facts, examples, statistics, testimony, and other information that support an assertion.

example an instance that serves to illustrate a point.

expert site a website offering expertise on requested topics.

explanation speech an oral presentation that explains a concept or situation.

extemporaneous method delivery of a speech from notes, following extensive preparation and rehearsal.

extended definition a rich, full elaboration of the meaning of a term.

F

fair use allowable and reasonable exceptions to copyright rules.

fallacy an argument based on a false inference.

false analogy creating a comparison that is exaggerated or erroneous.

false cause assuming that because two events are related in time, the first caused the second.

feedback verbal and nonverbal responses made by a listener to a speaker.

field research firsthand gathering of information.

flip chart a large book consisting of sheets (hinged at the top) that can be flipped over to present information sequentially.

follow-up question a question designed to stimulate elaboration.

full text every word of a document.

G

general purpose the broad objective of a speech.

H

handout material distributed to an audience as part of a speaker's presentation.

hasty generalization a conclusion that is based on inadequate evidence.

hearing the process by which sound waves are received by the ear.

hidden agenda an ulterior motive.

hypothetical illustration an imaginary scenario that illuminates a point.

hypothetical narrative imaginary story related to help listeners visualize a potential situation.

I

imagery words that evoke mental pictures or images.

impromptu method speaking with little or no preparation.

induction reasoning from specific evidence to a general conclusion.

infinitive a verb form beginning with "to."

inflated language words designed to puff up the importance of the person or thing being described.

information chart text material arranged as a series of key points.

inspirational speech an address that tries to stimulate listeners to a high level of feeling or activity.

interference anything that obstructs accurate communication of a message.

interlibrary loan sharing of materials and services among libraries.

internal summary a concise review of material covered during the body of a speech.

intonation the use of changing pitch to convey meaning.

J

jargon the technical language of a group or profession.

K

keyword a word looked for in a search command.

L

line graph a visual consisting of lines (charted on a grid) that show trends.

listener the receiver of the speaker's message.

listening the act of interpreting and evaluating what is being said.

M

main points key assertions made by a speaker to develop his or her central idea.

manuscript method delivery of a speech by reading a script.

Maslow's hierarchy of needs a ranking of human needs from simple to complex.

mean in a set of numbers, the sum of all figures divided by the number of figures.

median the number that falls in the middle of a numerical ranking.

message whatever is communicated verbally and nonverbally to the listener.

metaphor a comparison implying similarity between two things.

minutes written record of what occurred at a meeting.

mixed metaphor incongruously combined metaphors.

mode the figure that appears most frequently in a set of figures.

motivated sequence a series of steps designed to propel a listener toward accepting the speaker's proposition.

motivations the impulses and needs that stimulate a person to act in a certain way.

N

narrative a story that illustrates a point.

nonverbal communication transmission of messages without words.

O

open-ended question a question that permits a broad range of responses.

opinion a conclusion or judgment that remains open to dispute but seems true to one's own mind.

oral footnote a spoken citation of the source of one's material.

orienting material the part of the introduction that gives listeners the information they need to fully understand and believe the rest of the speech.

overt-response question a question asked to elicit a direct, immediate reply.

P

panel discussion consideration of a topic by a small group in the presence of an audience.

parallel language equivalent grammatical forms to express equivalent ideas.

parallel structure equivalent grammatical forms used to express ideas of equal importance.

paraphrase to restate material, using different words.

percentage a rate or proportion per hundred.

persuasion the process of influencing, changing, or reinforcing listeners' attitudes, beliefs, or behaviors.

pictorial graph a visual that dramatizes statistical data by means of pictorial forms.

pie graph a circle showing a given whole that is divided into component wedges.

pitch the highness or lowness of a sound.

plagiarism stealing the ideas or words of another and passing them off as one's own.

positive imagery visualization of successful actions.

positive nervousness useful energy.

posture the position of your body as you sit or stand.

preview a preliminary look at the highlights of a speech.

problem–solution pattern an arrangement of material that explores a problem and then offers a solution.

process speech an oral presentation that analyzes how to do something or how something works.

progressive revelation piece-by-piece unveiling of a visual.

pronunciation correct way of speaking a word.

public domain what is owned by the community at large; unprotected by patent or copyright.

Q

quote verbatim to cite the exact words used by a source.

R

reasoning using logic to draw conclusions from evidence.

red herring diverting listeners from the real issue to an irrelevant matter.

reference librarian a specialist in information retrieval.

reflective-thinking method a structured system for solving problems.

repetition repeating words or phrases for emotional effect.

rhetorical question a question asked solely to stimulate interest and not to elicit a reply.

royalty-free devoid of restrictions or fees.

S

scapegoat an individual or a group that innocently bears the blame of others.

search engine a service that lets you search for keywords on Web pages throughout the world.

self-actualization the need of humans to make the most of their abilities.

sexist language words based on gender stereotypes.

sex-related stereotype generalization that assigns roles or characteristics to people on the basis of gender.

signpost an explicit statement of the place that a speaker has reached.

simile a comparison, using *like* or *as,* of otherwise dissimilar things.

situation the setting in which communication takes place.

slippery slope one action will initiate a chain of events that will result in a tragic ending.

spatial pattern an arrangement of information in terms of physical space, such as top to bottom.

speaker the originator of a message sent to a listener.

speaking notes brief reminders of the points a speaker plans to cover during a speech.

specific purpose the precise goal that a speaker wants to achieve.

speech of acceptance oral remarks made by the recipient of an award or honor.

speech of introduction a brief talk that introduces a speaker to an audience.

speech of presentation an address designed to formally present an award or honor.

speech of refutation an oral counterargument against a concept or proposition put forth by others.

speech of tribute an oration in praise of someone or something.

speech to influence thinking an oral presentation aimed at winning intellectual assent for a concept or proposition.

speech to motivate action an oral presentation that tries to impel listeners to take action.

spotlight a device that alerts listeners to important points.

statement-of-reasons pattern a variation of the topical pattern in which a speaker gives reasons for an idea.

statistics numerical facts assembled to present significant information about a subject.

stereotype an oversimplified or exaggerated image.

straw man a weak opponent or dubious argument set up so that it can be easily defeated.

subject directory a list of websites categorized by subject.

summarize to give the substance of a statement in condensed form.

support material elements that illustrate or substantiate a point.

syllogism a deductive scheme consisting of a major premise, a minor premise, and a conclusion.

symposium a meeting featuring short addresses by different people on the same topic.

T

table numbers or words arranged systematically in rows and columns.

taboo an act, word, or object that is forbidden on grounds of morality or taste.

team presentation a well-coordinated presentation made by members of a group who focus on a common goal.

testimonial a statement supporting a benefit received.

testimony statement by a knowledgeable person, used by a speaker to explain or bolster a point.

topical pattern a division of a topic into components, types, or reasons.

topic outline a systematic arrangement of ideas, using words and phrases for headings and subheadings.

transition an expression that links ideas and shows the relationship between them.

transparency clear sheets on which visuals are drawn or printed, and then viewed by light shining from an overhead projector.

V

verbal fillers vocalized pauses in which a speaker inserts sounds such as "uh."

visual presenter a device capable of producing images of both two- and three-dimensional objects.

vivid image a description that evokes a lifelike picture within the mind of the listener.

vlog frequently updated video log.

End Notes

Preface

1. David E. Schneider, "Assessing the Readability of College Textbooks in Public Speaking: Attending to Entry Level Instruction," *Communication Teacher,* Vol. 25, Nos. 1–4, January–December, 2011, pp. 245–254.

Chapter 1

1. "Making a Difference: Abigail Hardin," NBC13.com, Birmingham, Alabama. Video, nbc13.com (accessed May 6, 2011); Abigail Hardin, e-mail interview, January 31, 2010; "Founder," Open My Eyes Foundation, www.openmyeyesfoundation.org (accessed May 6, 2011).

2. Abigail Cole Hardin, *Look at Me; I Am Just Like You* (Jackson, MS: Pecan Row Press, 2009), pp. 1–30.

3. The Sharpe quote appears on the book jacket of *Look at Me; I Am Just Like You.*

4. In author's e-mail survey (February–March 2000) of 742 business and professional speakers, 487 said that, in college, they had taken either a public speaking course or a communication course with a public speaking component; of the 487 who had received training, 91 percent rated the course as "highly valuable."

5. Gerhard Gschwandtner, *The Pocket Sales Mentor* (New York: McGraw-Hill, 2006), p. 199.

6. Ann L. Darling and Deanna P. Dannels, "Practicing Engineers Talk about the Importance of Talk: A Report on Oral Communication in the Workplace," *Communication Education,* January 2003, pp. 1–16; "Oral Communication Skills Rank First among Employers," results of survey of Fortune 500 companies by National Association of Colleges and Employers, www.naceweb.org (accessed March 15, 2008).

7. Marilyn Mackes, executive director, National Association of Colleges and Employers, e-mail interview, January 22, 2009.

8. Cristina Silva, human resources manager, Camillus Enterprises, Los Angeles, in "The Manager's Tutorial," www.managercoaching.org (accessed March 19, 2008).

9. Karen Walker was a student in the author's public speaking class.

10. John Locke, 17th-century English philosopher, "Essay Concerning Human Understanding," electronic text posted by Oregon State University, www.orst.edu/instruct/phl302/texts/locke/locke1/Book3a.html (accessed December 2, 2011).

11. Michael O'Malley, *Creating Commitment: How to Attract and Retain Talented Employees* (New York: Wiley, 2000), p. 59.

12. Slogan used in an advertisement by Hitachi, Ltd., Tokyo, Japan (undated).

13. David W. Richardson, management consultant, Westport, Connecticut, e-mail interview, May 9, 2000.

14. Jack Brilhart et al., "Ethics in Public Speaking," supplementary materials for COM115 at Southwest Missouri State University, com115.missouristate.edu/31374.htm (accessed January 25, 2009).

15. *Aesop's Fables—Online Collection,* www.pacificnet.net/~johnr/aesop (accessed March 16, 2008).

16. Will Rogers, quoted at *Quotation World,* s-2000.com/quoteworld (accessed March 16, 2008).

17. Corey Rangel, "Homeless Tempe Man Turns in Backpack with $3,300," KNXV-TV, Phoenix, Arizona, www.abc15.com (accessed November 8, 2011).

18. James ("Doc") Blakely, professional speaker, Wharton, Texas, e-mail interview, November 13, 2007.

Chapter 2

1. Carl Edwards, telephone interview, March 29, 2011.

2. Ibid.

3. The term *stage fright* originated in the world of theater, but it is used today to designate the nervousness or fear experienced by a person before or during an appearance in front of any kind of audience. Other terms that are sometimes used to describe this condition are *speech fright, speech anxiety,* and *communication apprehension.*

4. Graham D. Bodie, "A Racing Heart, Rattling Knees, and Ruminative Thoughts: Defining, Explaining, and Treating Public Speaking Anxiety," *Communication Education,* January 2010, p. 70; Lars Lindberg Christensen, *The Hands-on Guide for Science Communicators* (New York: Springer, 2007), p. 167.

5. Reggie Jackson, interview during an ABC sports telecast, October 2, 1984.

6. Garth Brooks, quoted by PublicSpeakingSkills.com, www.publicspeakingskills.com (accessed May 6, 2011).

7. Elayne Snyder, *Speak for Yourself—with Confidence* (New York: New American Library, 1983), p. 113.

8. I. A. R. Wylie, quoted by Pushp Lata, *Communicate or Collapse: A Handbook of Effective Public Speaking* (New Delhi: Prentice-Hall of India, 2007), p. 22.

9. Adair Linn Nagata, "Cultivating Confidence in Public Communication," *Journal of Intercultural Communication,* No.7, 2004, pp. 177–197.

10. Joel Weldon, professional speaker, Scottsdale, Arizona, e-mail interview, December 4, 2000.

11. Ibid.

12. Tammie Ronen, *The Positive Power of Imagery* (New York: John Wiley and Sons, 2011), p. 46.

13. "11 Celebrities You Would Never Guess Are Shy," The Frisky, www.thefrisky.com (accessed August 5, 2011); "Introvert or Extrovert," *Los Angeles Times,* February 25, 2003, p. 1; Philip Zimbardo, *Psychology and Life,* 11th ed. (Glenview, IL: Scott, Foresman, 1985), p. 448.

14. Joe W. Boyd, professional speaker, Bellingham, Washington, e-mail interview, December 4, 2000.

15. Johnny Lee, director of Peace at Work, Raleigh, North Carolina, personal interview, October 5, 2005.

16. Carlos Jimenez, member of Toastmasters International, quoted in Toastmasters District 39 (Northern California) online newsletter, www.district39.org (accessed October 3, 2005).

17. Matthew T. Feldner and Michael J. Zvolensky, " Prevention of Anxiety Psychopathology: A Critical Review of the Empirical Literature," *Clinical Psychology: Science and Practice,* December 2004, pp. 405–424.

18. Henry Heimlich, M.D., Cincinnati, Ohio, telephone interview, January 8, 2000.

19. Danielle Kennedy, professional speaker, Sun Valley, Idaho, e-mail interview, June 8, 2000.

20. Michael T. Motley, "Taking the Terror out of Talk," *Psychology Today,* January 1988, p. 49.

21. Colette R. Hirsch, et al, "Self-Images Play a Causal Role in Social Phobia," *Behaviour Research and Therapy,* August 2003, pp. 909–921.

22. Dick Cavett, quoted in "Talk Shows: Dick Cavett," www.talkshows .about.com/tvradio/talkshows/msubcavett.htm (accessed October 3, 2005).

23. David Segal, "Verdict: The Defense Can't Rest Too Often," *Washington Post On-Line,* www.washingtonpost.com (accessed April 5, 2008).

24. Earl Nightingale, *Communicate What You Think* (Chicago: Nightingale-Conant Corp., 2001), Audiocassette #11.

25. Maggie Paley, "Modern Image Signal: Voice," *Vogue,* August 1984, p. 412.

26. Motley, "Taking the Terror out of Talk," p. 49.

Chapter 3

1. Samantha Rudolph, Associate Director of Stats and Information, ESPN network, e-mail interview, February 15, 2011.

2. The professor who sent her class to the presentation requested that her name and college not be identified.

3. Keith Davis, quoted in "How to Be a Better Listener," The Small Business Knowledge Base, www.bizmove.com (accessed October 5, 2005).

4. Lyman K. Steil, "Your Personal Listening Profile," booklet published by Sperry Corporation, undated, p. 5.

5. Owen Hargie and David Dickson, *Skilled Interpersonal Communication: Research, Theory, and Practice* (New York: Routledge, 2004), pp. 170–173.

6. Quoted by James O'Rourke, *The Truth About Confident Presenting* (Upper Saddle River, NJ: FT Press, 2008), p. 62.

7. Rona F. Flippo and David C. Caverly, editors, *Handbook of College Reading and Study Strategy Research,* 2nd ed. (New York: Routledge, 2009), p. 236; Andreas Kapardis, *Psychology and Law: A Critical Introduction,* 3rd ed. (Cambridge: Cambridge University Press, 2010), p. 189.

8. Alex Williams, "At Meetings, It's Mind Your Blackberry or Mind Your Manners," *New York Times,* June 22, 2009, p. 1.

9. Helene Hembrooke and Geri Gay, "The Laptop and the Lecture: The Effects of Multitasking in Learning Environments," *Journal of Computing in Higher Education* 15 (Fall 2003), presented online at www.hci.cornell.edu (accessed October 8, 2005).

10. David E. Mayer, director of the Brain, Cognition and Action Laboratory at the University of Michigan, and René Marois, director of the Human Information Processing Laboratory at Vanderbilt University, as quoted by Steve Lohr, "Slow Down, Multitasker, Especially If You're Reading This in Traffic," *New York Times,* March 25, 2007, p. 1.

11. René Marois, PhD, Department of Psychology, Vanderbilt University, quoted by Dave Crenshaw, *The Myth of Multitasking* (San Francisco: Jossey-Bass, 2008), p. 18.

12. Christine Pearson, "Sending a Message That You Don't Care," *New York Times,* May 16, 2010, p. BU-9; Blue Avocado (Food-for-Thought for Nonprofits), "Ground Rules for the New Generation," www.blueavocado.org (accessed March 6, 2012); Donald G. Zauderer, "Workplace Incivility and the Management of Human Capital," *The Public Manager,* Spring 2002, pp. 36–42.

13. Christine Pearson and Christine Porath, *The Cost of Bad Behavior* (New York: Portfolio, 2009), p. 111.

14. Alex Williams, "At Meetings, It's Mind Your Blackberry or Mind Your Manners," *New York Times,* June 22, 2009, p. 1.

15. Sandra Chapman, "Judge Loses Job Over Texting During Hearings," wthr.com Eyewitness News (Indianapolis, IN), www.wthr .com (accessed September 21, 2011).

16. Hank London, "To Tweet or Not to Tweet?" Hank London's Blog, http://hanklondon.com (accessed February 5, 2012).

17. Anonymous speaker quoted by Ronald B. Adler and Jeanne Marquardt Elmhorst, *Communicating at Work,* 8th ed. (New York: McGraw-Hill, 2005), p. 125.

Chapter 4

1. Apolo Ohno, telephone interview, March 15, 2011.

2. Katherine Long, "Apolo Ohno Delivers Anti-Drinking Message at Bellevue School," *The Seattle Times,* March 12, 2010, p. 8.

3. Greg Anrig Jr., "Taxpayers' Revenge," in *How to Manage Your Taxes,* a booklet published by *Money* magazine, undated, pp. 2–3.

4. Ibid.

5. Kitty O. Locker, *Business and Administrative Communication,* 5th ed. (New York: McGraw-Hill, 2000), p. 45.

6. Fred Ebel, "Know Your Audience," *Toastmaster,* June 1985, p. 20.

7. Perry Garfinkel, "On Keeping Your Foot Safely out of Your Mouth," *New York Times,* July 13, 2004, p. C7.

8. "Cultural Diversity and Racial Sensitivity," Texas Commission on Law Enforcement Officer Standards and Education, www. utexas.edu/cee/dec/tcleose/cultdiv/chp2.html (accessed August 5, 2000); "Non-Verbal Communication Modes," article posted for Intercultural Business Relations course at Andrews University, www2.andrews.edu/~tidwell/bsad560/NonVerbal.html (accessed August 5, 2000).

9. Edward Daimler, travel agent, San Diego, California, telephone interview, September 12, 2005.

10. Axtell is quoted in Mary Ellen Guffey, *Business Communication,* 5th ed. (Mason, OH: Thomson South-Western, 2006), p. 116.

11. LaTresa Pearson, "Think Globally, Present Locally," *Presentations,* April 1996, p. 22.

12. Ibid., p. 27.

13. Scott H. Lewis, "Toastmasters of Disability," Toastmasters International Tips & Techniques, www.toastmasters.org (accessed September 11, 2010).

14. Unattributed advice was featured on an Easter Seals calendar, published by Easter Seals, an organization devoted to people with disabilities.

15. Deborah L. Harmon, *Serving Students with Disabilities* (Asheville, NC: Asheville-Buncombe Technical Community College, 1994), pp. 7–9.

16. Ibid., p. 9.

17. Ibid.

18. Helen Sloss Luey et al., "Hard-of-Hearing or Deaf," *Social Work,* March 1995, p. 177.

19. Harmon, *Serving Students with Disabilities,* p. 9.

20. Sharon Lynn Campbell, "Helping the Toastmaster of Disability," *Toastmaster,* February 1993, p. 15.

21. Thomas Leech, San Diego, California, consultant, "Tips and Articles," Winning Presentations, www.winningpresentations .com (accessed December 2, 2000).

22. Information about Dorsey's speech was gathered by the Marketing and Communications Department, Georgia Southern University, May 1, 2001.

23. Felicia R. Lee, "Comedian Conversation Falls Flat at 92nd Street Y," *New York Times,* December 1, 2010, p. A27.

24. John Naber, professional speaker, Pasadena, California, telephone interview, November 12, 2000.

Chapter 5

1. Christo Coetzer, e-mail interview, November 5, 2011.

2. Anne C. Paine, "Oberlin's First Volcanologist Seeks Answers to Eruptive Questions," Oberlin College, www.oberlin.edu/ colrelat/ats/story/castro.html (accessed April 11, 2003).

3. Michio Kaku, *Physics of the Future* (New York: Doubleday, 2011), pp. 160–164 [Kaku, a professor of theoretical physics at City College of New York, gathered ideas from more than 300 experts in many different scientific fields]; Marcus Hall (ed.), *Restoration and History* (New York: Routledge, 2010), pp. 288–230.

4. Adapted from an advertisement by United Technologies Corporation in *The Wall Street Journal,* date unavailable.

Chapter 6

1. Jennifer Zwilling, personal correspondence and e-mail, March 2008; "2007 BRICK Award Winner: Jennifer Zwilling," How-StuffWorks website, people.howstuffworks.com (accessed April 21, 2008); Linda Saslow, "Two Students Honored for Scientific Projects," *New York Times,* December 11, 2005, p. 14LI.8; Rhoda Amon, "Teen Spreads Awareness of Tourette," *Newsday* (Melville, NY), June 3, 2007. Posted on *Newsday.com* (accessed April 22, 2008).

2. Carole Campbell, former student in the author's public speaking class, personal interview, October 26, 2005.

3. Roberta Larson Duyff, *American Dietetic Association Complete Food and Nutrition Guide, 3rd ed.* (Hoboken, NJ: John Wiley & Sons, Inc., 2006), p. 409.

4. Kathy Herrlich, Research and Instruction Department, Northeastern University, "Search Tips," Northeastern University Library website, www.lib.neu.edu/online_research/help/search_ tips (accessed January 5, 2006).

5. The graphic was created by the author to represent what a typical preview looks like online; the words are by Walter Isaacson, *Benjamin Franklin: An American Life* (New York: Simon & Schuster, 2003), p. 36.

6. Jennifer Brooks, "VU Medical Students Slash Food Budgets for Week," *The Tennessean* (Nashville), www.tennessean.com (accessed July 16, 2011).

7. Kathleen Brady was a student in the author's public speaking class.

Chapter 7

1. Layla Merritt, "How to Train Your Brain," *Psychology Today* website, www.psychologytoday.com/articles (accessed August 8, 2011).

2. Scott O. Lilienfeld, Barry L. Beyerstein, et al., *50 Great Myths of Popular Psychology* (New York: Wiley-Blackwell, 2010). p. 22; Robynne Boyd, "Do People Only Use 10 Percent of Their Brains?" *Scientific American* online, www.scientificamerican.com (accessed October 18, 2011).

3. Allen St. John, *The Billion Dollar Game: Behind the Scenes of the Greatest Day in American Sport—Super Bowl Sunday* (New York: Random House, 2010), pp. 44–45; "Increase of Violence Against Women on Super Bowl Sunday is a Myth," SciNewsBlog, scinewsblog.blogspot.com (accessed July 9, 2011).

4. "Duct tape, warts and all," *Harvard Health Letter,* July 2007, p. 5.

5. Jared Sandberg, "Despite Success Stories, Working with a Spouse Is Very Risky Business," *The Wall Street Journal,* January 24, 2006, p. B1.

6. Kathy Frankovic, "To Tell the Truth to Pollsters," *CBS News,* (www.cbsnews.com), August 15, 2007, (accessed May 22, 2008); "Federal Elections 2004," Federal Election Commission, www. fec.gov (accessed May 21, 2008); Gordon S. Wood, "American Religion: The Great Retreat," *New York Review of Books,* June 8, 2006, p. 60.

7. José Ramón Sánchez, *Boricua Power* (New York: NYU Press, 2007), pp. 182–183.

8. Kathi Ames, "Lying with Polls," *Poll Watchers,* www.pollwatchers .com (accessed February 3, 2009); "Social Security," *ProCon.org,* socialsecurity.procon.org (accessed February 26, 2012).

9. "Overpasses and Tornado Safety – Not a Good Mix," National Weather Service, Dodge City, Kansas, www.crh.noaa.gov (accessed August 6, 2011); for an example of bad advice, see "The Big Tornadoes—Part1," uploaded to YouTube by ColonelAngus75, www.youtube.com (accessed August 6, 2011).

10. Michele Pullia Turk, "Ephedrine's Deadly Edge," *U.S. News Online,* www.usnews.com (accessed February 8, 2009).

11. "Moms for Mercury," *The Progressive,* December 2007, p. 10.

12. Laura Bird, "Corporate Critics Complain Companies Hide behind 'Grass-Roots' Campaigns," *The Wall Street Journal Online,* interactive.wsj.com (accessed January 28, 2006).

13. "Kidney Stealing Hoax," Hoax-Slayer website, www.hoax-slayer .com (accessed August 16, 2011).

14. Bunko Squad, "Quackery," Wellness Web, www.wellweb.com/ ALTERN/bunko/bunko.htm (accessed January 28, 2006).

15. Geoffrey Nunberg, "Teaching Students to Swim in the Online Sea," *New York Times,* February 13, 2005, p. WK-4.

16. "Purple Grape Juice May Help Prevent Heart Attacks," Reuters news report, March 18, 1997, at Electric Library, www.elibrary .com (accessed September 22, 2000).

17. David Emery, "Is a Dog's Mouth Cleaner than a Human's?" About. com (http://urbanlegends.about.com) (accessed August 23, 2011).

18. The Modern Language Association of America, *MLA Style Manual and Guide to Scholarly Publishing,* 3rd ed. (New York: The Modern Language Association of America, 2008), pp. 165–167; Rob Kitchin and Duncan Fuller, *The Academic's Guide to Publishing* (Thousand Oaks, CA: Sage Publications, 2005), pp. 32–34.

19. Codi Wilson, "Medical Dean's Convocation Speech Angers U of A Students," Edmonton Journal, June 13, 2011, www.edmontonjournal.com, (accessed August 24, 2011); Sarah Boesveld, "University of Alberta Medical School Dean Resigns After Plagiarizing Speech," National Post, June 17, 2011, http://news.nationalpost.com (accessed August 24, 2011).

20. The observation that over a dozen ministers had resigned is based on the number of different cases reported in articles in Internet news archives; Mike Woodruff and Steve Moore, "An Honest Sermon: Plagiarism, the Pulpit, and How to Appropriate Others' Ideas Appropriately," Christianity Today Library, January 1, 2003, www.ctlibrary.com (accessed May 6, 2008); Michael Luo, "Pastor Who Plagiarized Finds a Church Willing to Forgive," *New York Times,* July 28, 2006, p. A25; Richard C. Dujardin, "Minister resigns over plagiarized sermons," *Providence Journal,* April 28, 2007, p. 1; Suzanne Sataline, "That Sermon You Heard on Sunday May Be from the Web," *The Wall Street Journal,* November 15, 2006, p. 1.

21. Tamar Lewin, "Hamilton President Resigns over Speech," *New York Times,* October 3, 2002, p. B10; Jonathan Margulies, "Hamilton President Apologizes for Failing to Cite Sources in Speech," *Chronicle of Higher Education,* October 4, 2002, p. A34; Denise K. Magner, "Plagiarism Charge Prompts President of Hastings College to Retire," *Chronicle of Higher Education,* March 3, 2000, p. A39; Darrin Culmer, "COB Acting President's Term Extended," *The Bahama Journal Online,* January 11, 2006, www.jonesbahamas.com (accessed January 19, 2006).

22. "How to Avoid Plagiarism," Information Technology Services, Penn State University, tlt.its.psu.edu/suggestions/cyberplag/cyberplagexamples.html (accessed February 11, 2009).

23. "Erma Bombeck," The Quotations Page, www.quotationspage.com/quotes/Erma_Bombeck (accessed February 11, 2009).

24. The Modern Language Association of America, *MLA Style Manual and Guide to Scholarly Publishing,* 3rd ed. (New York: The Modern Language Association of America, 2008) pp. 34–59.

25. "When Works Pass into the Public Domain," University of North Carolina Library, www.unc.edu/~unclng/public-d.htm (accessed February 11, 2009).

26. "Copyright Information and Education," University of Minnesota Libraries, www.lib.umn.edu/copyright (accessed February 11, 2009).

27. Steven Blaize, "Who Owns Rita Hayworth? Multimedia Rights: Yours and Theirs," *Digital Video,* November 1994, p. 63.

Chapter 8

1. Sandi Doughton and Danny O'Neil, "Seahawks Fans' Frenzy Felt by Seismometer," *The Seattle Times,* January 10, 2011, p. 1.

2. Rebecca Hale derived her material from Bill Bryson, *A Short History of Nearly Everything* (New York: Broadway Books, 2003), p. 239.

3. Dave Sowders, "Potpourri," *Houston Chronicle,* June 3, 2008, p. A2.

4. The dolphin information was derived from Natalie Angier, "A Highly Evolved Propensity for Deceit," *New York Times,* December 23, 2008, p. D1.

5. "Miracle of Parisian Toddler Surviving Seven-Story Fall," *France Today,* www.france-today.com, posted November 3, 2010 (accessed October 21, 2011).

6. Katrina Benjamin was interviewed by student speaker Diane Woolsey.

7. Information was derived from Felicity Barringer, "Demand for Wind Spurs Ranchers to Join Forces," *New York Times,* November 28, 2008, p. 1.

8. Joshua Quittner, "Cracks in the Net," *Time,* February 27, 1995, p. 34.

9. Jessica M. Utts and Robert F. Heckard, *Mind on Statistics* (South Melbourne, Australia: Cengage, 2011), p. 123.

10. Arnold Barnett, professor, Massachusetts Institute of Technology, "How Numbers Are Tricking You," *Technology Review,* www.techreview.com (accessed February 11, 2009).

11. Astronomer Fred Hoyle, quoted in *Quotations Page,* www.quotationspage.com (accessed February 11, 2009).

Chapter 9

1. Erico Guizzo, "Meet Geminoid F, a Smiling Female Android." *IEEE Spectrum,* spectrum.ieee.org (accessed December 15, 2011).

2. Shu-Ling Lai, "Influence of Audio-Visual Presentations on Learning Abstract Concepts," *International Journal of Instructional Media* 27 (2000), pp. 199–206.

3. Experiment conducted by the author using two groups, each composed of 40 students; see also Mark Gellevij, et al., "Multimodal versus Unimodal Instructions in a Complex Learning Context," *Journal of Experimental Education* 70 (2002), pp. 215–39.

4. Rune Pettersson, *Information Design: An Introduction* (Amsterdam, The Netherlands: John Benjamins Publishing Company, 2002), pp. 103–104; Stephen Petrina, *Advanced Teaching Methods for the Technology Classroom* (Hershey, PA: Idea Group, Inc., 2006), pp. 12–13.

5. Linda Larson, instructor, Mesa Community College, personal interview, August 20, 2004.

6. Bill Howard, "On Technology: PowerPoint," *PCMAG.com,* pcmag.com (accessed February 17, 2009).

7. Kara Rogers, *The Eye: The Physiology of Human Perception* (New York: The Rosen Publishing Group, 2011), p. 192; "Colour Blindness," *Biology Online,* www.biology-online.org (accessed December 16, 2011).

8. Chris MacGregor, *The Flash Usability Guide* (New York: Springer, 2003) p. 7; Faber Birren, *Functional Color* (Whitefish, Montana: Kessinger Publishing, 2006), p. 46.

9. E. Michael Smith, M.D., Department of Psychiatry and Behavioral Sciences, University of Oklahoma Health Services Center, e-mail interview, June 3, 2008; Martin Lindstrom, *Brand Sense: Build Powerful Brands through Touch, Taste, Smell, Sight, and Sound* (New York: Simon and Schuster, 2005), pp. 99–110.

Chapter 9 Appendix

1. Jared Sandberg, "Tips for PowerPoint," *Wall Street Journal,* November 14, 2006, p. B1; Ellen Neuborne, "Top Four PowerPoint Gaffes," *Sales & Marketing Management,* June 2003, p. 22.

2. Lance Secretan, "Inspirational Teaching," *Industry Week,* May 21, 2001, p. 19.

3. Jan Caldwell, public speaking instructor, Asheville-Buncombe Technical Community College, e-mail interview, January 30, 2012.

Chapter 10

1. Astronaut José Hernández, telephone interview, January 4, 2011.

2. Wesley J. Smith, attorney, Los Angeles, e-mail interview, September 10, 2007.

3. Experiment, conducted by the author, replicates numerous psychologists' studies, which reach the same conclusion.

4. Miriam J. Metzger, Andrew J. Flanagin, Keren Eyal, Daisy R. Lemus, and Robert M. McCann (all of University of California, Santa Barbara), "Credibility for the 21st Century: Integrating Perspectives on Source, Message, and Media Credibility in the Contemporary Media Environment," *Communication Yearbook 27* (Mahwah, NJ: Lawrence Erlbaum Associates, Inc., 2003), p. 302.

5. "An Intolerable Fraud" [Editorial], *New York Times,* February 8, 2008, p. A.18.

6. Marti Davis, "Local Charity Called Bogus," Knoxnews.com, December 29, 2007 (accessed August 4, 2008).

7. Used with permission from student Wendy Trujillo, who derived her information from Jane E. Brody, "Health 'Facts' You Only Thought You Knew," *New York Times,* July 22, 2008, p. D7; "Ear Injuries," Data & Statistics Division, Centers for Disease Control and Prevention, www.cdc.gov/datastatistics (accessed July 3, 2008); John Wendle, "The Things We Put in Our Ears May or May Not Hurt Us," Columbia News Service, jscms.jrn.columbia.edu (accessed July 3, 2008); Laura Lee, *100 Most Dangerous Things in Everyday Life and What You Can Do About Them* (Sydney: Murdoch Books, 2004), p. 50; "Giants Linebacker Injures His Ear," *New York Times,* October 4, 2007, p. D2; "A Cotton Swab in the Ear Can Kill, Quebec Coroner Says," Canadian Broadcasting Corporation, www.cbc.ca/news (accessed July 3, 2008).

8. Marcia Yudkin, "Eschew Podium Odium," Toastmasters International Website, www.toastmasters.org (accessed September 10, 2007).

Chapter 11

1. Mike McCurley and Diana S. Friedman, attorneys, Dallas, Texas, in "The Art of Persuasion," American Academy of Matrimonial Lawyers, www.aaml.org/ (accessed September 22, 2008).

2. Michelle Roberts, Washington, DC, attorney, telephone interview, May 19, 2000; David Segal, "Verdict: The Defense Can't Rest Too Often," Washington Post On-Line, www.washingtonpost.com (accessed September 19, 2008).

3. Myrna Marofsky, president, ProGroup, e-mail interview, September 22, 2008.

4. The student's material was derived from Bill Bryson, *A Short History of Nearly Everything* (New York: Broadway Books, 2003), pp. 282–286, and an e-mail interview with Daniel Pauly, a marine biologist at the University of British Columbia in Vancouver.

5. Cynthia Wray, Western Carolina University, gave permission for this excerpt to be used.

6. Sullivan derived her material from R. C. Lewontin, "The Confusion over Cloning," *New York Review of Books,* October 23, 1997, p. 18.

7. Ingemar Svantesson, *Learning Maps and Memory Skills,* 3rd ed. (London: Kogan Page, 2004), p. 90.

8. Edward L. Friedman, quoted by Marlin Coast (Australia) Toastmasters Club, www.marlincoastcairns.com (accessed September 22, 2008).

Chapter 12

1. Bill Bryson, *At Home: A Short History of Private Life* (New York: Doubleday, 2010), p. 234.

2. Hans Friedrich Ebel, Claus Bliefert, and William E. Russey, *The Art of Scientific Writing* (New York: Wiley, 2004), pp. 88–89.

Chapter 13

1. "Living Up to Her Legacy: Alexandra Cousteau," The Outside Blog, *Outside* magazine, www.outsideonline.com (accessed January 25, 2012).

2. J. Alexander Tanford, Indiana University School of Law, *The Trial Process: Law, Tactics, and Ethics,* 3rd ed. (Newark, NJ: Lexis-Nexis, 2002), p. 47.

3. Anthony Pratkanis and Elliot Aronson, *Age of Propaganda: The Everyday Use and Abuse of Persuasion* (New York: Macmillan, 2001), p. 33.

4. Edward Dolnick, "Fish or Foul?" *New York Times,* September 2, 2008, p. A23.

5. C. J. Ducasse, quoted in Thoughts to Ponder, www.math.louisville.edu/~barnes/quotes.html (accessed October 7, 2008).

6. Unidentified speaker at EXPO 2008, August 19, 2008, in Zaragoza, Spain, reported by EXPO Zaragoza 2008 Blog, www.expozaragoza2008.es/theblog (accessed October 6, 2008).

7. Dennis Kessinger, "The Agents of Imagery," Toastmasters International, www.toastmasters.org (accessed March 4, 2008).

8. Technically, the term *wetland* can cover marshes and bogs as well as swamps, but in popular usage, *wetland* is a synonym for *swamp.*

9. Don Bagin, "Here's a Frightful Implication," Communication Briefings, www.briefings.com (accessed October 2, 2008).

10. William Raspberry, *Washington Post* columnist, quoted by Pellissippi State Writing Lab, www.pstcc.edu (accessed October 3, 2008).

11. John V. Thill and Courtland L. Bovée, *Excellence in Business Communication,* 7th ed. (Upper Saddle River, NJ: Pearson/Prentice Hall, 2007), p. 148.

12. Edward T. Thompson, "How to Write Clearly," reprint of advertisement by International Paper Company, undated.

13. William Zinsser, *On Writing Well,* revised. ed. (New York: HarperCollins, 2006), p. 68.

14. *Doublespeak* is a hybrid word based on "doublethink" and "newspeak" from George Orwell's novel *1984.*

15. Sheldon Rampton and John Stauber, *Trust Us, We're Experts!* (New York: Jeremy P. Tarcher/Putnam, 2001), p. 292.

16. William Lutz, *Doublespeak* (New York: Harper, 1989), pp. 2–3.

17. Eliza A. Comodromos, *Instructor's Manual for The Longman Writer Rhetoric and Reader,* 5th ed. (New York: Longman, 2003), p. 77.

18. Timothy Egan, "Political Parties See Votes in National Parks, and Park Veterans Join Debate," *New York Times,* June 19, 2004, p. A10.

19. Lutz, *Doublespeak,* p. 6.

20. Lutz, *Doublespeak,* p. 6.

21. "He's Not Old, He's Chronologically Gifted," Economist.com, www.economist.com, (accessed October 5, 2008).

22. "Domino's Careers," Domino's Pizza, www.dominosbiz.com (accessed October 20, 2008).

23. Janet Turpin, financial analyst, Chicago, personal interview, July 18, 2008.

24. Samuel Abt, "Armstrong's Lead Unchanged After the Pyrenees," *New York Times,* July 20, 2005, p. C21.

25. E. Gordon Gee, quoted in "Commencement 2005," *Chronicle of Higher Education,* July 1, 2005, p. B2.

26. Bergen Evans and Cornelia Evans, *A Dictionary of Contemporary American Usage* (New York: Random House, 1957), p. 258.

27. Lynn Quitman Troyka, *Simon & Schuster Handbook for Writers,* 3rd ed. (Englewood Cliffs, NJ: Prentice Hall, 1993), p. 425.

28. Mixed Metaphors, Calvin College English Department, www.calvin.edu/academic/engl/lang/mixmet.htm (accessed October 20, 2008).

Chapter 14

1. Helene Cooper, "Figure Skater Is New Envoy of Good Will Overseas," *New York Times,* November 10, 2006, p. 10; Gary Mihoces, "Kwan Skates to Ambassador's Role," *USA Today,* posted online on USA Today website, usatoday.com (accessed April 22, 2008); Michelle Kwan, interview on "The View," ABC, April 12, 2006; "Michelle Speaks to MKF," The Michelle Kwan Forum, www.mkforum.net/forum (accessed April 22, 2008).

2. R. T. Kingman, quoted by Thomas Leech, San Diego, California, consultant, in "Tips and Articles," *Winning Presentations,* www.winningpresentations.com (accessed April 6, 2007).

3. Waldo W. Braden, "Abraham Lincoln," in *American Orators before 1900,* ed. Bernard K. Duffy and Halford R. Ryan (New York: Greenwood Press, 1987), p. 267.

4. Simon Sebag Montefiore, *Speeches That Changed the World* (London: Quercus, 2006), p. 91.

5. Arnold "Nick" Carter, professional speaker, Niles, Illinois, e-mail interview, January 13, 2000.

6. "Intercultural Business Communication," RefBy website, www.ref.by (accessed October 30, 2008).

7. Most items in the table are adapted from Jeffrey C. Hahner et al., *Speaking Clearly: Improving Voice and Diction,* 6th ed. (New York: McGraw-Hill, 2002).

8. Yvette Ortiz, Ph.D., telephone interview, January 21, 2000.

9. Debi LaPlante and Nalini Ambady, "Saying It Like It Isn't: Mixed Messages From Men and Women in the Workplace," *Journal of Applied Social Psychology* 32 (2002), pp. 2435–2457; Robert D. Ramsey, *How to Say the Right Thing Every Time: Communicating Well with Students, Staff, Parents, and the Public* (Thousand Oaks, CA: Corwin Press, 2008), p. 214.

10. Janet Stone and Jane Bachner, *Speaking Up* (New York: Carroll and Graf, 1994), p. 62.

11. Dawn E. Waldrop, "What You Wear Is Almost as Important as What You Say," *Presentations,* July 2000, p. 74.

12. Jack Valenti, *Speak Up with Confidence* (New York: Hyperion, 2002), p. 84.

13. Danny Cox, professional speaker, Tustin, California, e-mail interview, February 15, 2000.

14. Dorothy Sarnoff, *Never Be Nervous Again* (New York: Crown, 1987), p. 43.

15. Cristina Stuart, *How to Be an Effective Speaker* (Lincolnwood, IL: NTC Business Books, 1990), p. 67.

Chapter 15

1. Cullen Jones, Olympic Gold Medalist, telephone interview, November 10, 2010.

2. Neurologist Richard Cytowič, "Synesthesia," Cytowič on Synesthesia website, http://cytowic.net (accessed November 19, 2008).

3. From "Our Bodies Are Like Machines," a speech delivered by Rosharna Hazel, Morgan State University, Maryland, in the 1995 Contest of the Interstate Oratorical Association, reprinted from *Winning Orations of the Interstate Oratorical Association,* 1995, pp. 45–47.

4. Chip Heath and Dan Heath, *Made to Stick: Why Some Ideas Take Hold and Others Come Unstuck* (New York: Random House, 2007), pp. 177–187; H. B. Reed, "Meaning as a Factor in Learning," *Journal of Educational Psychology,* December 1992, p. 395.

5. Suzanne Frey, "Nina Totenberg," *Toastmaster,* December 1993, p. 27.

6. Cornelia Dean, "Scientific Savvy? In U.S., Not Much," *New York Times,* August 30, 2005, p. D3.

7. "One in Seven Adult Americans Can't Find the U.S. on a World Map," *National Geographic,* June 2000, p. A-33.

8. Ted Gup, "So Much for the Information Age," *Chronicle of Higher Education,* April 11, 2008, p. A37.

9. Carl Bialik, "How Policy Makers Use Number Analyses to Turn Our Heads," *The Wall Street Journal,* September 7, 2007, p. B1.

10. "Ozone," American Lung Association, www.lung.org/healthy-air/outdoor/resources/ozone.html (accessed March 25, 2012).

Chapter 16

1. William Moss Wilson, "Just Don't Call Her Che," *The New York Times,* January 29, 2012, p. SR-5.

2. Carol Doniek Wydra and Thomas P. Sattler, "Success in Sales," *Fitness World,* www.fitnessworld.com/library (accessed June 16, 2008).

3. Dr. Jerry Tarver in "Writing for Results," *Speechwriter's Newsletter* archives, Lawrence Ragan Communications, www.ragan.com (accessed July 11, 2007).

4. Stuart Oskamp and P. Wesley Schultz, *Attitudes and Opinions* (New York: Psychology Press, 2005), p. 238.

5. Elliot Aronson, social psychologist, quoted by Mark R. Leary, Geoff MacDonald, and June Price Tangney in *Handbook of Self and Identity* (New York: Guilford Press, 2005), p. 283.

6. Linette Lopez, "Meet Molly Katchpole, The 22-Year Old Whose Campaign To Take Down The Big Banks Is Already Working," *Business Insider,* articles.businessinsider.com (accessed Feb. 20, 2012).

7. Tarver, "Writing for Results."

8.   The late Alan H. Monroe, a speech professor, was the author of *Monroe's Principles and Types of Speech,* first published in 1935 by Scott, Foresman.

9.   For ideas and inspiration, special thanks to one of my students, Justine Cucchiara.

Chapter 17

1.   Nate Freeman, "Marine Life Advocate January Jones Makes a Splash in the Huffington Post," *The New York Observer,* www. observor.com (accessed February 7, 2012).

2.   "California: Governor Signs Ban on Shark Fins," *New York Times,* October 8, 2011, p. A12.

3.   Josh Elliott, anchor, ABC Good Morning America, October 10, 2011.

4.   Sandra Blakeslee, "Why Vanishing Sharks Deserve Attention, and Even Affection," *New York Times,* September 6, 2011, p. D3.

5.   Scale adapted from one developed by Sandy Linver, founder of Speakeasy, Inc., a consulting firm with offices in Atlanta and San Francisco (www.speakeasyinc.com).

6.   Mildred M. Cody, Ph.D., R.D., L.D., Nutrition Division Head, Georgia State University, quoted by Kathleen Zelman, "9 Food Poisoning Myths," MedicineNet.com, www.medicinenet.com (accessed January 9, 2009).

7.   Pamela J. Kalbfleisch, Dafna Lemish, and Patricia Sue Parker, *Communication Yearbook 27* (Philadelphia: Lawrence Erlbaum Associates, 2003), p. 302.

8.   Used with permission from Patricia Caldwell.

9.   Diana Fisher, personal interview, October 25, 2005.

10.   Ibid.

11.   Elliot Aronson, *The Social Animal,* 6th ed. (New York: W. H. Freeman & Co., 1992), p. 90.

12.   Ibid., p. 91.

13.   Kenneth T. Broda-Bahm, Daniela Kempf, and William J. Driscoll, *Argument and Audience: Presenting Debates in Public Settings* (New York: International Debate Education Association, 2004), p. 186.

14.   Aristotle, Analytica Posteriora, Book I, in *Introduction to Aristotle* (New York: Modern Library, 1947), pp. 9–34.

15.   The speaker derived her material from Adam Liptak, "Inmate Count in U.S. Dwarfs Other Nations," *New York Times,* (April 23, 2008), p. 1.

16.   Sheryl Feinstein, *The Praeger Handbook of Learning and the Brain: Volume 2* (Westport, CT: Greenwood Publishing Group, 2006), pp. 340–348.

17.   Dolores Albarracin, Blair T. Johnson, and Mark P. Zanna, *The Handbook of Attitudes* (New York: Routledge, 2005), pp. 755–761.

18.   Abraham H. Maslow, *Motivation and Personality* (New York: Harper & Row, 1970).

19.   The speaker derived this story from Christine Dempsey, "Shopper Says Employee Helped, Then Took Card," *Hartford Courant,* www.courant.com (accessed September 24, 2008).

20.   Joe L. Kincheloe and Raymond A. Horn, *The Praeger Handbook of Education and Psychology* (Westport, CT: Greenwood Publishing Group, 2007), p. 593.

21.   Aronson, *The Social Animal,* p. 85.

22.   Albarracin, p. 470.

Chapter 18

1.   Amy Harris and J.B. Wogan, "Rachel Beckwith's Legacy," *The Seattle Times,* August 12, 2011, p. 1; Seattle Times Staff, "Girl's Favored Charity Raises $1.26 Million after Her Death," *The Seattle Times* online, seattletimes.nwsource.com (accessed February 22, 2012).

2.   Speech used with permission of Terry Triplett.

3.   "Wedding Quotations," Famous-Quotes-And-Quotations.Com, www.famous-quotes-and-quotations.com (accessed April 29, 2009).

4.   "Ogden Nash Famous Quotes," QuoteMountain.com, www. quotemountain.com, (accessed April 29, 2009).

5.   Lillian Hunt Chaney and Jeanette S. Martin, *The Essential Guide to Business Etiquette* (New York: Greenwood Publishing Group, 2007), pp. 100–101.

6.   Remarks courtesy of Dan Crenshaw, mental-health counselor.

Chapter 19

1.   Justin Ewers, "No Ideas? You're Not Alone," *U.S. News & World Report,* June 18, 2007, p. 50.

2.   Mary Ellen Guffey, *Business Communication: Process and Product,* 5th ed. (Mason, OH: Thomson South-Western, 2006), p. 42.

3.   Steve W. J. Kozlowski and Daniel R. Ilgen, "The Science of Team Success," *Scientific American Mind,* June/July 2007, pp. 54–61; Timothy S. Kiessling, Louis D. Marino, and R. Glenn Richey, "Global Marketing Teams: A Strategic Option for Multinationals," *Organizational Dynamics,* August 2006, pp. 237–250.

4.   Daniel Goleman, Paul Kaufman, and Michael Ray, *The Creative Spirit* (New York: Dutton, 1992), p. 121.

5.   Shri L. Henkel, *Successful Meetings: How to Plan, Prepare, and Execute Top-notch Business Meetings* (Ocala, FL: Atlantic Publishing Company, 2007), p. 146; Lesley Partridge, *Teams: Learning Made Simple* (Oxford, England: Butterworth-Heinemann, 2007), pp. 58–59.

6.   Quoted by Andy Goodman in "The Single Best Predictor of a Successful Meeting," Andy Goodman's website, www. agoodmanonline.com (accessed April 28, 2009).

7.   "ASME Guide to Starting a FIRST Team," American Society of Mechanical Engineers, www.asme.org, (accessed April 27, 2009).

8.   John Dewey, *How We Think* (Boston: Heath, 1933), pp. 106–115.

9.   Guy Gugliotta, "1-Hour Brainstorm Gave Birth to Digital Imaging," *Washington Post,* February 20, 2006, p. A-09.

Tips for Your Career

Tip 1.2 Survey by the author of 370 business and professional leaders, February–March 2011; Therese Myers, quoted in Bronwyn Fryer, "Pointers for Public Speaking," *PC World,* November 1991, p. 238.

Tip 4.1 Elizabeth A. Harris, "At Events Featuring the Governor of New York, the Forecast is Icy," *New York Times,* January 7, 2011, p. A16.

Tip 7.1 Dan Schawbel, "Business Myths You Can't Afford to Believe," *Forbes Online,* www.forbes.com (accessed February 28, 2012).

Tip 9.1 Preston Bradley, vice president, Graystone Corporation, personal correspondence with the author.

Tip 10.1. Ann Curry, "My Favorite Mistake," *Newsweek,* June 13, 2011, p. 84; e-mail interview, June 28, 2011.

Tip 12.1 "Employee Video," *Videomaker* magazine website, www. videomaker.com (accessed October 2, 2008); "American Preaching: A Dying Art?" *Time* magazine website, www.time.com (accessed October 2, 2008).

Tip 13.1 Ron Hoff, *"I Can See You Naked": A Fearless Guide to Making Great Presentations,"* rev. ed. (Kansas City, MO: Andrews and McMeel, 1992), pp. 224–225.

Tip 14.1 Cristina Stuart, *How to Be an Effective Speaker* (Lincolnwood, IL: NTC Business Books, 1989), p. 69.

Tip 14.2 Rosita Perez, professional speaker, Brandon, Florida, e-mail interview, September 14, 2007; Sandy Linver, *Speak Easy* (New York: Summit Books, 1978), p. 121; Steve Allen, *How to Make a Speech* (New York: McGraw-Hill, 1986), p. 120.

Tip 16.1 Sandra Stone Sundel, *Behavior Change in the Human Services: Behavioral and Cognitive Principles and Applications* (Thousand Oaks, CA: SAGE Publications, 2005), pp. 112–115.

Tip 17.1 Lincoln critic quoted by Clifton Fadiman, ed., *The American Treasury,* 1455–1955 (New York: Harper & Brothers, 1955), p. 152; Lilly Walters, *Secrets of Successful Speakers* (New York: McGraw-Hill, 1993), p. 37.

Tip 17.2 Douglas Hunt, *The Riverside Guide to Writing* (Boston: Houghton Mifflin, 1991), p. 158.

Special Techniques

How to Use Leave-Behinds: Jim Seymour, "The Importance of Leave-Behinds," ZD Net, www.zdnet.com (accessed September 16, 2008).

How to Use Humor: Jeff Valdez, quoted in The Quotations Page, www. quotationspage.com (accessed April 27, 2009); Marc G. Weinberger and Charles S. Gulas, "The Impact of Humor in Advertising," *Journal of Advertising,* December 1992, pp. 35–39; Carl Van Doren, *Benjamin Franklin* (New York: Viking, 1938), p. 650; Edmund Fuller, ed., *Thesaurus of Anecdotes* (New York: Avenel, 1990), p. 21; Laurie Schloff and Marcia Yudkin, *Smart Speaking* (New York: Henry Holt, 1991), p. 121.

Photo Credits

Chapter 1

Opener: © AP Photo/Robert Sutton, The Tuscaloosa News; p. 3(hippo): Courtesy of Abigail Hardin; p. 5: © Gabriel Bouys/AFP/Getty Images; 1.1: © iStockphoto.com/kupicoo; p. 9: © Darren Baker/Fotolia; p. 14: © Corel Stock Photos; p. 15: © Tomas Rodriguez/Corbis RF; p. 17: © PictureNet/Corbis RF.

Chapter 2

Opener: © AP Photo/Kathy Willens; p. 23: © Punit Paranjpe/AFP/Getty Images; p. 25: © iStockphoto.com/EdStock; p. 26: © Kurhan/Fotolia; p. 30: © Jason Brown, J.Brown Photography. All Rights Reserved; p. 31: © John MacDougall/AFP/Getty Images.

Chapter 3

Opener: © Kevin Dietsch-Pool/Getty Images; p. 38: Courtesy of Lucio Villa, The Daily Titan, California State University, Fullerton; p. 39: © Yuri Arcurs/Shutterstock; p. 43(top): © takayuki/Shutterstock; p. 43(bottom): © Shi Yali/Shutterstock; p. 44: © iStockphoto.com/Stockphoto4u; p. 46: © Marcin Balcerzak/Shutterstock; p. 47: © Renee Jansoa/Fotolia.

Chapter 4

Opener: © Barry Brecheisen/Getty Images; p. 54: © Dee Hunter/Shutterstock; p. 55: © iStockphoto.com/Juanmonino; p. 59: © iStockphoto.com/Figure8Photos; p. 60: © AP Photo/Wason Wanichkorn; p. 61: © AP Photo/Don Ryan; p. 63: © Robert Kneschke/Fotolia; p. 64: © Ingram Publishing; 4.2: Courtesy of Suzanne Oliver, Georgia Southern University; p. 67: Hamilton Gregory; p. 69: © Andrew Winning/Reuters/Corbis.

Chapter 5

Opener: © Photo by Foto24/Gallo Images/Getty Images; p. 74: © Alexander Joe/AFP/Getty Images; p. 75: © Beboy/Fotolia; p. 78: © Ingram Publishing; p. 81: © Ljipco Smokovski/Fotolia; p. 83: © iStockphoto.com/Brosa; p. 84: © Ruth Black/Shutterstock.

Chapter 6

Opener: © Tiffany Rose/Wire Images/Getty Images; p. 91: © Ingram Publishing; p. 92: © Kachalkina Veronika/Shutterstock; p. 93: Courtesy of Harvard Business Publishing; p. 97(top): © AP Photo/The Tennessean, Larry McCormack; p. 97(bottom): © Aaron Kohr/Shutterstock; p. 98: © AP Photo/The Grand Rapids Press, Paul L. Newby, II; p. 100: © Andrew Rodriguez/Fotolia.

Chapter 7

Opener: Courtesy U.S. Air Force; p. 113: © Benjamin Thorn/Shutterstock; p. 114: © Minerva Studio/Shutterstock; p. 115: © iStockphoto.com/VladimirCetinski; p. 116(bridge): Ingram Publishing/SuperStock; p. 116(tornado): Don Farrall/Getty Images; p. 117: © Lyle Leduc/WorkbookStock/Getty Images; p. 119: © Ingram Publishing; p. 125: © Ethan Miller/Getty Images.

Chapter 8

Opener: © Stephen Brashear/EPA/Corbis; p. 133: © iStockphoto.com/twohumans; 8.1: © Miguel Medina/AFP/Getty Images; 8.2: Hamilton Gregory; p. 138: © NBC Universal, Inc.; p. 140: © Kevin Wolf/AP Images for DRIVE4COPD.COM; p. 142: (Smartphone): © Ilker canikligil/Shutterstock; p. 142:(Photo on phone): © Andresr/Shutterstock; 8.4: © Corel Stock Photos.

Chapter 9

Opener: © Yoshikazu Tsuno/AFP/Getty Images; 9.8: © iStockphoto.com/Fotosmurf03; p. 159: © saiko3p/Shutterstock; p. 161: © AP Photo/Courier-Post, Douglas Bovitt; p. 162: © Simone van den Berg/Fotolia; 9.10: © Marco Secchi/Getty Images; p. 165: © Vovan/Fotolia; p. 166: Courtesy of Facebook; p. 169: © Patrick Hermans/Fotolia; p. 173: © iStockphoto.com/buzbuzzer; p. 174: © Maurizio Lagana/Getty Images; p. 175: © Netfalls/Fotolia; p. 178(Green background): © Shutterstock/riri; p. 178(coffee cup): Burke/Triolo Productions/Getty Images; p. 178(hot liquids): © iStockphoto/SensorSpot; p. 179(lions): © Corel Stock Photos; p. 179(African Girl): © Steffen Foerster Photography/Shutterstock; p. 179(zebra, baboon, cheetah): © Corel Stock Photos; p. 179(giraffes): © Anna Omelchenko/Shutterstock.

Chapter 10

Opener: © AP Photo/Houston Chronicle, Steve Ueckert; p. 185: © robynmac/Fotolia; p. 186: © Hamilton Gregory; 10.4: © pp76/Fotolia; 10.6: © Ingram Publishing; p. 191: © PeJo/Shutterstock; p. 193: © James Steidl/Fotolia; p. 194: U.S. Census Bureau.

Chapter 11

Opener: © AP Images/Rex Features; p. 204: © Olga Nayashkova/Fotolia; p. 206(top): © Madis Uudam/Fotolia; p. 206: © blinkblink/Fotolia; 11.1: © Linda Davidson/The Washington Post via Getty Images.

Chapter 12

Opener: © iStockphoto.com/craftvision; 12.1(computer): © iStockphoto.com/ronen; 12.1(hand): © Nikon'as/Fotolia; 12.1(silhouette): © Dan/Fotolia; p. 220: © oxygen64/Fotolia; 12.4(donut): © Fotolia/Qstock; 12.4(muffin): © Fotolia/Anton Prado; 12.6: © Igor Dutina/Shutterstock; p. 228: © AP Photo/The Canadian Press, Adrian Wyld.

Chapter 13

Opener: © Kris Connor/Getty Images; p. 238: © Brad Collett/Shutterstock; p. 240: © iStockphoto.com/Creativeye99; p. 243: © mikess/Fotolia; p. 245: © iStockphoto.com/Valerie Loiseleux; p. 246: Comstock Images/Jupiterimages.

Chapter 14

Opener: © Jim Watson/AFP/Getty Images; p. 255: © iStockphoto.com/endopack; p. 258: © AP Photo/Rogelio Solis; p. 259: © iStockphoto.com/sdominick; p. 263: © FogStock/Alamy; p. 264: © Garrett Ellwood/NBAE/Getty Images; p. 266: © iStockphoto.com/DSGpro; p. 267: © Jo Yong-Hak/Reuters/Corbis; p. 269: © Ingram Publishing; p. 270: Photographer Paul Patton, Wilmington University; p. 271: Comstock/Masterfile; p. 273: © iStockphoto.com/pederk.

Chapter 15

Opener: © AP Photo/Sharon Steinmann; p. 278: © khz/Fotolia; p. 279: © Hamilton Gregory; p. 281: © Sean Gladwell/Fotolia; 15.1: © William West/

AFP/Getty Images; p. 283: © Daniel Dempster Photography/Alamy; 15.2: © Kurhan/Fotolia; p. 287: © Norman Pogson/Fotolia; 15.3: © Hamilton Gregory; 15.4: © Lisa S./Shutterstock; 15.5: © Andres Rodriguez/Fotolia; 15.6: © Corel Stock Photos; 15.7: © Corel Stock Photos.

Chapter 16

Opener: © Stephanie Cadel/AFP/Getty Images; p. 299(top): © Sylvia Wolke/Fotolia; p. 299(bottom): © Dave Newman/Fotolia; p. 302(top): © iStockphoto.com/Ron Masessa; p. 302(middle): © Richard Carey/Fotolia; p. 302(bottom): Donna Dewhurst, U.S. Fish and Wildlife Service; p. 303(top): Photo by Goncalo Veiga, Wikimedia; p. 303(middle): Jerron Barnett, U.S. Air Force; p. 305: Don Mason/Blend Images LLC; p. 307: © Ingram Publishing; 16.2: © AP Photos/Jae C. Hong; 16.A: © iStockphoto.com/Oleg Prikhodko.

Chapter 17

Opener: Courtesy of Oceana, © Tim Calver; p. 321: © ryanking999/Fotolia; p. 322: © Peter Hopper Stone/ABC Family/Getty Images; 17.1: Courtesy of Diana Fisher; p. 326: © Chip Somodevilla/Getty Images; p. 327: © iStockphoto.com/DanielBendjy; p. 328: © Petr Malyshev/Fotolia.com; p. 330: © Yuri Arcurs/Shutterstock; p. 336: ballyscanlon/Getty Images.

Chapter 18

Opener: © Jemal Countess/Getty Images; p. 348: © AP Photo/Huntington, Ind., Herald-Press, Jeff Morehead; p. 353(top): Jamie Grill/Iconica/Getty Images; p. 353(bottom): © EastWest Imaging/Fotolia; p. 354: © AP Photo/Reed Saxon, Pool.

Chapter 19

Opener: ©John Lund/Sam Diephuis/Blend Images LLC; 19.1: © auremar/Shutterstock; p. 366: © Hamilton Gregory; p. 369: © Spencer Platt/Getty Images.

Appendix

Figure A-1: © Nathalie Rocchia/Fotolia; A-2: Photo courtesy of Steph Davis; A-3: Photo courtesy of Damon Corso (www.petrala.com); p. 378: Hamilton Gregory.

Index